Life and Bronze

Life and Bronze

A Sculptor's Journal

RUTH ABERNETHY

GRANVILLE ISLAND PUBLISHING

Library and Archives Canada Cataloguing in Publication

Abernethy, Ruth, author, artist
Life and bronze : a sculptor's journal / Ruth Abernethy.

Includes index.

Issued in print and electronic formats.
ISBN 978-1-926991-73-3 (hardback).—ISBN 978-1-926991-74-0 (ebook)

1. Abernethy, Ruth. 2. Women sculptors—Canada—Biography. I. Title.

NB249.A23A3 2016 730.92 C2016-905928-6
C2016-906098-5

Editor: Angie Littlefield
Indexer: Bookmark: Editing and Indexing
Proofreader: Neall Calvert
Book Designer: Maggie Woo

Granville Island Publishing Ltd.
2 – 1656 Duranleau St. Granville Island
couver, BC, Canada V6H 3S4

-688-0320 / 1-877-688-0320
ro@granvilleislandpublishing.com
www.granvilleislandpublishing.com

First published in 2017
Printed in South Korea

This book is dedicated
to remarkable collaborators,
with whom I've worked
on projects large and small.
Here's to making statements
much larger than us all!

– Ruth Abernethy

Table of Contents

Foreword

You become an admirer when you stand in front of a work by Ruth Abernethy. She is a gifted portraitist with an extraordinary ability to capture physical likeness in wax, clay and bronze. Her list of public commissions is long and impressive. She has immortalized notable Canadians from prime ministers to artists and heroes—in public landmarks across the country. I became an admirer through a modest, private commission.

Ruth designed an athletic trophy commemorating my late husband, Paul Stothart—a trophy I donated to Queen's University for use by their men's varsity hockey team. Working from a few family photographs, Ruth created a ten-inch-tall bronze figure of Paul skating. The portrait likeness of his face, modeled by hand and no more than an inch-and-a-half in scale, was utterly perfect. Ruth mounted the original work on a sheet of glass which she suspended above a block of century-old maple from near the arena where he played. Her inspired use of materials, design, craftsmanship and history was deeply moving to me.

To speak with Ruth is to discover her gentle curiosity and interest in people, her enthusiasm for stories and her theatre background.

Years of designing and building complex stage sets and props early in her career, for the likes of The National Ballet and The Stratford Theatre, infused her work with an effortless and subtle sense of narrative. This unique formula of exquisite portraiture and theatrical sensibility is her signature.

It was a rare pleasure to come to know Ruth and I am gratified that this book celebrates her numerous accomplishments. A gifted artist, a sublime craftswoman and a compassionate human being, Ruth has a story that is still unfolding.

Karen Colby-Stothart
CEO of the National Gallery of Canada Foundation

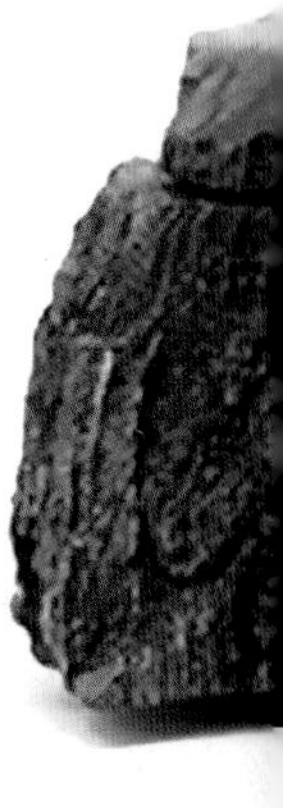

Paul Stothart Memorial Award, 2013

Awarded annually for academic and athletic excellence to a member of the Gaels, the Men's Varsity Hockey Team, Queen's University, Kingston, Ontario

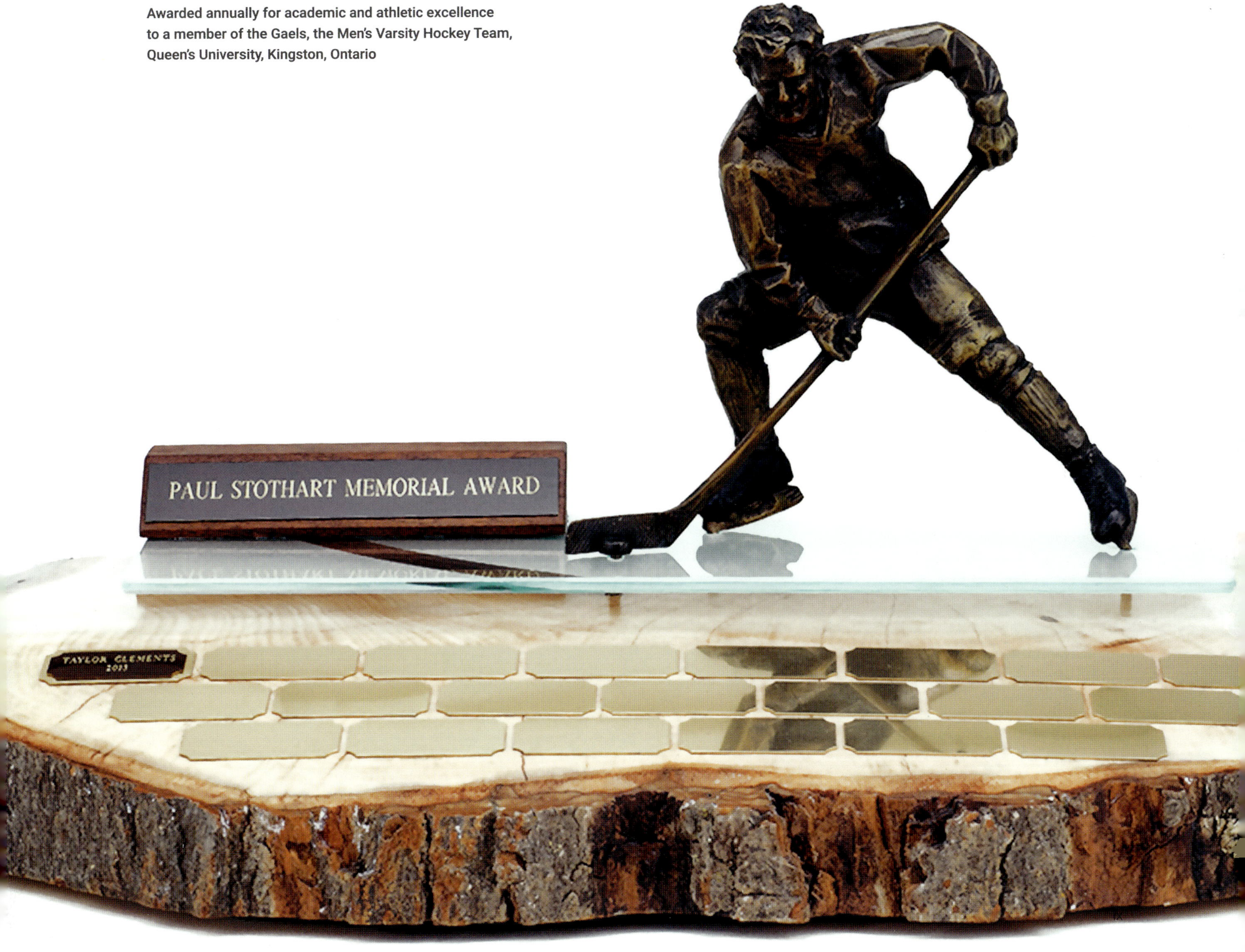

Creativity

If I knew where the good songs came from, I'd go there more often.

– Leonard Cohen

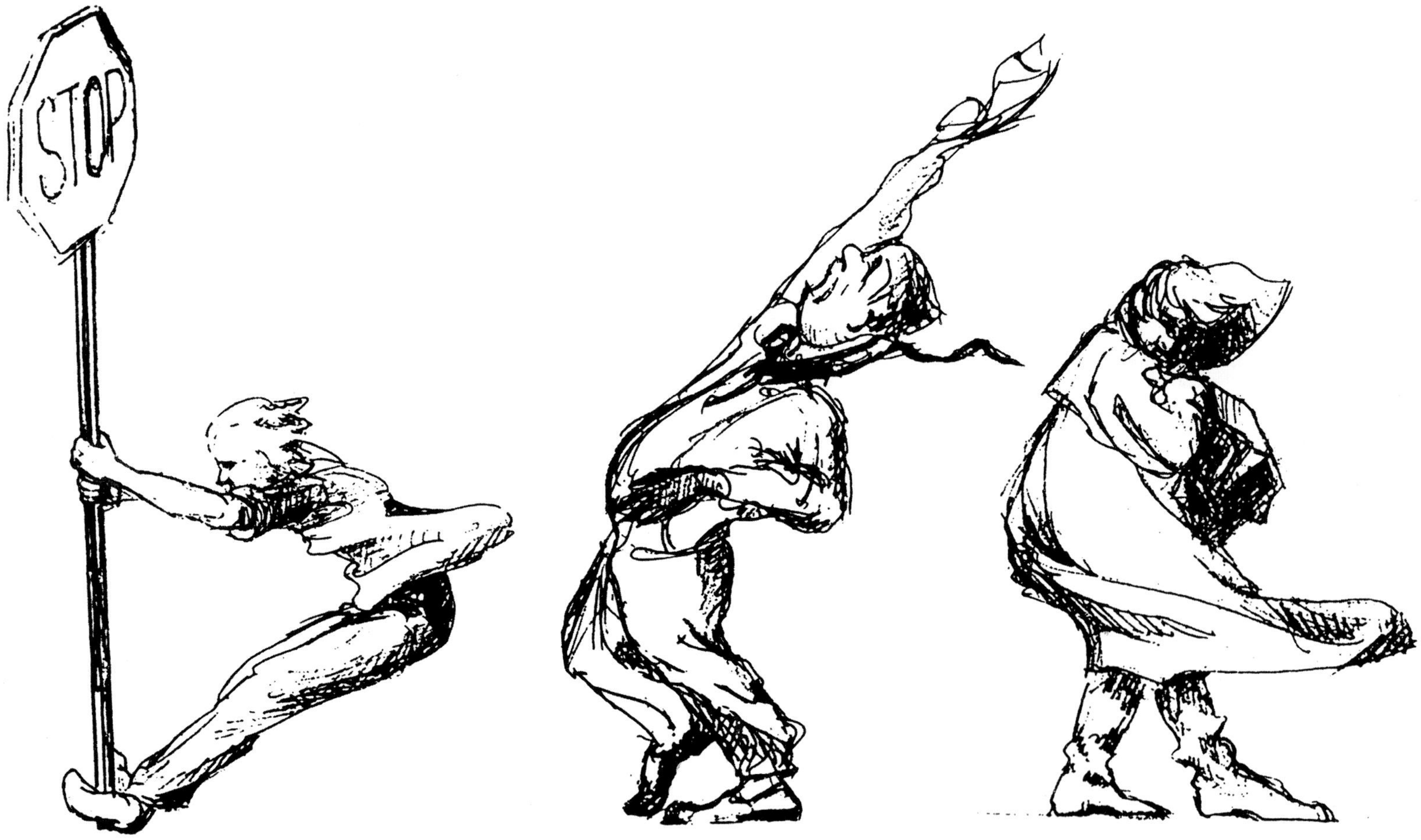

The 'struggle' of an artist has nothing in common
with the effortless arrival of a good idea!

Ideas are instant things of air.
They're as soothing as a breath or as exciting
as finding a new room in your home.
They're quizzical thoughts, allowed lateral drift in the mind
to bump against each another.

Music floats emotion.
Fragrance transports to another time and place.
Encountering art is like nudging a tray of marbles
and seeing glass ideas roll into new patterns
and reflect in each other fresh ways to see
things already seen.

Ruth Abernethy

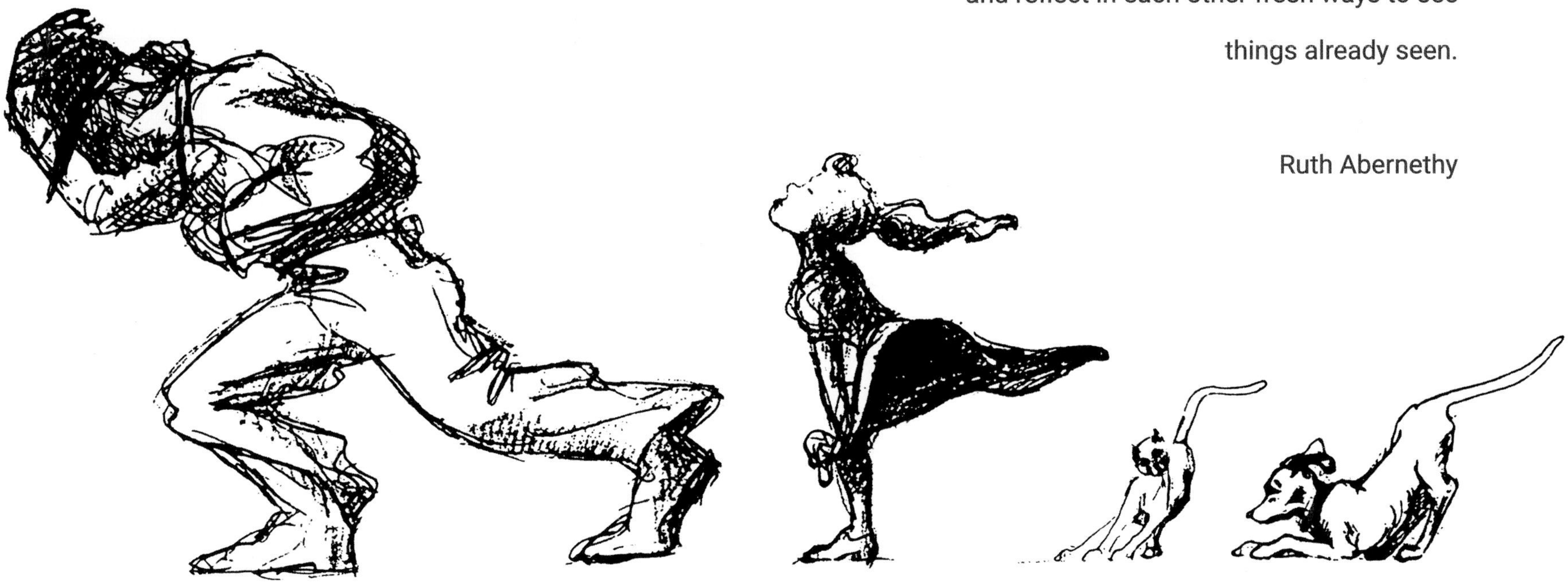

PART ONE

Early Works

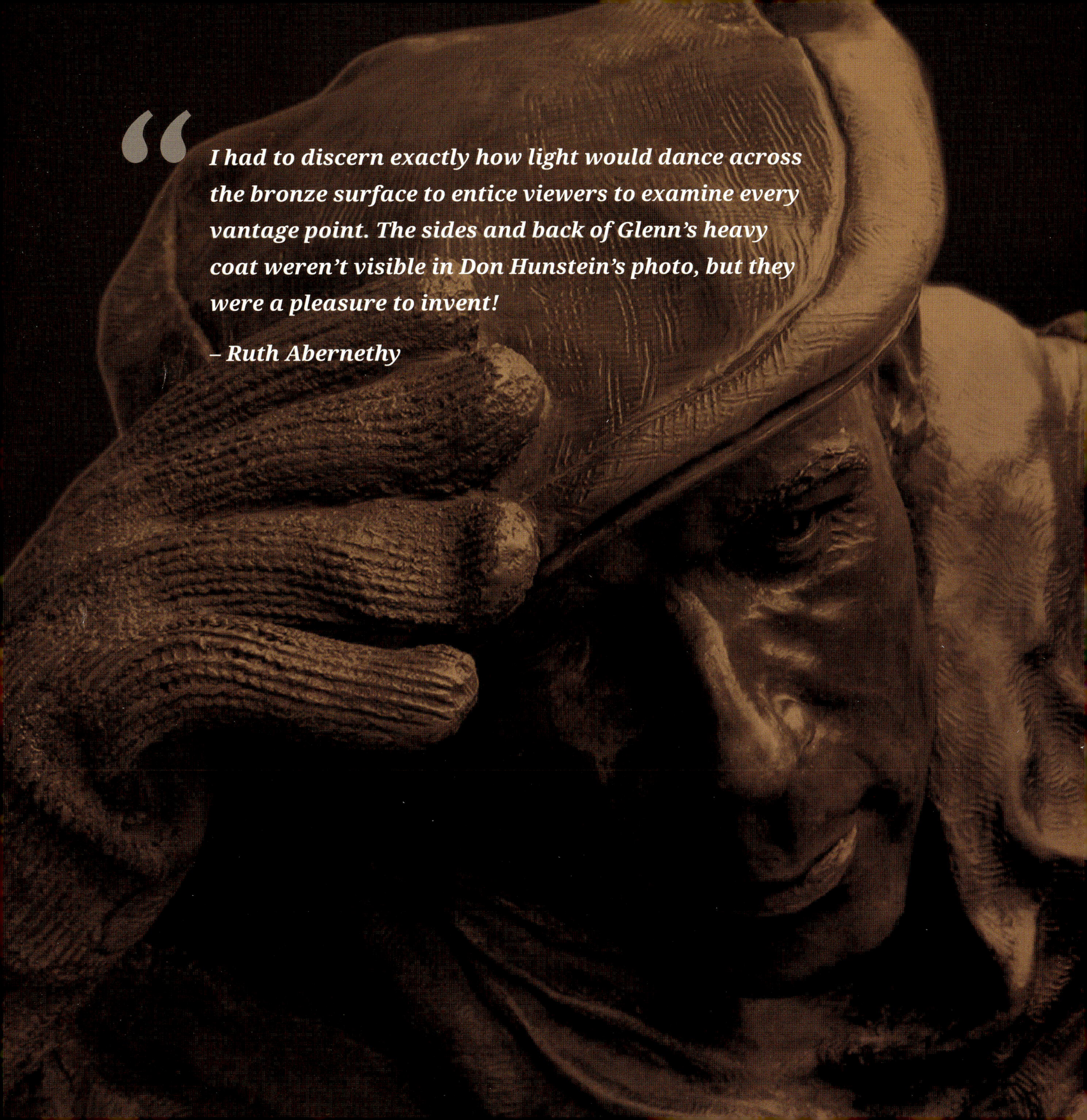

"I had to discern exactly how light would dance across the bronze surface to entice viewers to examine every vantage point. The sides and back of Glenn's heavy coat weren't visible in Don Hunstein's photo, but they were a pleasure to invent!

– Ruth Abernethy

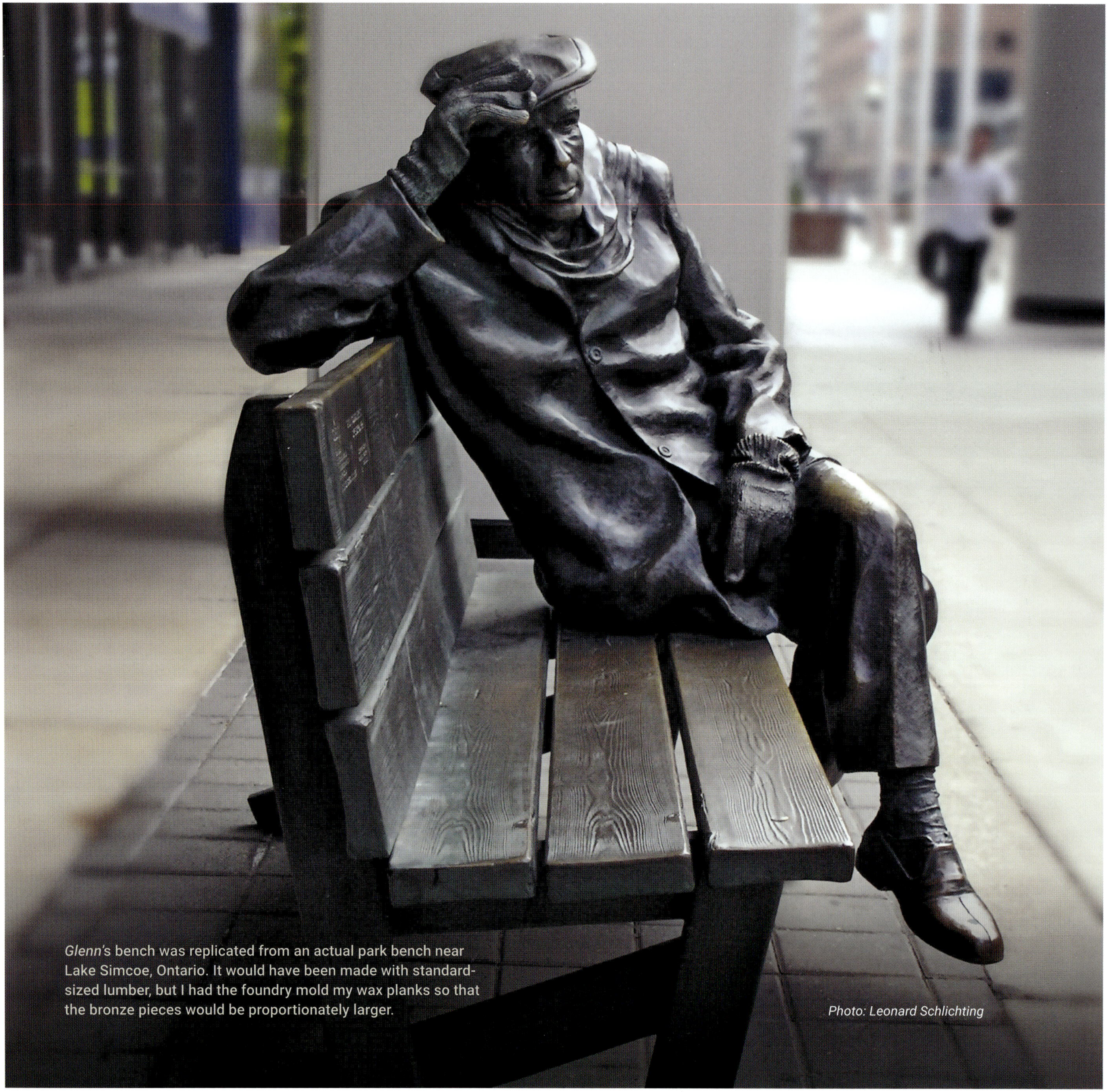

Glenn's bench was replicated from an actual park bench near Lake Simcoe, Ontario. It would have been made with standard-sized lumber, but I had the foundry mold my wax planks so that the bronze pieces would be proportionately larger.

Photo: Leonard Schlichting

Glenn Gould

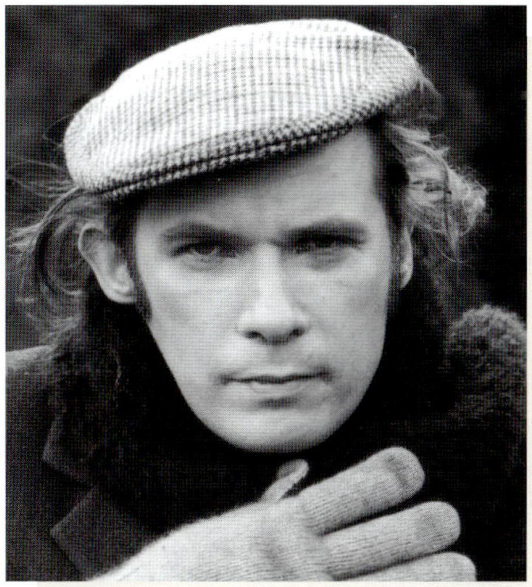

Glenn Gould (1932–1982)

Canadian Pianist

At the age of three, Glenn Gould had absolute pitch. By age five, he composed and performed original piano works. He graduated from Toronto's Royal Conservatory of Music with the highest honours at age 14. Known for his technical proficiency, perfect accuracy and unique technique, he became the first North American to play in the USSR. His playing prowess is celebrated around the globe and beyond. One of his recordings was sent skyward aboard the Voyager I spacecraft, now the furthest man-made object from Earth.

In July 1997, several weeks after celebrating the installation of the Stratford figures, I received a phone inquiry from John Miller, then administrator of the Glenn Gould Foundation. Would I be interested in sculpting Glenn Gould, the famed classical pianist from Toronto? John wanted a bronze portrait as a permanent marker for the Glenn Gould Gathering, a conference he was planning for 1999. I was astonished and thrilled.

Mr. Miller didn't need the portrait for many months and, almost jokingly, I suggested we talk again the following year. Such a long timeline was unheard of in the Stratford prop shop where I still worked. Over that year John and I had time to look at photos and discuss how to portray Glenn's quirky character. As a world-renowned performer, Glenn was meticulously documented. He was also a master of crafting his public image. He selected all his promotional shots with great care.

At the Gould Foundation in Toronto, Glenn's friends considered various ideas. For simplicity's sake, I suggested we work directly from a photo taken by Columbia Records photographer Don Hunstein. This talented man had captured Glenn sitting, poised on the end of a wooden plank bench, during an outing near Lake Simcoe. It was one of Glenn's favourite images, taken in one of his favourite locations in Canada's 'North'. I smiled at the idea that Glenn considered Lake Simcoe the Canadian North . . . but, the photo was perfect.

> *"When I recall sculpting Glenn, most striking in memory is the calm of working in my home studio in Wellesley, Ontario rather than building props at the Stratford Festival as I'd done for nearly 15 seasons. Only Glenn Gould's exquisite music in the air stirred the winter afternoons. My acquaintances assumed I was hard at work at my prop table . . . I wasn't. Except for morning and afternoon routines to deliver my sons, Glen and Alex, to and from daycare, the days were my own. I had few interruptions and the phone simply never rang.*

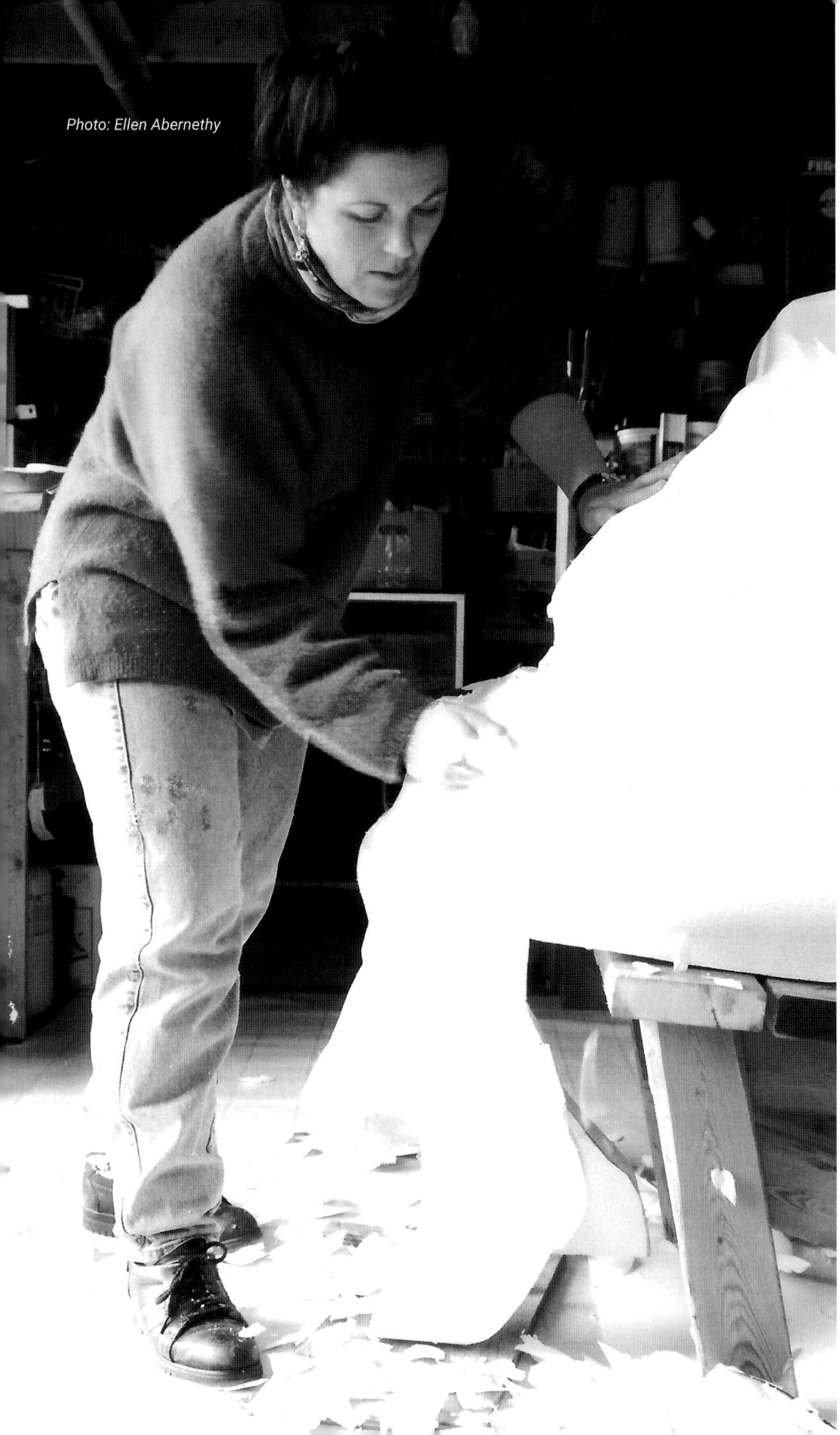

Photo: Ellen Abernethy

The winter weeks slid by and *Glenn*'s likeness took shape. My husband, Mark Smyth, remembered a point where Mr. Gould 'became a presence'. We'd speak to him as we walked through the studio or apologize for bumping him on our way by. Only once did I fail to find the necessary details in my array of photos but, luckily, a performance video showed exactly which cheek muscle to define.

When I felt I'd captured the Gould I'd imagined, I placed the heavy head on a wheeled cart and headed to Toronto. It was nerve-racking to transport the delicate sculpted head. A heavy foot on the brakes or one misjudged revolving door would mean weeks of repair. Arriving at the downtown address, I carefully manoeuvred my head-trolley into the elevator and rose to the client's suite. Glenn's long-time friend Ray Roberts offered a most memorable compliment: "If I stand right here, I'm sure I can hear him speak!" *Glenn* and I departed in high spirits.

Gloves and a woolen overcoat were Glenn's standard dress; he'd wear them even during summer months. My key reference photo showed the distinctive outfit, though only from the front. Any photograph can only show perhaps 60 of the 360 degrees in a three-dimensional form. The sculpted 3D portrait I was creating had no 'upstage side', meaning that no part of the sculpture would go unnoticed by a public that could approach from all directions. My task was to recreate the garments as they were, beyond the camera's view. I had to discern exactly how light would dance across the bronze surface to entice viewers to examine every vantage point. The sides and back of *Glenn*'s heavy coat weren't visible in the Hunstein photo, but they were a pleasure to invent! I've always loved fabrics, and carving clunky styrene into lush folds of wool was excellent fun.

Glenn's incredible hands would be inside woolen gloves—those too would need to be four-percent oversized. I found a close-up

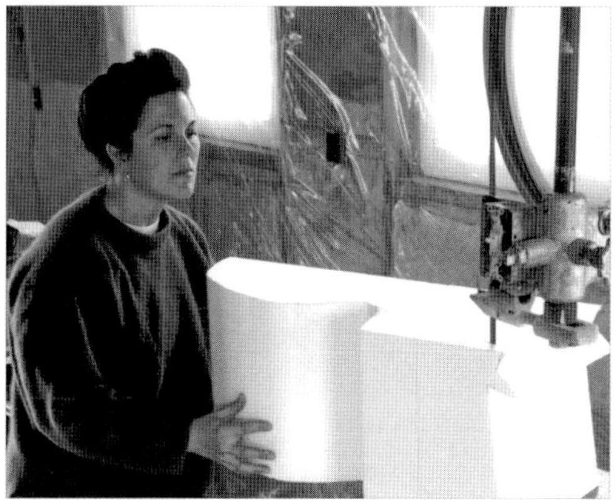

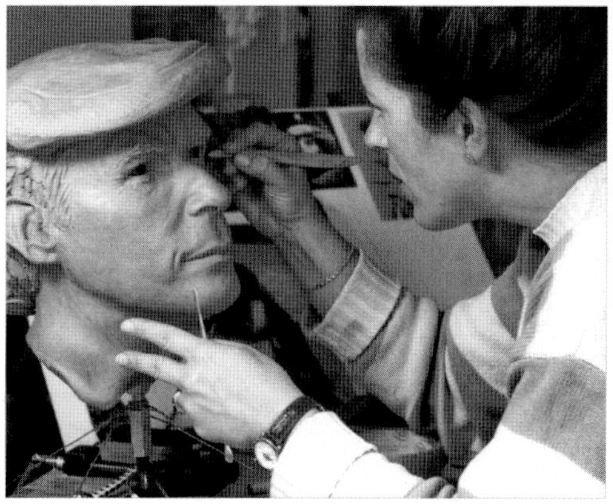

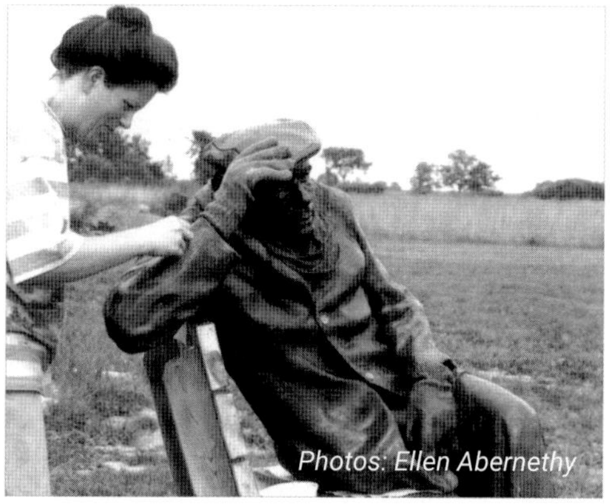
Photos: Ellen Abernethy

> *It took meticulous planning to make the figure seated on the wooden bench look as it did. Gould had to appear life-size as people sat with him, but a literally sculpted 'life-size' figure would shrink as the molten bronze cooled. The resulting sculpture would be diminutive in a public space. To compensate, I created this portrait to be four percent larger than life—after shrinkage. I also had to resolve a perfect fit between the oversize figure and my replica of an actual bench which was most certainly made of standard size lumber. My solution was to design oversized wax planks that the foundry molded in sections. The resulting wax 'lumber' in Glenn's bench had the correct proportions and it fit the figure as precisely as it did in the photograph.*

image of Glenn's hands in an album centre-fold; I had all the reference I needed. I shopped for the style of leather-palmed, oatmeal-coloured gloves Glenn wore and bought them in the largest size. With linings removed, I fit them over delicate hands that I'd carved with scissors out of upholstery foam. The knitted gloves and leather palms provided surface texture when cast in bronze.

John Miller stopped by to see my progress. On one occasion he mentioned that this pianist had no patience with lace-up shoes. Glenn's simple solution was to force down the backs of his shoes and wear them as slip-on footwear. Once I knew this detail, no other solution would be as interesting. Rubber shoe covers were difficult to find, but a friend located and bought a pair in the hardware store in the small town of Haliburton, several hours' drive north of Toronto. I added this final distinctive detail.

When I felt my rendering was complete, Joan Chalmers and John Miller planned a studio visit. Joan was a legendary arts supporter and a stalwart early member of the Glenn Gould Foundation. Clarice Chalmers, her sister-in-law, had provided portrait funding in memory of her husband, Wallace. Before Joan and John's arrival, my sister Ellen and I carried Gould's wax figure into the backyard and set him on the little plank chair I'd created for *Glenn* in the studio.

Joan and John were delighted with the work. We shared a sense of celebration that the sculpting stage was completed and they departed in high spirits. The figure stayed on the lawn. My sister Ellen, the project photographer, documented the day and asked about bringing *Glenn* inside. I stalled; I was completing some other task. Ellen returned a half-hour later to report that dear Mr. Gould was changing colour. The wax was pale and had become mushy in the hot sunshine. Only Ellen's vigilance saved my pianist from certain destruction.

There is no description for the heady freedom of delivering a large project to the foundry. With relief, my wax-covered styrene sculpture will be carefully handed to a team of technicians who'll spend months recreating its exact likeness in bronze. I liken it to stumbling into a vacuum after months of leaning against a strong wind. The Artcast Foundry did a remarkable job with the figure, the bench and the fit between the two. *Glenn* now rests comfortably outside the Canadian Broadcasting Corporation's Glenn Gould Studio at the Front Street headquarters in Toronto. He's become an icon in the city.

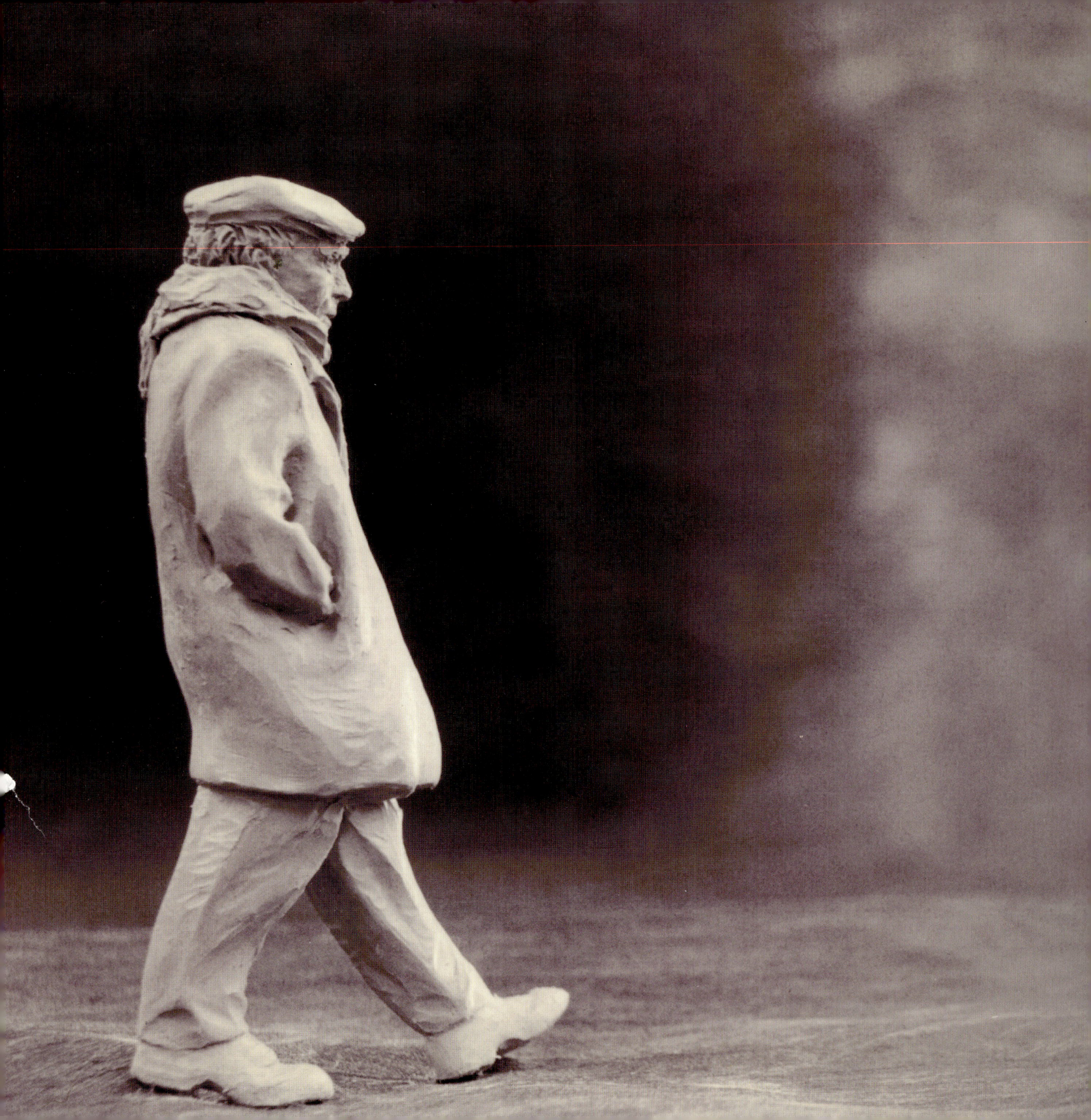

CRAFTING A SMALL PORTRAIT

During the spring of 1998, as I worked on the large portrait of Glenn Gould, I had numerous conversations with John Miller. John wanted a signature item to present to the winner of the Glenn Gould Prize. The Gould Foundation awarded this every three years to extraordinary musicians for their lifetime contributions. Prior recipients had received unique commissioned craft items made from a variety of materials. The Foundation sought something distinctively Gouldian that could be reproduced in perpetuity.

I was focused on the large portrait but John continued to prompt. His plans for the upcoming Glenn Gould Gathering at CBC Toronto were a celebration of the man and his ideals. Events included the presentation of the new distinctive award to cellist Yo-Yo Ma and John felt a literal portrait would be perfect.

That summer Gallery Stratford presented archival photos from Columbia Records that photographer Don Hunstein had taken of Glenn Gould. In the exhibit I saw a photograph of Glenn walking through snow toward the camera. He was wearing his winter galoshes, cap and overcoat—which I'd just finished sculpting for the large bronze. The photo inspired me to begin by building a wire armature on a square of masonite board. Then, over a few nights, while watching the evening news with Mark, I sculpted a six-inch-tall figure in clay, striding across the small board on my lap. It wasn't difficult. The forms and textures of Glenn's outfit were implanted in my imagination. I told John Miller about my 'little Gould' and he kindly borrowed the source photo from Don's collection. It was great to have a second look, but really I'd done the sculpting to my satisfaction.

I took the small figure to Toronto to show the Gould Foundation board members. In the elevator, heads turned. Immediate recognition of my tiny Glenn was reassuring. Yo-Yo Ma received the first bronze of my small portrait following his memorable concert at the Glenn Gould Gathering in September 1999.

Photo: Ellen Abernethy

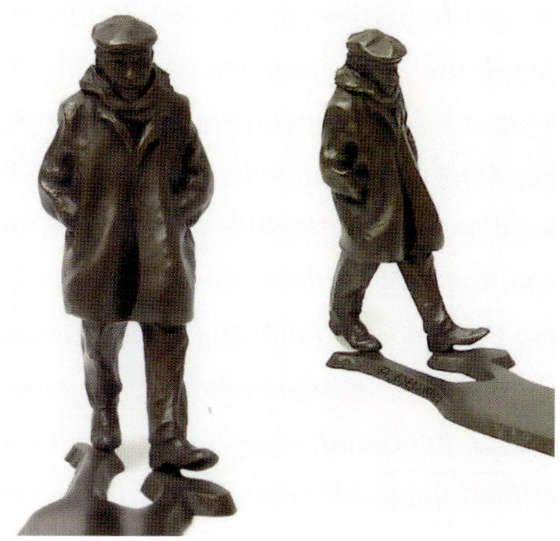

GLENN GOULD PRIZE LAUREATES

1987	R. Murray Schafer, Canada
1990	Yehudi Menuhin, US/Swiss/Britain
1993	Oscar Peterson, Canada
1996	Toru Takemitsu, Japan
1999	Yo-Yo Ma, France/United States
2002	Pierre Boulez, France
2005	André Previn, Germany/United States
2008	José Antonio Abreu, Venezuela
2011	Leonard Cohen, Canada
2013	Robert Lepage, Canada
2015	Philip Glass, United States

Spirit of Zorba

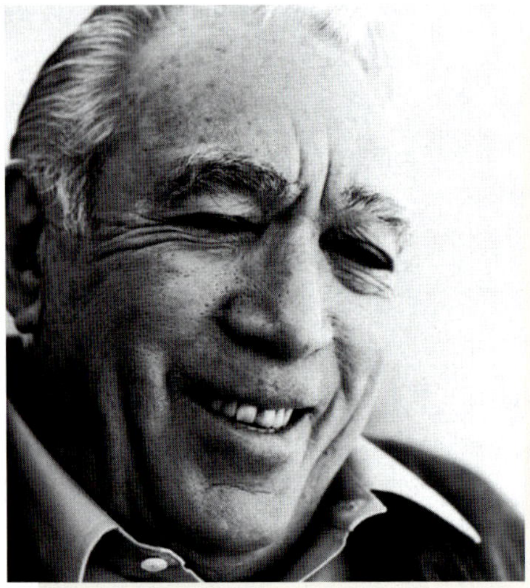

Anthony Quinn (1915–2001)

American Actor

Anthony Quinn's first film in 1936 launched an acting career that spanned six decades. He won two Academy Awards and appeared in more than 200 films. Of Irish-Mexican descent, he created dynamic and charismatic characters, one of whom was Zorba in *Zorba the Greek* (1964).

> ***I have lived in a flurry of images, but I will go out in a freeze frame.***
> ***– Anthony Quinn***

Eric Knoespel of Artcast Foundry called me early in 1999 to ask if I'd consider enlarging a nine-inch bronze for an 'unnamed American artist'. The small bronze had a tangible energy. Its surface had been shaped by powerful finger strokes in clay. The original sculpture had a tiny face, only the suggestion of features. I had to render this in a much larger scale using believable new forms. It was a delicious dilemma. In three intense weeks, I transferred the dynamic original piece into a 72-inch replica and delivered it to the foundry as promised.

Eric snapped photos of the sculpture and drove immediately to Toronto to meet with Anthony Quinn—the actor, the film star . . . and the client. An excited Quinn waited in the hotel lobby. On seeing the fresh photos of my work, Quinn loudly demanded, "But I want to see photos of the big piece!" With a chuckle, Eric was delighted to answer, "But Mr. Quinn, *this is the big piece!*" When Mr. Quinn saw the head life-size, he asked if he could have his own features on it in time for the upcoming show.

While the clock ticked down to opening night at the Columbus Centre in Toronto, I took an Italian magazine with a photo spread of Mr. Quinn and retreated to the studio. After my husband and sons were in bed, the house was silent and for a few hours time seemed to stop.

The visual rhythm of Quinn's features became obvious. I simply sculpted what I saw. I don't know that I'd ever felt as rewarded by a creative session.

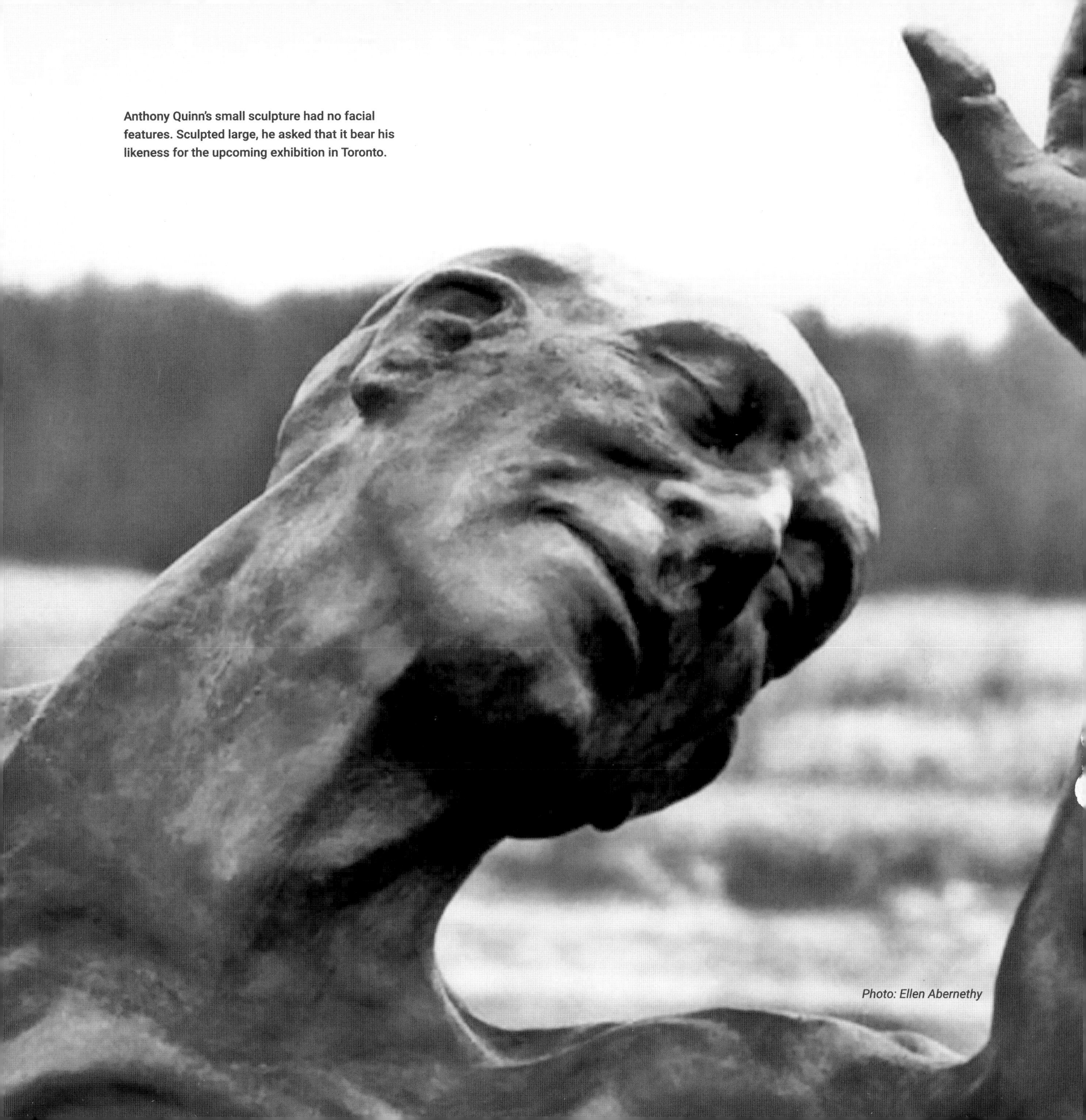

Anthony Quinn's small sculpture had no facial features. Sculpted large, he asked that it bear his likeness for the upcoming exhibition in Toronto.

Photo: Ellen Abernethy

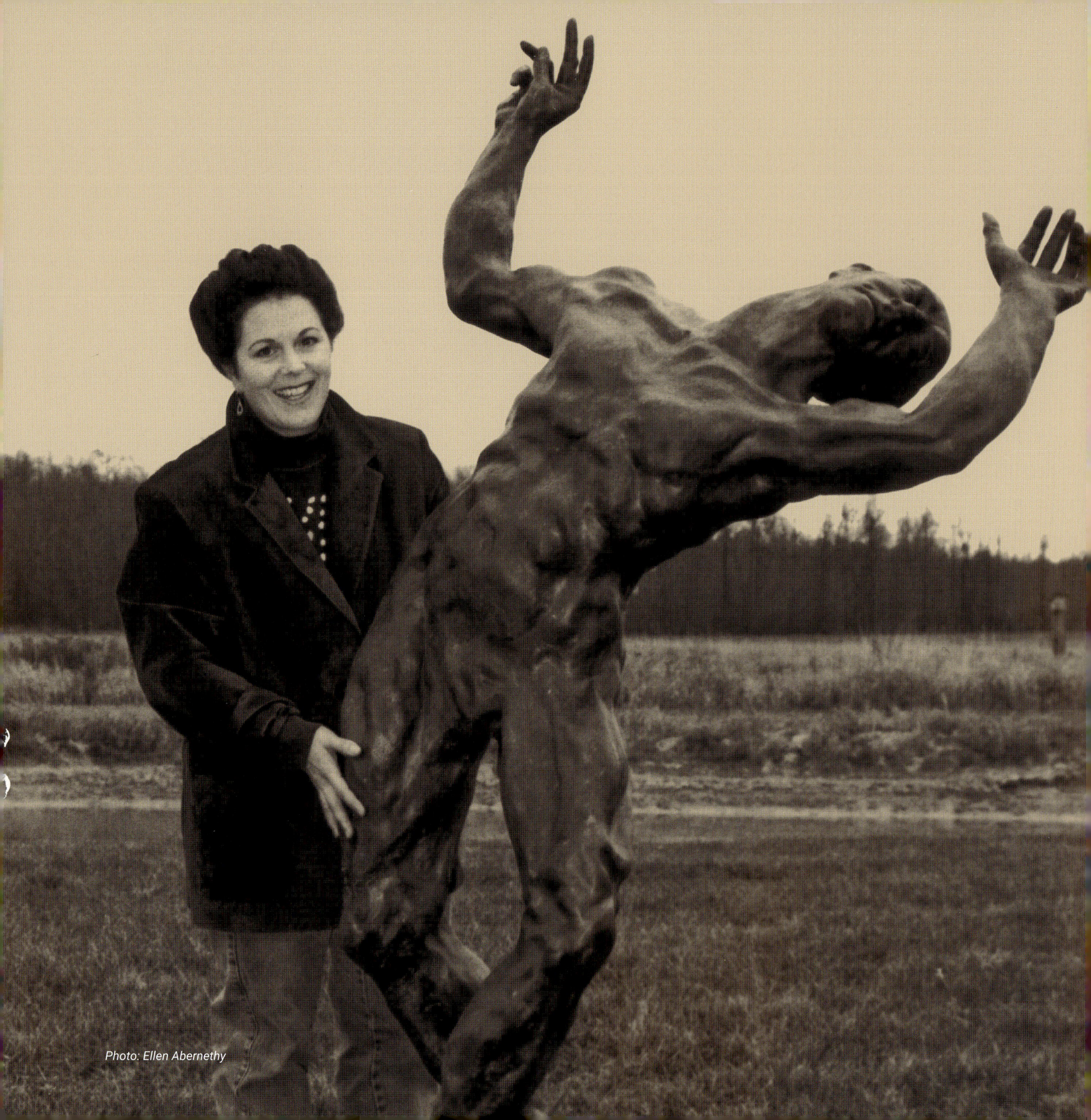

Photo: Ellen Abernethy

With the figure of Zorba in my car, I headed to Toronto to meet with Mr. Quinn. At the gas station, the attendant peered inside the van and caught a glimpse of the large body. I overheard him comment, "Well, I don't know what he died of, but he was fit!" Sculpted in styrene and wax, The Spirit of Zorba *was a cornerstone work for the exhibition "My Time" in Toronto.*

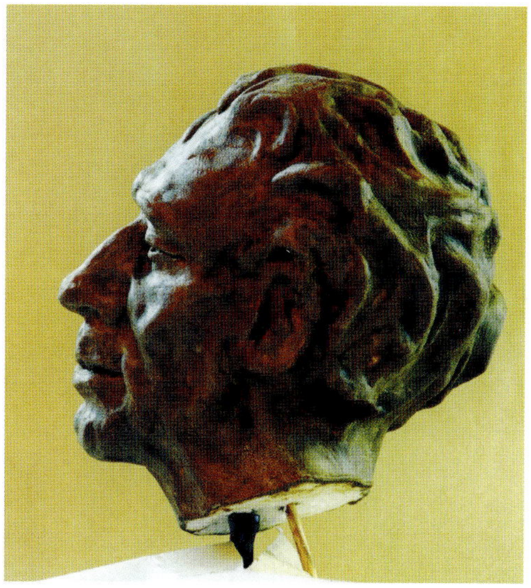

Mr. Quinn and I enjoyed a rare quiet moment to view the completed work. What had simply been a dancing figure at nine inches tall was an imposing nude at 72 inches tall. In short order, Quinn caught my attention and gestured to the very centre of the figure. "The poor fellow looks a bit light on the front here," he declared gruffly. "See what you can do about that."

Mr. Quinn was fascinated by my methods. He understood how important it was to create 'fresh' bronzes with the simplest steps. Making a bronze without a mold was of great interest to him.

He invited me to visit him and his family in Rhode Island to discuss and experiment. The invitation included my sons, seven-year-old Glen and five-year-old Alex. Quinn's own children were then aged eight and four.

Unable to find a bulk styrene supplier near Quinn's home, I strapped large foam pieces from my own stock onto the top of the car, put Glen and Alex inside and headed for the US border. Crossing the huge Niagara Gorge, in the middle of the Rainbow Bridge, a clasp on our roof rack failed and the bulky styrene blocks bounced wildly across the roadway. Insisting that the boys stay inside the car, I scampered through traffic to collect my cargo. Once gathered, I talked Glen through the complex rigging of straps to hold the blocks on the roof and we began what felt like an interminable drive to Buffalo at 10 pm, all the while looking for a shop where we could buy vice grips.

Rhode Island lingers in memory as a magical time. The boys and I combed the beach between studio sessions. The summer days were long. Quinn's son, Ryan, was learning to ride a tiny bicycle and his daughter, Antonia, charmed us all. Glen, Alex and I became regulars at one of the cafés in Bristol and there were afternoons of frolic with the Quinn family. I worked on small items by hand while Mr. Quinn, his wife Katherine and our children paddled in the pool.

Mr. Quinn's thoughts on human nature, creativity and capturing the life force, defy my writing skills. My fleeting hours with him were a treasure. Tony and Katherine's stunning property over the water was a home filled with affection and astonishing art. The immaculate 'barn' brimmed with Quinn's collection and his own sculptures and paintings. His bright whitewashed studio nearby always had a project taking shape on the table.

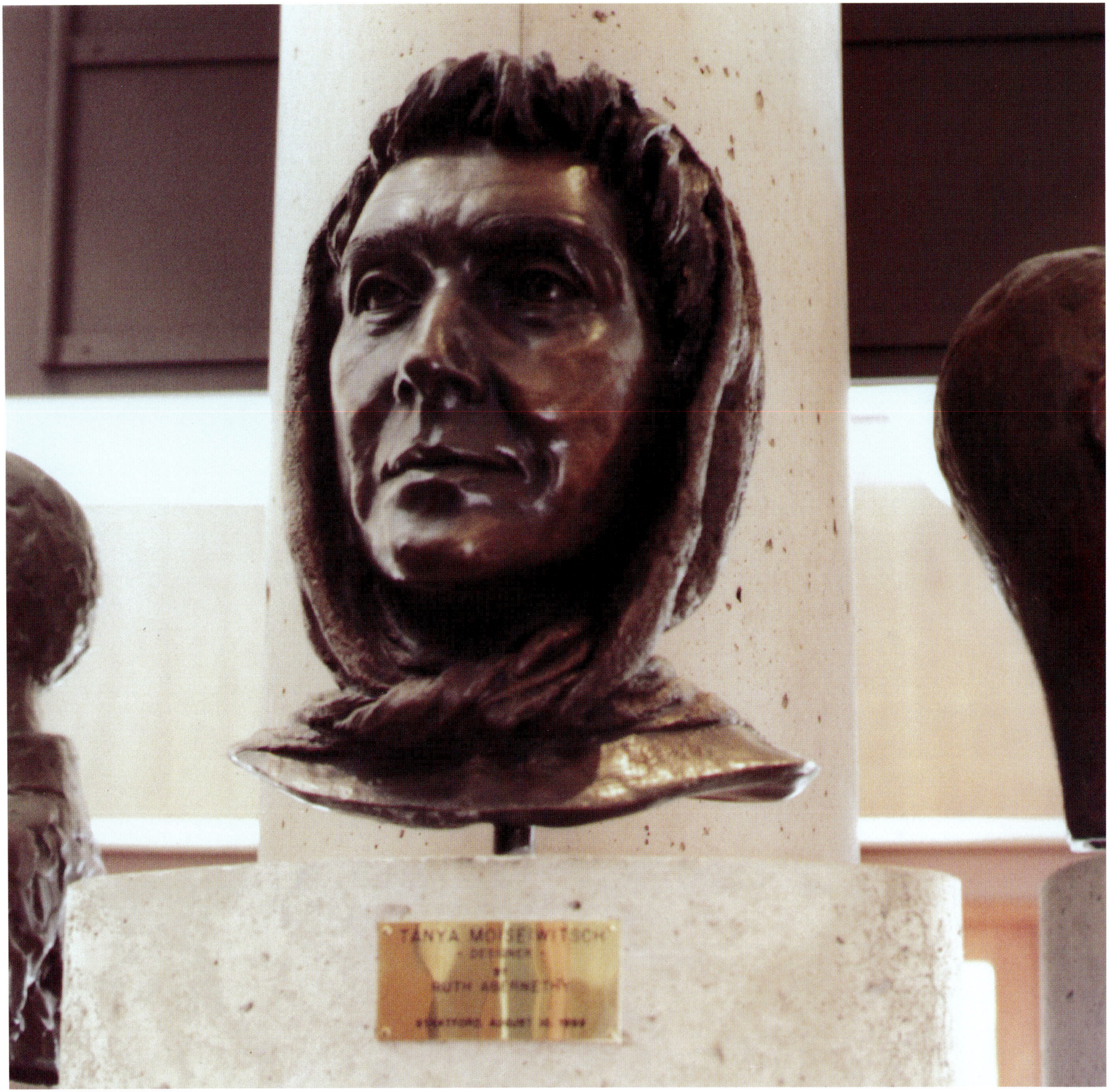

Tanya Moiseiwitsch

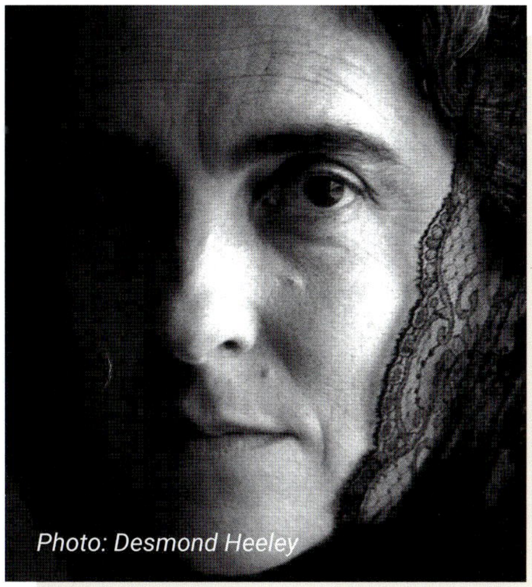

Tanya Moiseiwitsch (1914–2003)

Theatre Designer

The Stratford Festival story could not be told without introducing brilliant theatre designer Tanya Moiseiwitsch. She and director Tyrone Guthrie created innovative productions in London and Dublin before reaching Stratford, Canada in the early 1950s. Part of Tanya's contribution was the design of the Festival Theatre and its famous thrust stage. It altered Shakespearean theatre profoundly and changed productions of the classical repertoire across the world.

> *If ever there was a woman who moved my heart, it would be Tanya Moiseiwitsch.*

My first season in Stratford was 1981. That year Tanya Moiseiwitsch designed *Misanthrope*, for which I was asked to place a crucifix in the centre of a transom window above a door. I was mortified when Tanya, walking through the shop, asked me why I hadn't managed to find the window's centre. The crucifix was already firmly fixed, and onstage it went. The following day, Tanya took time to stop by the shop to apologize for her criticism. She assured me that once she'd seen the cross in position, it was perfect. I will never forget her astute praise and the gracious gesture of the apology.

The invitation to sculpt Tanya's portrait came nearly 20 years after I'd worked for her. I asked that the portrait commission include a brief trip to England. Over tea at her flat in London, Tanya was as thoughtful and charming as ever. "I look in the mirror and I scarcely recognize myself any more," she told me. "Just work from the photos. I am in there." I was surprised to register just how diminutive she had become.

She loomed large in my remembrance. Tanya's appearances in the prop shop were treated with such awe that it felt like the docking of the *Queen Mary*.

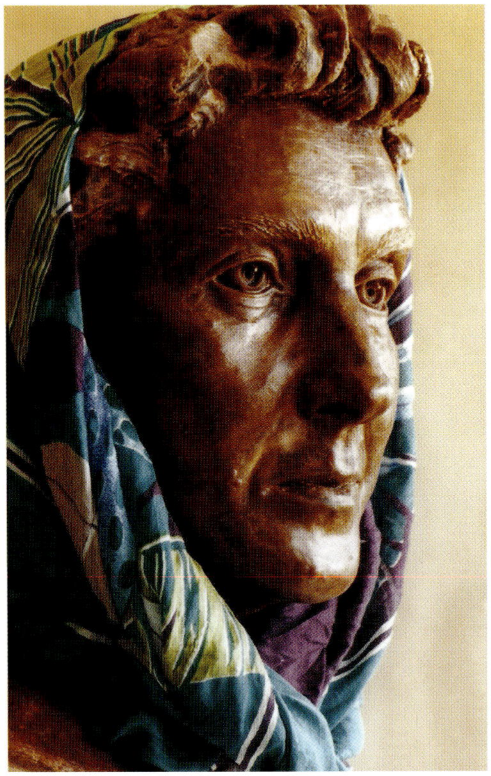

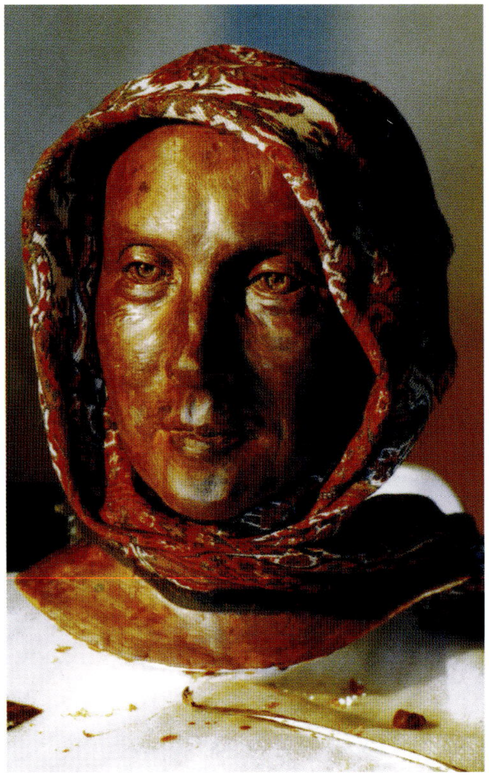

I found an excellent photo taken by Tanya's close friend and one-time assistant, Desmond Heeley. In it Tanya wore a knowing half-smile and a beautiful lace mantilla. Without question, it was to be my primary reference image. I set to work.

Tanya had explained to me that wearing a scarf was easier than trying to arrange her very fine hair. I paused in my work on the project when Desmond commented that a sheer scarf would be impossible to sculpt. His comment unleashed a 'Eureka moment'. I realized that 'sheer' in sculptural terms was really just seeing two things at the same time. I formed the bronze to effect glimpses of hair interlaced with the texture of silk crepe.

Project sponsors Sandra and Jim Pitblado were delighted to have Tanya's portrait placed in the Festival's main foyer. Flanked by previously sculpted portraits of Tom Patterson and Tyrone Guthrie, Tanya's bust completed an installation of the three Stratford Festival founders. It was dedicated in August 1999.

4. sept. 2000
Dear Ruth – This floral card comes
with my thanks, long overdue, for
your letter & my disappointment
for not getting in touch when I was
in Stratford – It was a wildly enjoy-
able visit but every moment seemed
to be action-packed. I'm still jet-
lagged, although we got back on 24th
of August – My sister adored everything
about Canada & vows she'll return in
2002 – I'm not making any long term
plans! Best good wishes for your work
& health – love from Tanya –

Leap of Faith

> ***I designed these teenagers to symbolize* hope**
> ***—a fitting entrance into the new millennium.***

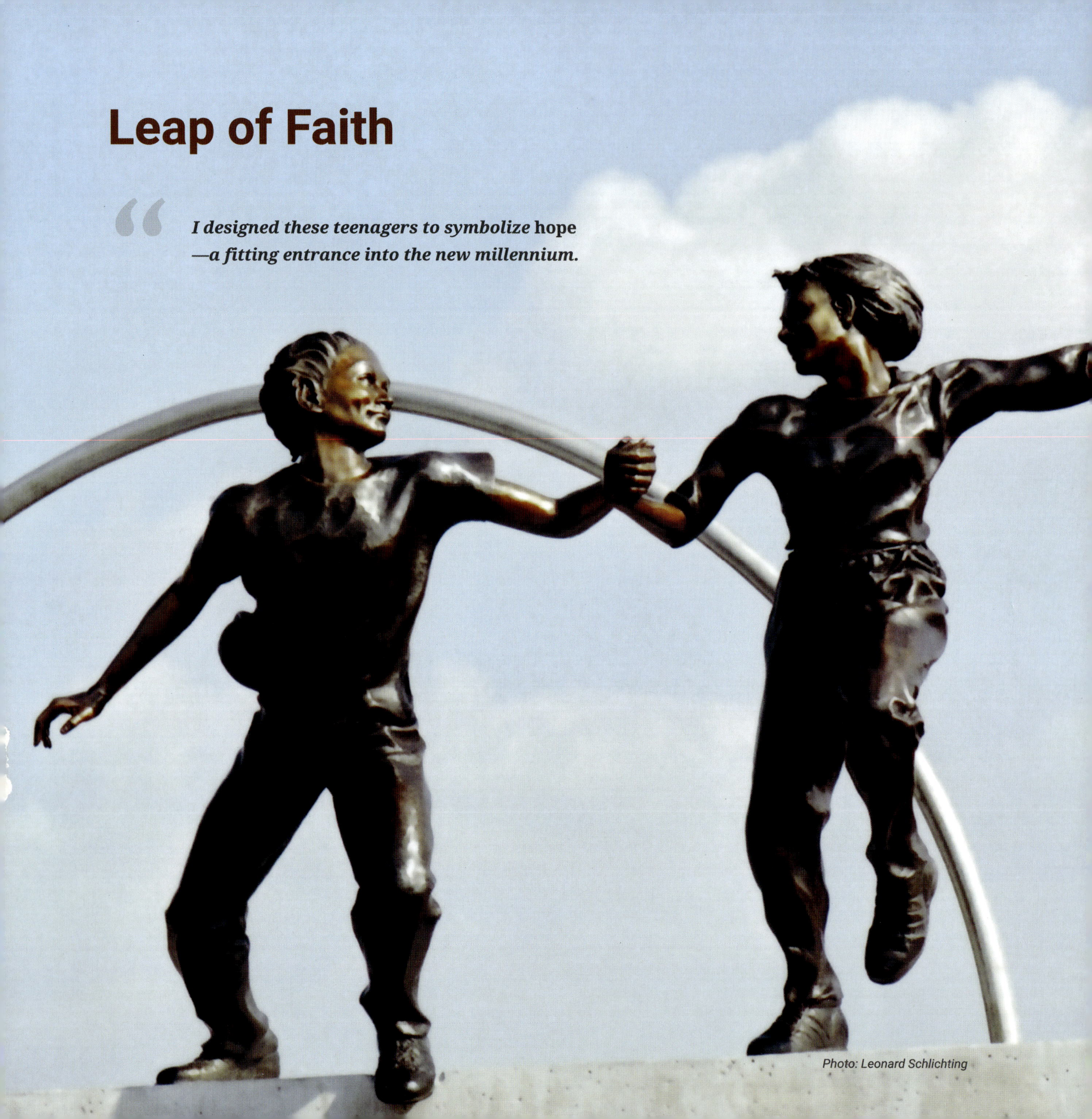

Photo: Leonard Schlichting

One sunny autumn day my neighbour Sarah Richardson met me at the mailbox. She outlined a Wilmot Township proposal to celebrate its 150th anniversary—which fell in step with the millennium. Lisa and Stephen Yantzi had offered a half-acre of land for a millennium park on the site of the township's first meeting hall.

German Mennonites from Pennsylvania had settled the township, west of Waterloo, in the 1820s. It remained largely agricultural. A commemorative bronze plowman was suggested, but I sought a more inclusive concept. My rural upbringing assured me that all successful farmers in the 1800s had wives with a formidable talent to multitask. The contributions of wives and mothers in the township's development would be hard to overstate. Women had to be a part of the bronze picture.

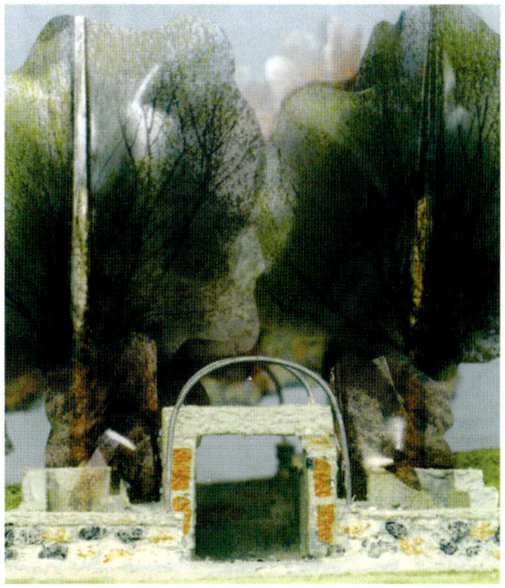

I presented a scale model in the township's elementary schools to introduce the millennium project. The kids' excitement was a reward in itself. Several years later I overheard one student telling a younger friend about the park and of the teenagers made of bronze. With pride, she declared, "That's us!"

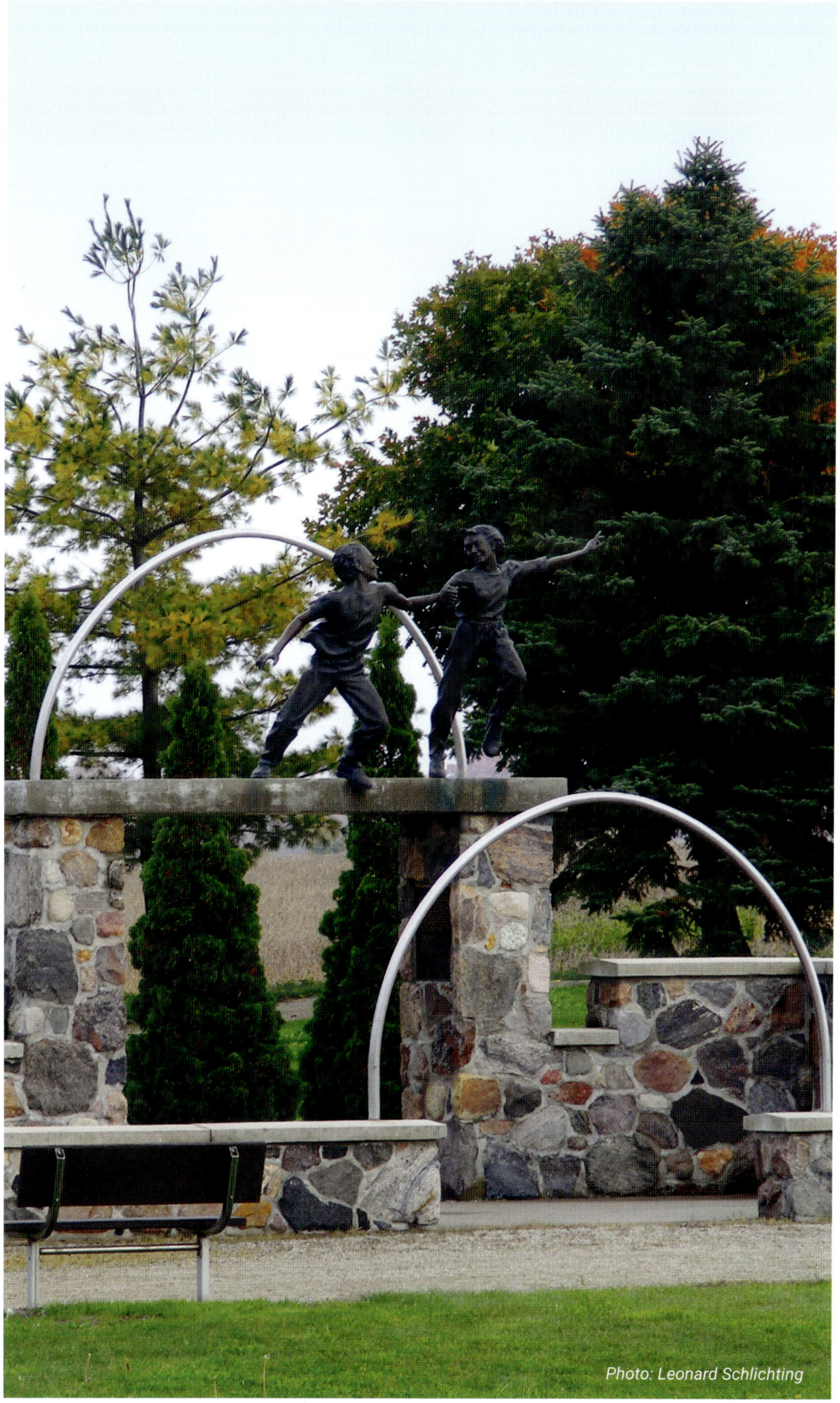

Photo: Leonard Schlichting

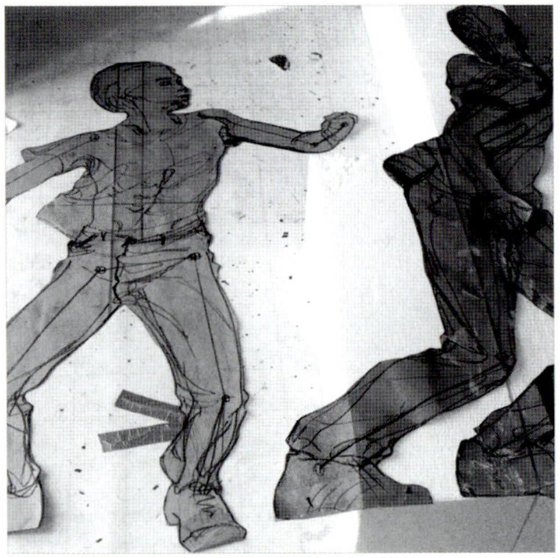

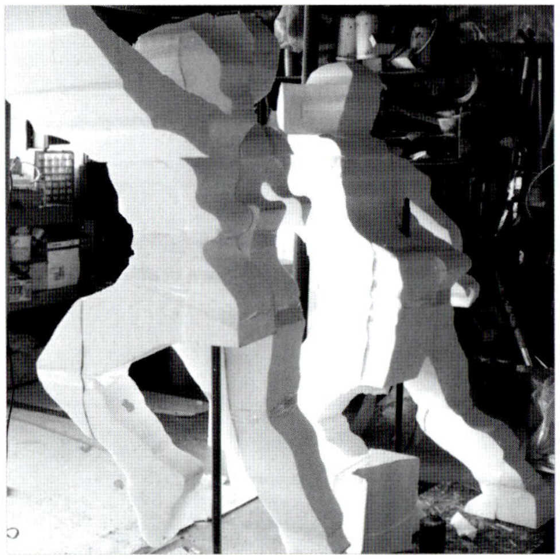

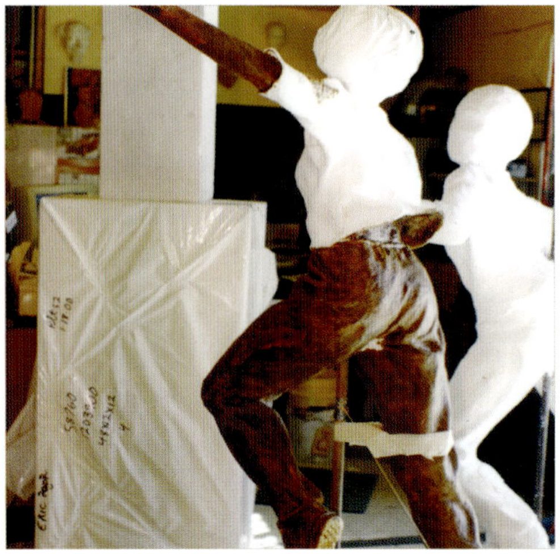

I considered what our arrival in the millennium meant. It was a moment of passage, an unavoidable entrance—best done with grace. My first goal would be to offset the anxiety then circling that year-2000 programming limitations would cause worldwide computer failure. I focused on hope. I began to imagine a pair of teenagers whose entry into adulthood reflected our unstoppable march into the future. I wanted a dynamic duo who'd dreamed up an adventure. The young man believed in his own strength and had concern for his partner's safe landing. The young woman was sure that, together, they could fly. These figures were a sculptural duet at every stage of creation.

The park's footprint had been proposed as a square, but Wilmot Township roads intersect at acute and obtuse angles. I designed a triangular park with roadside exposure for people driving by. The field's corner site had easy parking and access from a lesser-used side road. The original cropland was relieved of a narrow wet corner that was hard to work with large machinery. The three-sided park then had a view of the heritage farm to the east.

I had a fully formed image of the sculpture in my mind, but watching the excavators shape the landscape of my idea was exciting beyond measure.

The park, named *Oasis in the Centre*, required dedicated and inventive fundraising from a local population of only 22,000 people. Committee chairperson Marilyn Sararus was unstoppable. She and her group demonstrated the integrity and sense of purpose that distinguished this community. *Leap of Faith* was a perfect metaphor for this group's efforts to raise funds for the bronze and for the park.

I managed to include family and friend in *Leap of Faith*. The bronze girl had the proportions of my niece Dana Abernethy; I based the face on our neighbour Leah Schwartzentruber, then in grade three. The young man was a composite of Sasha Knight and Eric Lankin, both of whom have family ties in Wilmot Township. On the bronze boy's pant leg, I signed: "Especially for Glen and Alex. Love, Mom"

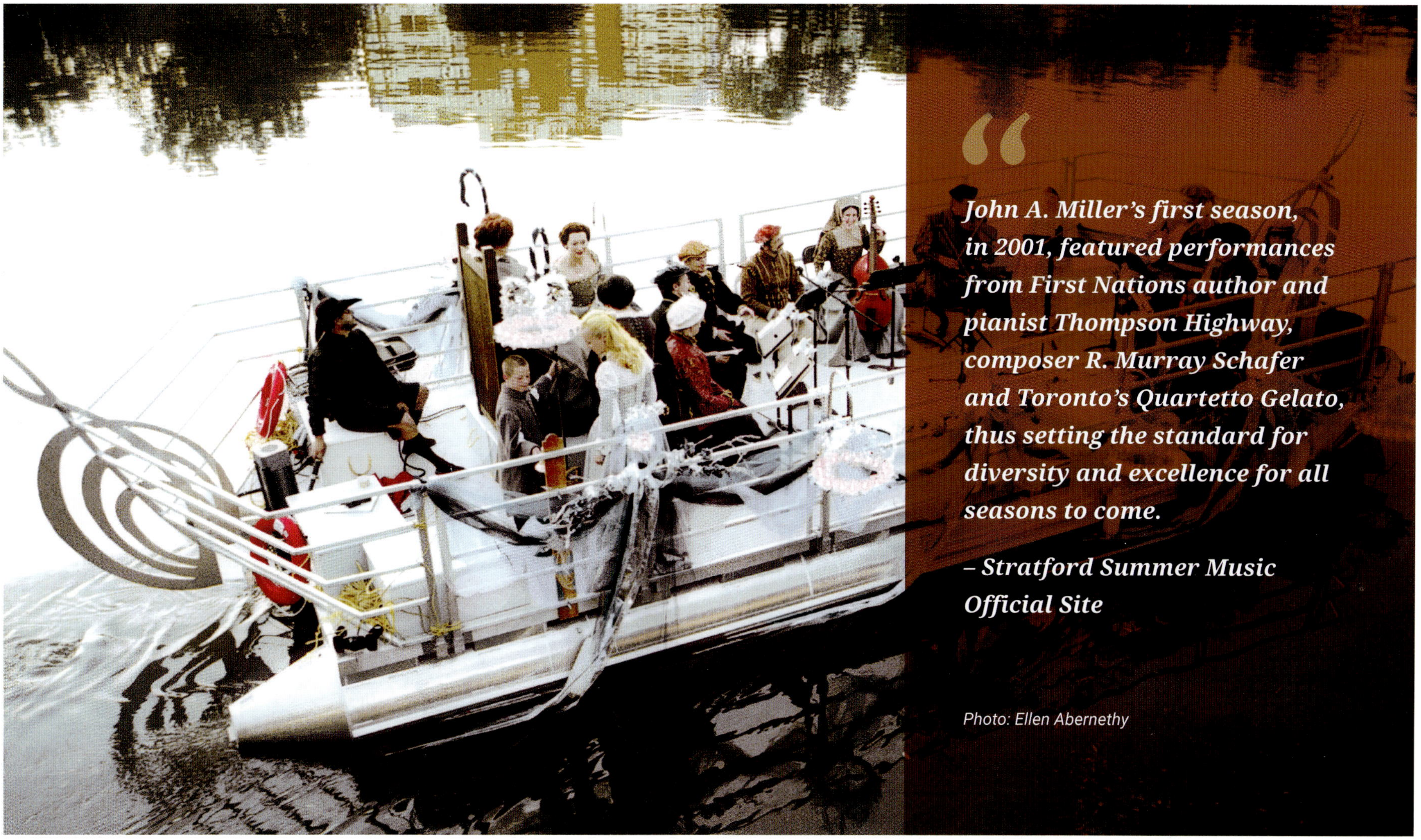

> *John A. Miller's first season, in 2001, featured performances from First Nations author and pianist Thompson Highway, composer R. Murray Schafer and Toronto's Quartetto Gelato, thus setting the standard for diversity and excellence for all seasons to come.*
>
> *– Stratford Summer Music Official Site*

Photo: Ellen Abernethy

Stratford Summer Music

John Miller, the administrator of the Glenn Gould Foundation, reappeared on his return to Stratford as Artistic Director of Stratford Summer Music. For the 2001 opening, John imagined a fanciful water pageant on the small lake in the town centre—reminiscent of royal evenings on the Thames River in London, England. Performers were to float into position for a first-night gala on Tom Patterson Island. The raft would then serve as a performance stage for musical groups during a six-week festival.

Even on the oversized pond in central Stratford, a watercraft required approvals and had to meet many safety requirements. Most significantly for John, the power system for the raft needed to be silent so that performers' music could be heard across the water. Knowing my husband Mark had experience with electric power systems, John asked the two of us to design the craft.

We began with a commercial kit for a pontoon boat. Mark devised a superb power system and he and I addressed safety measures and operating requirements to carry passengers. I'd designed the railings of the craft as musical notation with upright bars and a five-rail stave pattern. I cut stylized treble clefs from flat stainless steel for the bow and stern. I hinged these so that the tops folded down to allow the raft to float beneath a street-level bridge. On opening night and for many nights since then, our little craft has floated musical magic to Tom Patterson Island.

Al Waxman

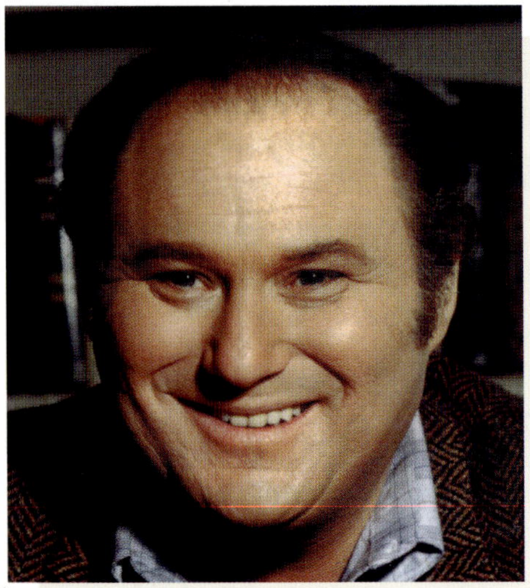

Albert Samuel Waxman (1935–2001)

Canadian Actor and Director

Al Waxman starred in *King of Kensington*, a very popular TV series across Canada. He played a variety store owner who helped his multicultural neighbours solve problems and find a foothold in their Canadian community. Internationally, he was better-known for his roles on *Cagney & Lacey* and in many films, but his iconic character will always be associated with Toronto's Kensington Market.

> *“Kensington Market is an ever-changing and colourful kaleidoscope in the heart of Toronto.*

The merchants of Kensington Market in Toronto, led by Tom Mihalik, the owner of Tom's Place, commissioned a portrait of actor Al Waxman. They were spurred on by an outpouring of emotion from Canadians across the country who responded to Al's sudden death in January of 2001. I began Al's portrait very soon after his death. The timeline for the project spanned his family's first year of adjustment and I have to say, they were courageous. His wife, Sara, was an excellent collaborator.

My visits to the Kensington Market area during the course of the project illustrated two striking things: First, the planetary difference between my rural childhood and that of the Waxman children in downtown Toronto. Second, the ever-changing demographic in Canadian cities.

Al's own childhood in Kensington had been culturally European. By the year 2000 the same area was home to new Canadians primarily from East Asia and South America.

The Market was rich with aromas from the cheese shops, the fish stores and the chocolate vendors. Garden produce was piled high on sidewalk tables; storefront windows along the packed streets offered every conceivable item for sale.

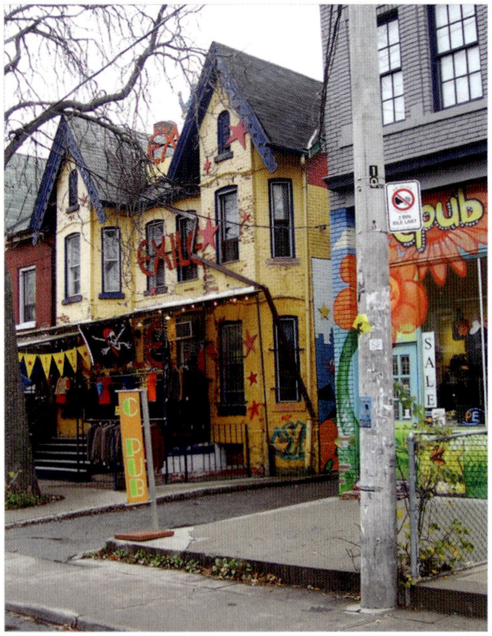

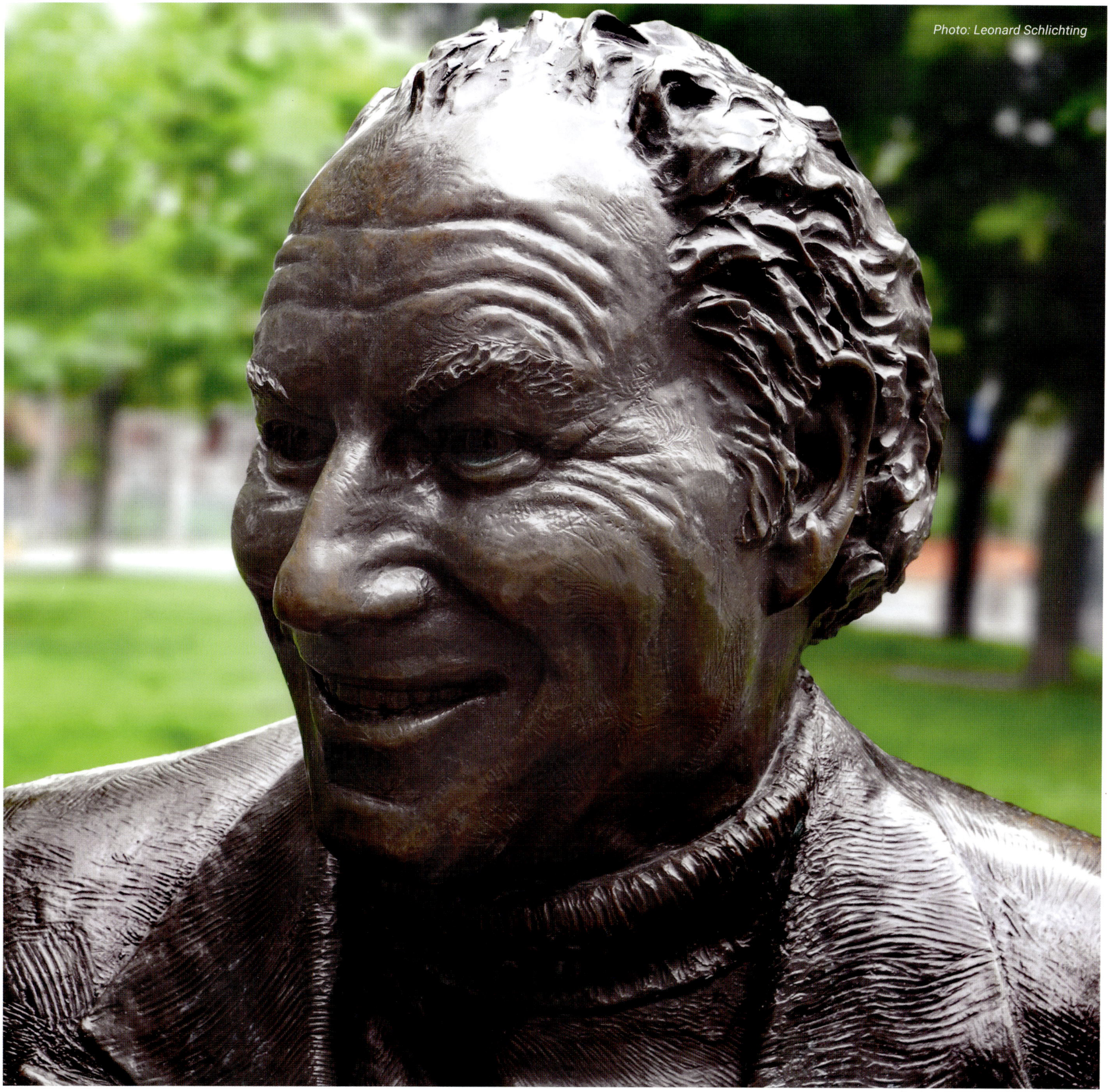
Photo: Leonard Schlichting

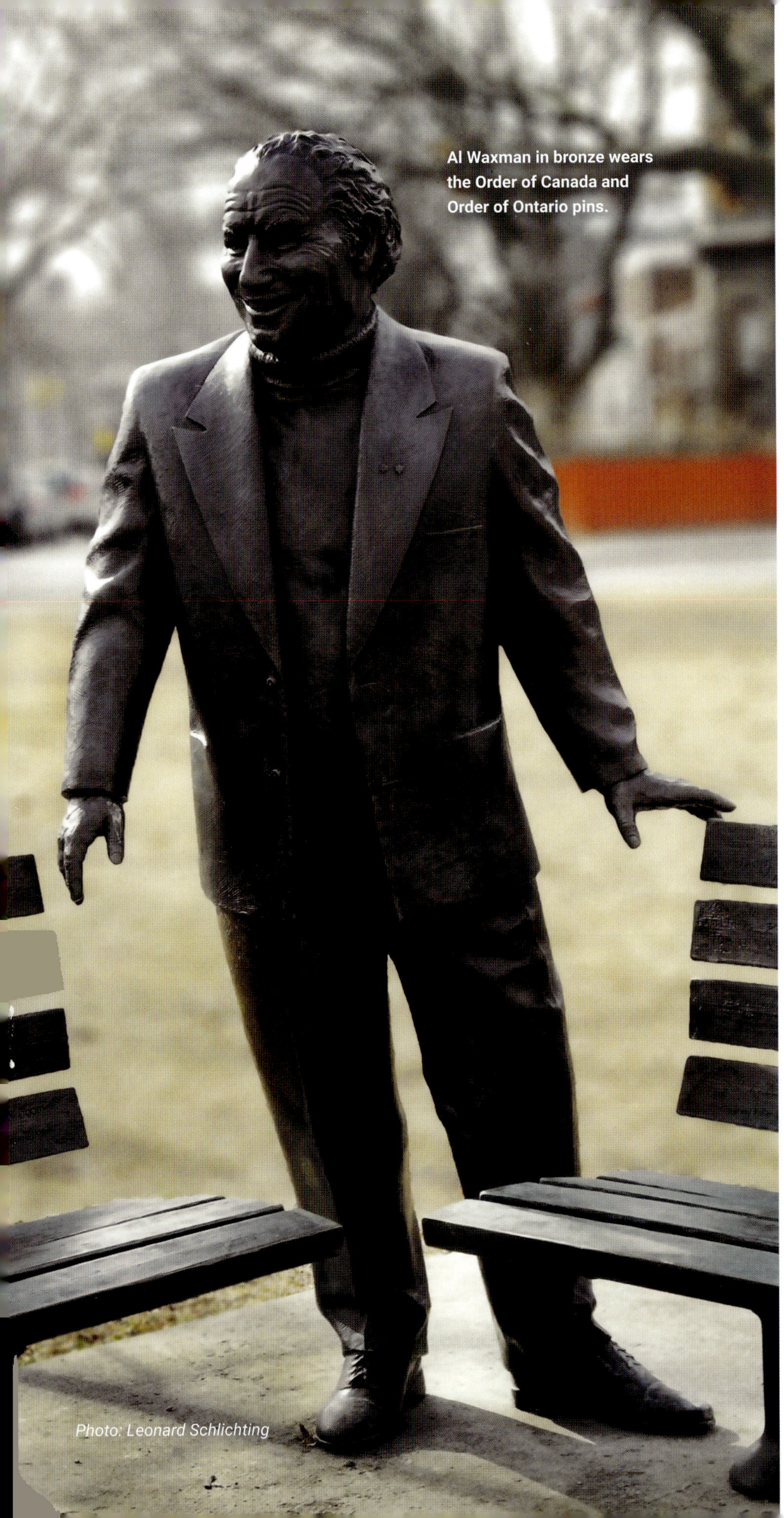

Al Waxman in bronze wears the Order of Canada and Order of Ontario pins.

Photo: Leonard Schlichting

Early in discussions of Mr. Waxman's portrait, his family and I determined a location for the figure in Bellevue Park near Al's community synagogue and peripheral to Kensington Market, the setting for his signature role. I posed the question to Al's son Adam, "Why is this man in this place, at this time?" Adam's face lit up as he exclaimed, "You want me to set the scene!" Thank you, Adam, I thought. In addition to portraying familiar features, I needed to set the scene for a true moment of encounter with Al.

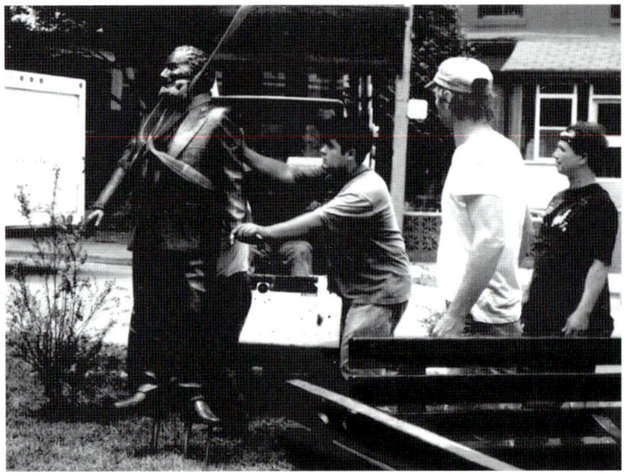

At the end of the market block, Al stands as though gathering with friends for coffee. He's flanked by two bronze benches. Into the bench's back planks are etched the names of his fans, friends and family. This colourful corner in Bellevue Park in Toronto remains the perfect location for Al Waxman, forever the King of Kensington.

"

There's lots to do down the road; there's always more. Trust your gut instincts. In small matters, trust your mind, but in the important decisions of life—trust your heart.

– Al Waxman
as inscribed on a flagstone at the portrait site

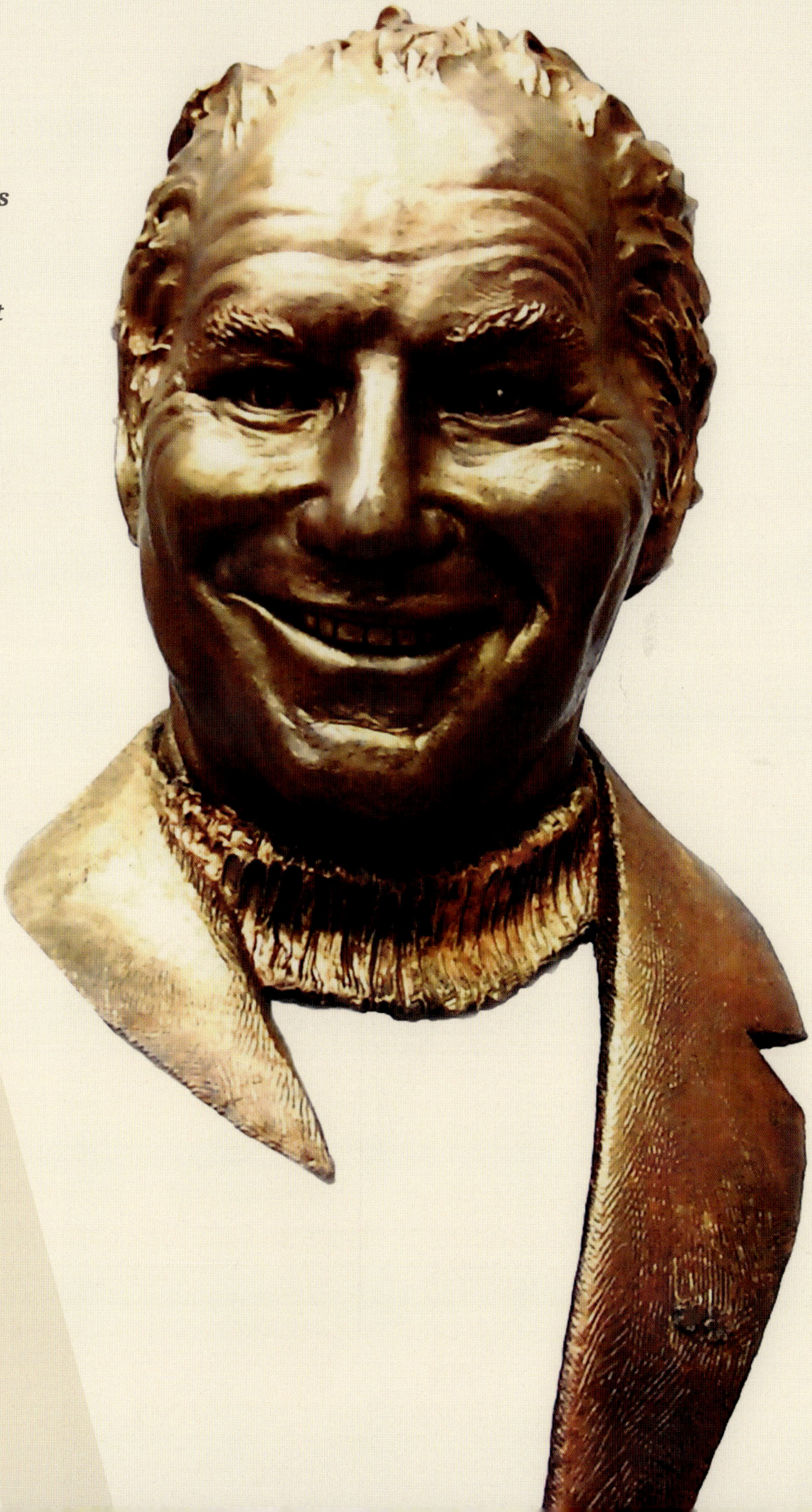

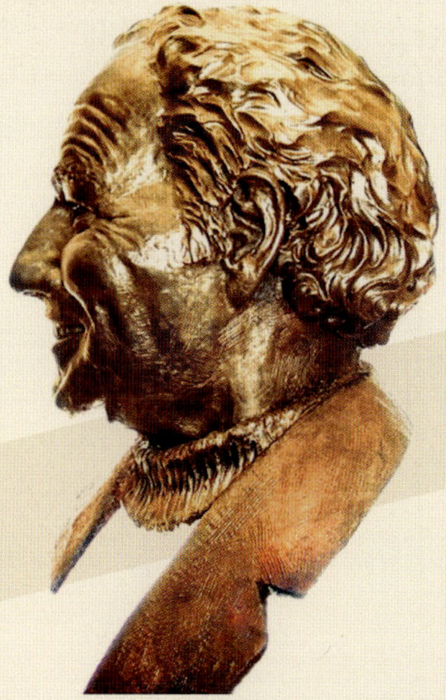

Al's head study was formed as a portrait bust. Shown here in wax, the finished bronze was acquired by the Canadian Portrait Collection in 2007.

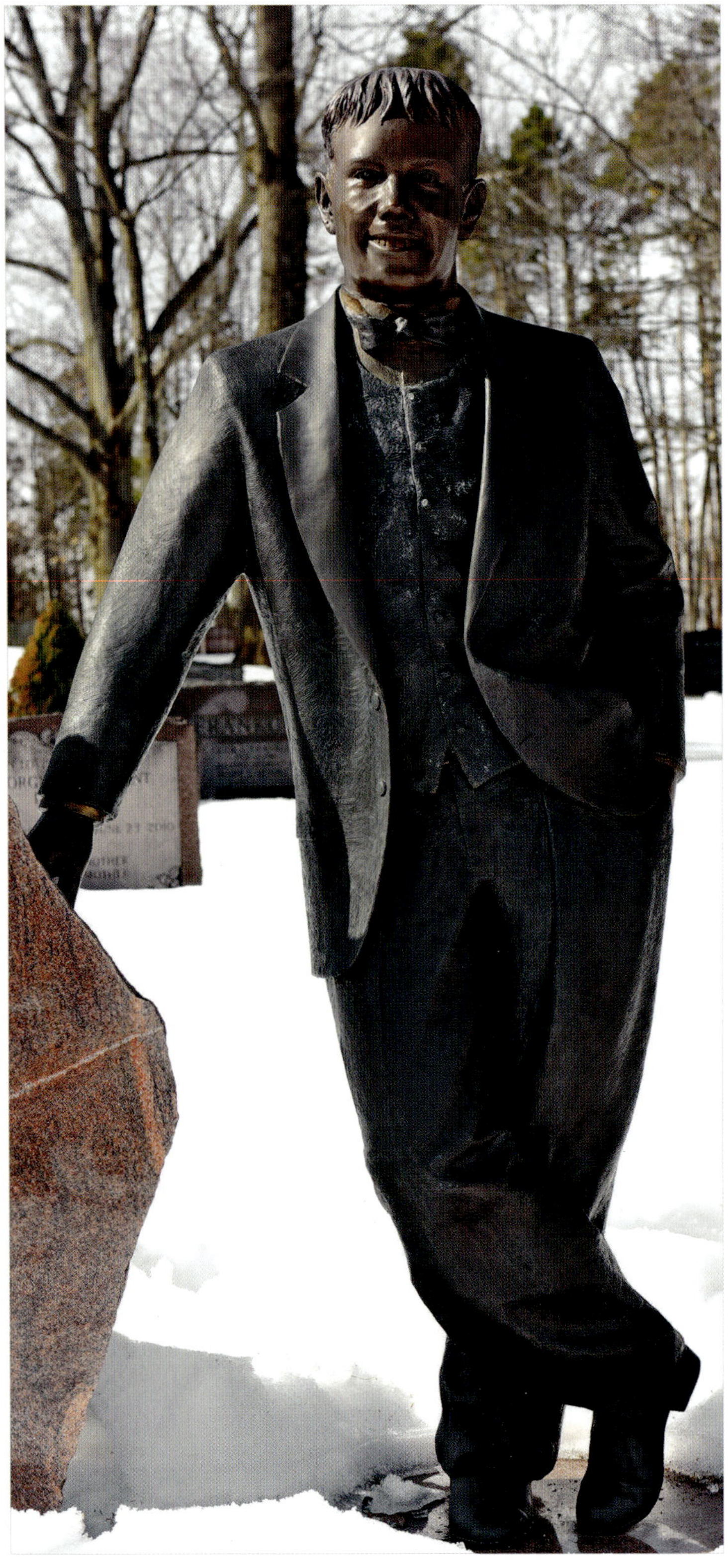

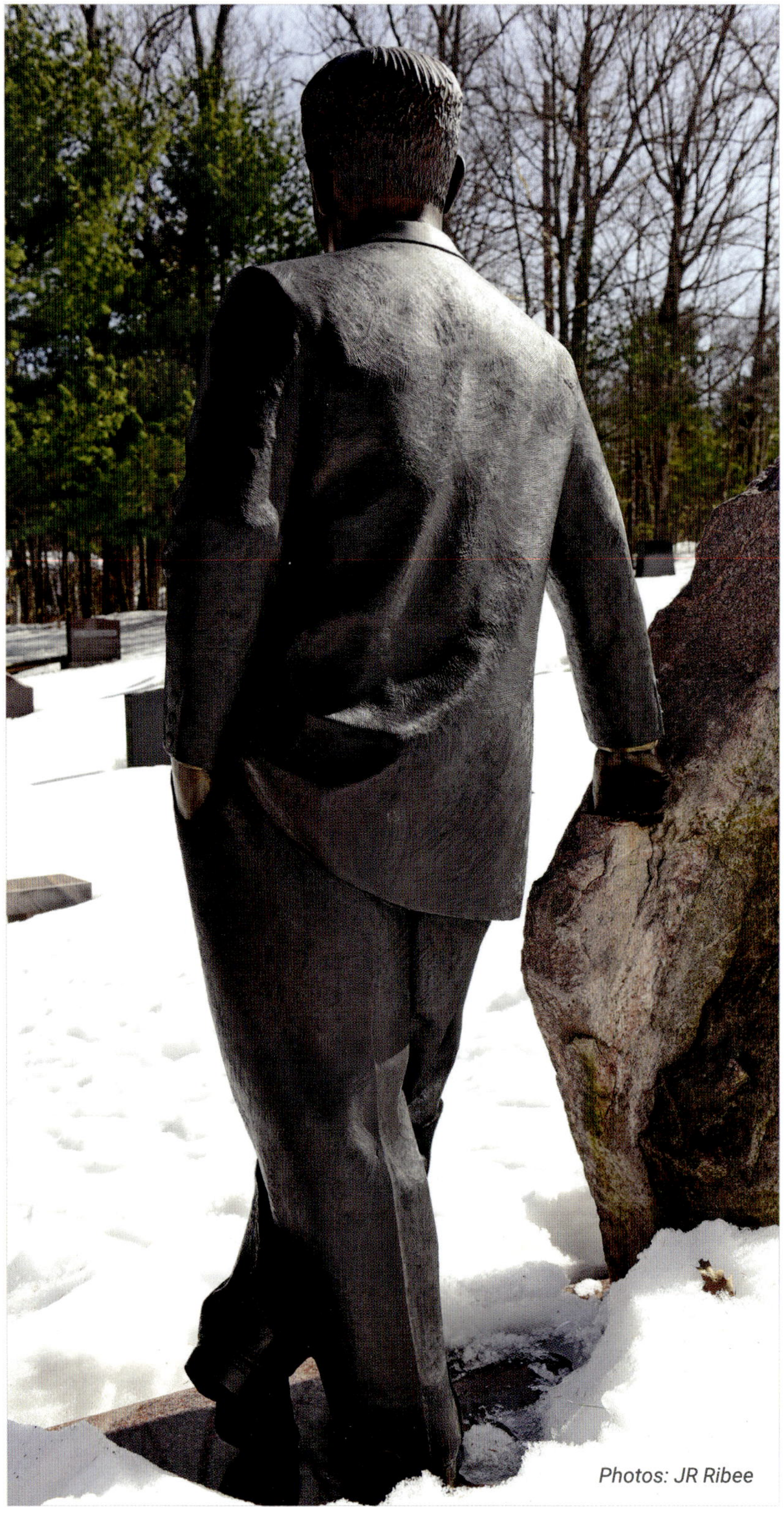

Photos: JR Ribee

Adam Elliott

> *Sculpting Adam involved hours of trying to reconcile loss and trying not to imagine vacant space no longer filled by people you love.*

Inquiries about a bronze portrait led the grieving Elliott family from the foundry to me. Adam, the eldest of four children, had died after a snowmobile accident just weeks after his 16th birthday. The accident was a tragic reminder of how instantly and drastically life alters.

On a golden afternoon, sitting with Adam's parents in my studio, an unusual level of calm prevailed. We pored over photographs, sharing tears and ideas. The table was covered with photos of people who truly loved one another. One candid shot caught Adam at a wedding. He was obviously attending his first 'grown-up' event, for which he wore a slightly oversized tuxedo and an enchanting smile. That was my reference.

For me, this portrait was a time of recommitment to Glen and Alex. My work was lit with glimpses of how immensely I loved them and shadows of how fleeting my time with them might be. Creating Adam was a striking illustration of how meaningful my portraiture can be.

The morning of September 11, 2001 was crisp and bright. Alex was in grade two. Pulling away, after a few hours at his school, I was unable to sort out disturbing narratives on the car radio. At home, I switched on the TV news to see the Twin Towers smoking. By early afternoon I heard more from a close friend whose son had arrived home from kindergarten. His questions to her haunt me still: "Why didn't that plane turn, Mommy? It could've just turned, and it didn't. Why?"

Grand Reassurance from Chandler, Arizona

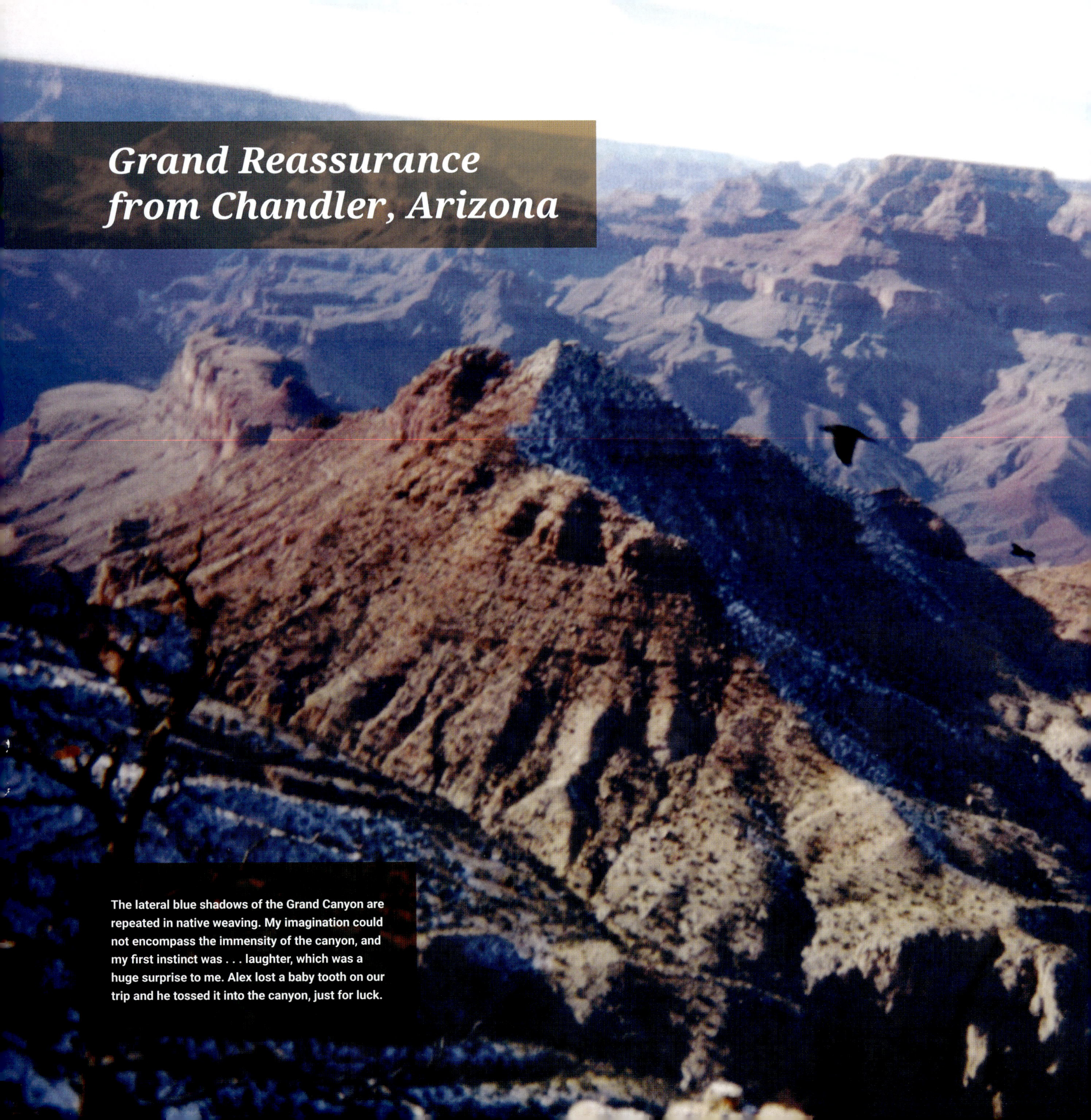

The lateral blue shadows of the Grand Canyon are repeated in native weaving. My imagination could not encompass the immensity of the canyon, and my first instinct was . . . laughter, which was a huge surprise to me. Alex lost a baby tooth on our trip and he tossed it into the canyon, just for luck.

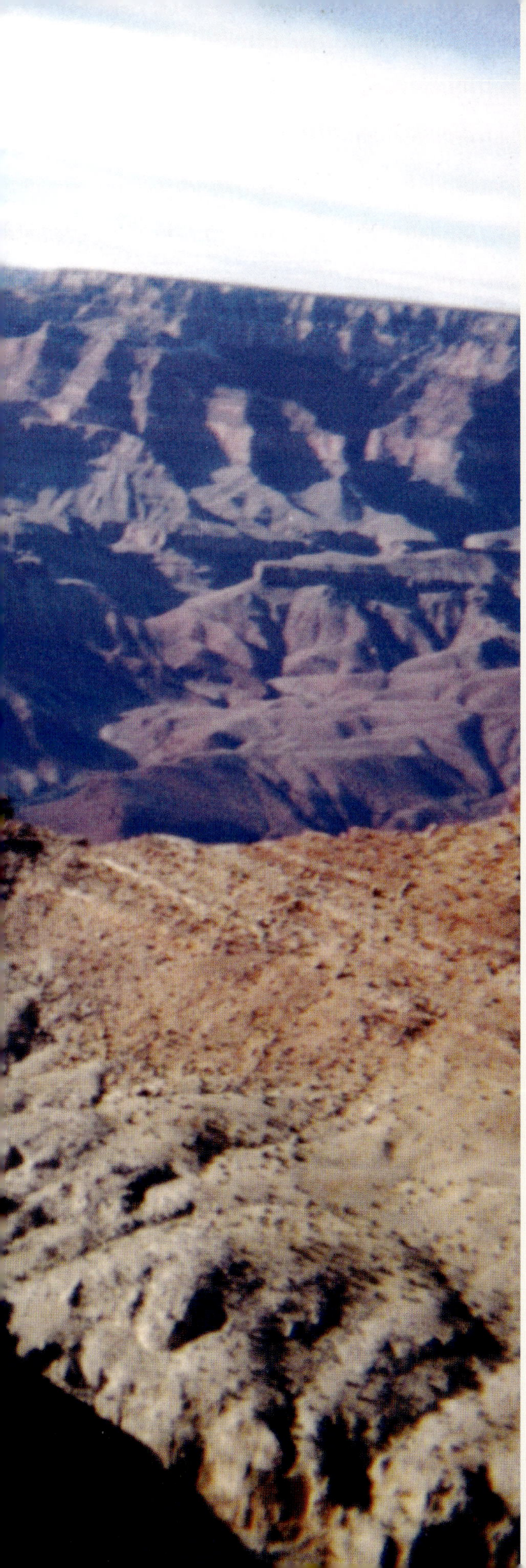

My early clumsy use of the internet brought occasional success. Somehow I found a Call to Artists from Vision Gallery in Chandler, Arizona. Chandler was named after Canadian veterinarian Dr. Alexander John Chandler, who had travelled to the American southwest to counsel cattle ranchers. He hated the desert and could hardly wait to leave but his departure was delayed by a thunderstorm. Watching the arid land spring to life after drenching rains, he fell in love with the place. The sculpture commission was to honour the Rosales, a Hispanic family who worked for Mr. Chandler building canals and irrigation systems to support farming (and golfing) south of Phoenix.

Vision Gallery greeted my design with excitement. As a finalist, I was to present my concept and a small 3D model called a maquette—in person. The Rosales commission went to Emanuel Martinez, a senior and well-established Hispanic artist from the American southwest. His work is represented at the Smithsonian Museum. I was honoured to be in such company.

With a delicate maquette in hand, Mark and I, with Glen and Alex in tow, headed to the airport. There, four-year-old Alex was randomly picked for a security check! With his pillowcase of travel toys tucked under his arm, he was stoic as the red-faced flight staff thoroughly patted him down.

While doing these early projects, I faced the incongruous choice of completing a sculpture that might last ten thousand years and the necessity of taking time to make a peanut butter sandwich that wouldn't last ten minutes.

I chose both, always, as best I could. I remember musing that I could perhaps 'have it all'—just not all at the same time.

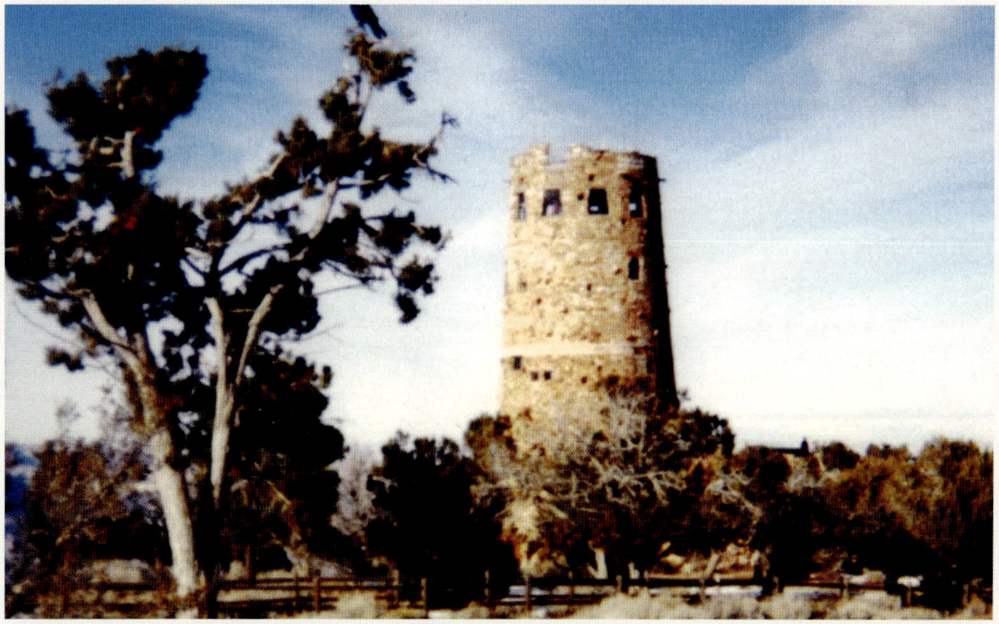

Franklin Children's Garden

In 2003 I got a phone call from Leslie Coates, a planner for the City of Toronto. Leslie had arranged the Music Garden installation on Toronto's waterfront some years earlier and was planning a children's park on Toronto's Centre Island. She had an imaginative landscape design by Janet Rosenberg which included a real turtle pond. Leslie hoped I might sculpt the animal characters from children's books about Franklin the Turtle. Glen, Alex and I loved Franklin; he and his gentle friends had a place in our hearts.

Brenda Clark, creator of the images of Bear and Beaver, Goose, Rabbit and tender-hearted Snail, was to come to Wellesley to be my studio consultant. I'd be rendering Brenda's ideas and she'd ensure they were true to her illustrations. My task was to imbue the creatures with the animal energy that would bring them to life; the characters would not be effective if they looked like stuffed toys. Working with Brenda on a 3D resolution held revelations. She and I had wonderful head-scratching conversations in which we invented new adjectives.

What Brenda drew as a line, I needed to resolve as a contour. It was an exhilarating mental workout through which she and I travelled to the third dimension!

Project timing dictated that foundation concrete for the bronzes in the park be installed months before the animals were cast. I'd have to get the spacing just right between the pairs of characters for their relationships to be believable. Leslie was a joy to work with and she managed every detail—to perfection. On unveiling day, Toronto Mayor David Miller and scores of children whisked away the hand-printed covers and brought *Franklin Children's Garden* to life.

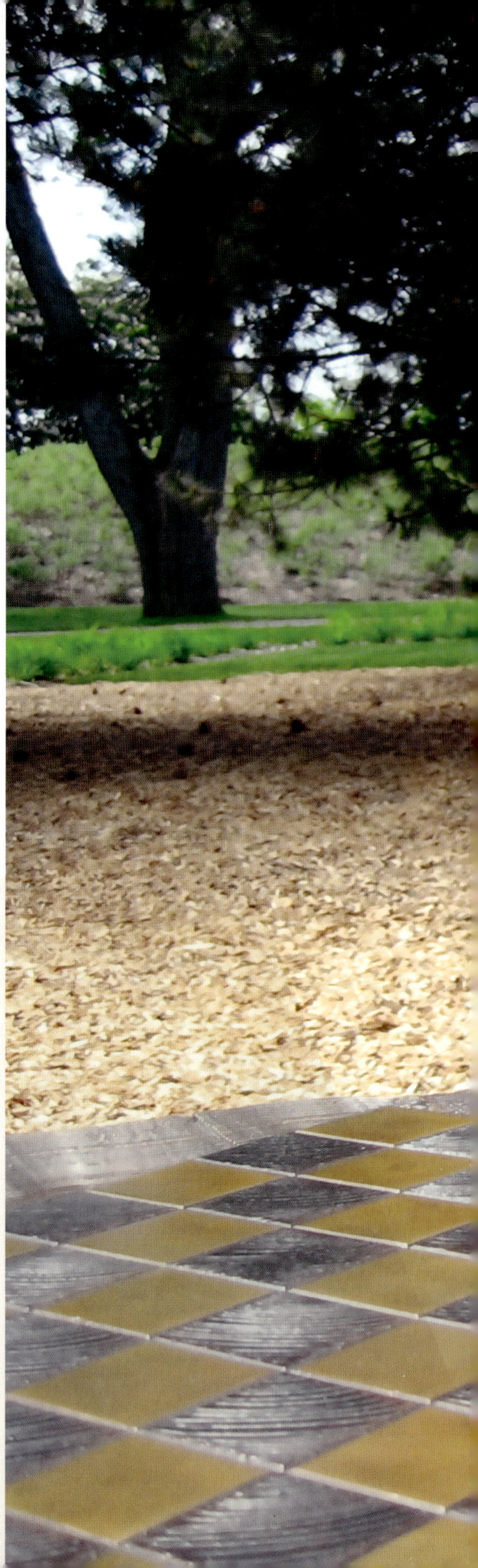

Franklin the Turtle is every young child's friend. Children instantly connect with his sense of adventure and they enjoy watching him solve familiar problems with friends in his own unique way. Created and illustrated by Brenda Clark and written by Paulette Bourgeois, the Franklin stories number more than sixty million copies in print. The books are sold in over thirty languages and Franklin has friends all over the world.

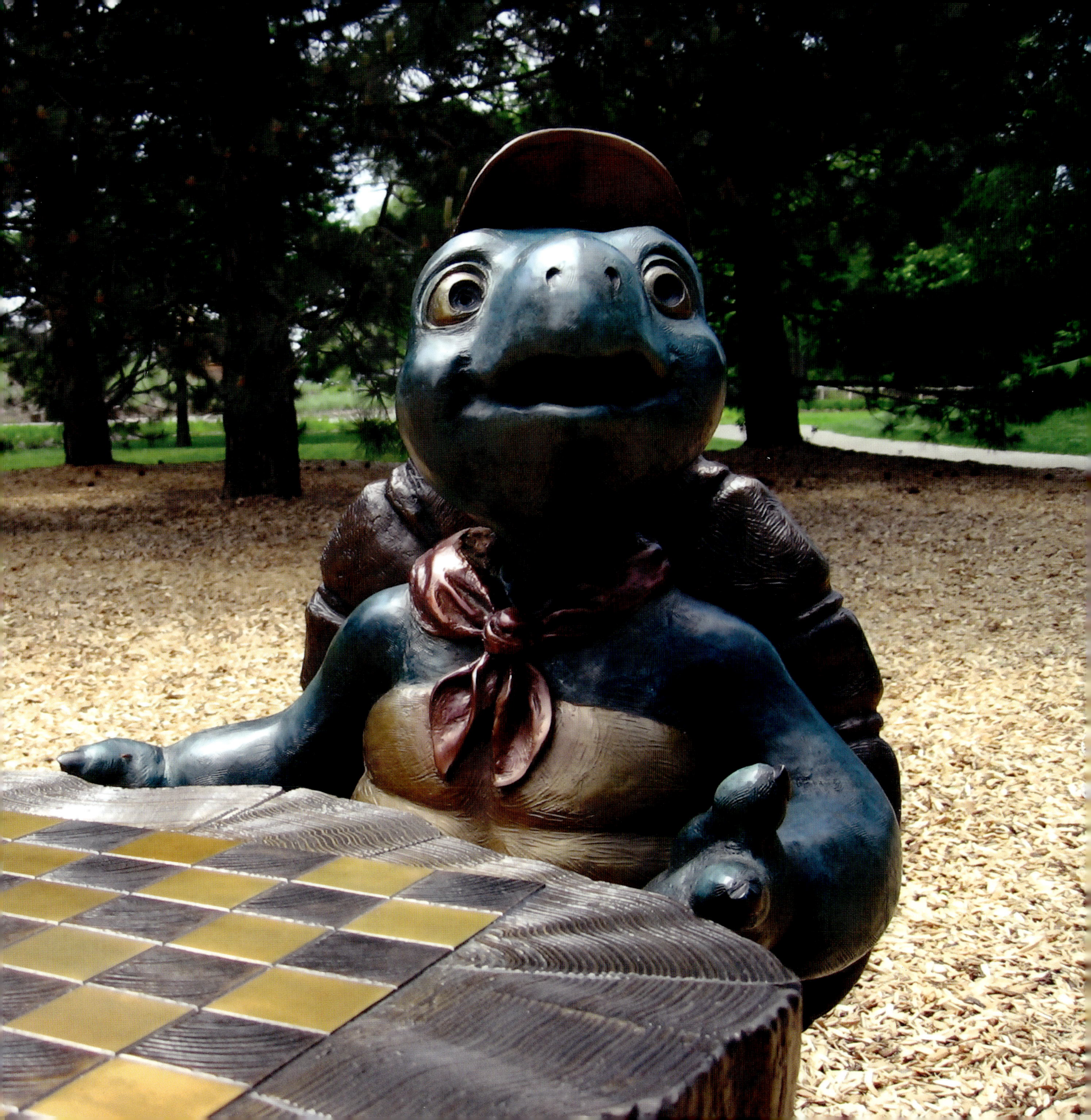

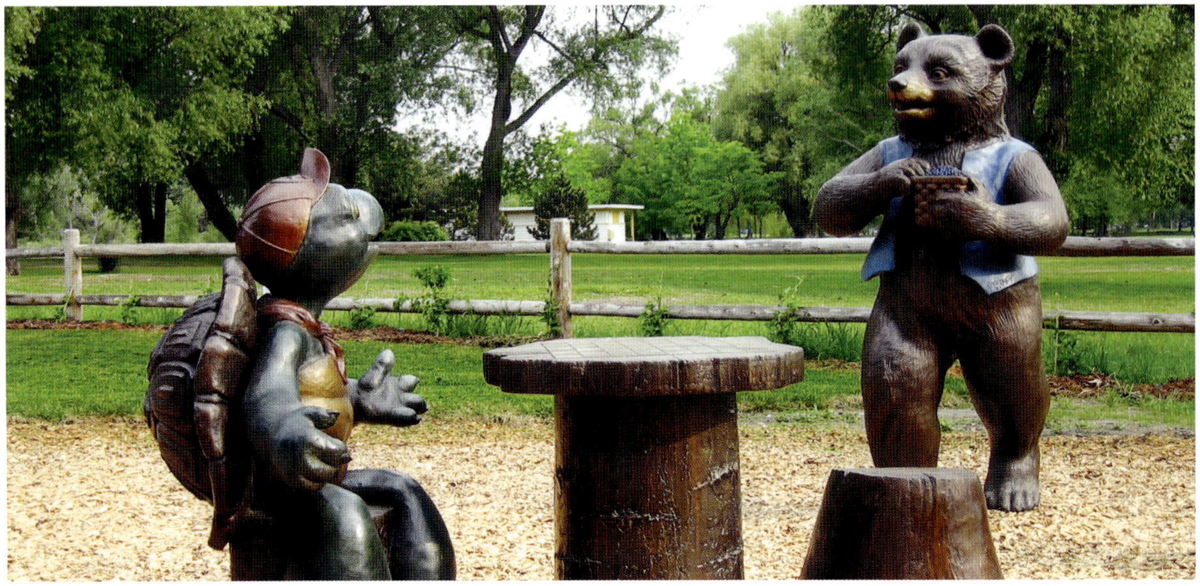

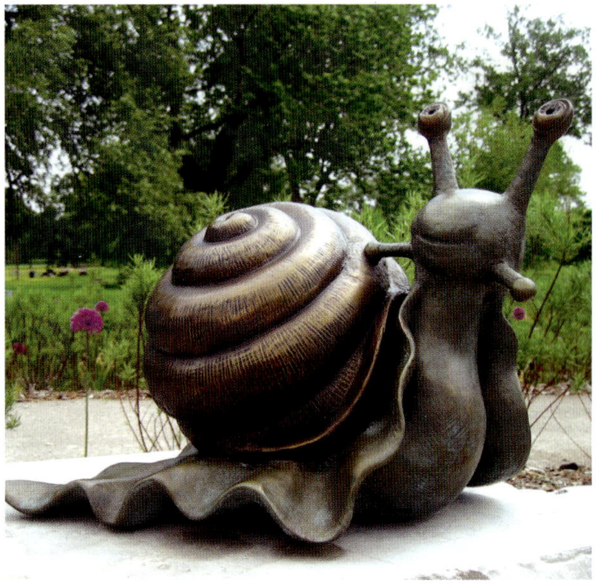

> *The garden is divided into seven sections where children can enjoy gardening, storytelling, exploring wildlife and visiting seven child-accessible sculptures from the Franklin the Turtle series.*
>
> *– City of Toronto website*

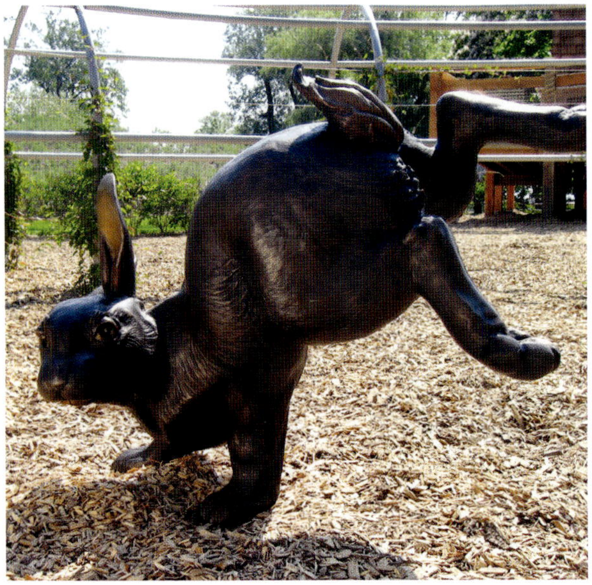

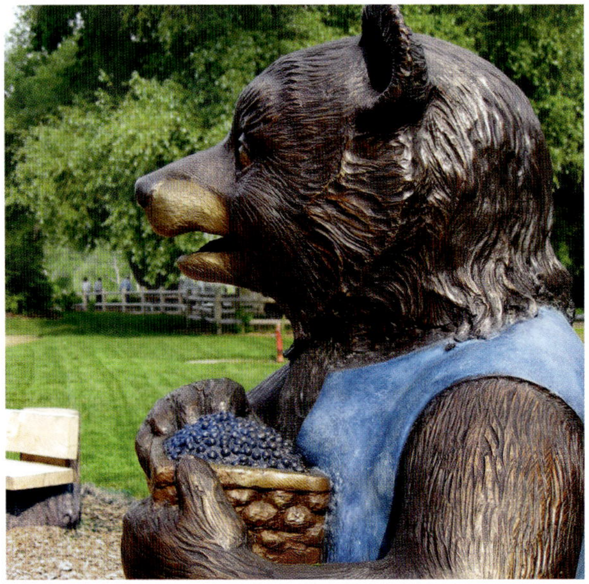

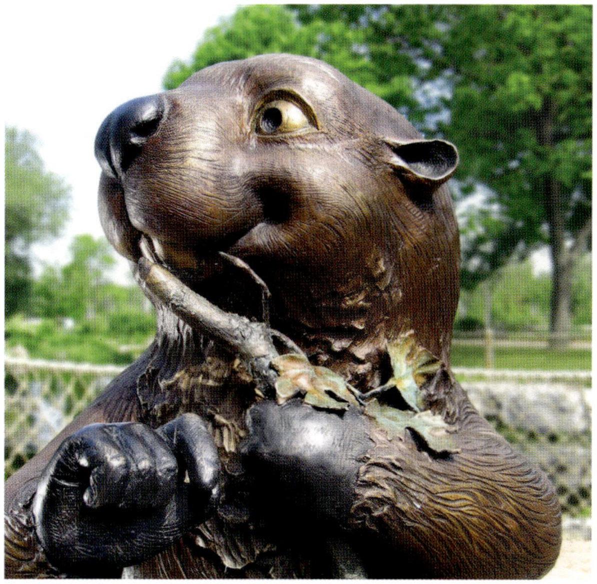

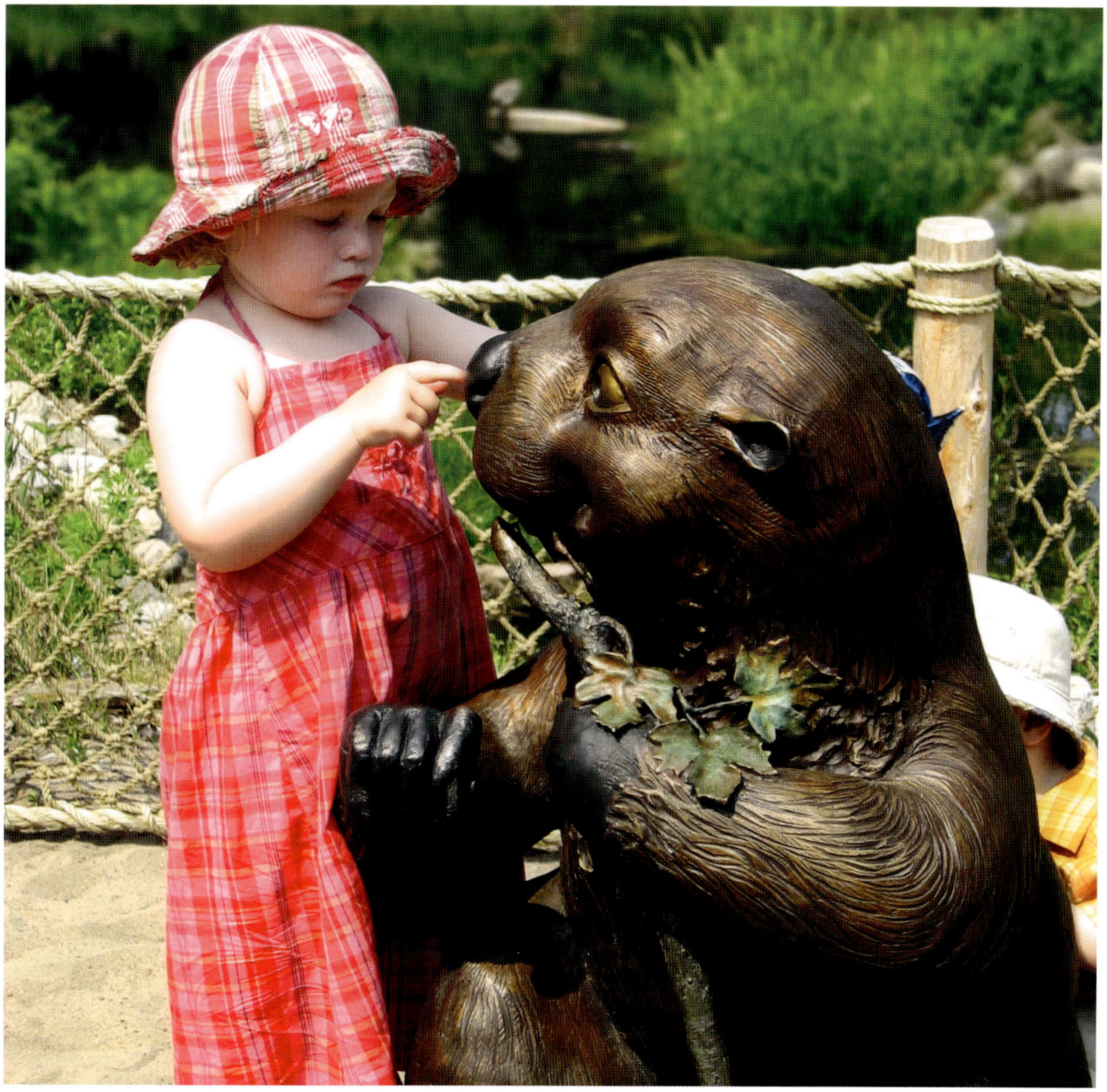

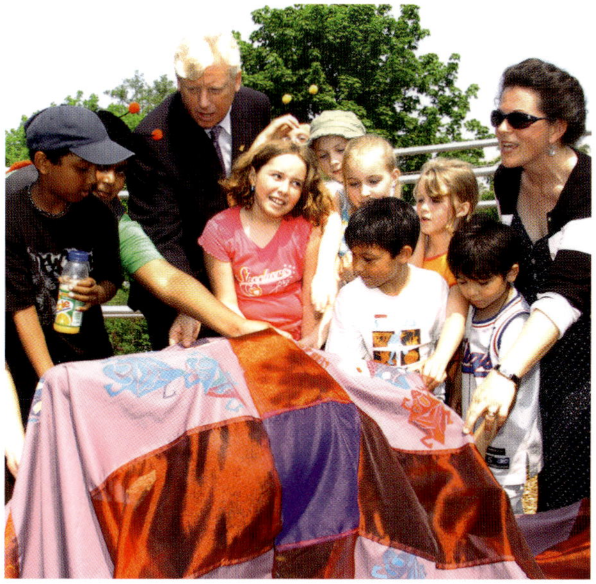

While I worked on the Franklin characters, we received word that Glen and Alex's small primary school was slated to close. Staff and students at North Wilmot P.S. were charmed at a terrific 'show and tell' of the animals I'd sculpted during the school's final term. Our unveiling team was led by Toronto Mayor David Miller.

Arnold Palmer

Nicknamed "The King", Arnold Palmer is one of golf's most popular stars and its most important trailblazer. He was the first superstar of the sport's television age which began in the 1950s.

In 1955 Arnold won his first PGA tournament at The Weston Golf and Country Club in Ontario. A photograph that embodied Palmer's spirit showed him at a podium joyfully embracing the Seagram's Cup. Palmer glowed with fresh energy; I did not need to look further for reference.

The massive podium, on which the Seagram's Cup rested, did present a problem. It would be expensive to replicate and I did not want to portray Arnold as an itinerant preacher beside a pulpit. I considered the image at length and resolved a believable composition. Arnold could sit on a black granite plinth and have just enough 'lap' to support the large cup.

The success of the Palmer portrait was all about balance. I was inventing the physical balance of Arnold's figure, transposing his standing position in the original photo to a comfortably seated bronze one. The finished Arnold seemed every bit as joyful about his success as he was in the original club photo.

Behind the scenes, I scrambled to find studio hours for this and several other projects—between requests to drive two sons from place to place. Few people saw that balancing act.

It's difficult to convey to clients just how many months it takes to move a complex portrait project from an idea to a finished item. Smoking timelines recur like a theme! Each endeavour develops a unique trajectory, but there is seldom a moment to lose. Mine was a pragmatic process of resolving forms that held their meaning and satisfied a legacy. More and more, I appreciated my years of meeting theatre deadlines where the first, and almost only rule, was not to panic.

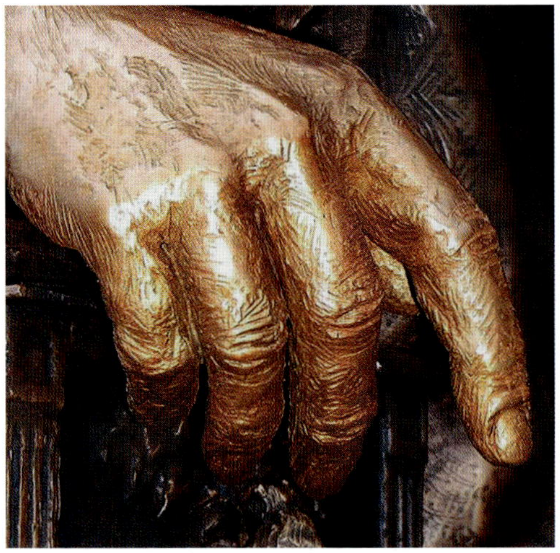

I love the challenge of sculpting hands and was particularly pleased with Arnold's. Hands are worked last to avoid them being damaged when the piece is moved and rotated for waxing. It's a relief to finally cut the hands free of the figure and sit down to sculpt them.

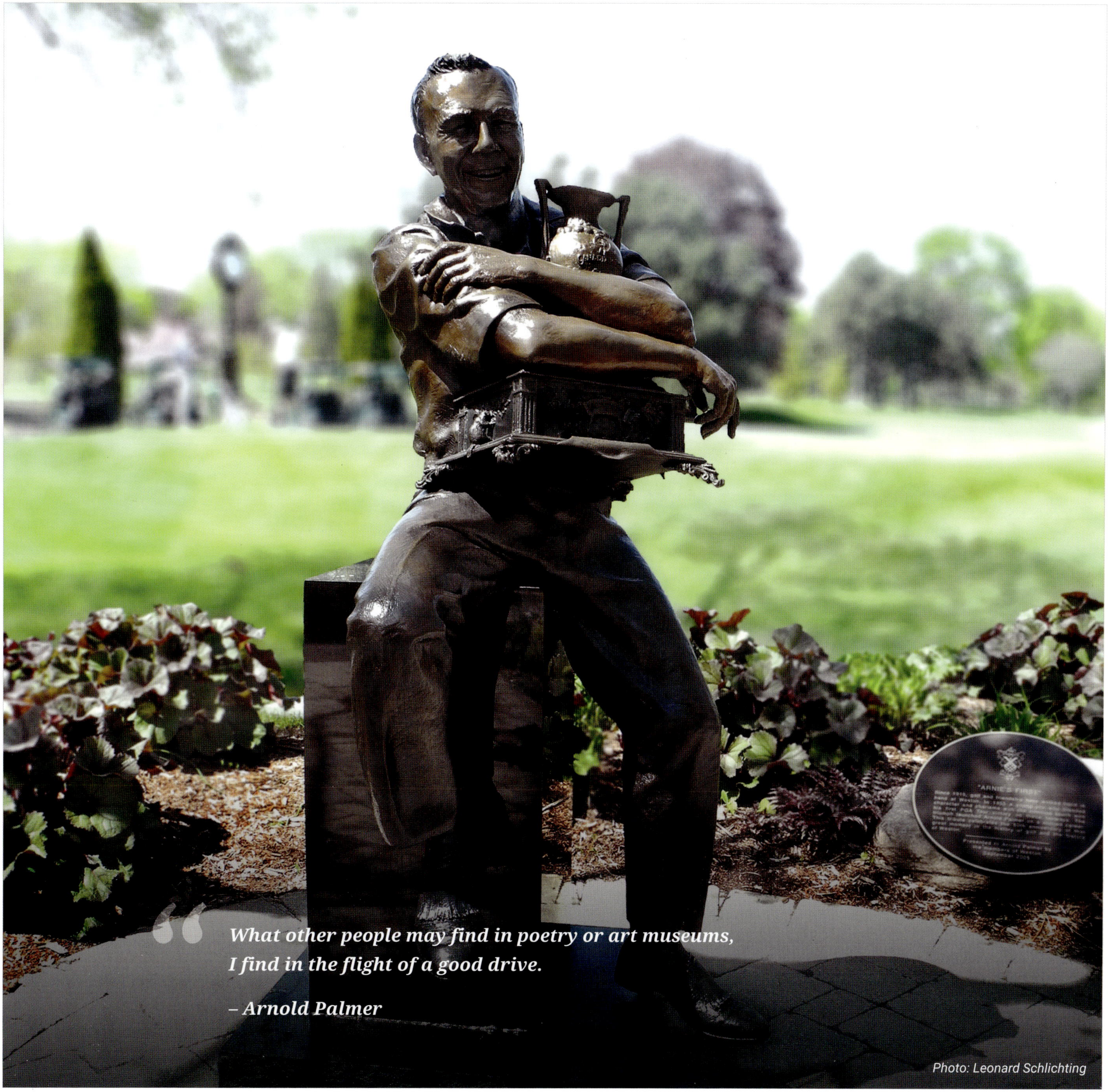

What other people may find in poetry or art museums, I find in the flight of a good drive.

– Arnold Palmer

Photo: Leonard Schlichting

Big Ben

Big Ben was a remarkable show-jumping horse, recognized in 1999 as a Canadian icon when Canada Post honoured him on a stamp. He was inducted into the Ontario Sports Hall of Fame and joined racehorse Northern Dancer as one of the only two horses in the Canadian Sports Hall of Fame.

A local committee in Perth, Ontario imagined a very large bronze of a very large horse in Codes Mill Park. The gorgeous grounds and rippling creek were just minutes from Millar Brooke Farm, the home of Ian Millar, his family and, of course, Big Ben the Belgian-bred show jumper.

By the time I was asked to put my hands to sculpting Big Ben and his rider Ian Millar, time was of the essence. Pattern-maker Stewart Smith had created a maquette of Big Ben and Ian but I suggested we get input from a true equine artist to proceed further. My sister Jean was the perfect candidate. She'd drawn horses since she could hold a pencil and sustained a career as a uniquely qualified horse illustrator.

I booked a flight for Jean from Marietta, Georgia, relieved she'd overlay her understanding of horse anatomy onto the sculpting process. We headed directly from the airport to the studio. In his workshop, enlarging sculptor Stewart Smith had done an admirable job of laying out the horse's form on an enormous jig. Jean sat astride Big Ben, pointing and instructing as Stewart and I sliced and shaped. Jean had watched Big Ben's career and was thrilled to have a hand in his rendering. Her few studio days were more intense than Christmas. I tackled the huge wax surface, refining shapes and textures for the whipping mane and tail and the rider's leather boots and flipping tailcoat.

As the three of us worked away furiously, Ian Millar and his wife, Lynn, made time in their demanding schedules for the five-hour drive from Perth to New Hamburg to see the making of *Big Ben*. They loved the work and their passion helped sustain our energy to the finish line. As luck would have it, the queue of work at the foundry stalled. While the clock ticked loudly for us, another artist's delicate wax sculpture had just began casting. We'd gained two additional weeks! Every second made a difference.

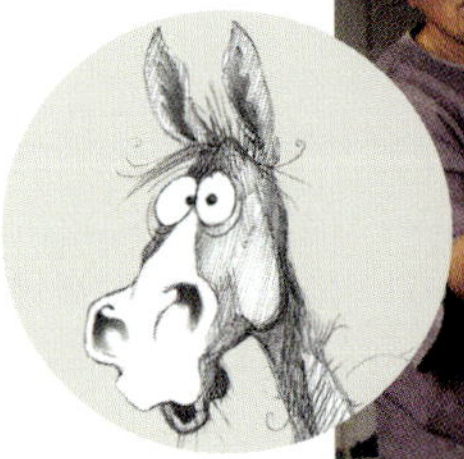

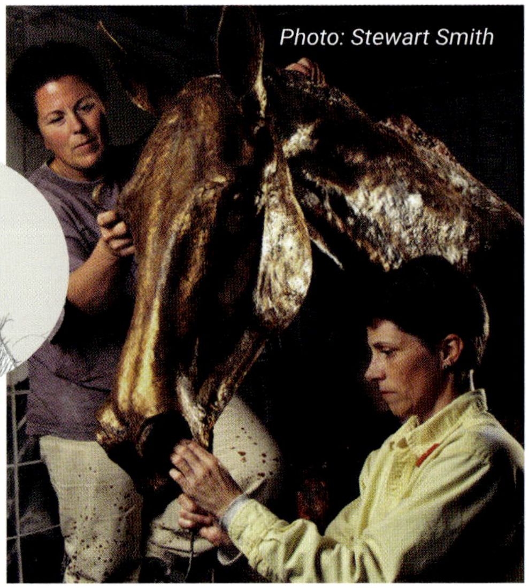

Photo: Stewart Smith

My sister Jean is an equine illustrator and her expertise guided the shaping of *Big Ben*. Her animated character Fergus has romped through horse publications for decades.

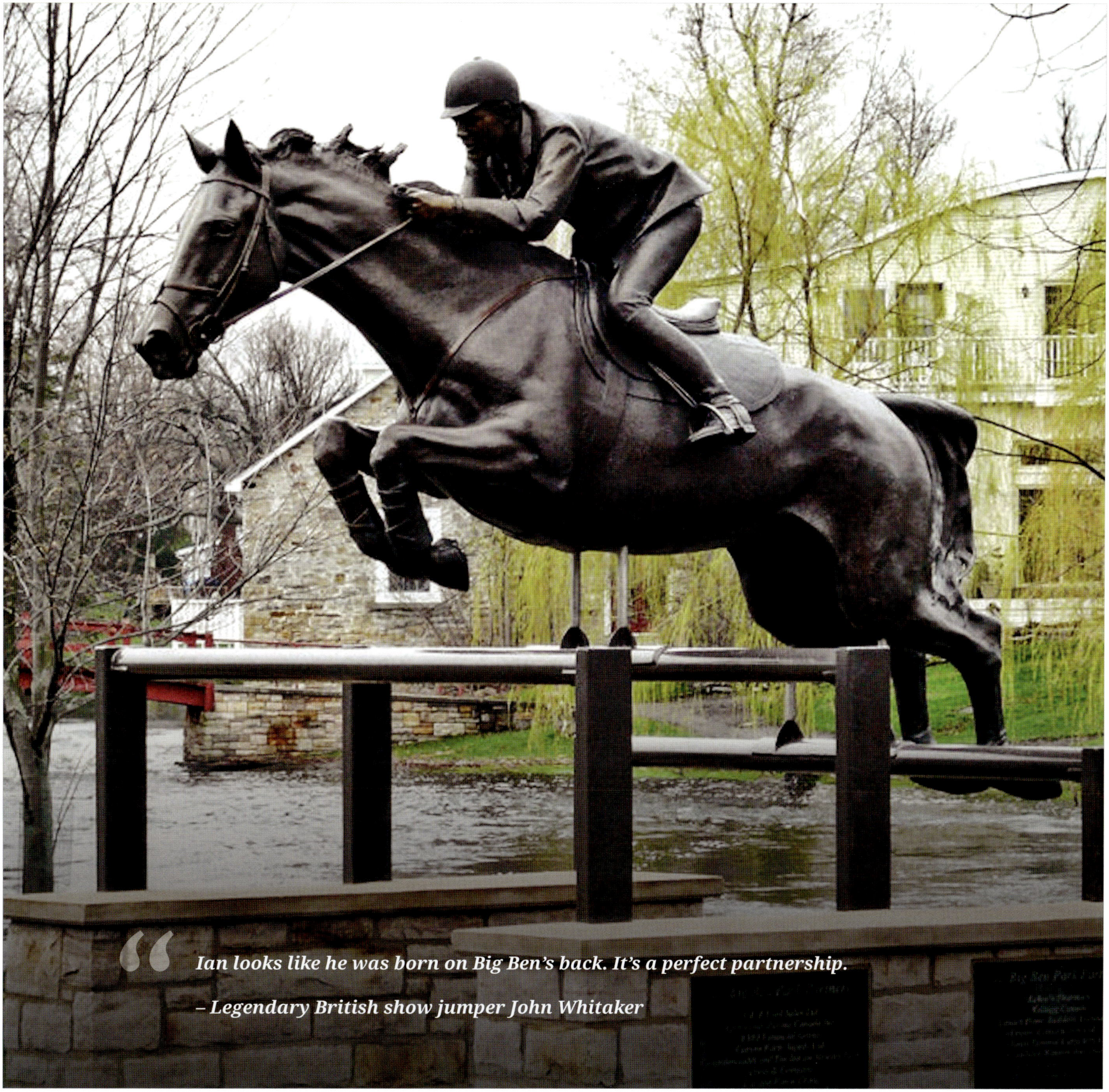

> *Ian looks like he was born on Big Ben's back. It's a perfect partnership.*
>
> *– Legendary British show jumper John Whitaker*

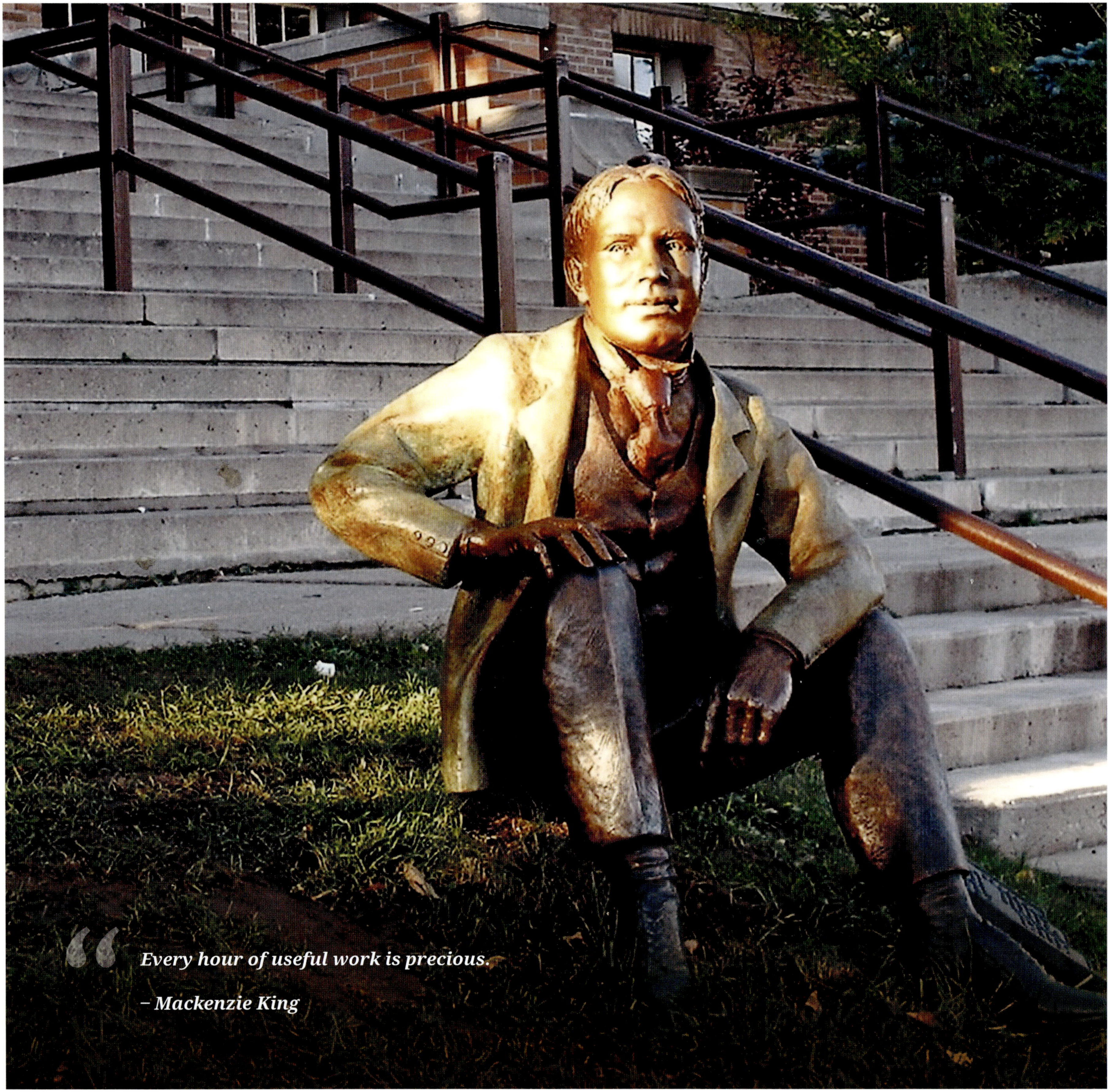
Every hour of useful work is precious.
– Mackenzie King

Mackenzie King

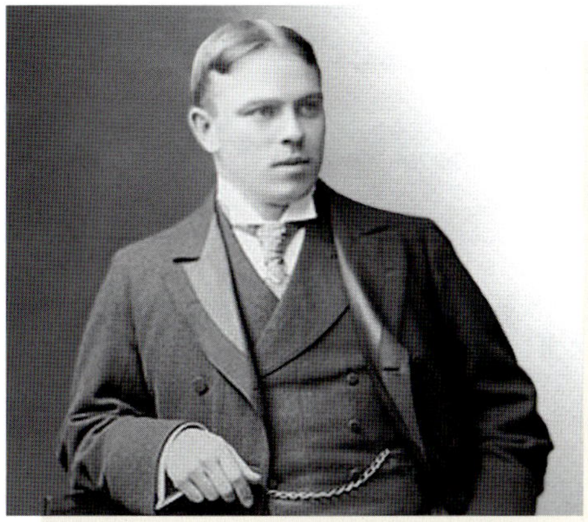

William Lyon Mackenzie King (1935–2001)

Prime Minister of Canada

Mackenzie King was Canada's longest-serving Prime Minister. He was the only leader in the British Commonwealth re-elected after World War II. King graduated from the University of Toronto in a new field of study called Political Science. He was our only PM to earn a PhD (from Harvard).

Alison Rodger taught at Forest Glen Public School in New Hamburg, where I'd presented the Wilmot Millennium Project and the sculpture *Leap of Faith*. Alison's husband, Jim, was principal of Kitchener Collegiate Institute. Jim called the studio one day to discuss a figure portrait of school alumnus and former Prime Minister, William Lyon Mackenzie King. He wanted it for his school's 150th anniversary.

Reading about Mackenzie King left me acutely aware that in contemporary Canadian lore he suffered from misrepresentation. It reinforced my idea that the context surrounding any life is difficult to convey, but it is also critical to understanding the person. How easy it was to overlook the fact that once upon a time, discussions of séances and eugenics were cutting-edge dinner table conversation. I suspected that our current conversations might sound misguided in another hundred years.

Tragically, King had reason to be interested in séances. His parents and one sister died within months of each other in the influenza outbreaks following WW I. King's surviving brother suffered poor health and relocated to Arizona. These losses in his close-knit family left King keen to explore connections with departed loved ones.

I compared these trials in his adult life with King's earlier childhood happiness in Kitchener. That dichotomy helped me imagine a moment that would make Mackenzie King approachable. Rather than a middle-aged man with a paunch and softening features, I sculpted a young man stealing a moment between classes at school. Situated on the embankment near the school's entrance, King's simple portrait reminds us of any young person who might someday make a difference.

To my unending delight, the finished bronze of Mackenzie King is loved by all and has been polished by many hands.

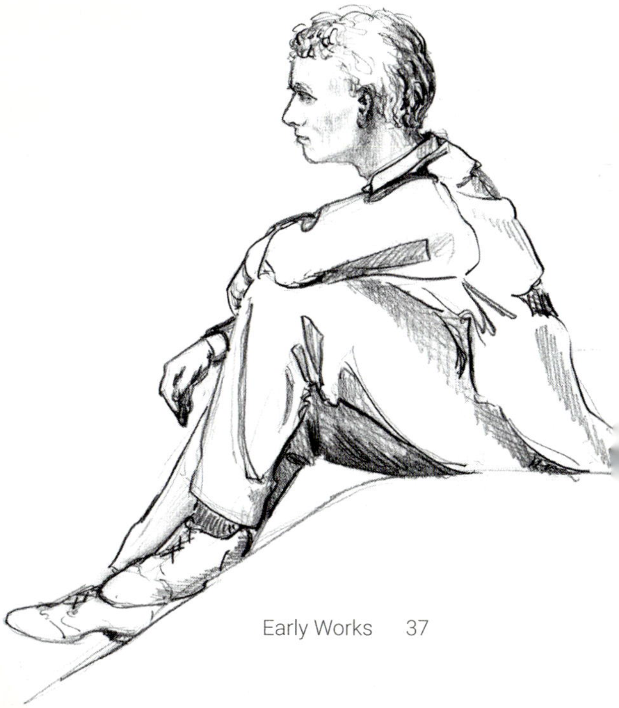

PART TWO

The Canadiana Collection

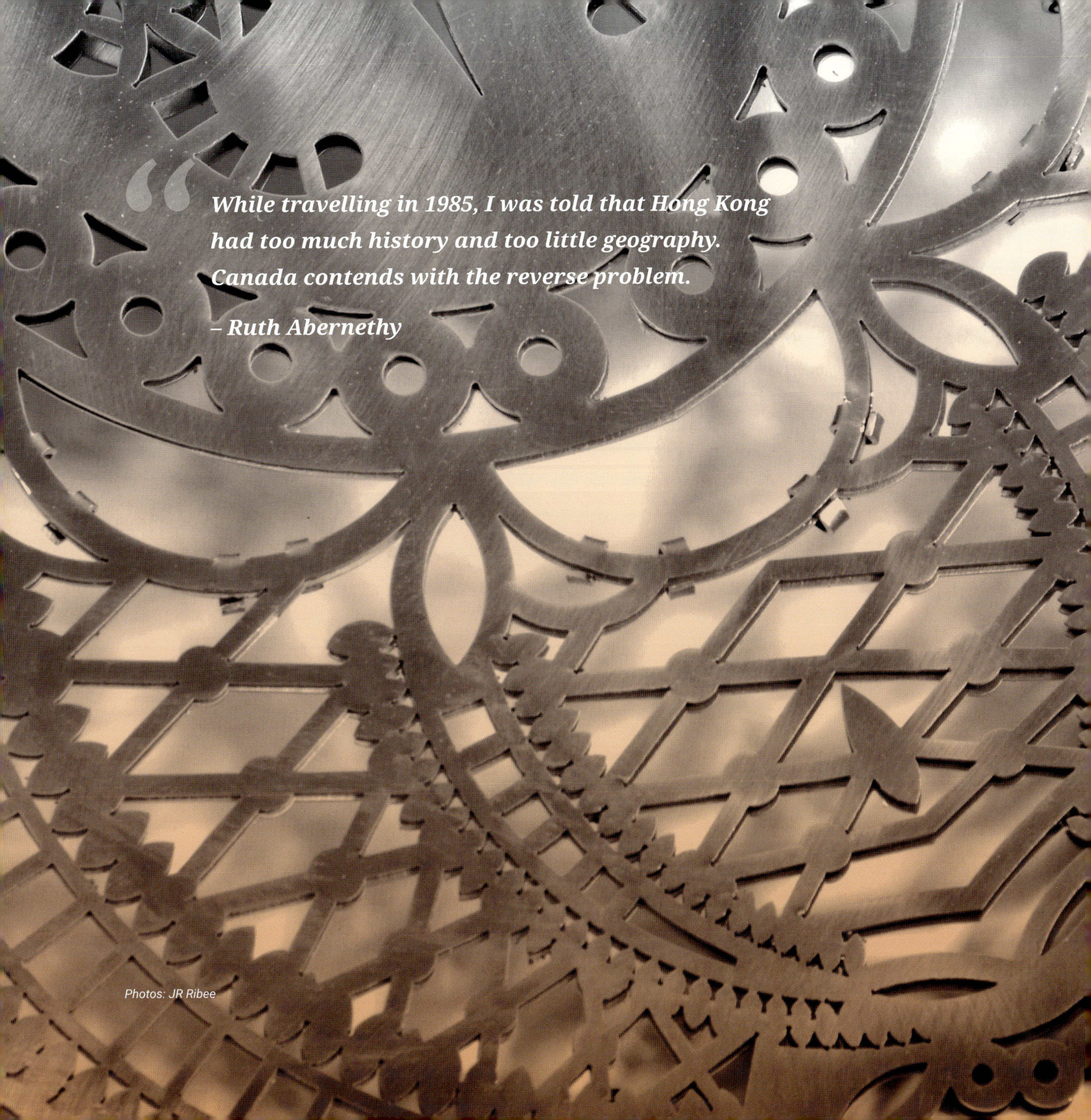

> *While travelling in 1985, I was told that Hong Kong had too much history and too little geography. Canada contends with the reverse problem.*
>
> *– Ruth Abernethy*

Photos: JR Ribee

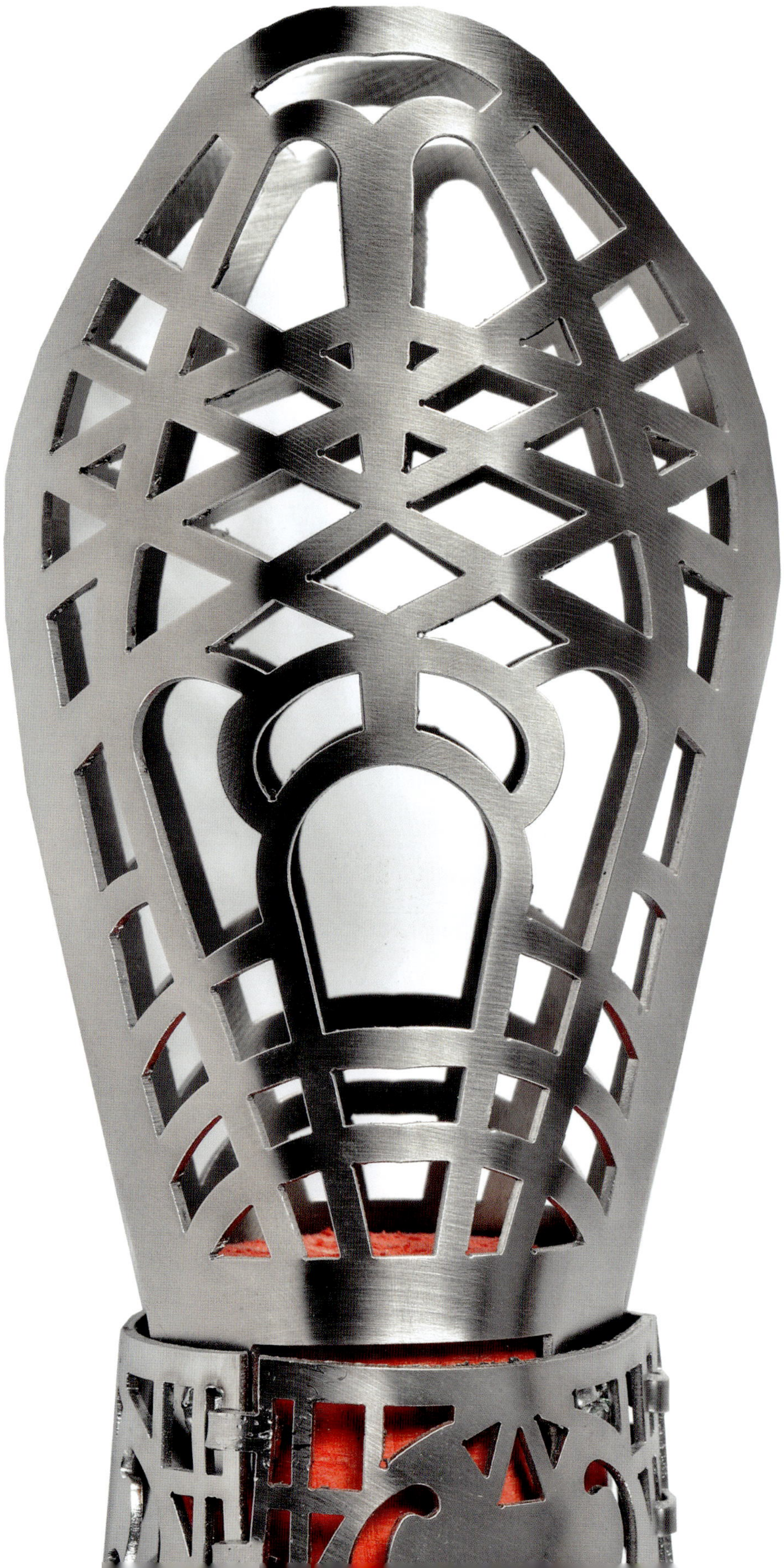

Recant Hook

52" x 3" x 15"
Canadian Collection
Photo: JR Ribee

Collection Overview

The Canadiana series is an exploration of settlement life through the tools, implements and craftwork used in helping to shape this country.

All the objects broadly allude to the pioneers' quest for 'civilization', but more pointedly address the role of women in building community.

Reference to handiwork (tatting, lace patterns) regarded typically as female transforms items conventionally evocative of men's labour—a hatchet, hammer, cross-cut saw or cant hook. *Canadiana #1*, for example, is fashioned with a scalloped edge blade, perforated in a lace pattern. The hatchet, often used by pioneer women in keeping the hearth fire constant, is thus reclaimed from the purview of men. In *Nuptials #1*, the hammer head is draped in a veil of silk organza and tatted cream lace. If the bridal veil references marriage, the partnership in making a home, it also alludes to the relationship between woman and her built environment and her strength in maintaining it. The apparent delicacy of The Canadiana Collection hammer is underlined by the power it nevertheless wields, evident in the spike it has bent.

While these works subvert the usual dichotomy between 'male' and 'female' labour, the hand-tatted Canadian flag in *Network* is the conceptual thread that links the domestic sphere, community and nation. The choice of tatting as means of construction is significant. Its basic stitch is comprised of two knots, reversed. Essentially a pair, the foundation stitch suggests cooperation, underlined by the title *Network* and its implied extension to activities beyond the home, to the local and national. As with all of the handicraft elements, the laborious production of tatting was carried out by the artist herself. In feminizing typically 'male' implements, Abernethy reinserts the presence of women into the story of settlement. In combining national symbols with typically female work, she makes the case for the essential role of women in building community.

Arlene Gehmacher, PhD
Curator, Canadian Art, Royal Ontario Museum

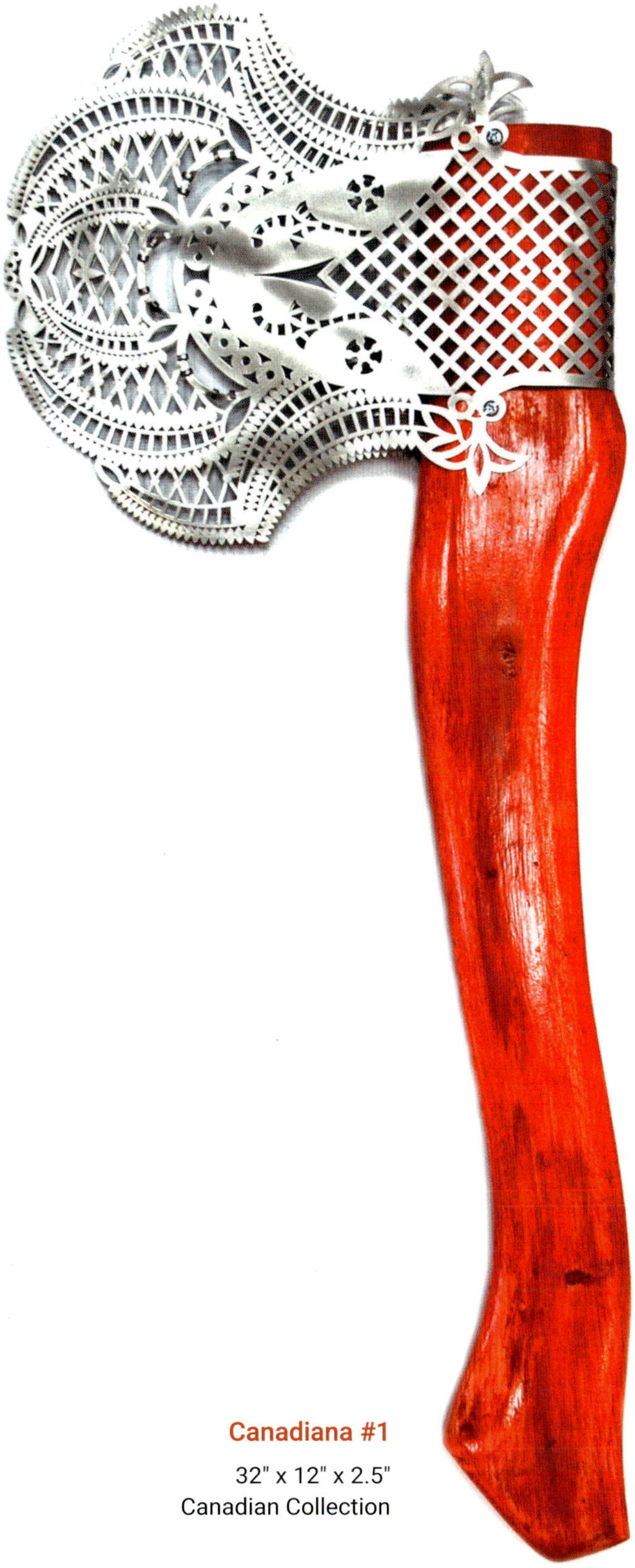

Canadiana #1
32" x 12" x 2.5"
Canadian Collection

These three works celebrated beautiful partnerships. I saluted their symmetry and balance and gently challenged the stereotypes of the traditional marriage, of lesbians in lumberjack shirts and gay friends out on the town in pearls.

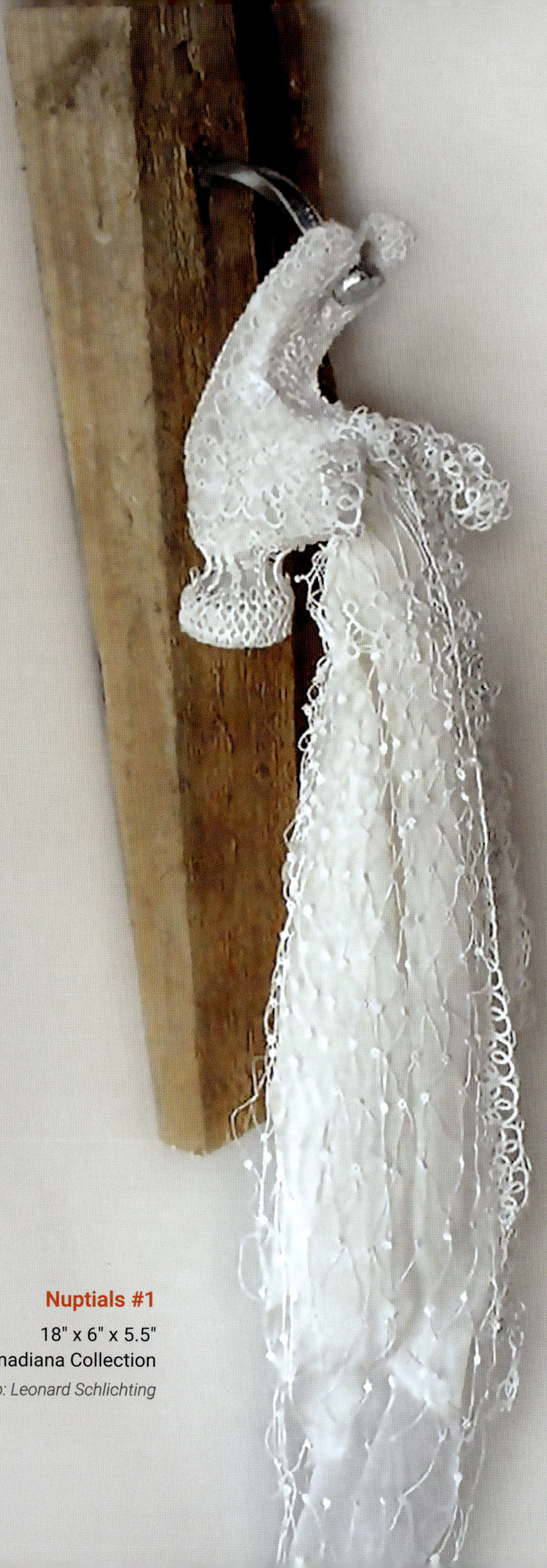

Nuptials #1

18" x 6" x 5.5"
Canadiana Collection
Photo: Leonard Schlichting

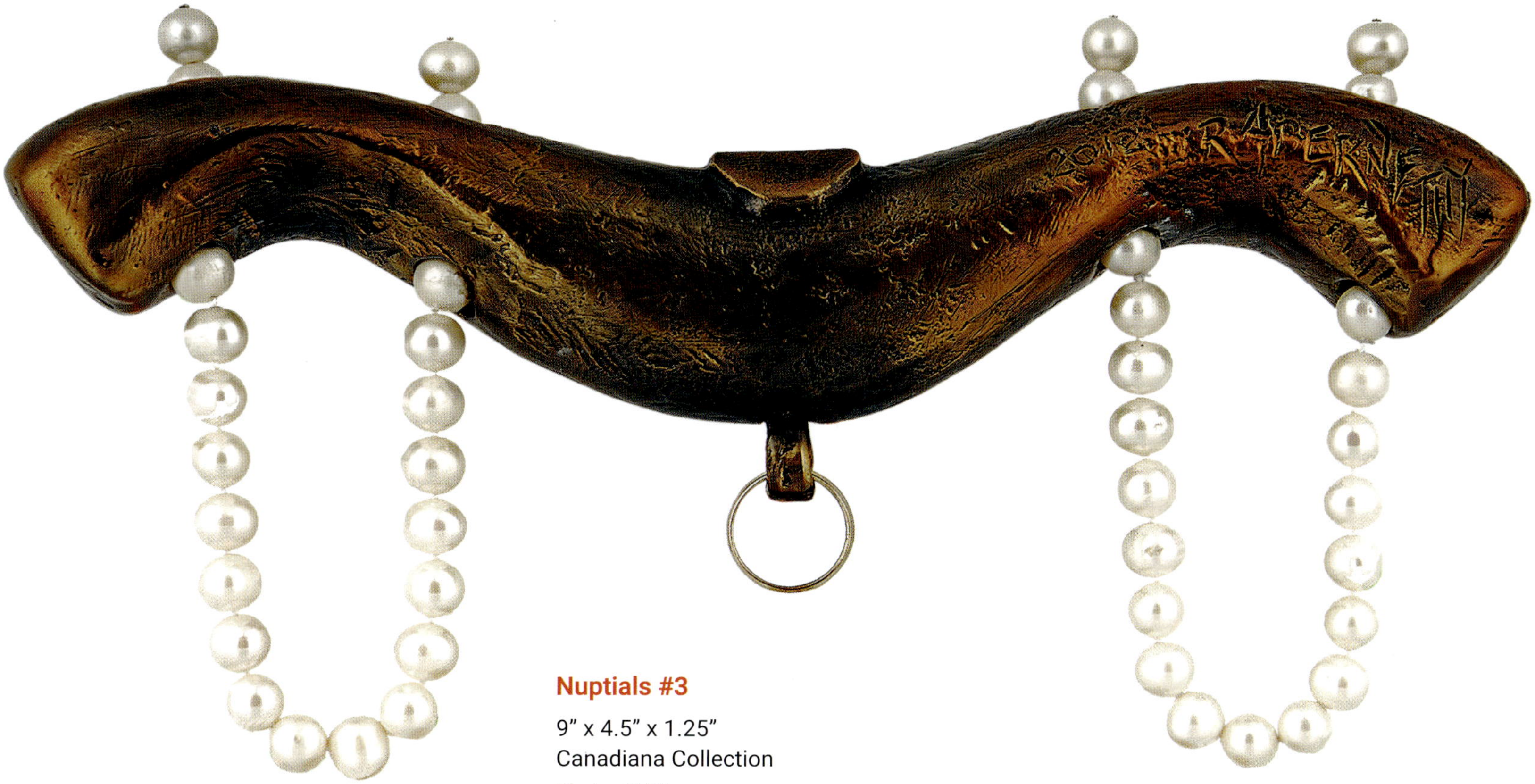

Nuptials #3

9” x 4.5” x 1.25”
Canadiana Collection
Photo: JR Ribee

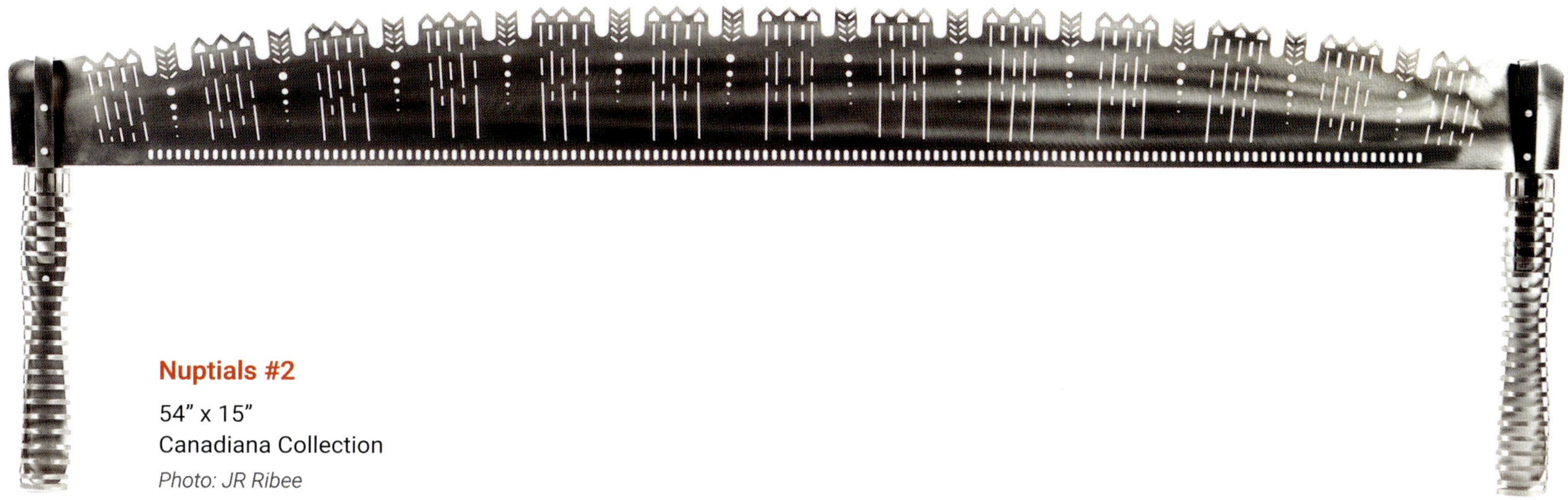

Nuptials #2

54” x 15”
Canadiana Collection
Photo: JR Ribee

Home

7" x 4"
Canadiana Collection

In complete contrast to the formal order of lace or the finesse of craftsmanship, *Home* is simply formed from rough-hewn shapes. I collected these crude pieces from a wind-fallen poplar tree and added cavities to suggest bird feeders, evocative of safety and collective nurturing. There is no slick 'home-front handbook' that guarantees order and domestic harmony. Homes are often crafted on the fly with whatever parenting skills and materials are at hand.

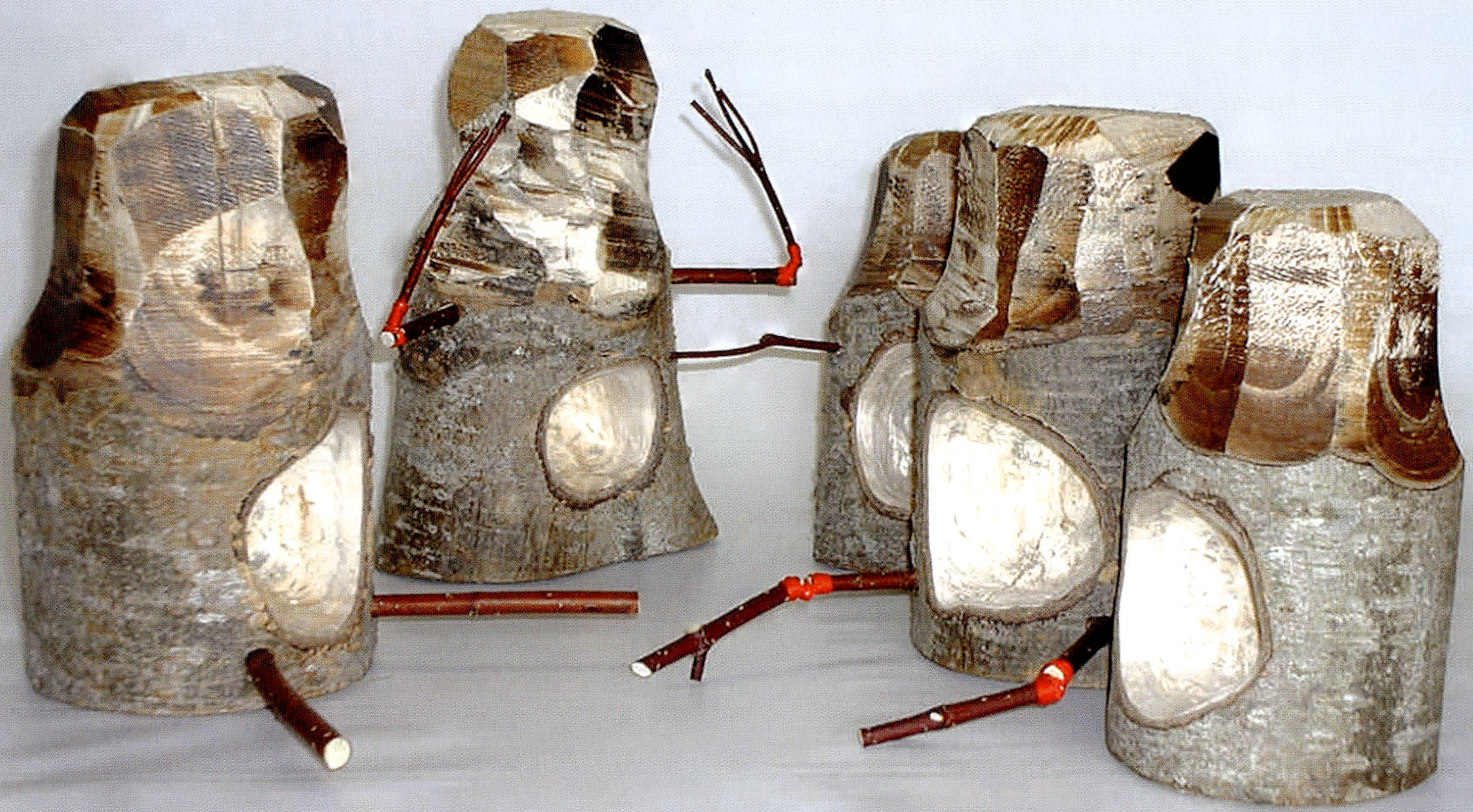

The globe went missing from its place on my sons' homework shelf. I rescued the empty stand. This potent structure which once held the world, begged to reestablish its authority. I'd inherited a plumb-bob from my grandfather. A plumb-bob is a carpenter's tool used to transfer an exact point vertically, using gravity.

In essence it's a weight suspended on a string. *En pointe* and clad in a tutu, this feminine plumb-bob was establishing a new place for 'herself' within the world.

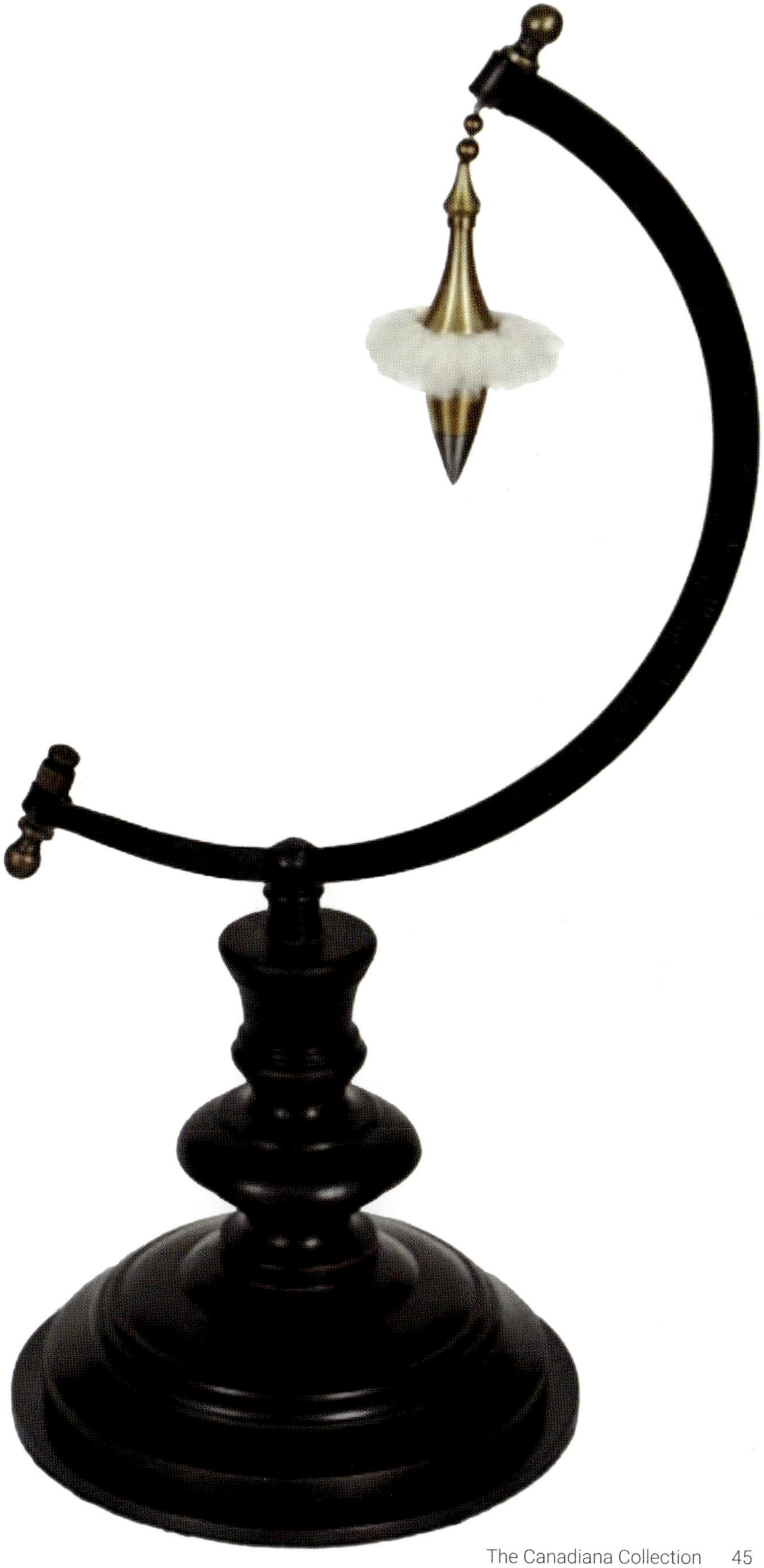

GPS

18" x 17" x 7"
Canadiana Collection
Photo: JR Ribee

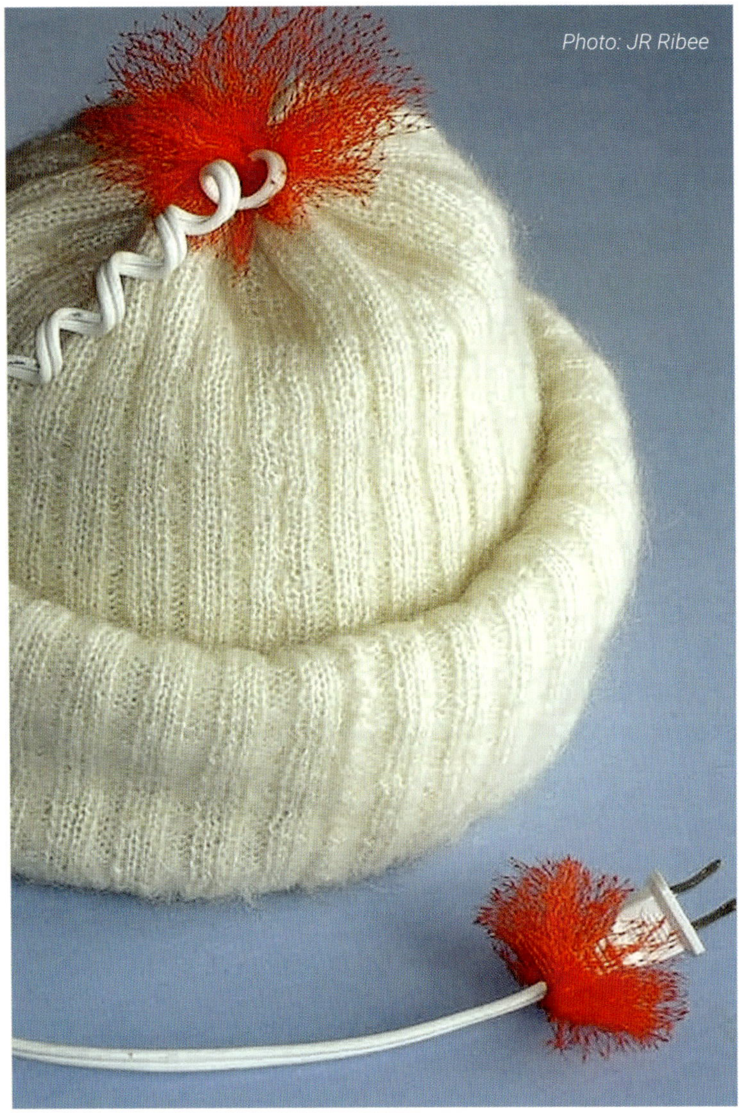

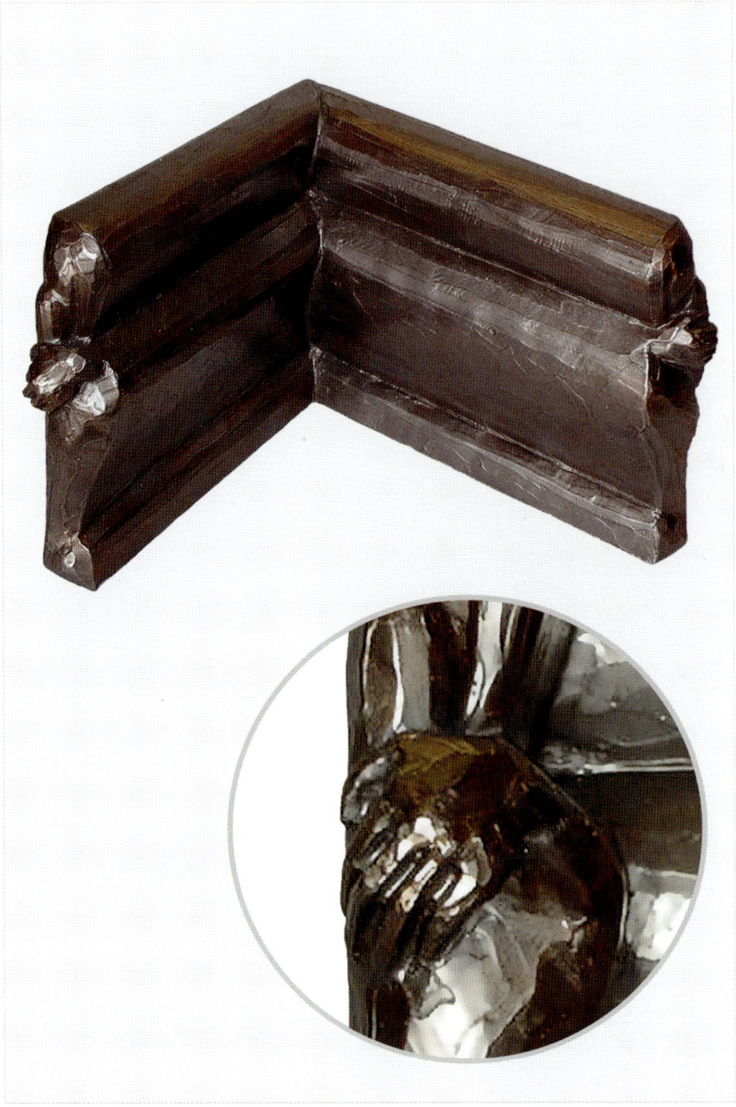

Outlet

11.5" x 10", Canadiana Collection

The cozy toque, reflecting winter isolation in Canada, is a heartfelt salute to those unplugged pioneers who maintained their dignity, intelligence and humour in a solitude that's now difficult to imagine.

Cope

7.25" x 9" x 9", Canadiana Collection

The summer of 2007 was filled with public discussions of same-sex marriage. Many heated exchanges managed to bypass the power and strength of all great partnerships. A coping saw is specifically intended to cut the fine contours of one wooden molding into another so that they fit together in a strong and seamless juncture. I created two bronze moldings, gave them delicate human details and cast them permanently together. *Cope* was not an expression of compromise or endurance, but a statement of affirmation, accommodation and strength.

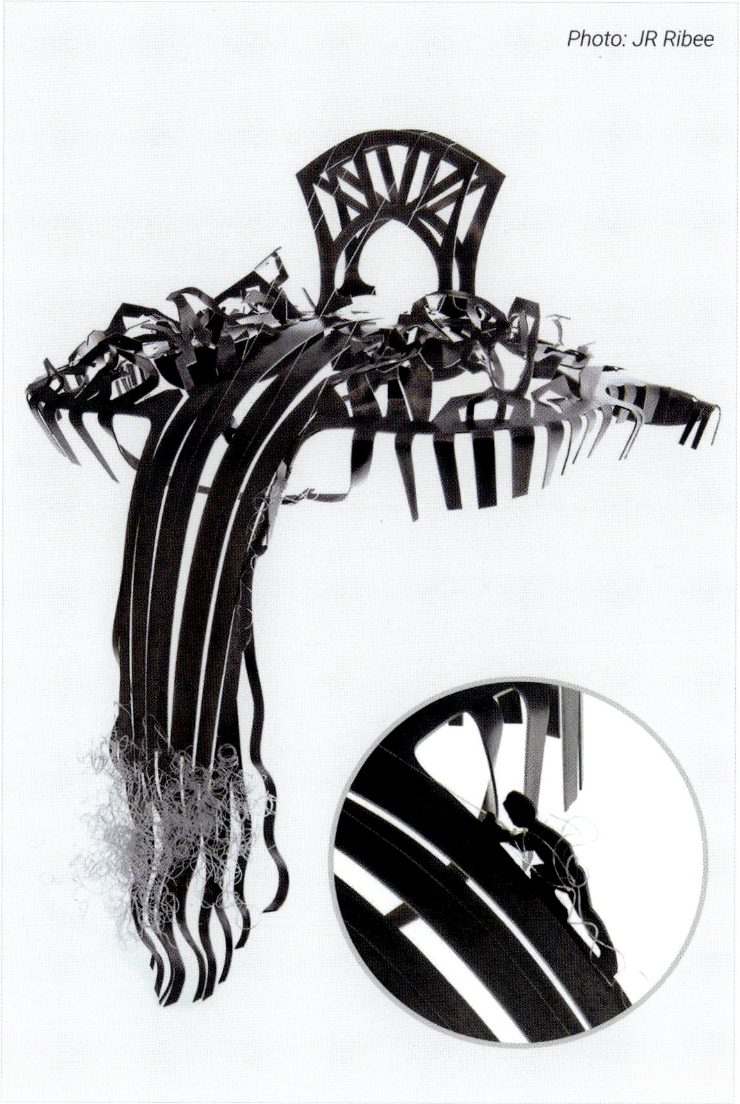

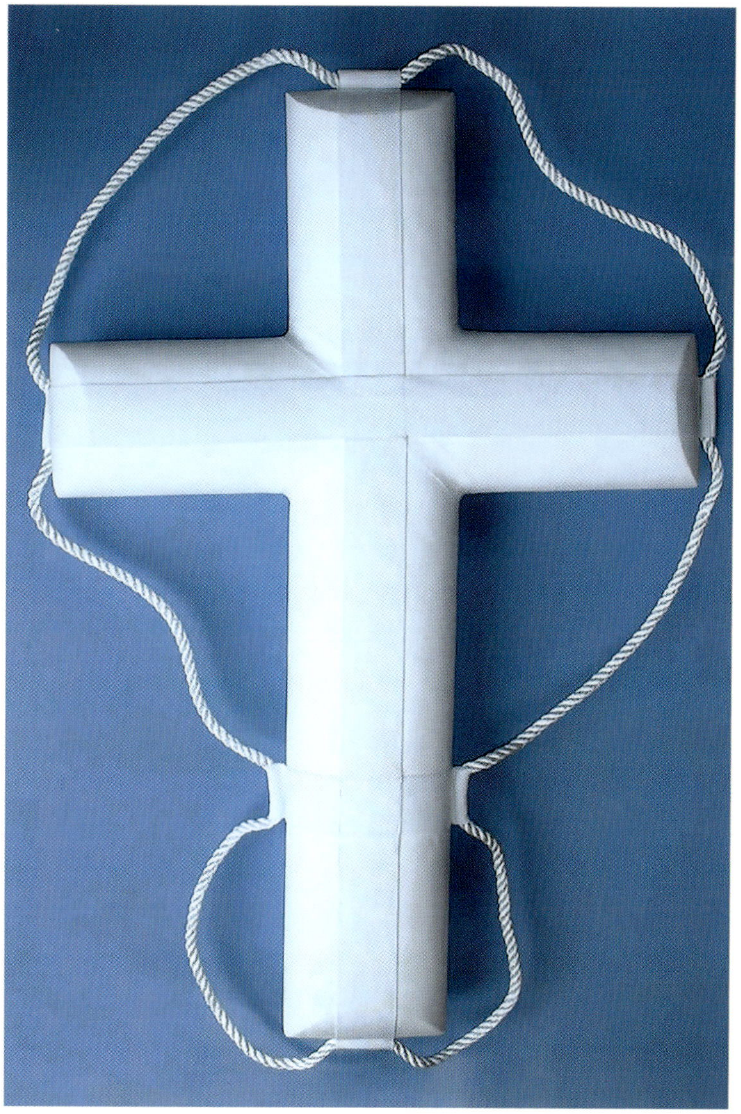

Scale

18" x 14" x 14", Canadiana Collection

I imagined the intensity of hearing live music after wintering in a sod shanty. *Scale* is a play on words. The steel pattern is shaped like a violin and the top surface has been torn into rugged landscape. The neck of the fiddle descends as a waterfall and strings connect the falls to grid towers suggesting communication, power and connection. A tiny figure scales the cliff in determined ascent.

Preservance

42" x 28" x 5", Canadiana Collection

My grandmother's Bible had pages so worn that they were unreadable. Endless handling had turned it into a potent symbol of refuge and sustenance. Her rearing of ten children during the 1930s no doubt held moments in which religious conviction was her best and only lifeline. I likened her faith to this life-saving device, effective because the viewer imbued it with the capacity to be so.

PART FOUR

International Highlights

Ladies – Size 8	Sydney, Australia
r Evolution	Casuarina, Australia
One Basket	Dublin, Ireland
v – Passion Flower	Beijing, China
Gathering	Chicago, USA

> *You are incredibly lucky to work on projects to which people bring their very,* very *best!*
>
> *– Mark Smyth*

Ladies – Size 8

Sculpture-by-the-Sea, Sydney, Australia

East Sydney, Australia, clusters around Bondi Beach where the 2000 Olympic Games staged volleyball matches. Beautiful Bondi links to neighbouring Tamarama Beach along a winding seawall where, for millennia, the surf has sculpted sandstone cliffs. Each October an installation of outdoor sculptures dots the sands and cliffs along this ocean walkway.

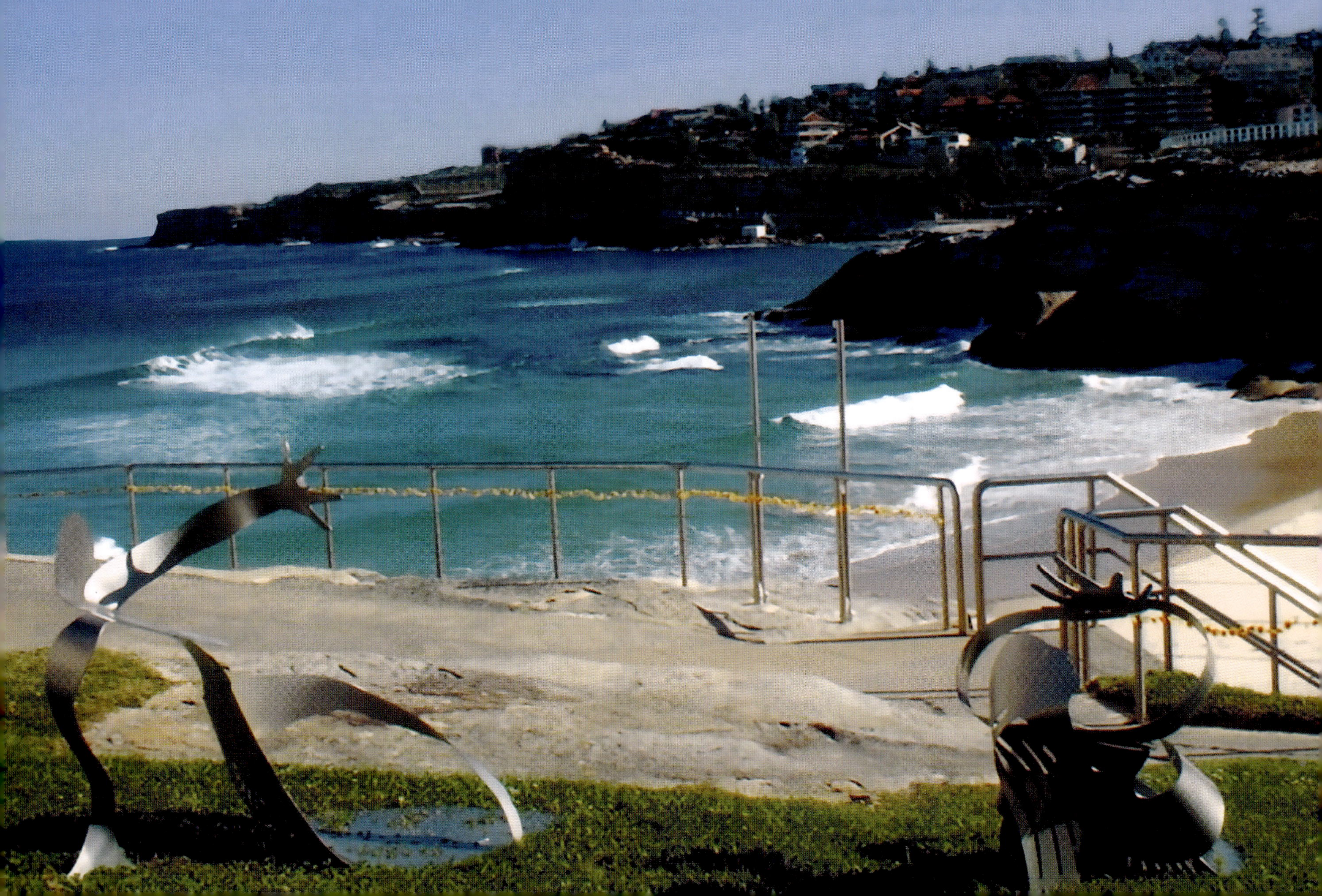

As Sculpture-by-the-Sea's first Canadian participant, I was one of 28 overseas artists in a show with over 100 juried participants. The majority were professional artists but people of all ages submitted excellent installation ideas. I was awarded a small bursary by the Canadian Consulate in Sydney. I was also rewarded by the sale of the three shoes on the second day of the show. Somewhere on the grounds of an estate home in the Southern Highlands, 70 miles southwest of Sydney, the Ladies gracefully work on their tans.

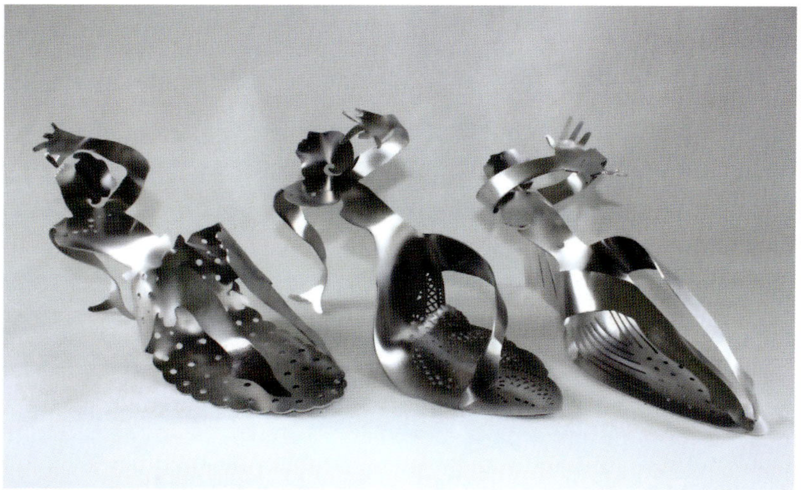

I don't remember how I became aware of Sculpture-by-the-Sea in Sydney, but this thriving exhibition attracts hundreds of thousands of visitors each year. Founded by David Handley, the sculpture walk is in its second decade.

I presume that in the early years of internet in the studio, I'd entered 'sculpture' just to see what would appear—and sun-washed Australian beaches had appeared. While reading the 2003 Call to Artists, the glimmering sands of East Sydney gave me a new vision of a work I'd already made, called *Ladies – Size 8*.

I'd created *Ladies – Size 8* in 1997 for a gallery fundraiser. The stylized footwear was laser-cut from sheets of stainless steel. I'd shaped the flat patterns by hand into three unique shoe designs that were also women. The Call from Australia shifted my imagination. The ladies were not footwear-sized anymore, but now life-sized sunbathing beauties on the warm sands of Bondi Beach.

I submitted my proposal and luckily my first bid was unsuccessful. Without sponsorship, the cost of shipping a trio of large crates to Australia was prohibitive. I really had no means for an overseas adventure. Still, *Ladies* lingered in my imagination and by the following season I had a solution. The first paper shoe designs had been plotted into a digital cutting pattern. I could simply *email* my sculptures across the Pacific for fabrication in Australia.

My second show proposal was successful and months of planning began. Exhibition staff arranged that a metal fabricator in Sydney would donate its laser-cutting time if I'd purchase their sheets of steel. Staffers contacted a second workshop that cleared a workspace for my husband, Mark, and I to shape the huge flat patterns into three-dimensional shoes, each nearly six feet long.

Bending flat metal cutouts into small shoes had become a familiar routine, but translating this into a critical sequence of curves on a large scale was a task I could only have done with Mark. One contour made out of step would make subsequent shaping impossible. We had to think fast and furiously ahead of ourselves. The staff at Sculpture-by-the-Sea seemed prepared for anything and a little delivery truck arrived at the workshop the moment we completed our pieces. The pre-arranged site was high on the cliff side, overlooking the surf and Tamarama's horseshoe-shaped beach.

There's a back story, of course. Mark and I had been delighted by my acceptance in the Australian show but our budget could only stretch to a single overseas flight. Mark was stoic. I found it hard to believe we'd not have this adventure together. Serendipity played a role once again. A surprise sale of artworks and several small projects materialized to provide extra funds. These were easy to keep secret. I began plotting to surprise Mark with a ticket to Sydney. One glance showed me that his passport was expired and also, we'd been told that the church in Quebec with his birth registry had burned to the ground. Prompting Mark to renew his passport would be too obvious. Resourcefully his workmates invented a mythical business trip and got paperwork underway—with great delight and astonishing subterfuge. They also joined us for an 'impromptu' lunch at which I presented Mark with his ticket to the land Down Under.

r Evolution

Casuarina, Australia

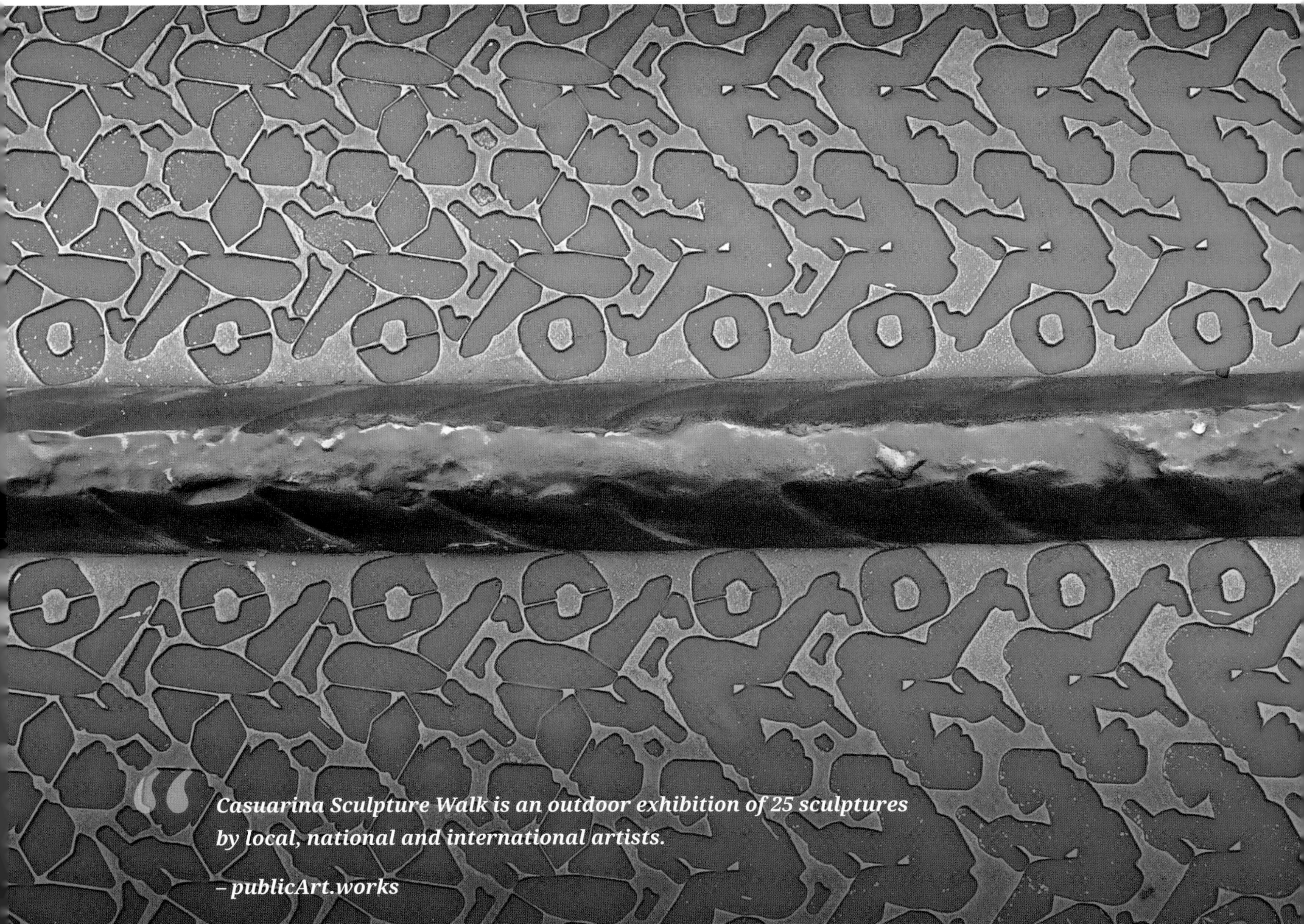

Mark and I had been heartbroken that we couldn't take Glen and Alex with us to Australia in 2004. We promised we'd never go again without them. Our Sydney hosts, Bev and Les Brandon, had become dear friends and a positive experience with Sculpture-by-the-Sea kept Australia on our radar.

I'd kept in touch with two SxS staff members who'd relocated further north near the Queensland border, to manage a new exhibition. I was excited to receive their invitation to the Casuarina Sculpture Walk. An hour's drive south of Brisbane, this walk meandered along a stunning beach and resort area that had been developed on the site of a disused sand-mining operation.

At that time in my life I was considering commuter culture in southern Ontario and our human imprint on the planet. Those thoughts led me to the design of *r Evolution*. It seemed perfect for Casuarina.

I measured the dual wheels on a local tow truck and with those dimensions I drew a tread pattern showing little commuters driving anxiously hither and yon. Over the span of one wheel rotation, the pattern's particles dispersed and coalesced into the drivers' silhouettes. This was a bronze 'anti-sculpture'. I imagined it installed as an irreverent scar on perfect turf: a permanent human imprint.

The *r Evolution* idea seemed ideal for the show, but shipping a bronze to the south Pacific was no simple matter. I prepared myself to solve problems as they arose, and again serendipity played a role. This time I bought four tickets to the land Down Under.

As an island continent, Australia would only accept imported goods in certified, heat-treated crates. After my family and I arrived via Sydney, I took an exhausting truck trip with a gregarious driver from our resort to the Brisbane Airport to retrieve my 400-pound crate. On the highway, the trucker's complaints about terrible traffic seemed laughable. In my view, there was no traffic congestion at all, even as we neared a major airport. I could scarcely suppress a chuckle when my driver carefully explained that Aussies simply don't like having a long drive to work.

My sculpture was well received and I was fascinated by the perspective of the Australian audience. The commuter culture I'd examined in Canada was all but unknown near the surfing beaches of the Gold Coast. Show patrons saw the recessed tire tread and were reminded of childhood outings. Driving the beaches in the back of a jeep, they'd leave miles of tire tracks behind in the sand.

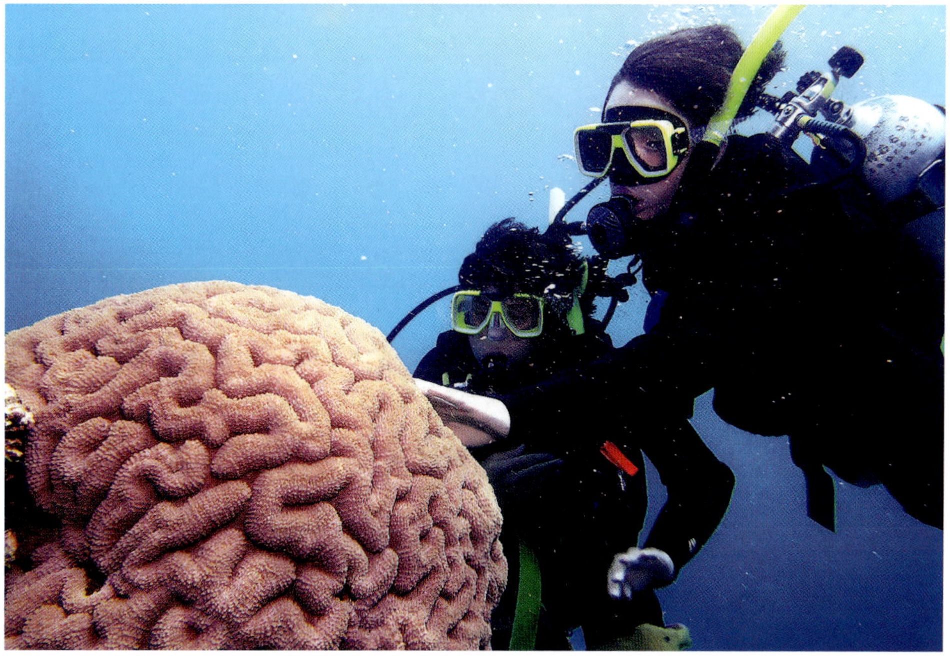

My family and I were enthralled with the tropical landscape. Snorkelling on the Great Barrier Reef was fantastical for us all. While hiking near our rustic mountain lodge in Binna Burra, we had wallabies bouncing past us with their heavy padding strides. Every new plant and birdcall was a delight to the senses. The steep mountain roads, that hadn't a guardrail in sight, left me wide-eyed! My own tiny place in the world was starkly stated when I stared at the night sky, unable to recognize a single constellation.

One Basket

Dublin, Ireland

One day, a Call to Artists appeared via email. It was from Anna Duncan, who was arranging an exhibition in Dublin, Ireland. Sculpture in Context requested proposals for artworks to be installed in the National Botanic Gardens. I had never been to Ireland, but I had strong impressions of it. I'd grown up hearing news reports of violence during Ireland's troubled 1970s. To me, the Irish setting seemed resonant with prickly religious issues. I began to prepare an idea that had been gestating in my imagination.

I was intrigued by the common ground among the Christian, Judaic and Islamic religions but, at the same time, their ancient religious doctrines seemed somewhat removed from current environmental concerns. To resolve these ideas, I structured 'delicate' eggshells, 24 inches long in stainless steel. Each was created with symbols representing one of the three faiths. The shapes were strong, detailed and enticing. As forms, they could be described as empty . . . but perhaps they brimmed with invisible content!? Contained within a barbed-wire 'basket', the prickly nest kept them effectively separated from the rest of the world.

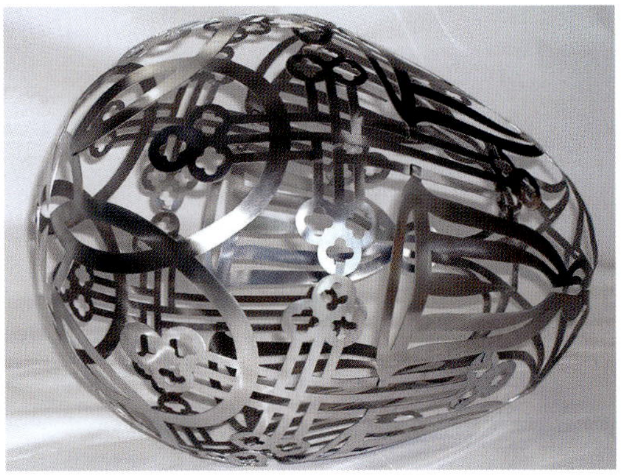

Christian fish,
chalice and cross

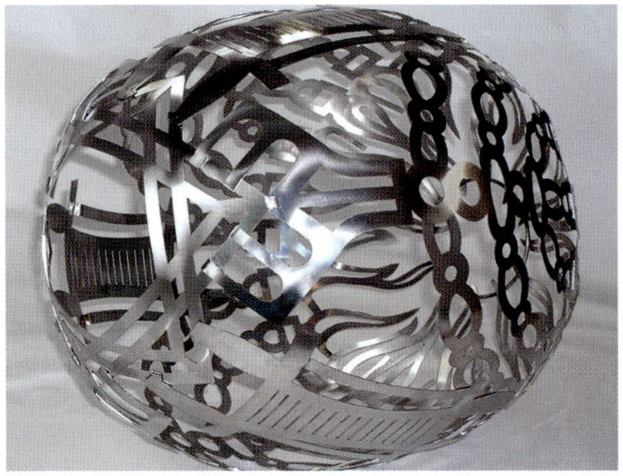

Judaic menorah,
with perpetual flame and tablets

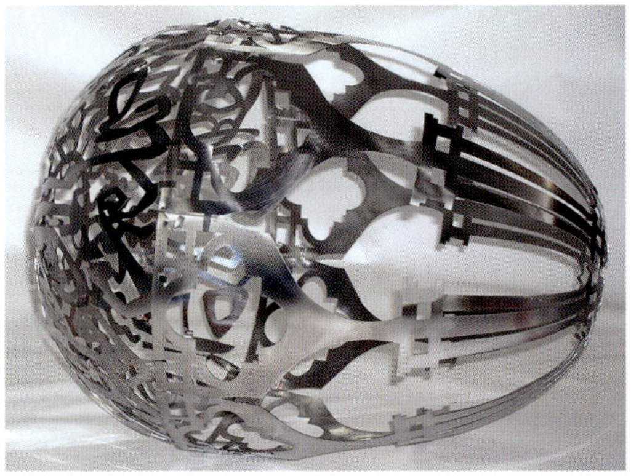

Islamic minarets,
with script from heritage tablet

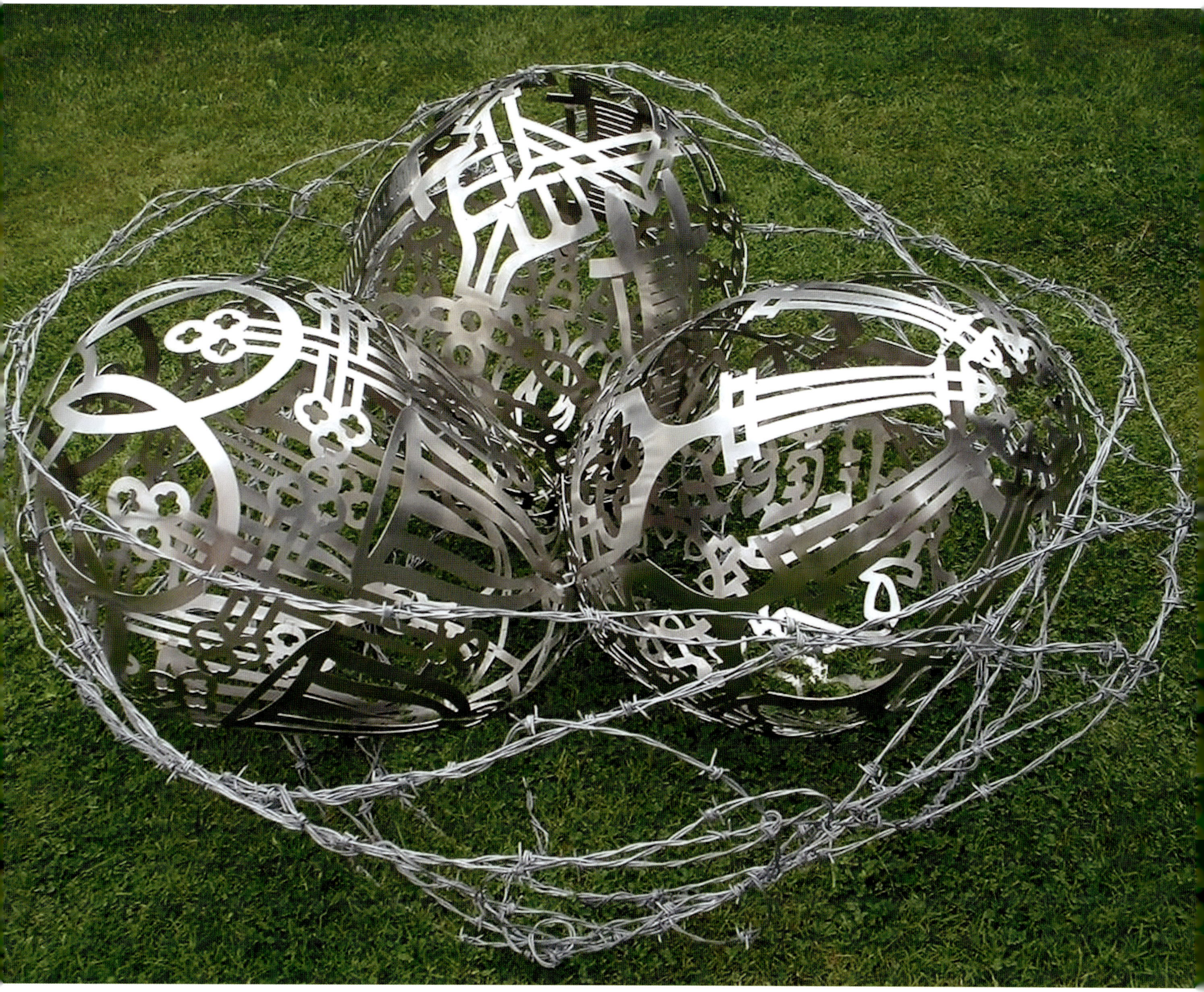

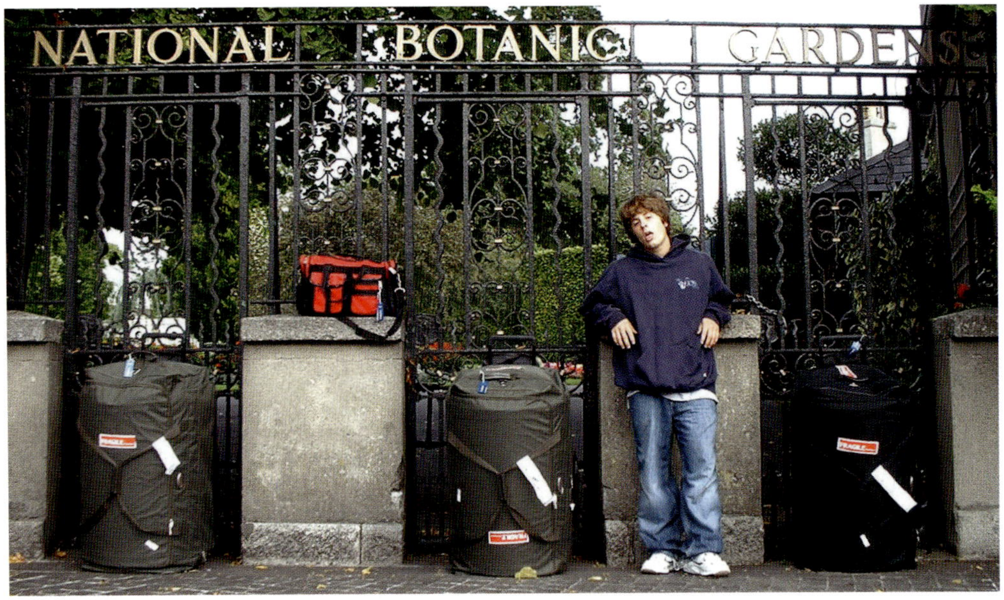

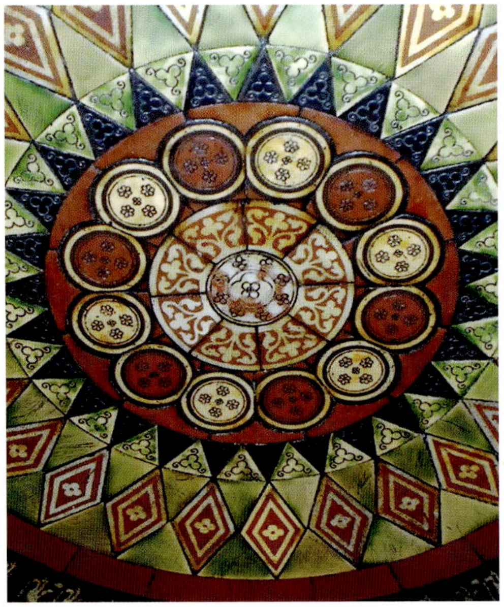

My trusty travel assistant Glen and our three large 'egg cartons'. It was a long haul from Toronto!

The Irish jury accepted my proposal despite its possible safety issues. Shipping barbed wire through international airports was ill-advised. Organizers of the exhibition secured a large spool of wire for me in Dublin. I packed several sets of wire cutters and heavy leather work gloves, hoping my tool kit wouldn't draw unwanted attention from airport security. I built large shipping cartons and custom packing to contain the eggs. I then shopped for three giant duffel bags for their overseas flight.

My son Glen was designated exhibition assistant. With his help, we trundled three huge packs across Dublin to the Botanic Gardens. The gardens themselves were a gorgeous oasis in the heart of north Dublin. I was pleased and rather surprised to be the first Canadian exhibitor.

Glen and I delighted in Irish stew, which was suspiciously like my mother's cooking—though my Abernethy ancestors are from Scotland. We explored Dublin's cathedrals, where richly-coloured tile mosaics spread like quilts across every floor and surface. I savoured my morning coffee at a café beside the River Liffey, and Glen had his first taste of Guinness.

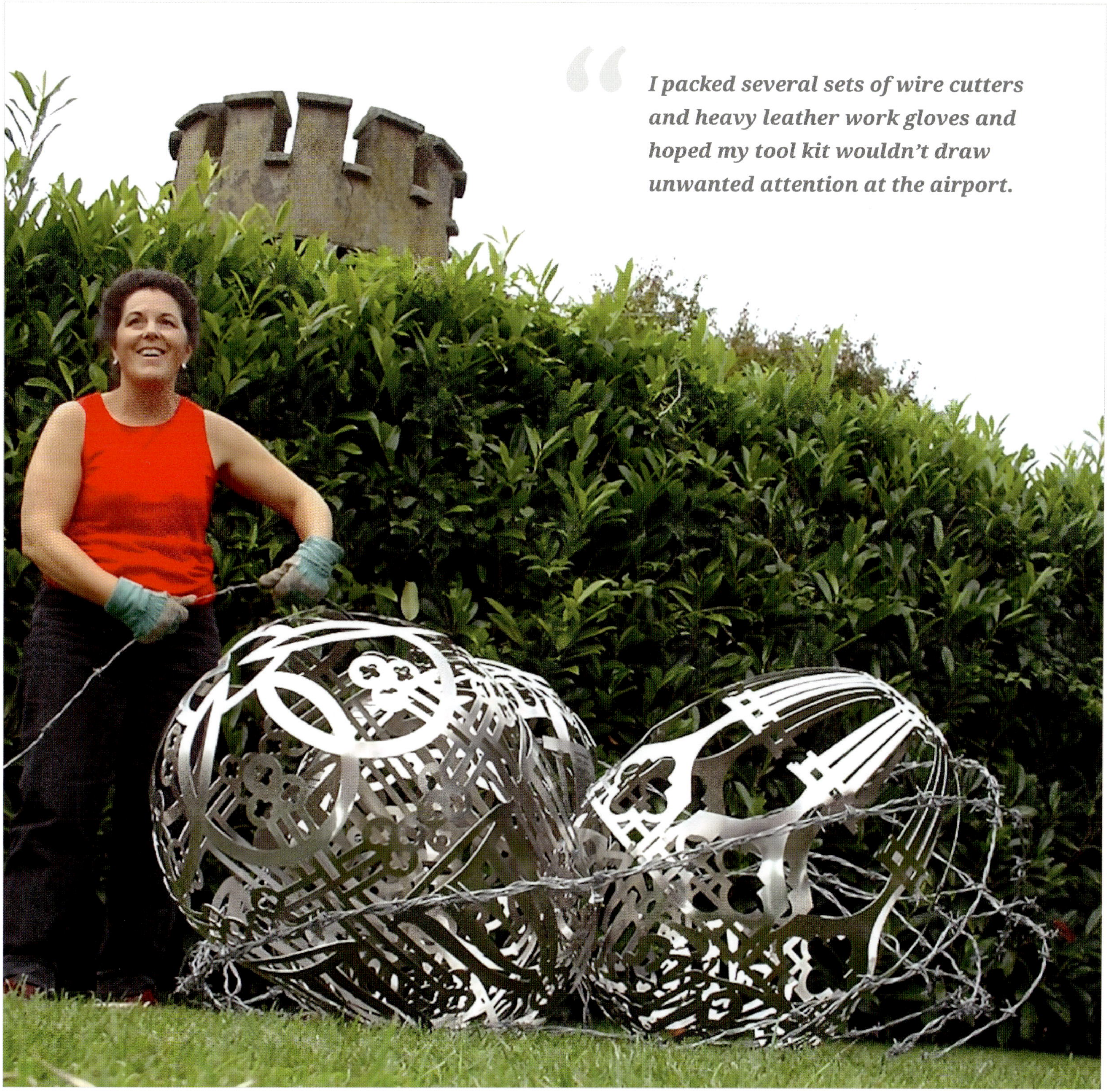

"I packed several sets of wire cutters and heavy leather work gloves and hoped my tool kit wouldn't draw unwanted attention at the airport.

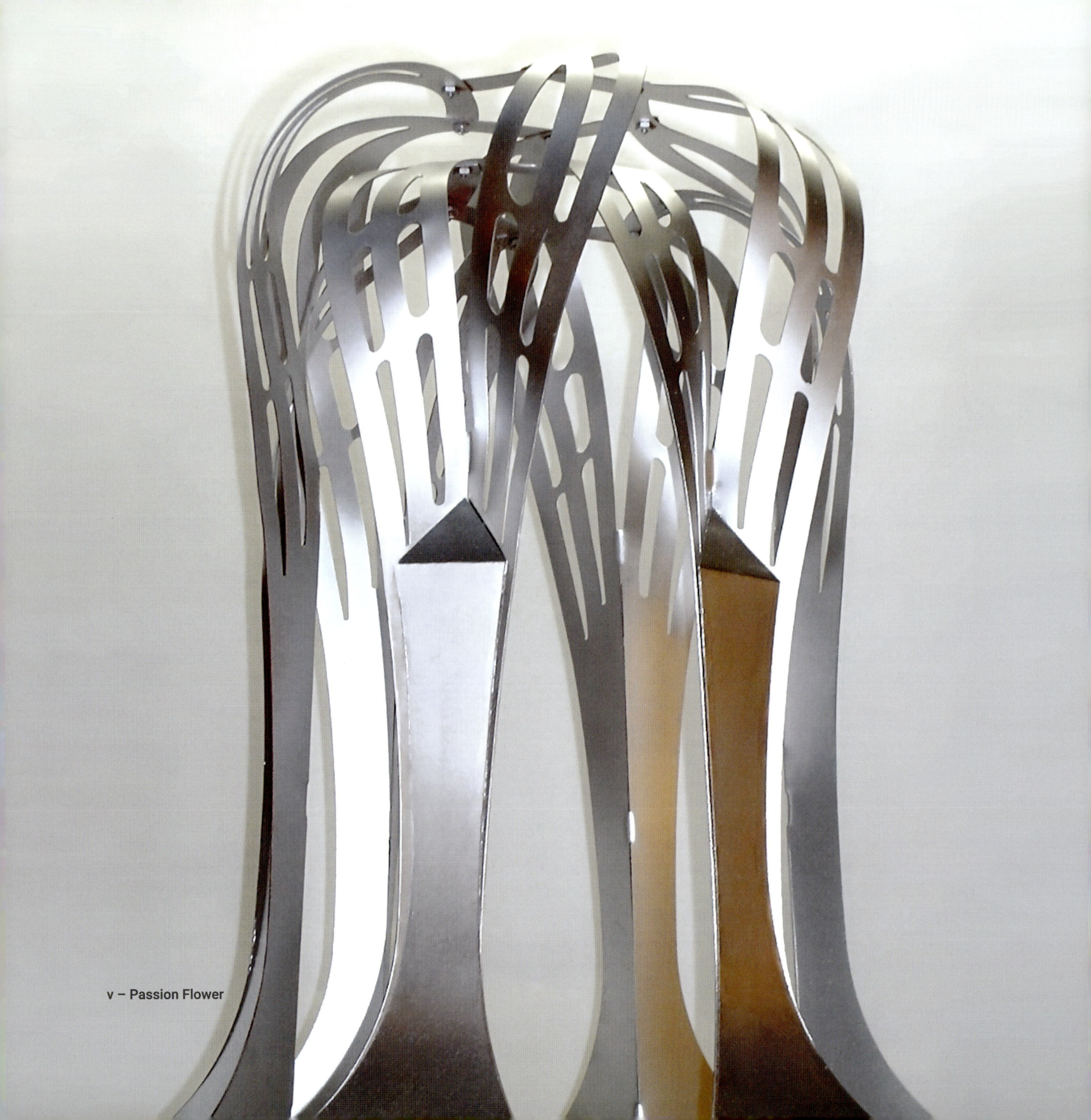

v – Passion Flower

v – Passion Flower

My emergent steel sculpture was short-listed for the 2008 Beijing Olympic Sculpture Competition. The *v – Passion Flower* maquette was exhibited across China and internationally, with other finalists, in the months before and after the games. The design won an "Excellent Works Award." It reminded me of Bird's Nest Stadium, which became the visual image of the Beijing games two years later!

Repeated phone calls in 2007 from the Olympic Landscape Sculpture Competition finally focused my attention on China. I had several projects underway in the studio, but I made time to consider *v – Passion Flower* as a submission piece. I'd designed the work in 2006 for a commission in Waterloo where it was a favoured proposal. Ironically, stainless steel prices had doubled because of the upcoming Beijing games and the sculpture could not be built in Waterloo within the modest project budget.

My concept melded wordplay into the intriguing structure of a Passion Flower blossom. A grammatical shift from noun to verb reframed passion as action. I'd designed the forms to suggest collective endeavour, and these themes aligned with Olympic ideals. How serendipitous that I had a finished maquette in the studio and a digital pattern ready for fabrication. I proposed the work for the Beijing Sculpture Competition.

I'd sized the sculpture maquette generously for the Waterloo site, which was near my home, but I was defeated at the shipping office by the price of getting this large carton overseas. An engineer friend, Gang Pan, offered to deliver the crate. He was leaving within days on a business trip to China. Gang faithfully delivered the piece despite needing an extra-large cab for every burdened step. Thank you, Gang!

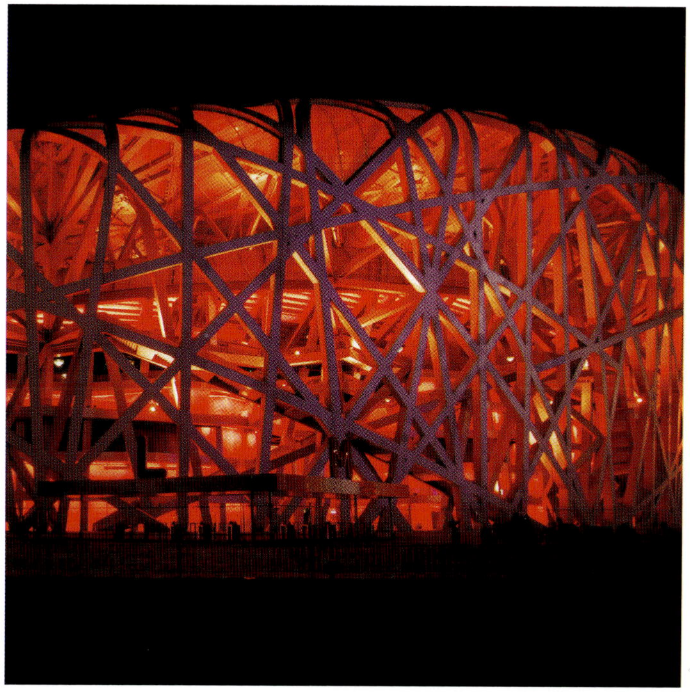

The Bird's Nest, or Beijing National Stadium

Gathering

11 o'clock one evening in 2007, the phone rang and I began a conversation with Jerry Horn, who lives in Chicago. The engaging Mr. Horn sought a sculptor to create portraits of family members who had perished during the Holocaust. Jerry shared ideas for placing the sculpture and told me about his elderly parents, for whom he was undertaking the commission. "We mustn't delay," Jerry insisted. "My entire family is keen."

As we spoke, the idea came to me that three people holding hands would form a triangle. Done twice, these entwined triangles would form the Star of David.

I described my concept with excitement and Jerry and I were enthralled. He introduced his family members to me on the phone. I'd be forming each triangle to depict his grandparents and one of their children, holding hands. The structure and symbolism of the design were hugely satisfying. The artwork would be integrated into renovations at the synagogue.

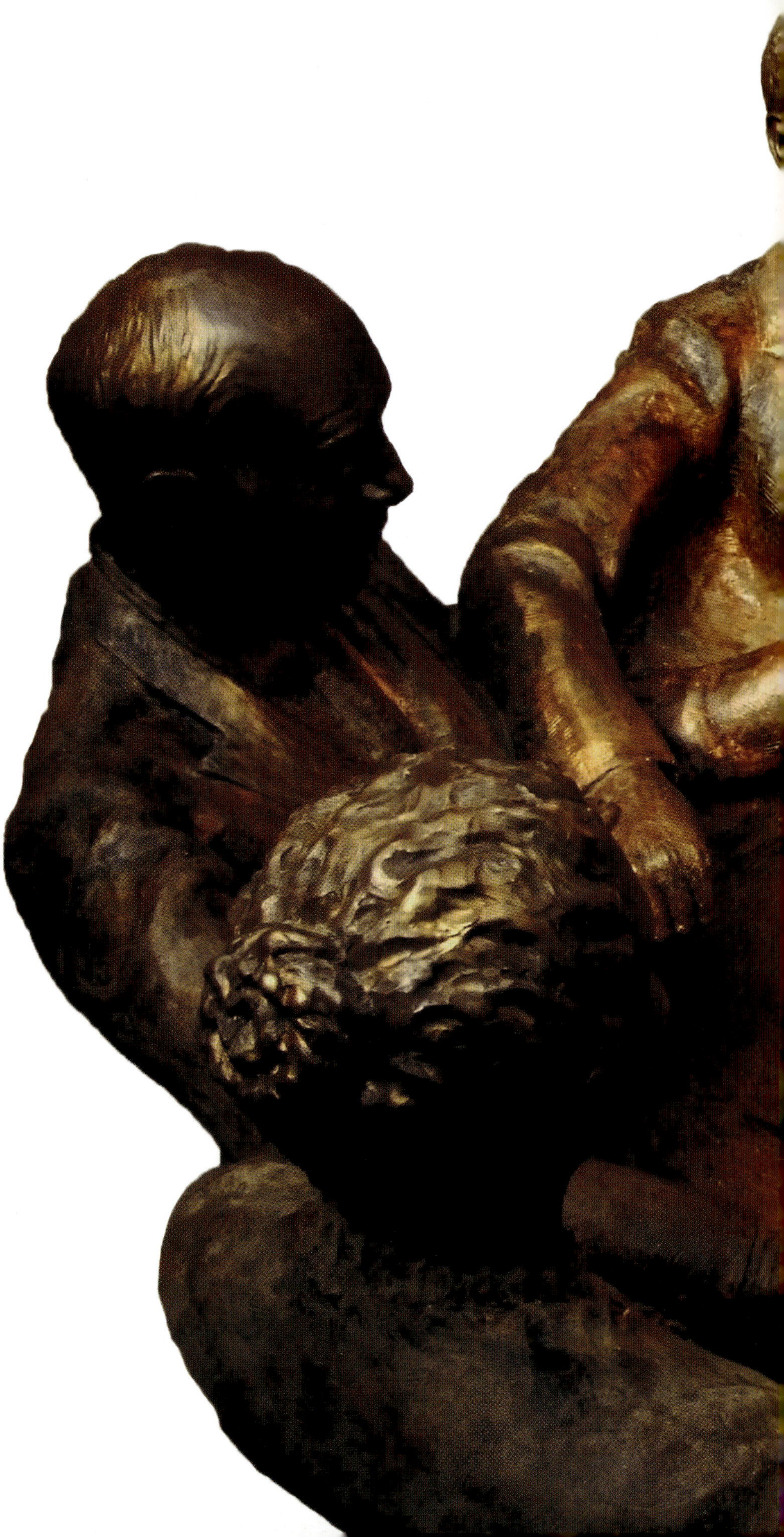

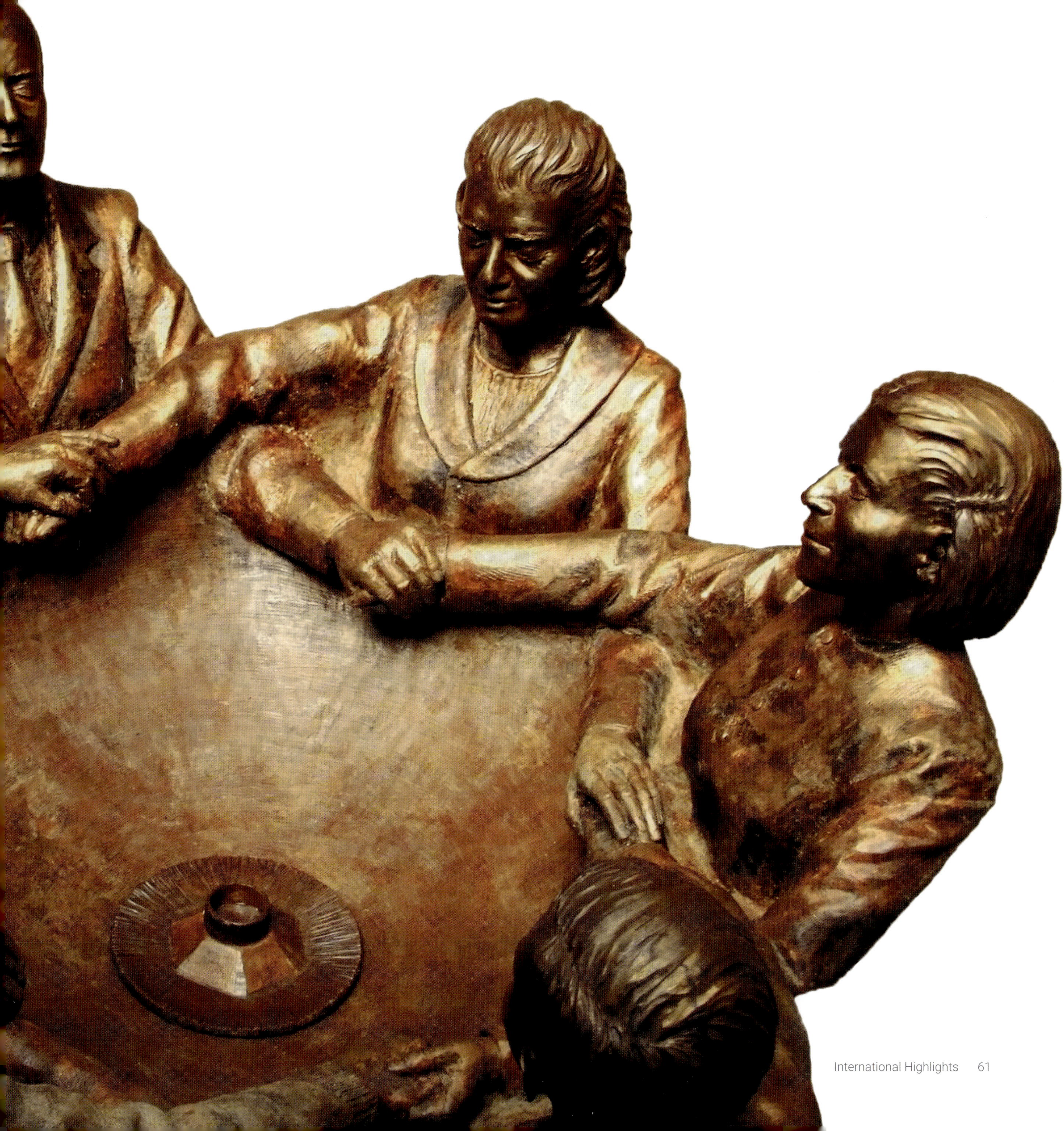

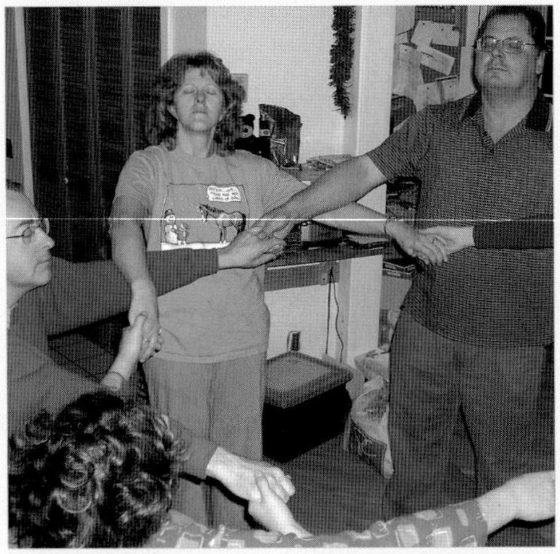
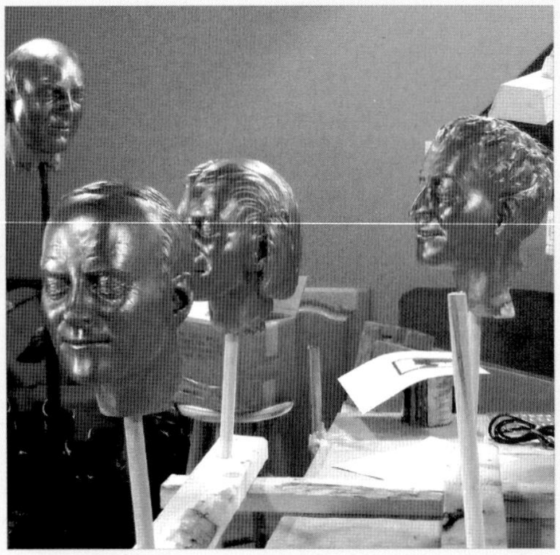
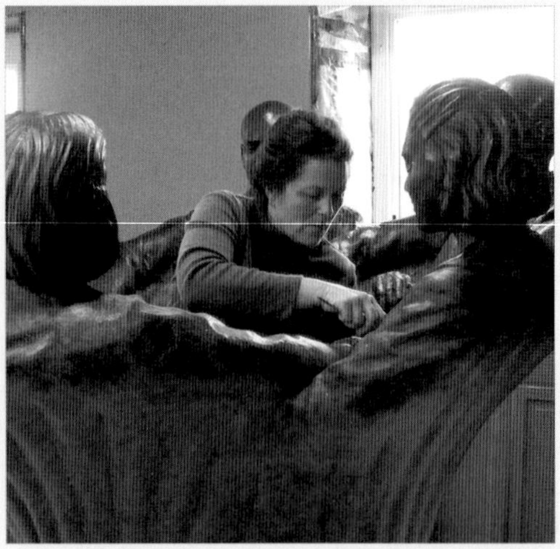

Initially the architects were keen to place the bronze outside the main entrance. If the building had been in Miami I might have been receptive, but it was too distressing to imagine a family outdoors in a chill midwestern winter. We opted for the serene and central foyer, for which I worked out the sculpture's size precisely using floor plans. The architects agreed to have a star-shaped mahogany base built in Chicago. I mailed a paper template to show exact proportions. I shipped the bronze with its approved internal light fixture by truck to North Chicago, where it would be mounted on its custom base.

It was important for me to absorb this family's story and establish a basis of trust for the commission. For their peace of mind and my own, I planned an eight-hour drive from Wellesley to Chicago. With a sense of great accomplishment, the family and I found our chosen restaurant. We also found each other in a very large and busy dining room. There was much to share. Jerry's parents, well into their 80s, were feisty and funny! They told remarkable stories and I was moved by their courage and humour.

My task was to create six portraits, although there were photos of only five. I'd have to sculpt them using only the single reference picture for each one. These precious images had been miraculously saved by neighbours and returned to the family after World War II.

I gleaned what details my clients could remember of their loved ones. I pored over the photos, letting ideas and impressions stir and take shape. We pieced together a likeness for the undocumented young woman.

One of the mothers in the photos looked like a dancer, with elegant neck and shoulders and beautiful hands. She was slim and I was compelled to dress her in a sweater to keep her warm. The second mother had been a dentist. Absorbing her character through the aged image, I imagined a softly-tailored professional jacket and hoped she'd be pleased. I clad each father in a simple suit coat and gave them as much dignity as I could summon.

The last subject was a young boy named David, photographed at the age of six when he started school. He was a gorgeous child. Jerry told me there was a striking resemblance between this lost boy and his own son, who was then about the same age. Weeks after sculpting David, I stood in the synagogue foyer and Jerry's young son scooted into the room. My intense response to his familiar features took me by surprise. It was all I could do to keep from scooping him up in my arms.

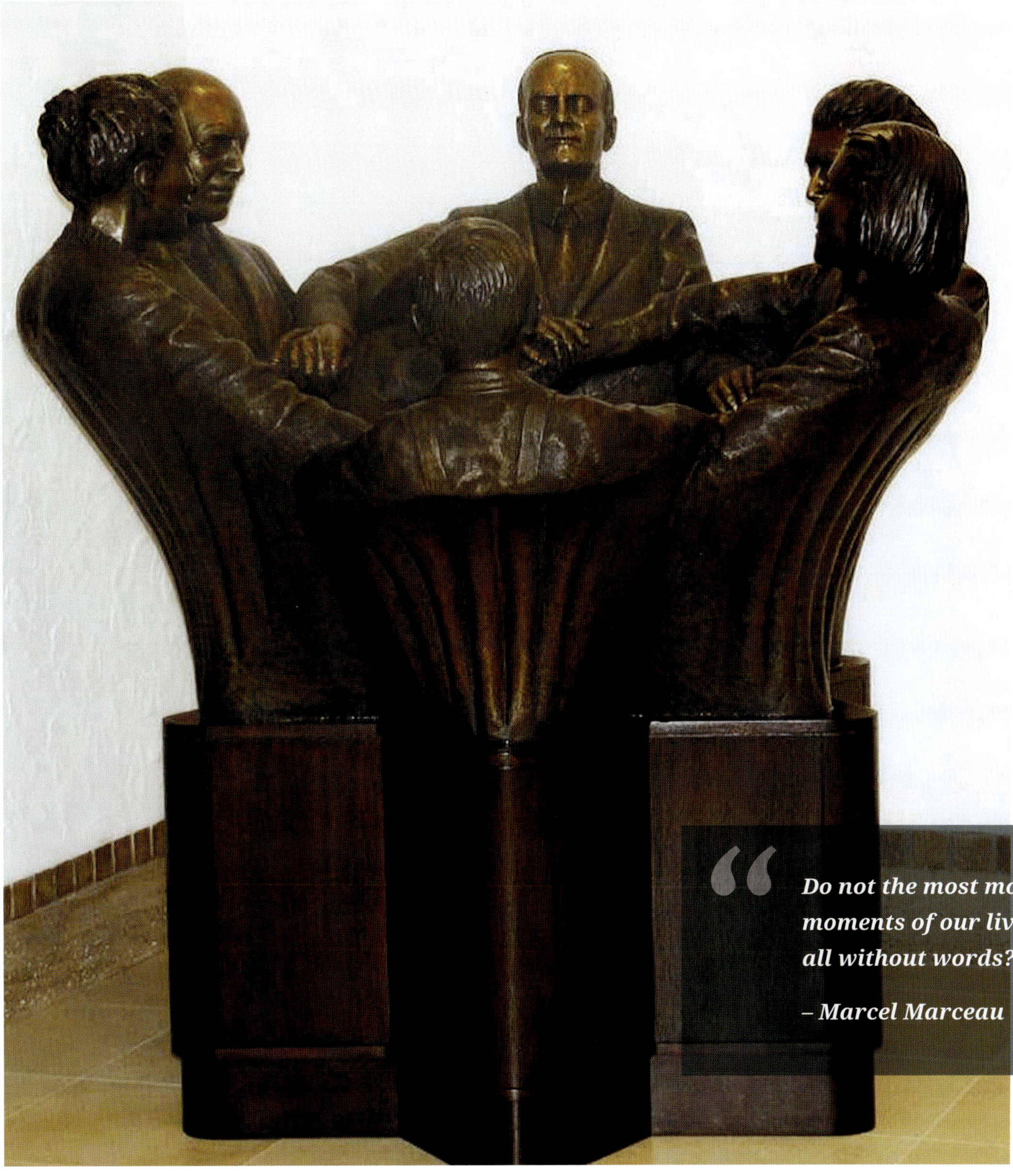

> **“** ***Do not the most moving moments of our lives find us all without words?***
>
> ***– Marcel Marceau***

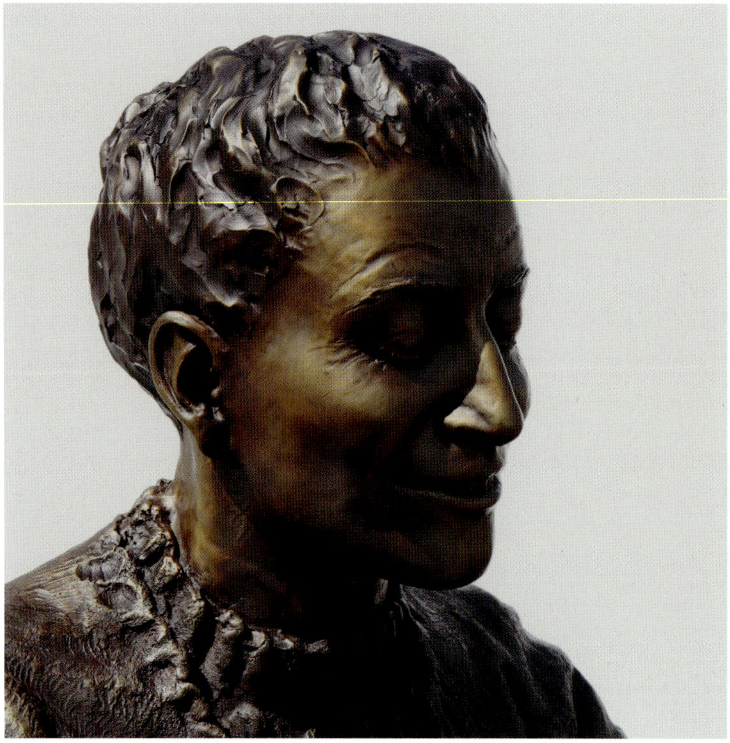

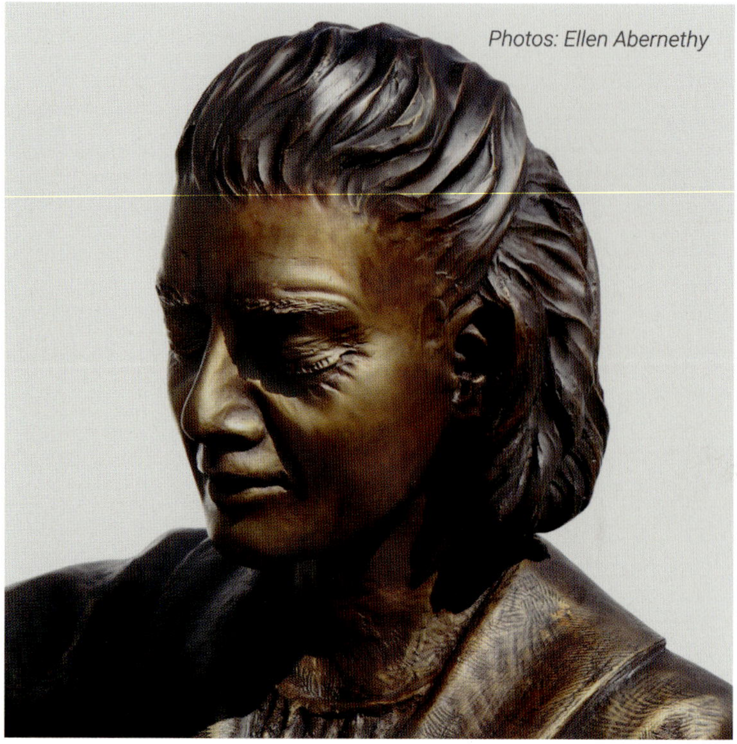

With every portrait, the act of memorizing facial features links me forever to my subject. I'd tried on occasion to put a name to the powerful bond I developed while sculpting, but shied away from the idea of being 'in love' with my portraits. The connection was just as powerful but it was not emotionally accurate. That day in Chicago I finally identified the link between creator and subject. It was devotion—perhaps utter devotion.

Mark and I flew to the Windy City for the November dedication service, on the anniversary of *Kristallnacht*. I'd been asked to speak. The service was moving. Haunting music filled the synagogue. Though I'm usually comfortable speaking to people, I could scarcely keep my composure.

Before my introduction, the client's father rose to address the congregation. With tears and delight, Felix Horn expressed how powerful the portraits were for him and how meaningful it was to share his missing family, at last, with his children and grandchildren. His gracious words brought the calm I needed to convey how honoured I was to have shared his family. I could not imagine life without my own. Later that night, my husband made a comment that rings beautifully true: "You are incredibly lucky to work on projects to which people bring their very, *very* best!"

I sculpted the characters in *Gathering* with their eyes closed. I wanted their interconnection to focus on physical touch and collective intention rather than 'across-the-centre' eye contact. The calm, inclusive presence of the families drew people in the synagogue to stand with them, to offer physical affection and to create moments of shared reflection.

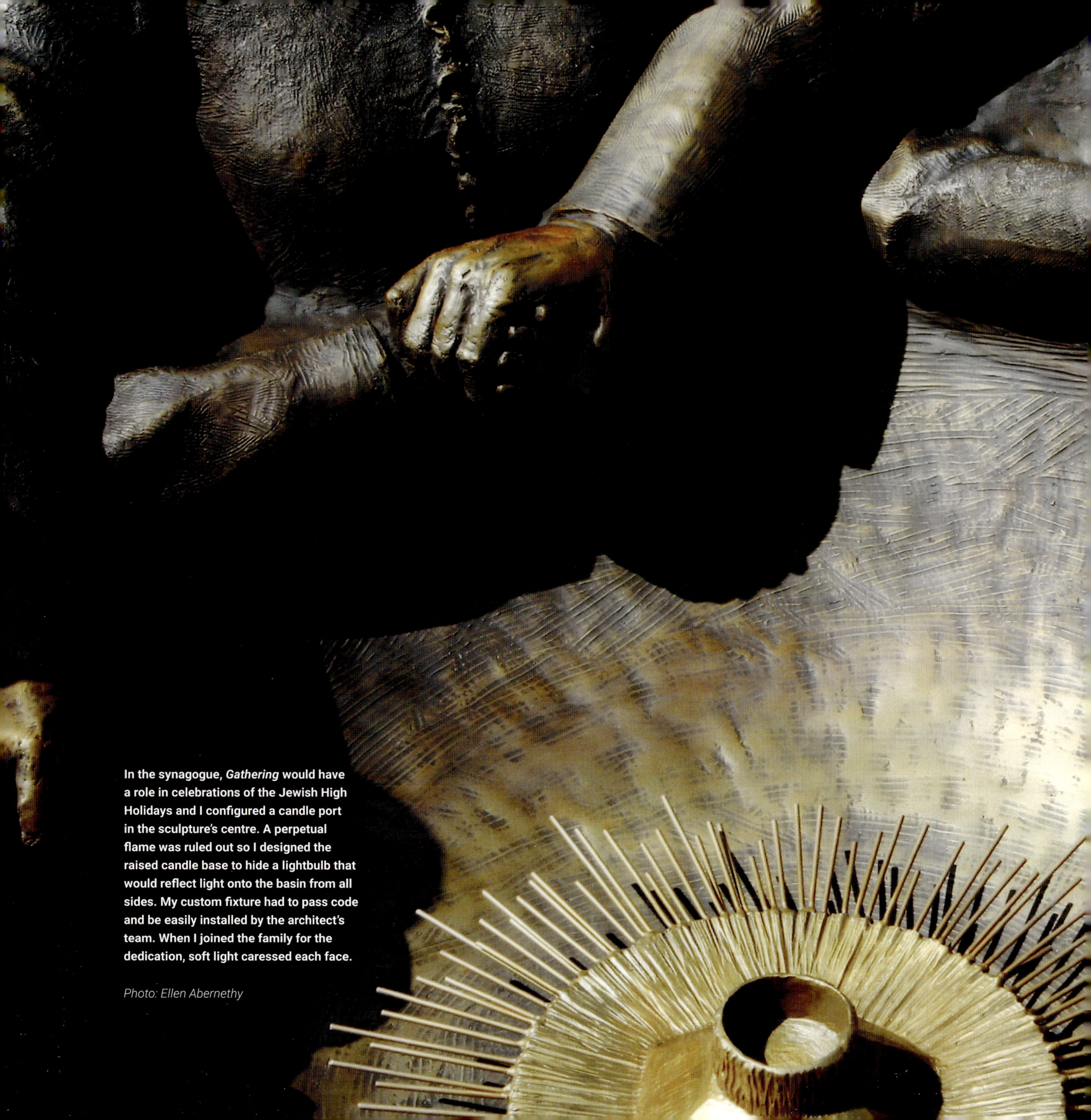

In the synagogue, *Gathering* would have a role in celebrations of the Jewish High Holidays and I configured a candle port in the sculpture's centre. A perpetual flame was ruled out so I designed the raised candle base to hide a lightbulb that would reflect light onto the basin from all sides. My custom fixture had to pass code and be easily installed by the architect's team. When I joined the family for the dedication, soft light caressed each face.

Photo: Ellen Abernethy

PART THREE

Later Works

John A.'s portrait had charm and youthful energy right from the start.

– Ruth Abernethy

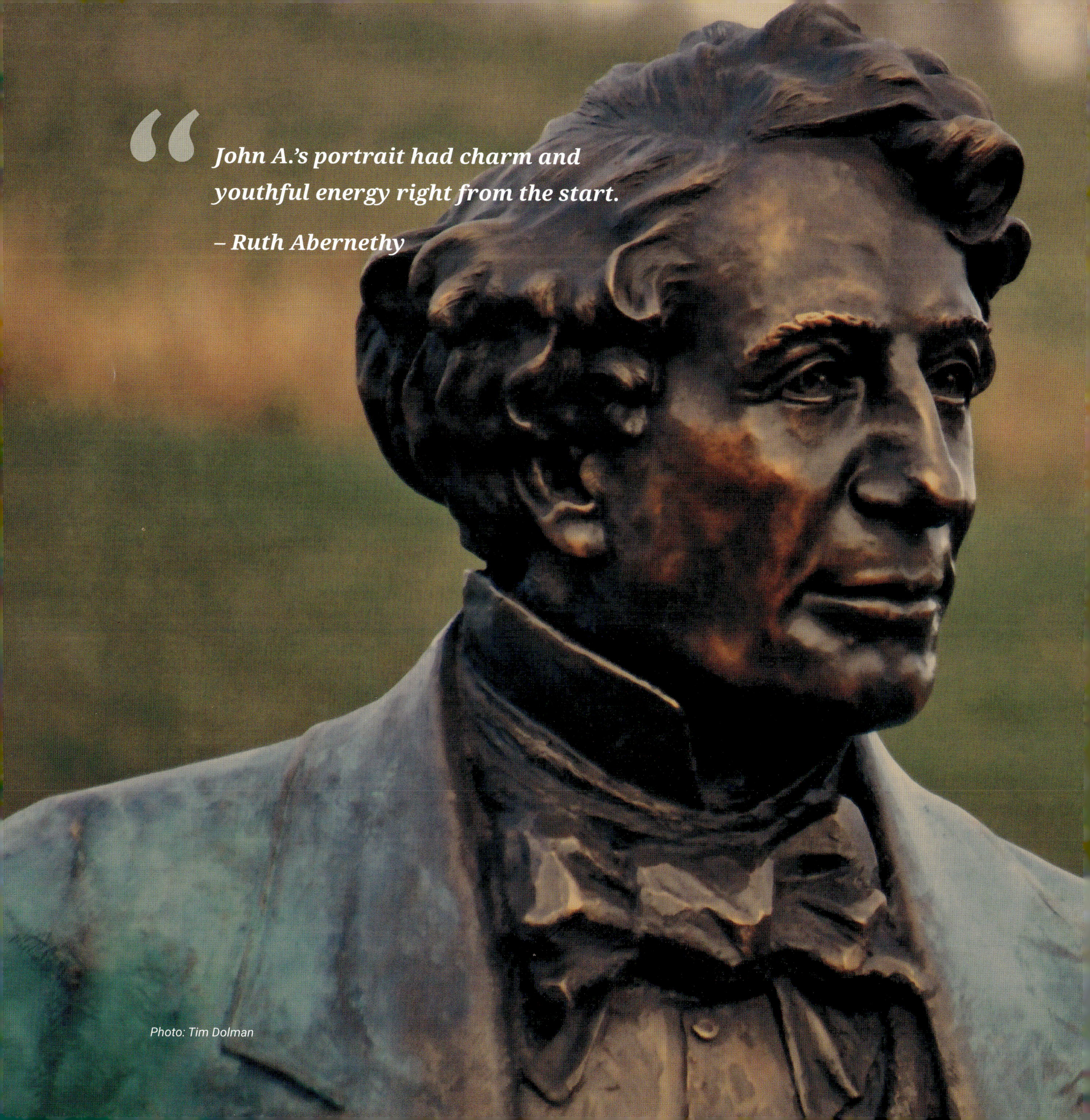

Photo: Tim Dolman

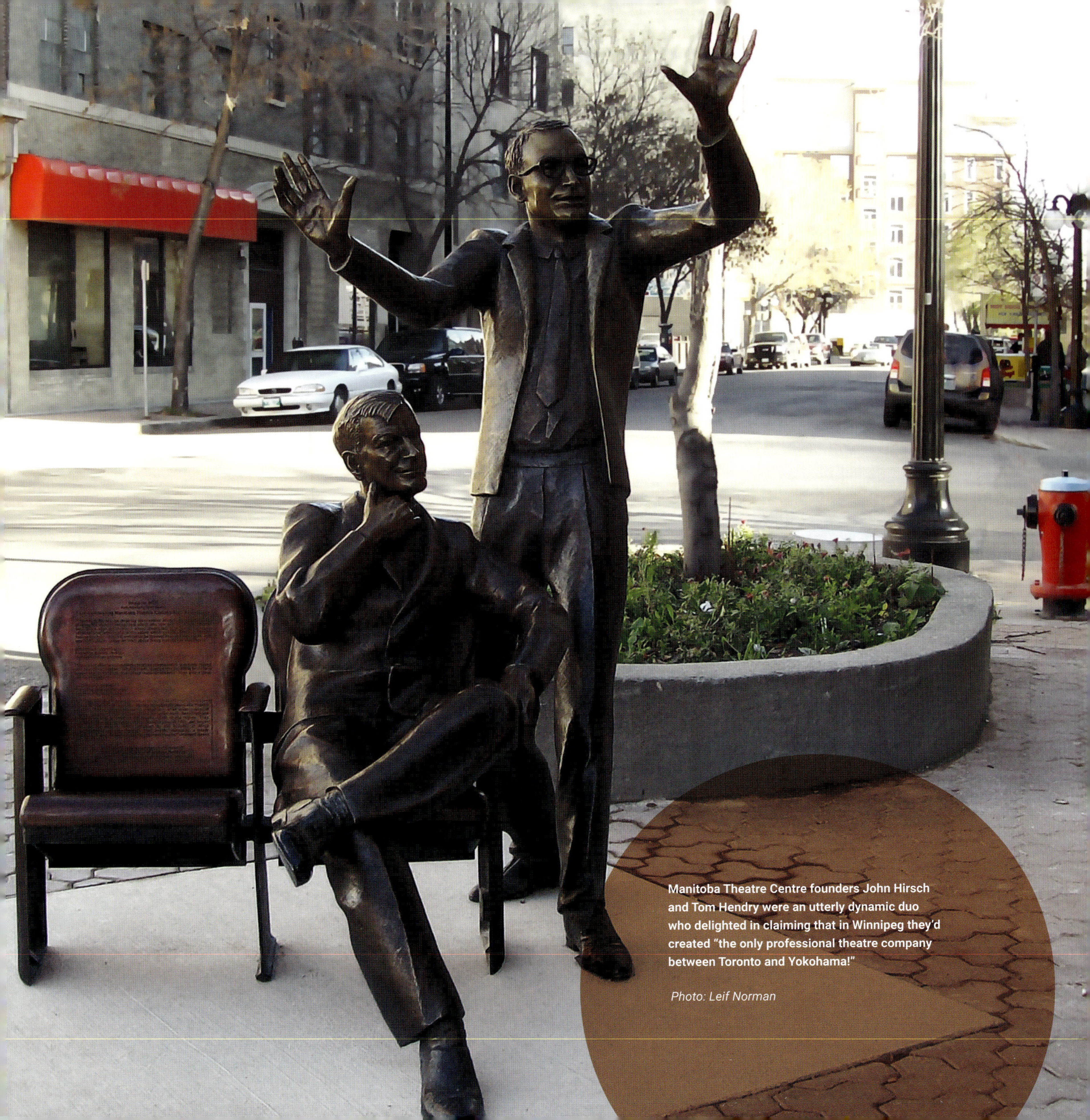

Manitoba Theatre Centre founders John Hirsch and Tom Hendry were an utterly dynamic duo who delighted in claiming that in Winnipeg they'd created "the only professional theatre company between Toronto and Yokohama!"

Photo: Leif Norman

John Hirsch and Tom Hendry

In 2008 the Manitoba Theatre Centre prepared to celebrate its 50th anniversary. Behind the scenes, Gail Asper, patron and long-time supporter of the theatre, insisted there be a permanent marker. After commissioning a new play for the theatre patrons, MTC launched the portraits of John Hirsch and Tom Hendry for their Winnipeg streetscape.

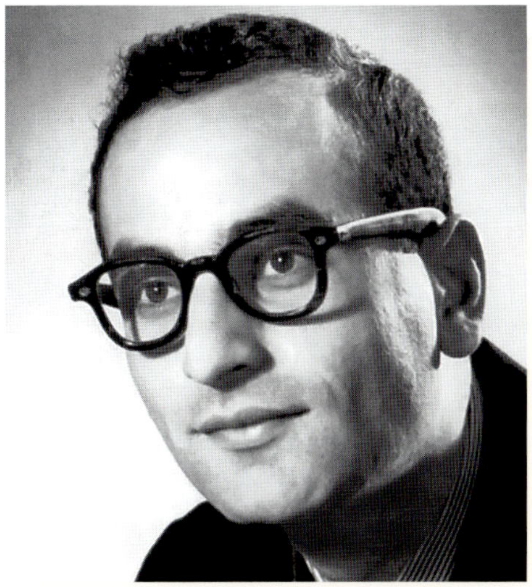

John Hirsch (1930–1989)

Theatre Director

John Hirsch's privileged Hungarian family died in the Holocaust. He arrived in Winnipeg at age 17 as a homeless war refugee. He was taken in by the Shack family, with whom he remained close for the rest of his life. Following success with the Manitoba Theatre Centre, John's career as a stage director brought him international acclaim. He was brilliant and demanding. He was also loved, feared and celebrated.

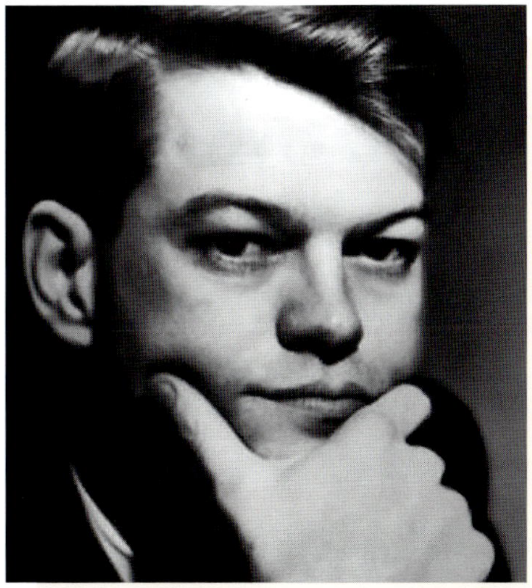

Tom Hendry (1929–2012)

Playwright and Theatre Administrator

Tom Hendry was born in Winnipeg and trained as an accountant. His financial talents were matched by his people skills and his passion for theatre, all three fundamental to his success as a Canadian playwright. Tom co-founded Toronto Free Theatre and the Banff Playwrights Colony. He wrote numerous successful plays and was a screenwriter for several television series. He was awarded the Order of Canada in 1995.

Hendry's play *Fifteen Miles of Broken Glass* (1975) won a Lieutenant Governor of Ontario Medal.

I had my own early career history with MTC's first artistic director, John Hirsch. By the time I arrived in the shops at Manitoba Theatre Centre, Hirsch had gone on to successes in Toronto, Los Angeles and New York. But in 1981 John became the first Canadian artistic director of the Stratford Festival, where I'd just arrived in the prop shop.

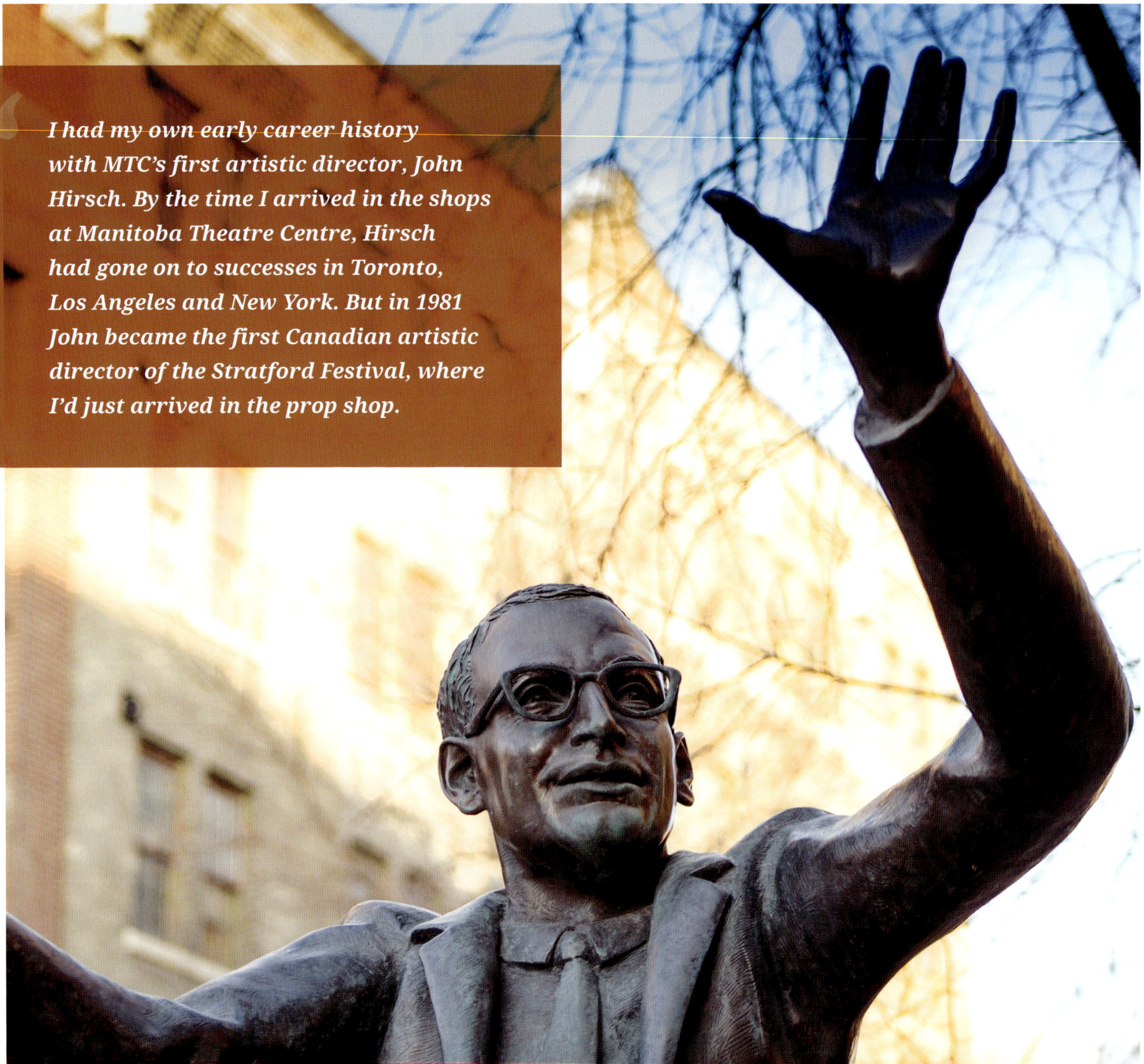

Photo: Leif Norman

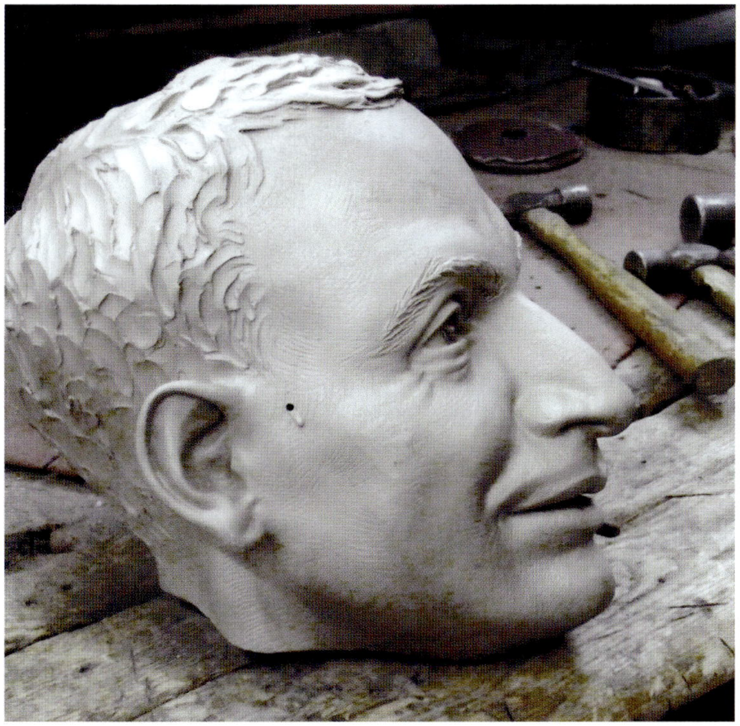

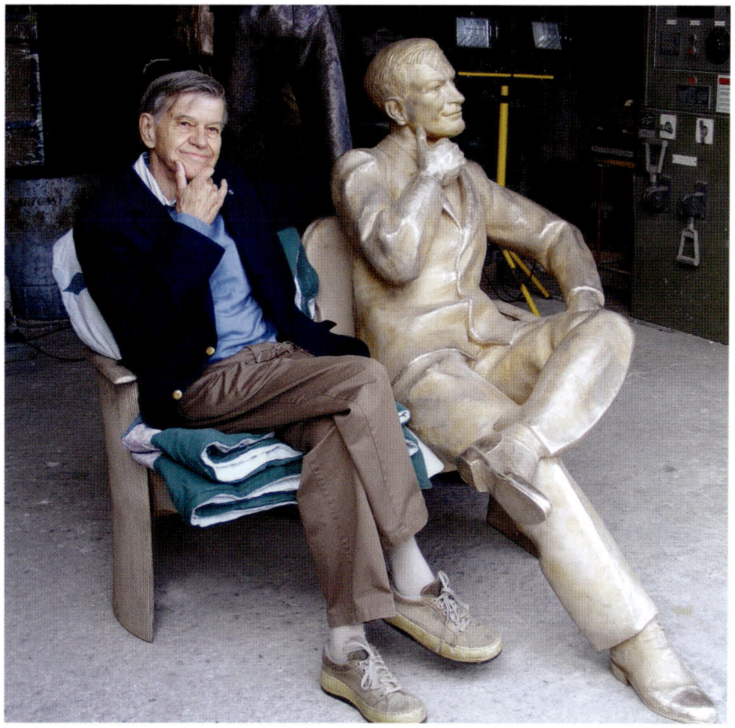

Through the dark months of winter I sculpted John Hirsch and absorbed his story. The process of assimilating it meshed profoundly with the Horn family's portraits that were underway at the same time for the work *Gathering*. The studio was a perfect place to develop their intersecting narratives of loss and regeneration.

I put finishing touches on John's head study in the living room of John's friend, the playwright Tom Hendry. As I worked, Tom described Winnipeg in the 1950s and a particular group of people who would appear without fail at arts events across the city. He and John referred to them as 'the Formerlies' since their introductions followed a pattern: "Formerly the Head of Sciences at . . .", "Formerly a lecturer for . . ." or "Formerly the conductor of . . ." These 'Formerlies' were transplants from a European culture destroyed by Hitler and WW II.

Tom Hendry was intelligent about art, human nature, and money management. After his theatre success in Winnipeg, he turned down dozens of job offers from around the world. He held the firm conviction that he would do his best work in Canada.

My hours with him were filled with glimpses of people who'd laid the foundations of the theatres I'd encountered across the country. He was a unique and gentle man with whom I shared a poignant sense of homecoming through this project.

Choice

The City of Waterloo and its surrounding region are a fascinating study. The Mennonites in the area descend from Swiss-Pennsylvanian Mennonite pioneers. Numerous community sects include distinctive Old Order groups that run large, efficient farms reliant on horse-drawn equipment. Horses also pull buggies alongside the highways and their drivers, in traditional garb, are distinguishing aspects of Waterloo Region. The Old Order presence is an exquisite counterpoint to state-of-the-art technologies and engineering sectors that also thrive in the region. In 1857, Waterloo's year of incorporation, prayer caps and hats of all sorts were standard dress. For those who choose to wear them still, the traditional, meticulously hand-made caps indicate nuanced Mennonite activities.

In 2006 the City of Waterloo requested sculpture proposals to celebrate its upcoming 150th anniversary. I proposed four styles of stainless steel 'bonnets' made in a large scale that would serve as public seating near a city centre park.

The underlying logic of the design was that these bonnets represented our personal capacity to choose when, and whether, traditional dress is meaningful in an ever-evolving Canadian society.

I borrowed paper bonnet patterns from my neighbour, then scanned and enlarged them. I replicated the weave of the material in a fabric cap by perforating flat steel pattern-pieces with a custom punch made in Chicago. It was essential to keep the stamped square holes of the 'weave' away from the edges of the steel pieces so that welded seams would be smooth and safe. The digital processes of scanning, electronic enlargement, photography and mechanized fabrication were satisfying high-tech steps towards the presentation of the 80-inch-tall heritage forms of the bonnets, entitled *Choice*.

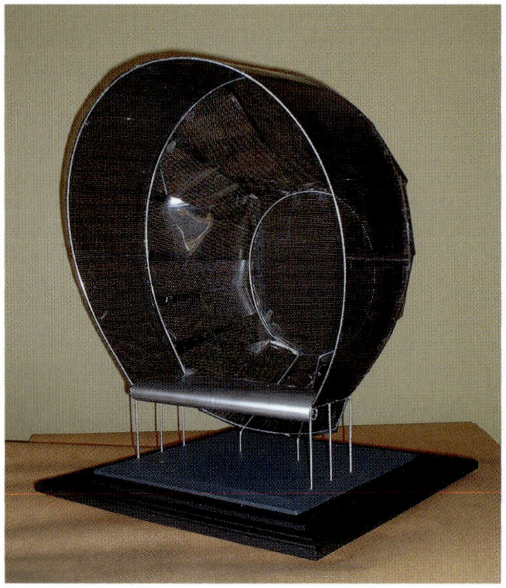

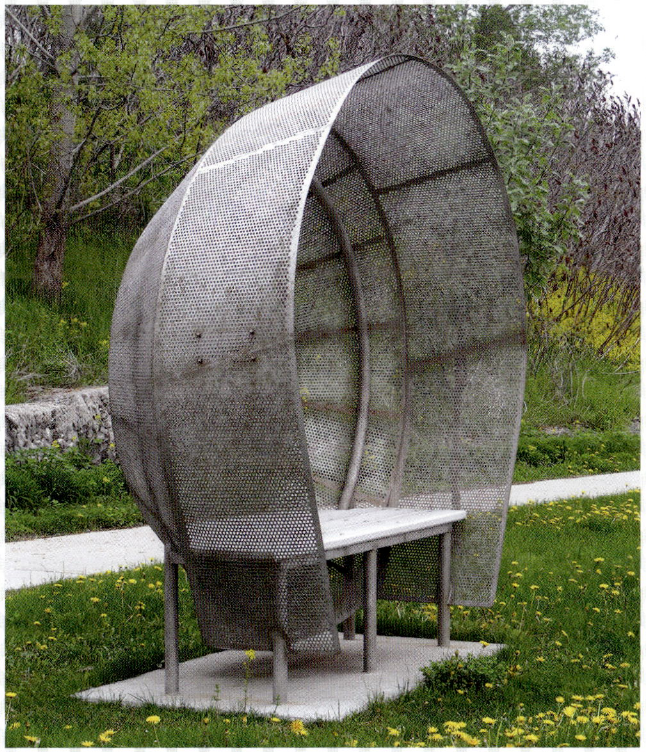

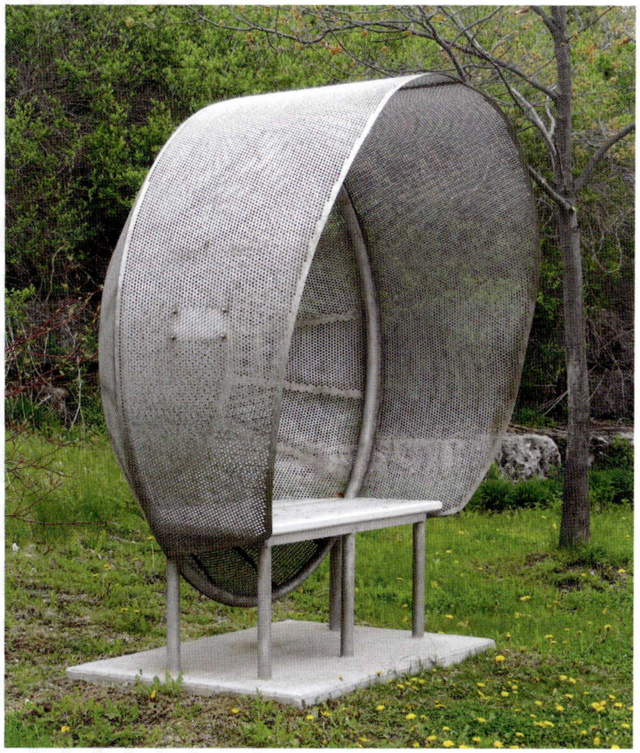

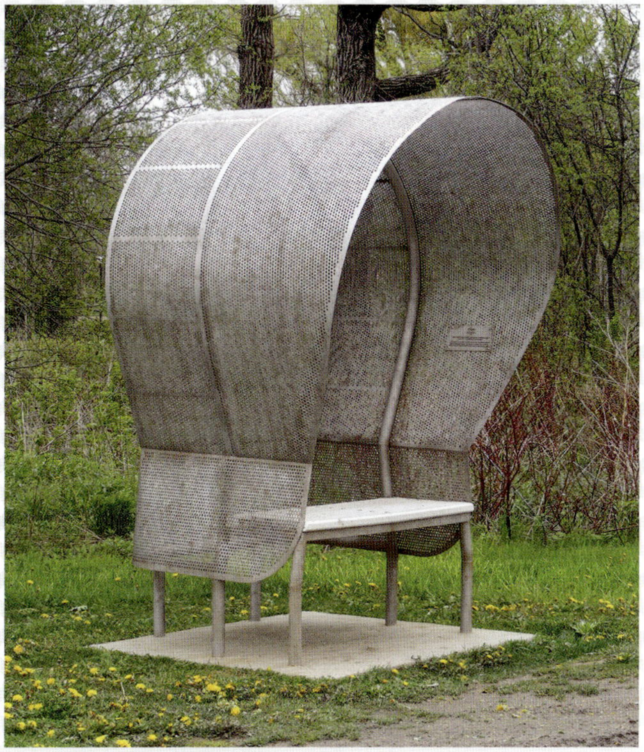

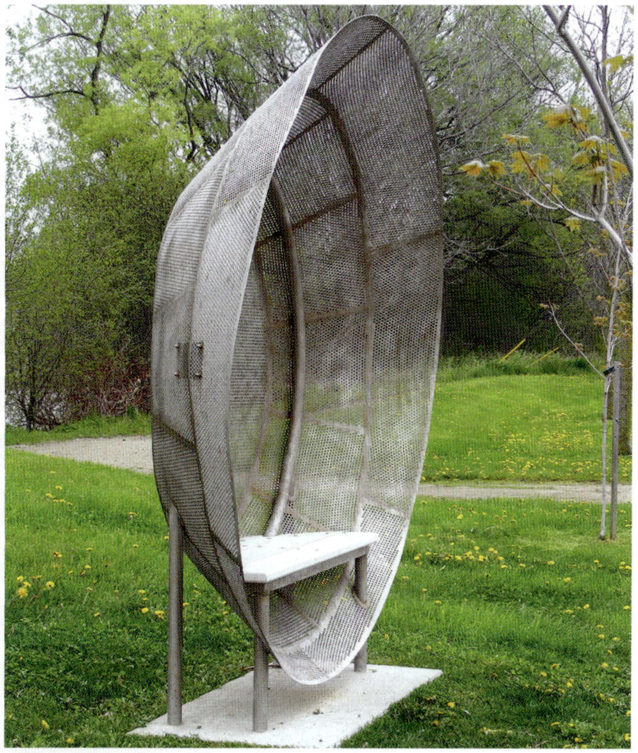

Photos: Leonard Schlichting

Meanwhile In The Studio...

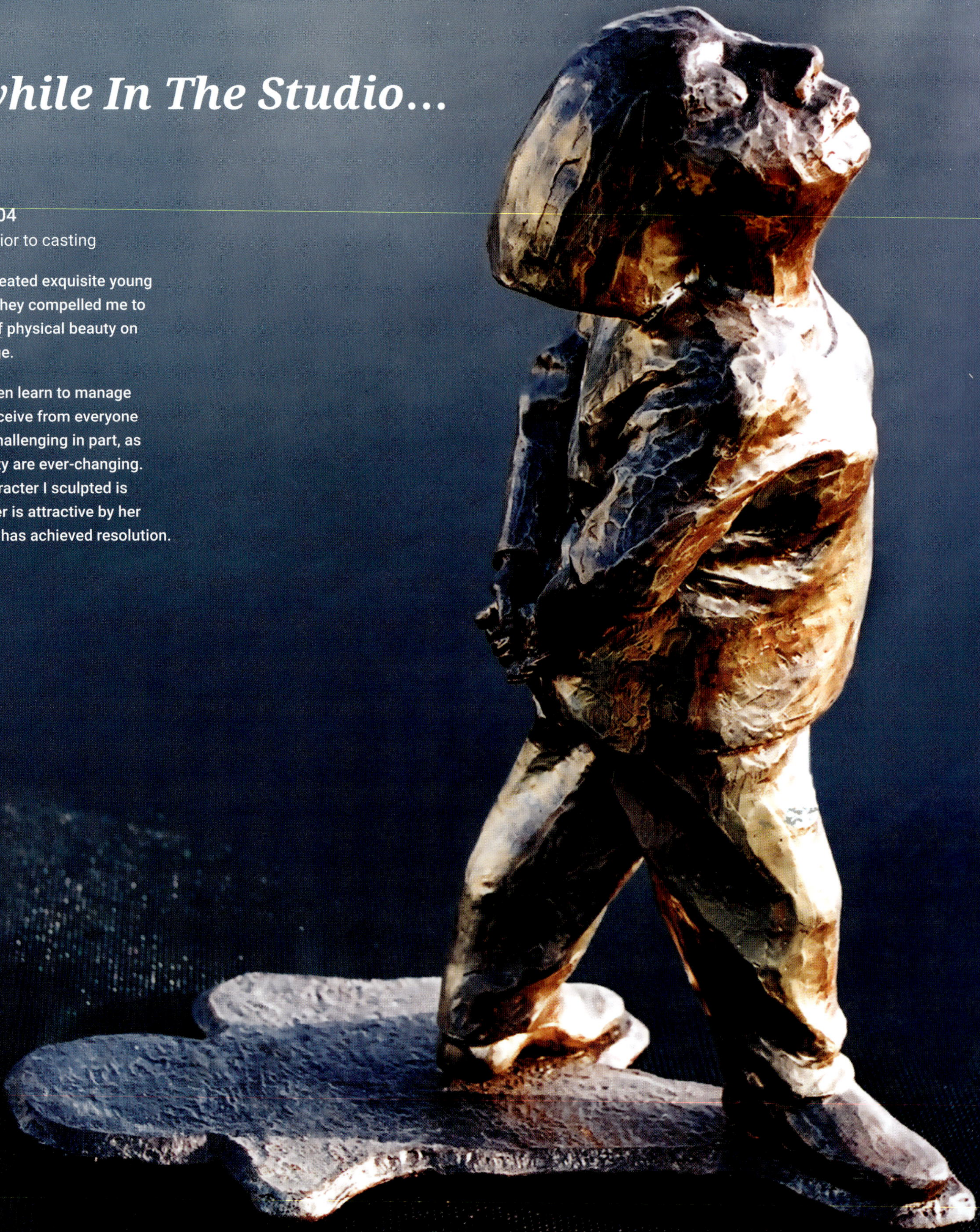

Not a Ballerina, 2004
14", Shown in wax, prior to casting

The sculptor Degas created exquisite young ballerinas in bronze. They compelled me to consider the impact of physical beauty on interpersonal exchange.

From childhood, women learn to manage the responses they receive from everyone they encounter. It is challenging in part, as assessments of beauty are ever-changing. The beauty of the character I sculpted is internal. This character is attractive by her own assessment; she has achieved resolution.

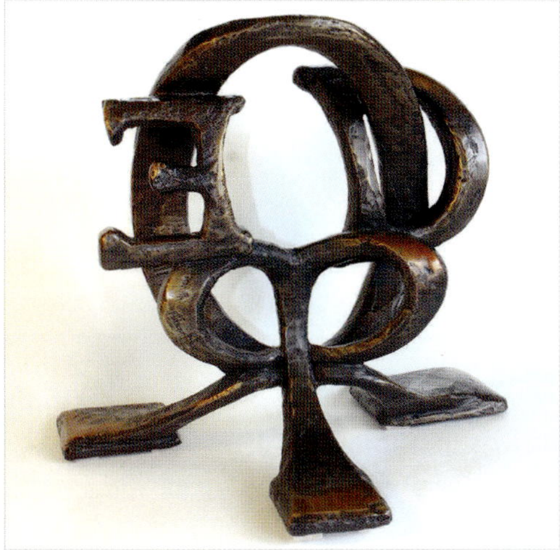

Order, 2010

14" x 14" x 11", Bronze

Photo: Cassandra Koch

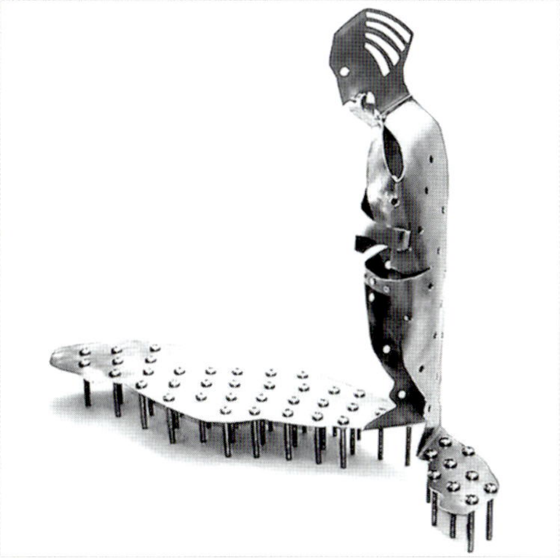

Big/Small, 2000

32" x 16" x 8", Stainless steel

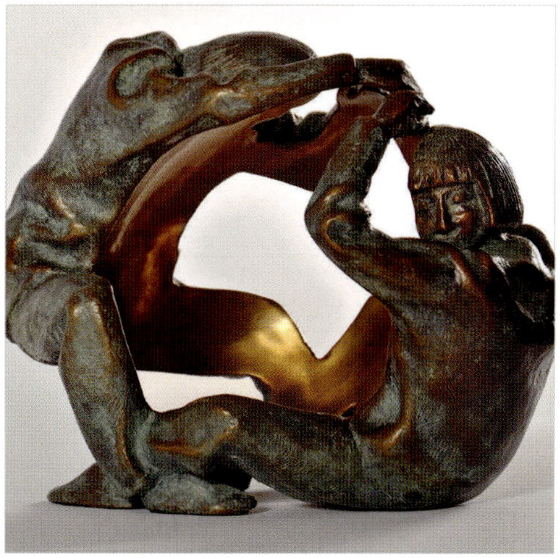

Pas D'Oeuf, 2004

10" x 8" x 6", Bronze

Photo: JR Ribee

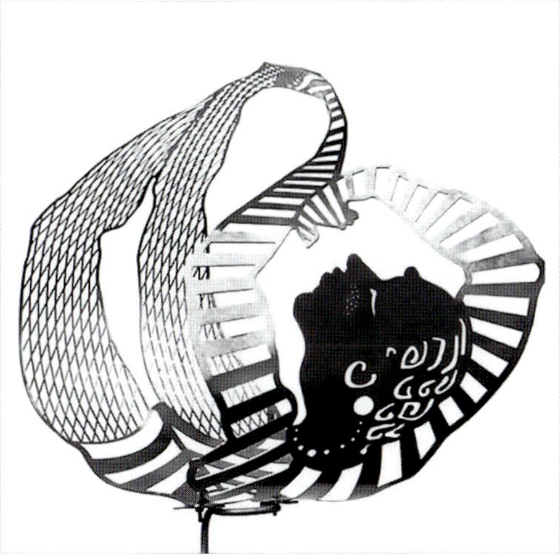

Moebius Stripper, 2003

32" dia. x 14" deep, Stainless steel

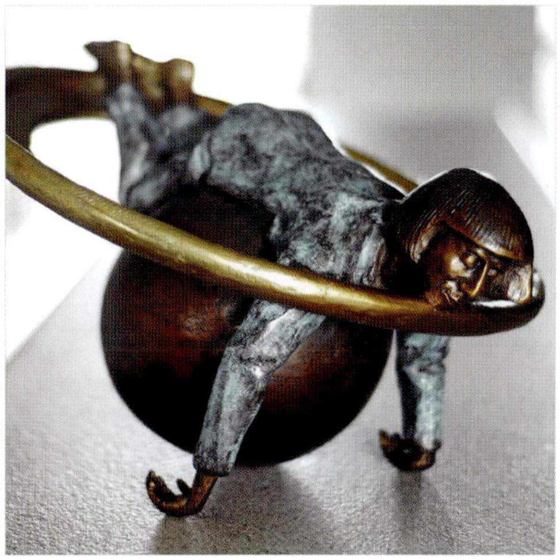

Citizen, 2005

14" dia. x 8.5" high, Bronze

Photo: JR Ribee

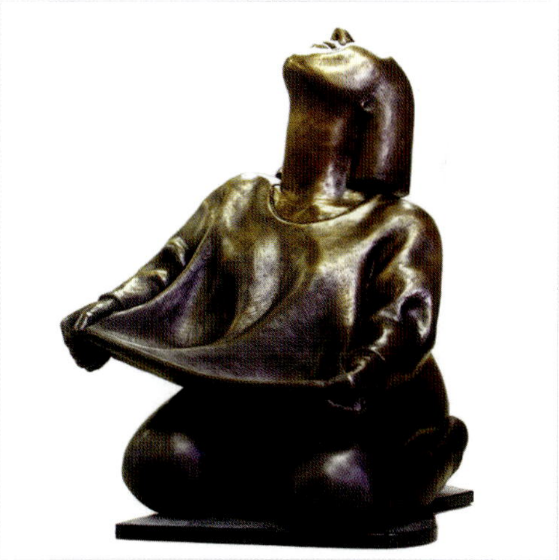

Emily's Bounty, 2003

28" x 16" x 16", Bronze

Photo: Eric Knoespel

> *I have an idea—I think we should organize an ambulant blood transfusion service.*
>
> *– Norman Bethune*

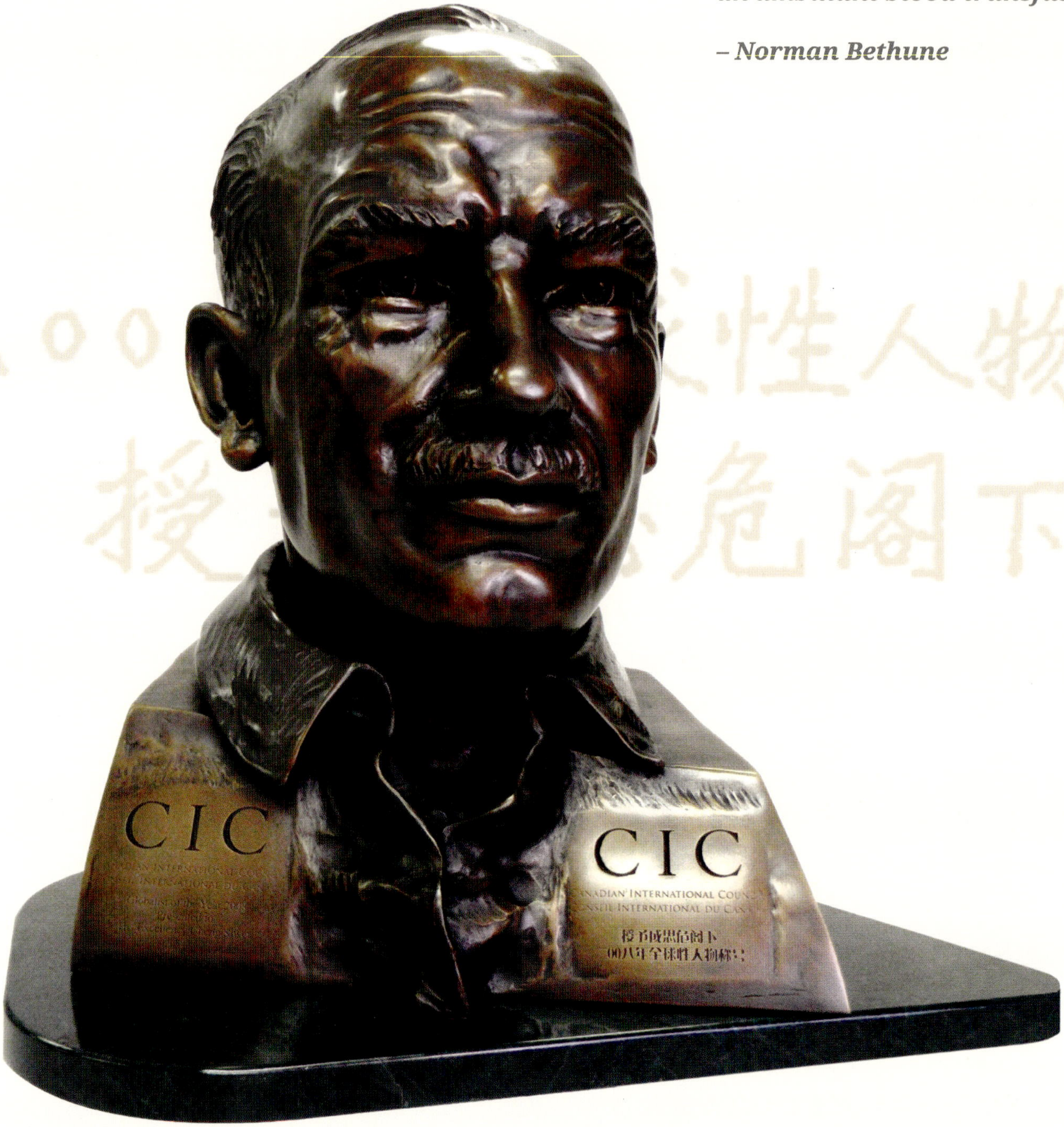

Photo: Eric Knoespel

Dr. Norman

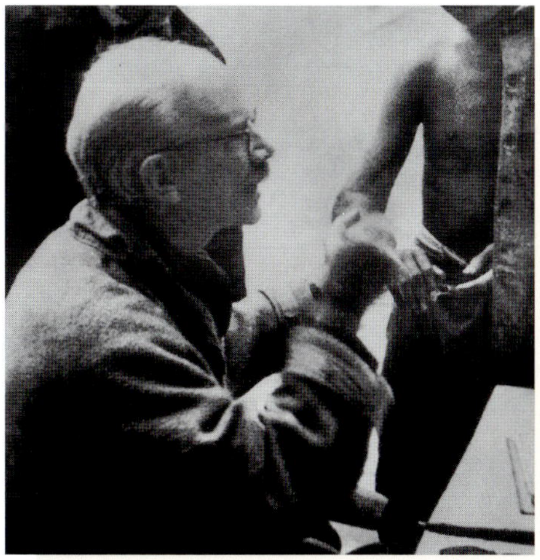

Norman Bethune (1890–1939)

Physician

Born in Gravenhurst, Ontario, Norman Henry Bethune was a Canadian physician and medical innovator who developed mobile blood transfusion units at the frontlines in the Spanish Civil War. He brought western medicine to rural China in the 1930s. He often treated sick villagers as well as wounded soldiers. He made such a powerful and long-lasting impression that statues in his honour are found in cities throughout China.

Shortly after sculpting *Glenn* Gould in 1999, I was asked to propose a portrait concept for Norman Bethune for his hometown of Gravenhurst, Ontario. I was confident the commission would go to Brenda Goulais, an artist from the Gravenhurst area. As a virtually unknown sculptor, I was pleased to be considered a candidate. I read Bethune's biography and prepared my submission. When Brenda was awarded the commission, I tucked my research photos into a file and turned my attention elsewhere.

A decade later, Mark and I began a long-planned addition to our house, which we'd named Ash Flats. We'd imagined this as a summer job for Glen and Alex but building permits were delayed. When the excavator arrived in early September we wondered if we were mad to proceed. Two weeks later I had a phone request for a portrait bust of Norman Bethune, to be presented at a gala evening in late October. The extreme deadline left no possibility of preparing a finished bronze. The best option was to sculpt the portrait, have it molded and provide a fine wax copy for presentation.

I was wide-eyed at tackling an exacting portrait while drastic changes were made to our house, but there was not a moment to lose. I was reminded of a busy period in 2003 when I'd articulated the idea that moments of time were like points on a line. Between any two moments was an infinite number of *smaller* moments! Under the circumstances, I prized every one of those infinite, smaller moments.

The good doctor would certainly have understood the value of focusing on nothing but the task, and making good use of those infinite, smaller moments!

The doctor's portrait was to be awarded as the "Globalist of the Year Award" (2008), the brainchild of Jim Balsillie, founder of, among other things, the Canadian International Council (CIC), based in Toronto. In Waterloo, a sister organization, the Centre for International Governance Innovation, or CIGI, was presenting a lecture series on China prior to the Beijing Olympics. Jim was insistent that guest diplomat Cheng Siwei receive this custom award. I set to work, relieved in small measure that house renovations only needed my attention during daylight hours.

With reference material at hand, Dr. Norman came together in a heartbeat. English and Chinese texts were proofed and prepared for molding. In late October former Governor General Adrienne Clarkson addressed a banquet room of VIPs at the Royal Ontario Museum in Toronto and presented the Bethune-portrait award.

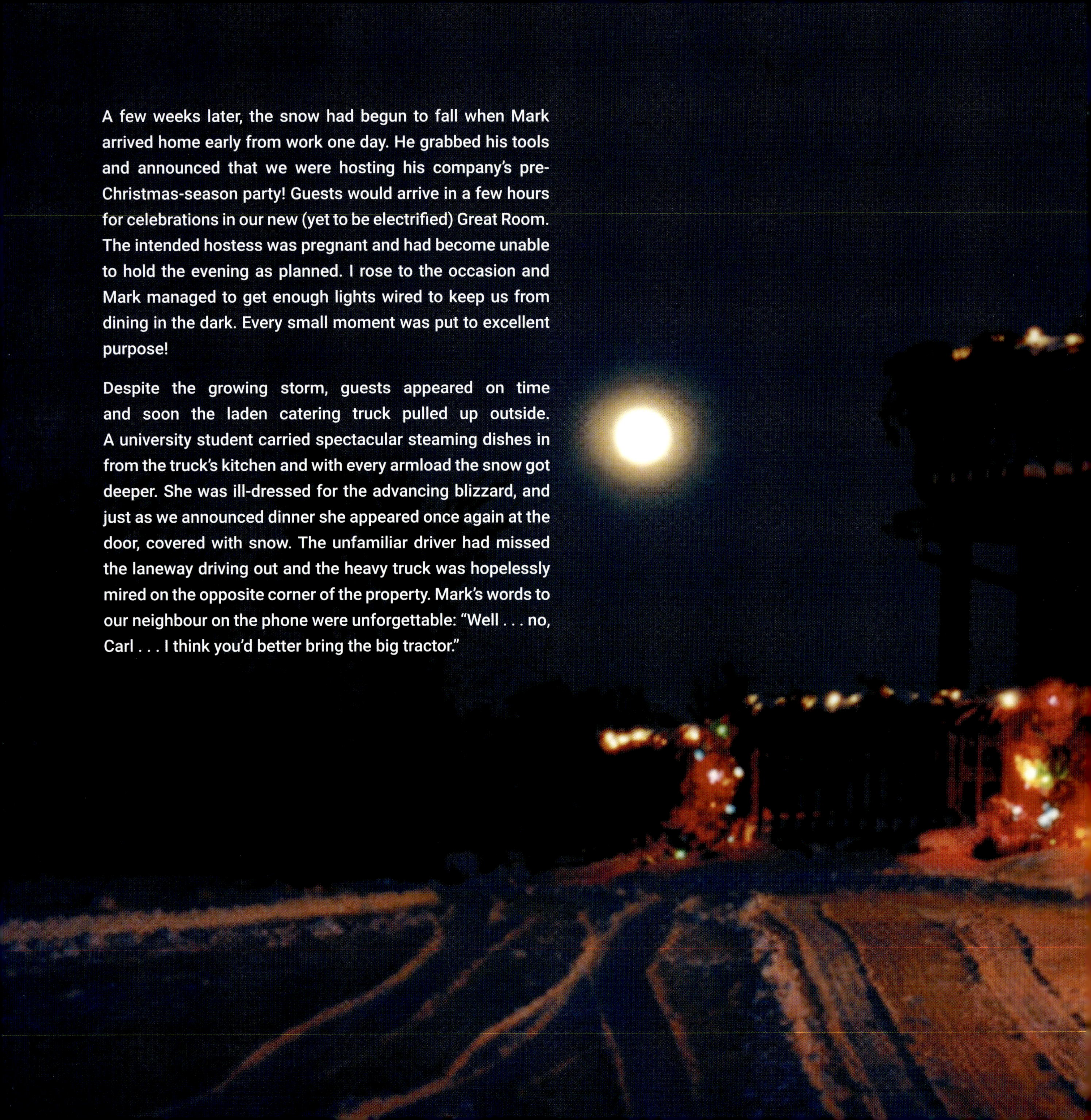

A few weeks later, the snow had begun to fall when Mark arrived home early from work one day. He grabbed his tools and announced that we were hosting his company's pre-Christmas-season party! Guests would arrive in a few hours for celebrations in our new (yet to be electrified) Great Room. The intended hostess was pregnant and had become unable to hold the evening as planned. I rose to the occasion and Mark managed to get enough lights wired to keep us from dining in the dark. Every small moment was put to excellent purpose!

Despite the growing storm, guests appeared on time and soon the laden catering truck pulled up outside. A university student carried spectacular steaming dishes in from the truck's kitchen and with every armload the snow got deeper. She was ill-dressed for the advancing blizzard, and just as we announced dinner she appeared once again at the door, covered with snow. The unfamiliar driver had missed the laneway driving out and the heavy truck was hopelessly mired on the opposite corner of the property. Mark's words to our neighbour on the phone were unforgettable: "Well . . . no, Carl . . . I think you'd better bring the big tractor."

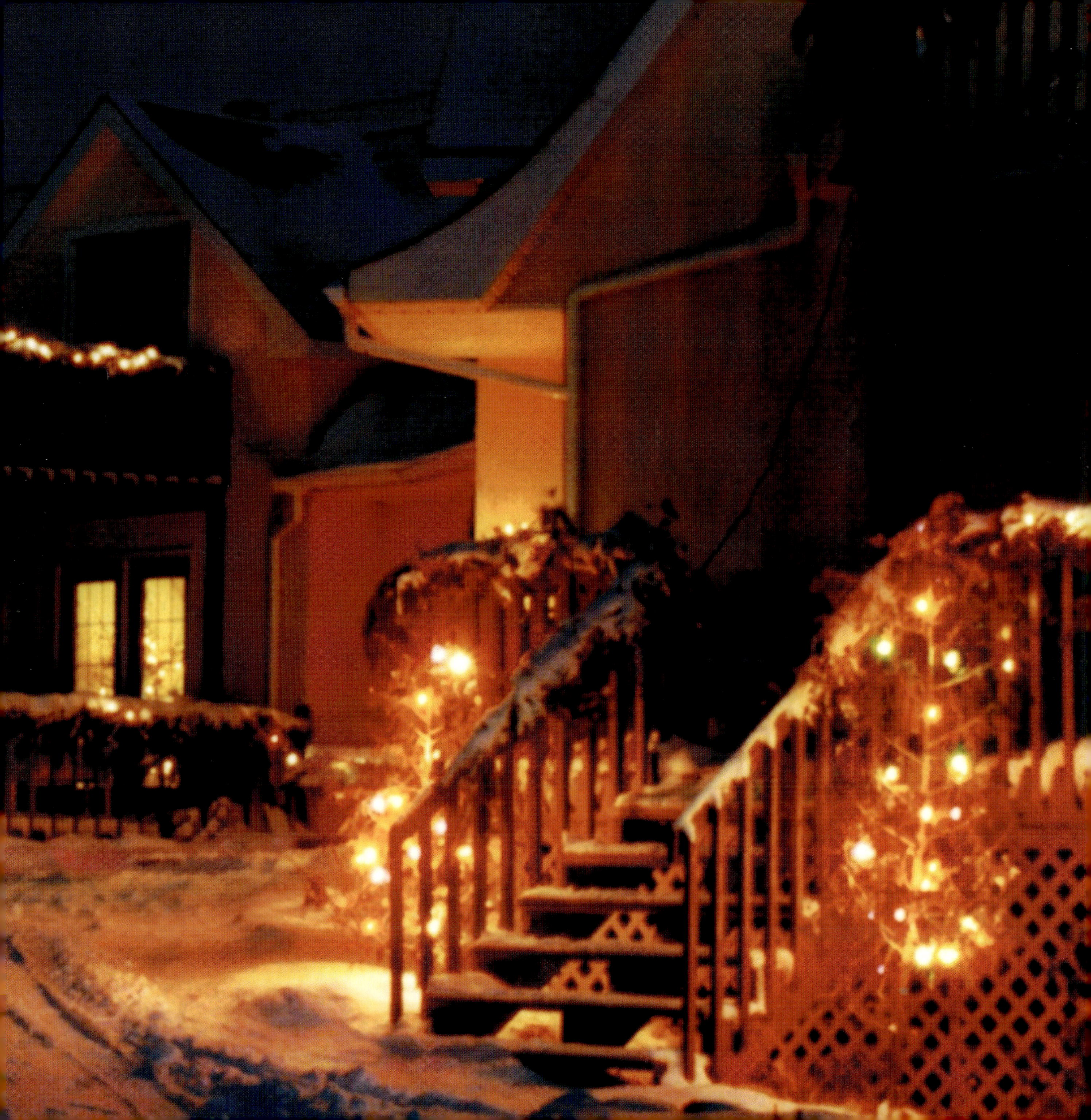

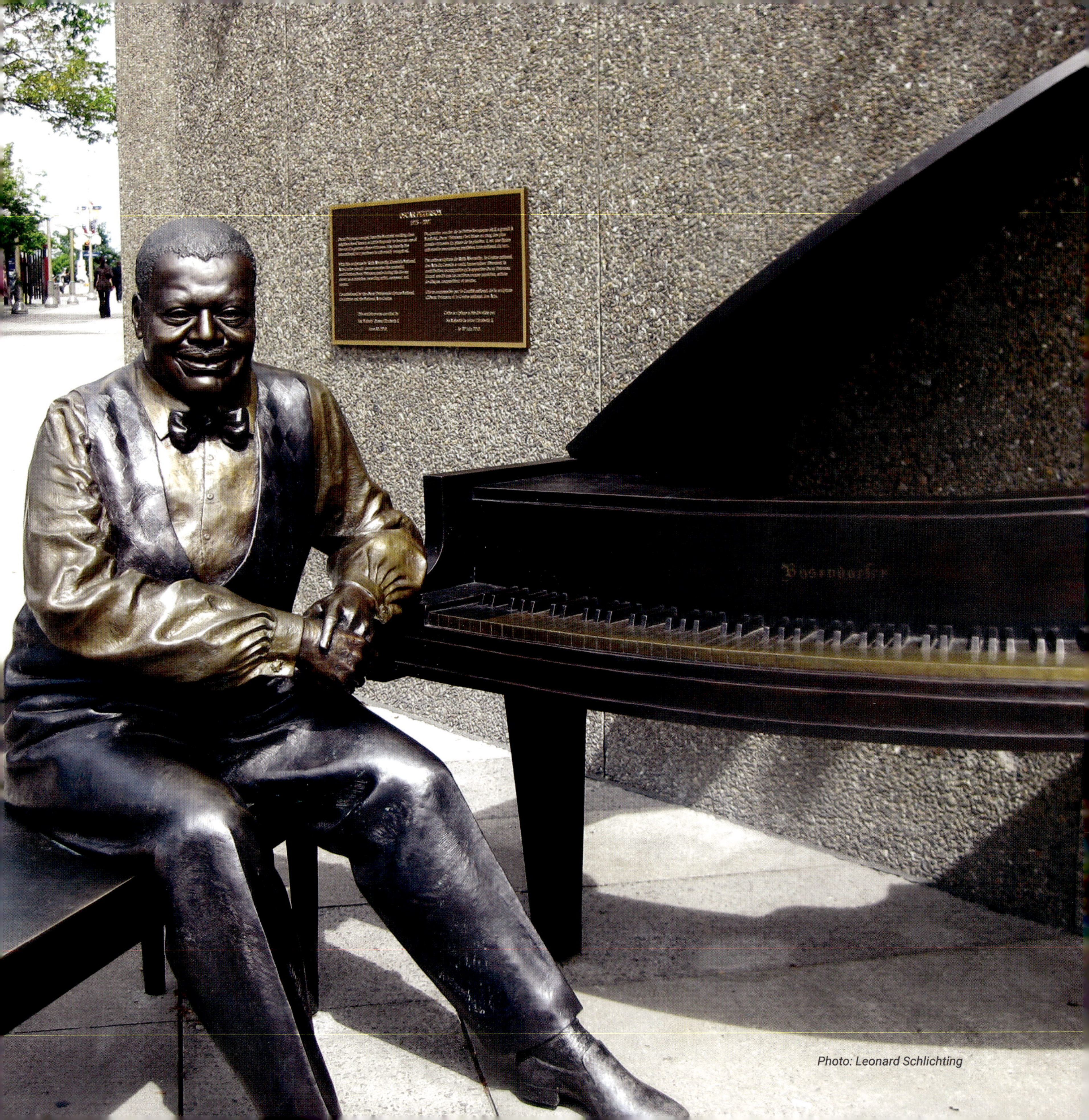
Photo: Leonard Schlichting

Oscar Peterson

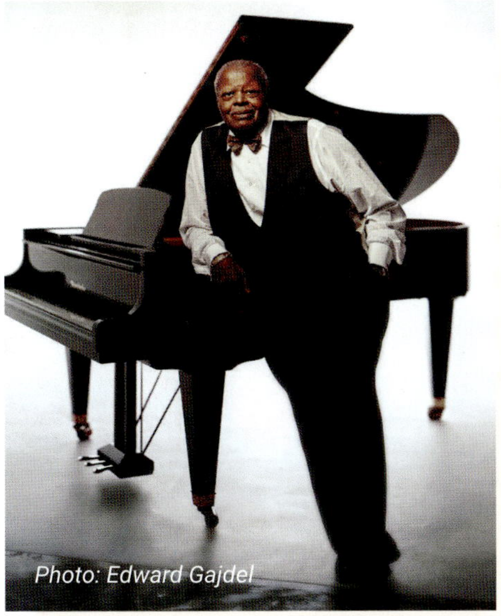

Photo: Edward Gajdel

Oscar Peterson (1925–2007)

Jazz Pianist

Internationally renowned jazz pianist and composer Oscar Peterson was born in Montreal to parents of Caribbean origin. Playing piano from age eight, he released more than 200 recordings in his 60-year plus career. His signature style inspired musicians and audiences alike. His accolades were countless: the first recipient of the Governor General's Performing Arts Award, the first living non-monarch to appear on a Canadian stamp and the first inductee to the Canadian Jazz and Blues Hall of Fame. Peterson was an Officer of both the Order of Canada and the Order of Arts and Letters in France. His other honours included the International Jazz Hall of Fame, Canada's Walk of Fame, the Canadian Music Hall of Fame and Grammy and Juno awards.

It was a deep blue Christmas Eve. My extended family was preparing for an evening church service near my parents' home. We slid into the car just as the radio host announced that Oscar Peterson had passed away. Time stopped. The full moon lit up every branch of every tree, silver with ice. I struggled to accept the news. It seemed that the world shifted beneath my feet. Mr. Peterson held a large corner of my Canadian tapestry. His death was a jarring reminder that the cultural backdrop to my own experience was fragile and fleeting.

At the time of Oscar's death, my days and studio were filled with the Chicago sculpture and the Hirsch/Hendry portraits. While working on these, I listened to radio updates on the Peterson tribute concert to be held in Toronto's Roy Thomson Hall. I wished that I, too, could be standing in line to get a seat. Shortly afterward, Martin Knelman in *The Toronto Star* demanded there be a portrait of Oscar, "just like that of Mr. Gould!" I got several calls from encouraging friends and then John Miller, who had requested the Gould portrait, connected me to the organizers of Oscar's memorial concert.

I made time to write to Peter Herrndorf, Brian Robertson and Bob Rae. If the tribute trio were interested in portraying 'Canada's other finest pianist', I would be thrilled to speak with them. Later that spring I met with Peter Herrndorf; I understood immediately why his staff at the National Arts Centre in Ottawa admire his leadership.

Later in April, NAC archivist Gerry Grace and I scouted locations for the portrait. We explored the many terraces and entrances of the Arts Centre, ending up at last on the corner of Albert and Elgin Streets.

We viewed the surrounding corners with laughably high snow banks while we stood on a sidewalk swept bare. The angled exterior wall of the theatre reflected light and heat and the sloped sidewalk drained away moisture. Gerry and I were delighted! On this site Oscar and his music would create memorable moments with visitors in every season.

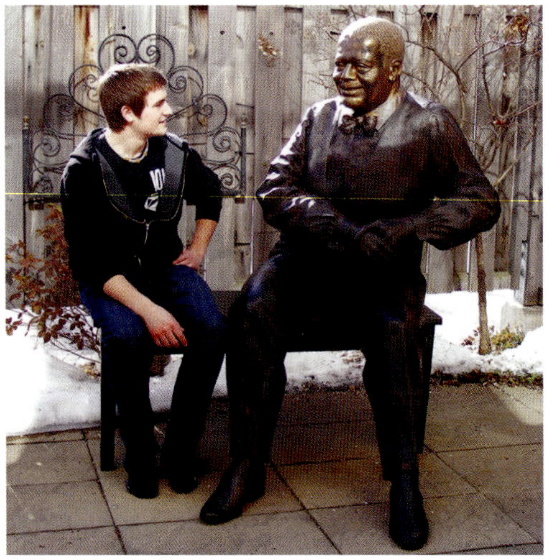

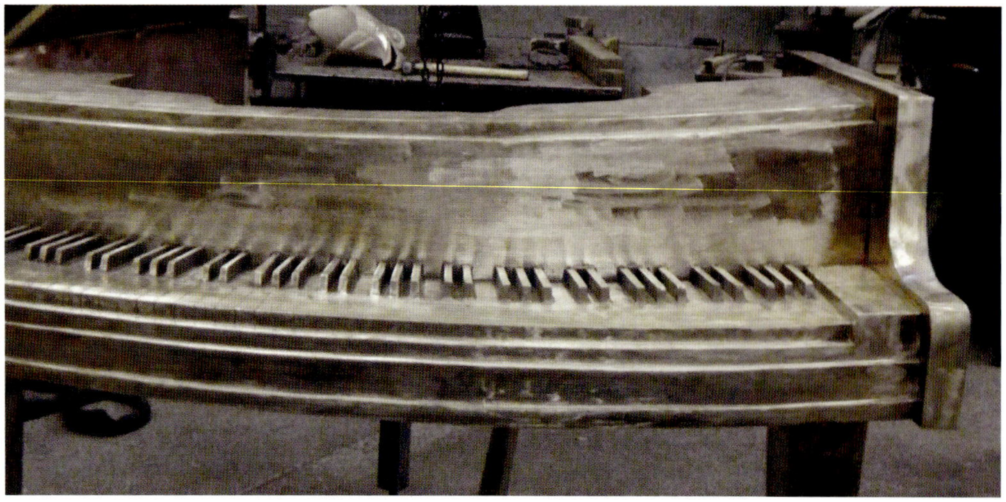

In Oscar's portrait, I wanted to create a personal moment that could be publicly shared, like so many moments in his life. I imagined Oscar playing his composition *Hymn to Freedom*, which became an anthem for Martin Luther King's Civil Rights Movement. Oscar's heart is laid bare as he floats through the melody. Once the final notes are adrift, Oscar slides back his bench and casts his gaze beyond the piano to see with whom he's shared his musical idea.

The sculptural moment I planned with Oscar had to ring true for those who knew him and for the uncountable fans who'd never have that opportunity. The piano was Oscar's first love and having him seated by the keyboard seemed only natural. Casting from an actual piano didn't interest me. It was costly and unimaginative. Oscar's brilliance was inventing music beyond the familiar notes of piano study. I'd learned from Kelly Peterson, Oscar's wife, that his piano of choice was the Bösendorfer Imperial 290, equipped with an additional bass octave made with all black keys! What a perfect signature detail for my design.

I resolved a seamless integration between the sculpture and the distinctive architecture of the National Arts Centre, which featured 30- and 60-degree angles. Oscar's figure was central in my design, but I planned all other structures of the sculpture to increase incrementally in size toward the south slope. One piano leg would be nearly three inches taller than the other and neither bench nor piano would have square, 90-degree corners. Many of these non-standard shapes, 'obnoctagons' as my father Sandy drily named them, can be found in Ash Flats. Every aspect of the piano was calculated and skewed. Delineations between the white keys disappeared along the advancing octaves while the narrow black keys grew larger in four incremental sizes. The stylized half-piano had a curved keyboard, suggesting a runway and a point of musical departure.

The intensity of the Winter Olympics in Vancouver set a perfect context for this portrait. I watched the games with Oscar's amazing hands taking shape in my lap. Surely I'd win a spot in the Sculptors' Olympics! The excitement surrounding the Peterson portrait continued to grow. At a Christmas gathering with the National Portrait Committee in Ottawa, it was whispered that Queen Elizabeth might have a hand in the unveiling. By February, the Oscar Peterson project had developed unique momentum.

The Queen's dedication of the newly-restored Museum of Natural History aligned perfectly with a stop at the National Arts Centre for her to unveil Oscar's portrait on June 30th, 2010. Oscar's followers rose to the occasion financially—in step with the unceasing efforts of Rosemary Thompson, Head of Communications at the NAC. The National Portrait Committee kept funds trickling in for the exciting and ever-expanding celebration.

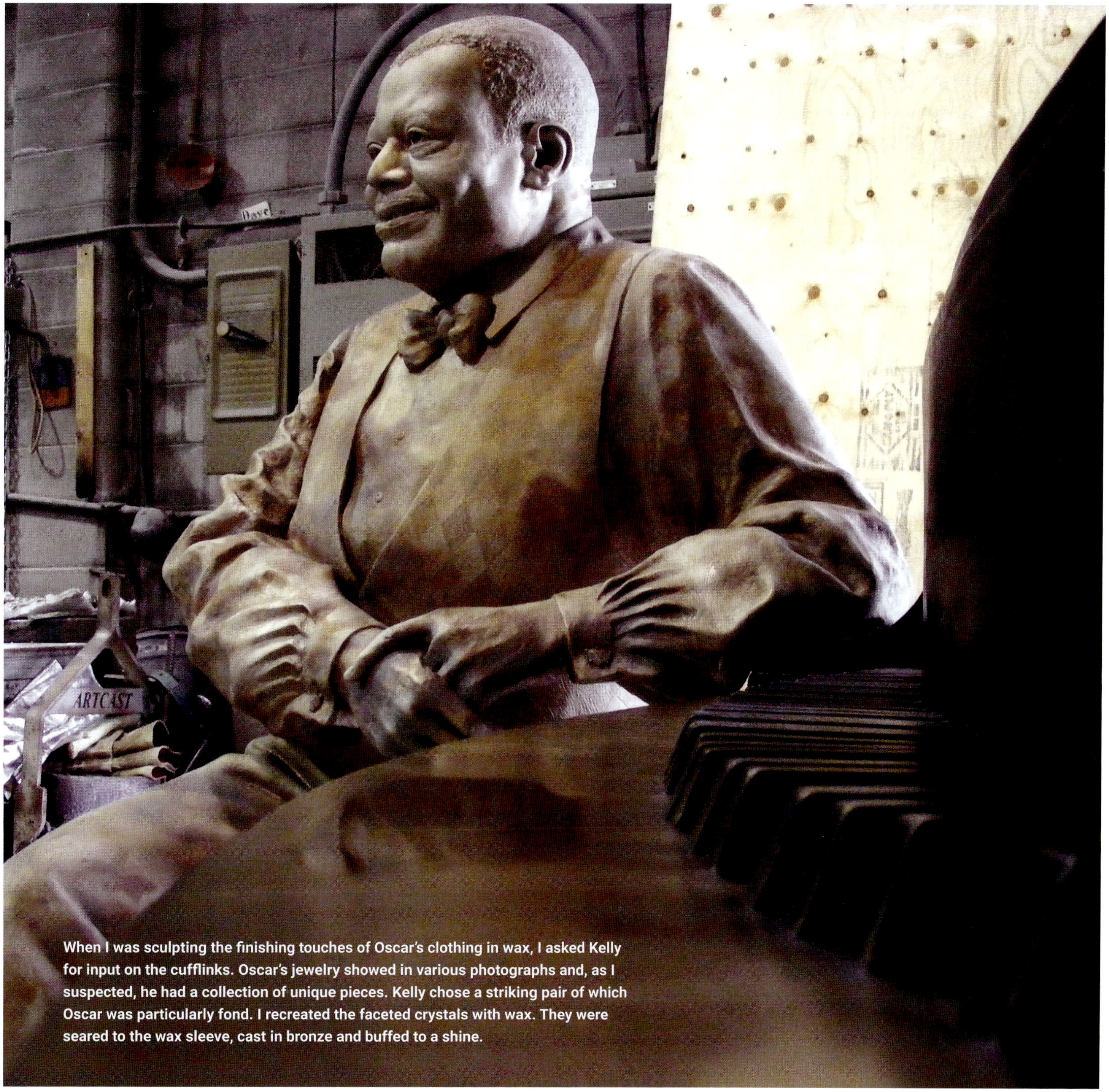

When I was sculpting the finishing touches of Oscar's clothing in wax, I asked Kelly for input on the cufflinks. Oscar's jewelry showed in various photographs and, as I suspected, he had a collection of unique pieces. Kelly chose a striking pair of which Oscar was particularly fond. I recreated the faceted crystals with wax. They were seared to the wax sleeve, cast in bronze and buffed to a shine.

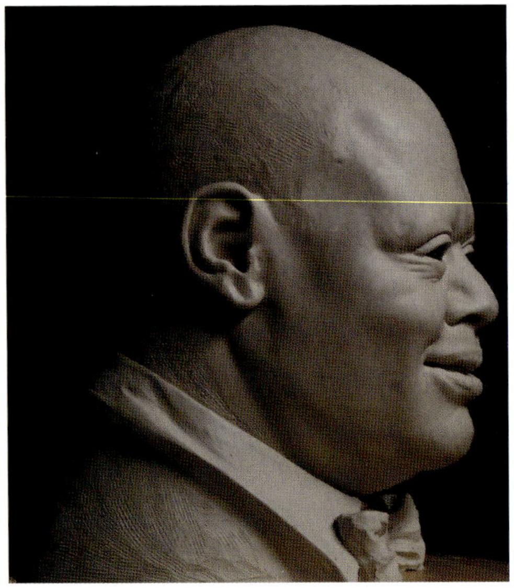

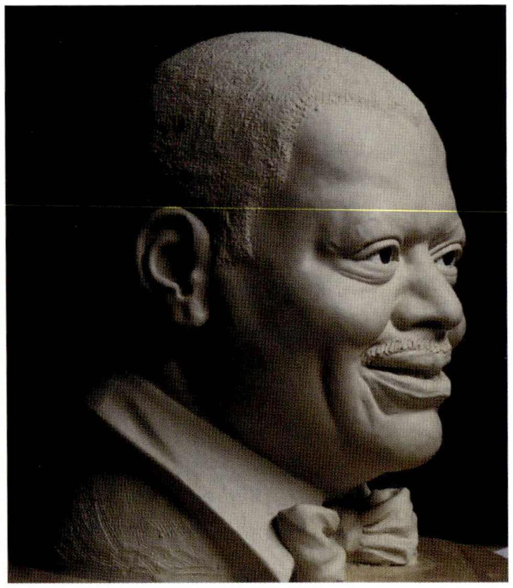

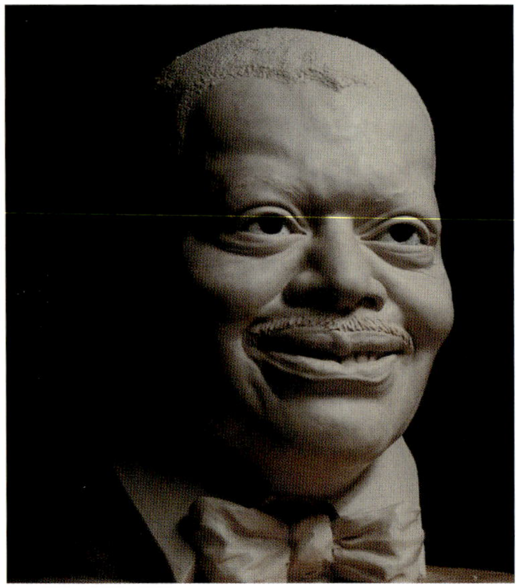

My portrait process involves an instinctive eye and a lot of 'proportional math'. When extrapolating from photographs, the ratios eventually gel and one number is generated again and again no matter which reference image is used. I stopped in my tracks when the number that recurred for Oscar Peterson was 3.14—the magical pi!

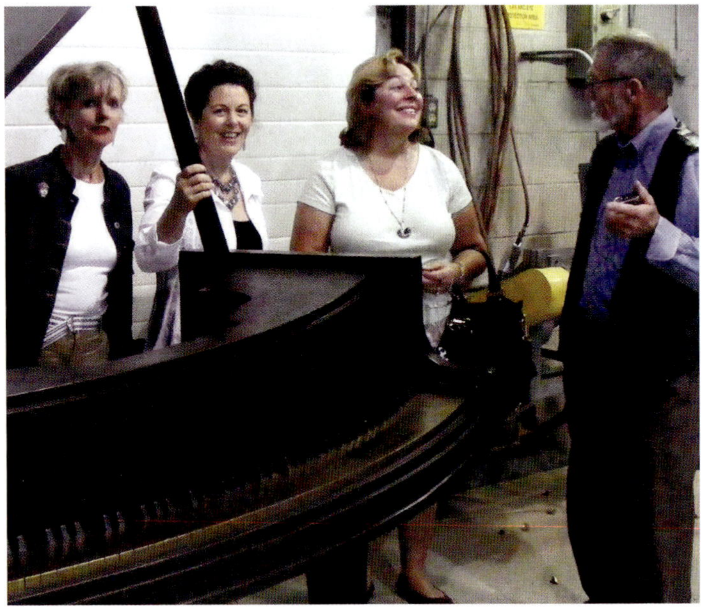

Kelly Peterson, Oscar's wife, was central to the portrait process and several times I trundled the heavy sculpted head to Mississauga for her to see. On one early session, I reached the house, settled Oscar's portrait in the living room and waited for Kelly to join me. The family's three dogs had been out walking and they arrived home while I waited. On seeing Oscar's pale sculpted likeness they let out an intense clamour! They were anxious and vocal, afraid to approach the familiar face, yet compelled to do so. Kelly and I stared in disbelief. They barked; they darted near for a sniff, only to jump away in fright. Their anxiety continued for nearly half an hour. It was surely the most authentic compliment I'd ever received.

A foundry session to see Oscar being assembled. From left to right: Cheryl Griffin, Ruth Abernethy, Oscar's wife Kelly Peterson, and Eric Knoespel/"Mr. Artcast"

> *If you have something to say of any worth, then people will listen to you.*
>
> *– Oscar Peterson*

The National Arts Centre staff understood *presentation* and they made innumerable great decisions. In the hands of these master event-planners and impeccable hosts, every step of the day was flawless. On the side, I arranged a jam session at a pub in the Byward Market for my extended family entourage the night before the unveiling.

At the end of June, the bronze pieces went to Ottawa and a talented team, aided by my now-very-experienced husband Mark, undertook the installation. As usual, the key successes in my design were invisible after the fact. Like the multifaceted components in Stratford's *Raising the Tent* (see page 158), the pieces, the pieces of the Peterson portrait slid together and into place without a hitch, seamlessly and deceptively simply.

'OSCAR NIGHT' IN STEP WITH HOLLYWOOD

In early March of 2010, I stalled my delivery of the Peterson portrait by a few days to host an 'Oscar Party', in step with awards night in Hollywood. My assistant at the time, Cheryl Griffin, had a loft in Waterloo that we used as a small gallery space. Our 'sneak peek' invitation brought fans and friends to celebrate the Peterson legacy. I'd finished Oscar's piano bench and had it cast in bronze months earlier to help me create an exact fit between the figure and the bench. Cheryl and I placed the wax portrait on the bronze seat and hosted a gala photo-op evening. Oscar's albums provided the soundtrack. We gave awards and our guests took lots of photographs.

The following day I arrived to retrieve the portrait and, in lifting Oscar from his bench, discovered someone had spilled a drink across his lap. The acidic liquid had settled beneath the figure and the bronze bench was unbelievably stained! The foundry tackled the patina and did an admirable job but the stubborn mark was permanent. Thankfully, we'd placed my wax Oscar in the exact position he'd have when bronzed. Once bolted to the bench his figure covered the irreversible stain and Oscar's adoring fans never had to know of our anxious moments.

On seeing my preliminary sketch, Kelly, Oscar's wife commented that he had no patience with lace-up shoes. She offered a gorgeous sample slip-on shoe, and told me Oscar had his footwear made by Foster & Son in London, UK. This borrowed shoe guided my carving. My assistant Jordan had a "Cinderella moment" in the studio when his foot slid perfectly into Oscar's leather pump.

On an icy winter street, road salt would stain the polished finish on a patent bronze shoe; I opted instead for ageless 'textured suede'. After installation, Kelly thanked Jordan for his work on the portrait and, thoughtfully, her gift package to him contained . . . both shoes.

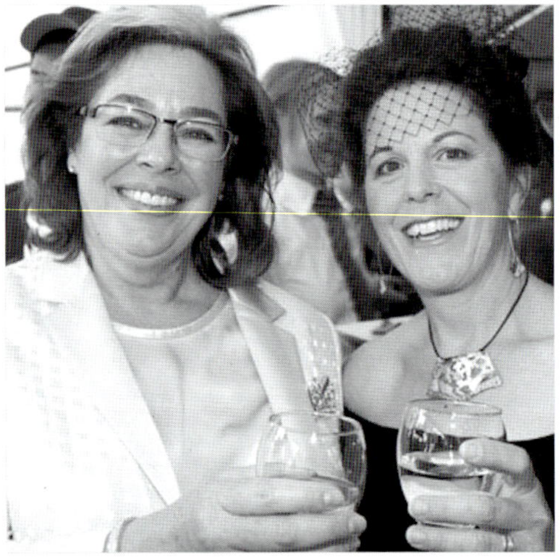
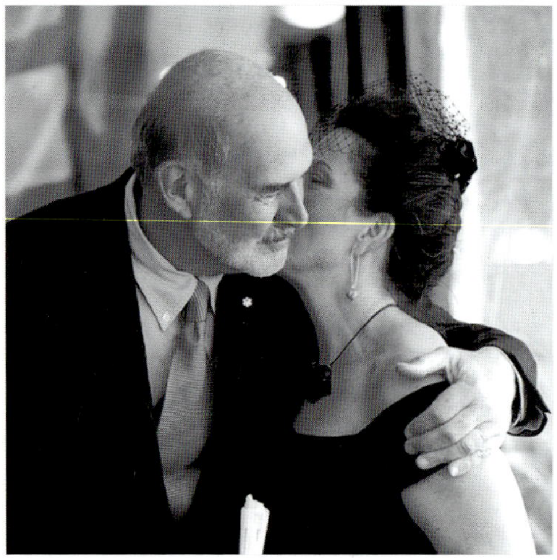
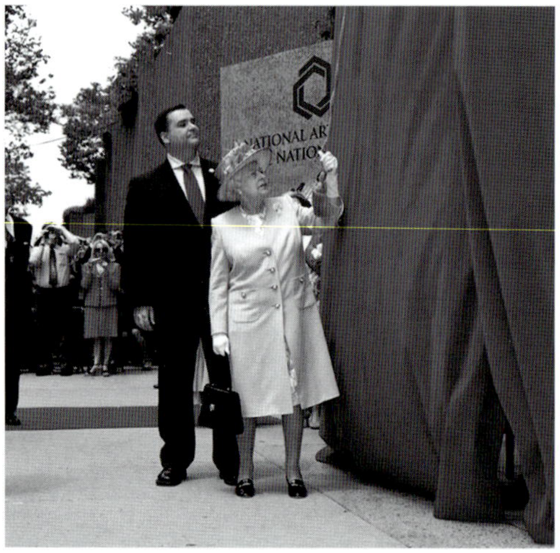
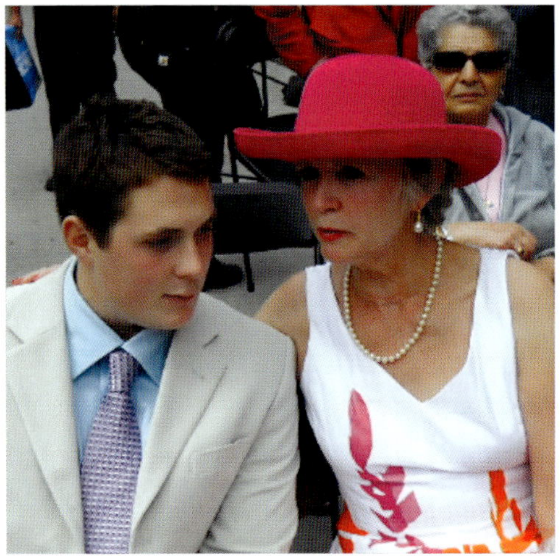
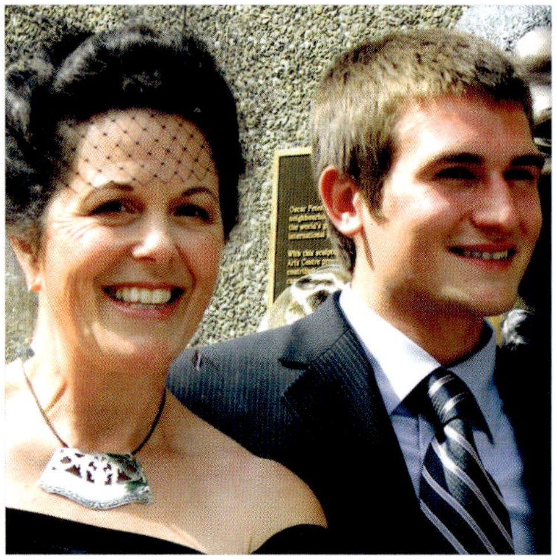
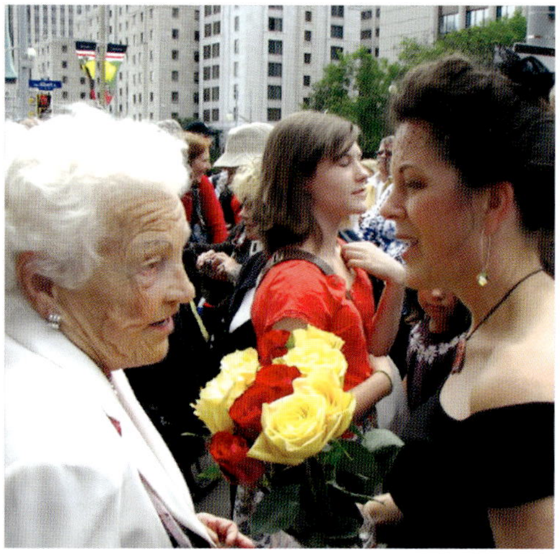

Peter Herrndorf, CEO, and Julia Foster, Head of the NAC Board, met Queen Elizabeth and Prince Philip at their car and made introductions to distinguished guests. They escorted the royal couple to the regal crimson drapery, where a heavy golden tassel was set to release Oscar's cover. At a royal touch, yards of material magically whisked out of sight and Oscar was a public figure at last. Queen Elizabeth turned to Oscar's daughter Céline, who presented a bouquet of flowers. Beside her, Kelly was poised and prepared with a gracious greeting.

The Queen then turned to me, offered a firm handshake and asked, "How do you create such beautiful metalwork?" Taken aback, I burst into a laugh. The casting process is so complex that I'd never dream of attempting to describe it in one sentence. Additionally, metalwork is done by foundry staff—and *not* by me. Hoping to avoid a witless answer, I simply said, "That's an endeavour for which I don't need to be an expert, but I do need to *know* one!" We shared a delicious chuckle before she commenced to the walkabout, freeing Prince Philip to circle back. He was genuinely curious about how the portrait had been made. I was relieved to have a second opportunity to explain my sculpting process. Queen Elizabeth and Prince Philip had focus and energy as tangible and memorable as her firm handshake.

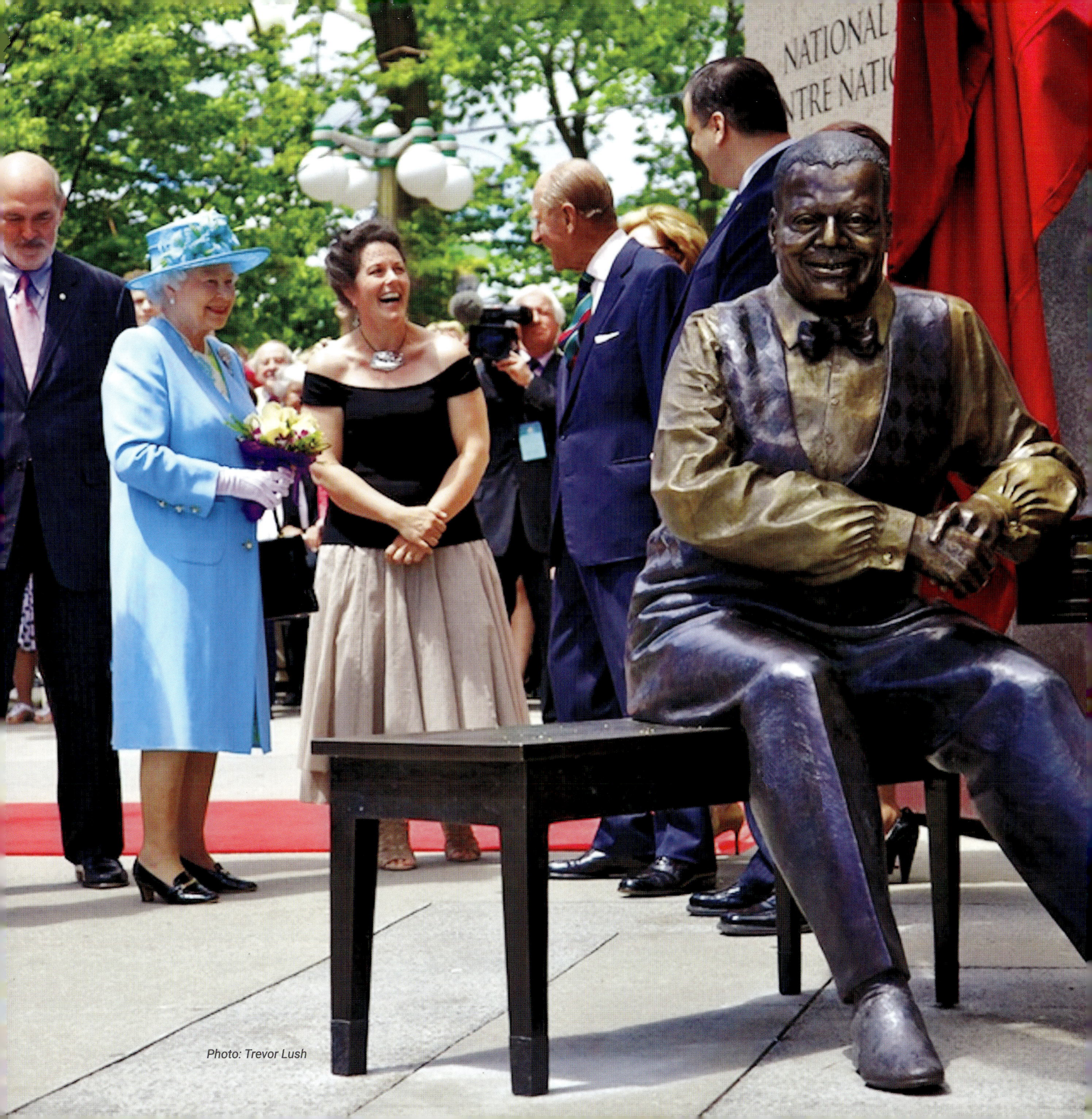

Photo: Trevor Lush

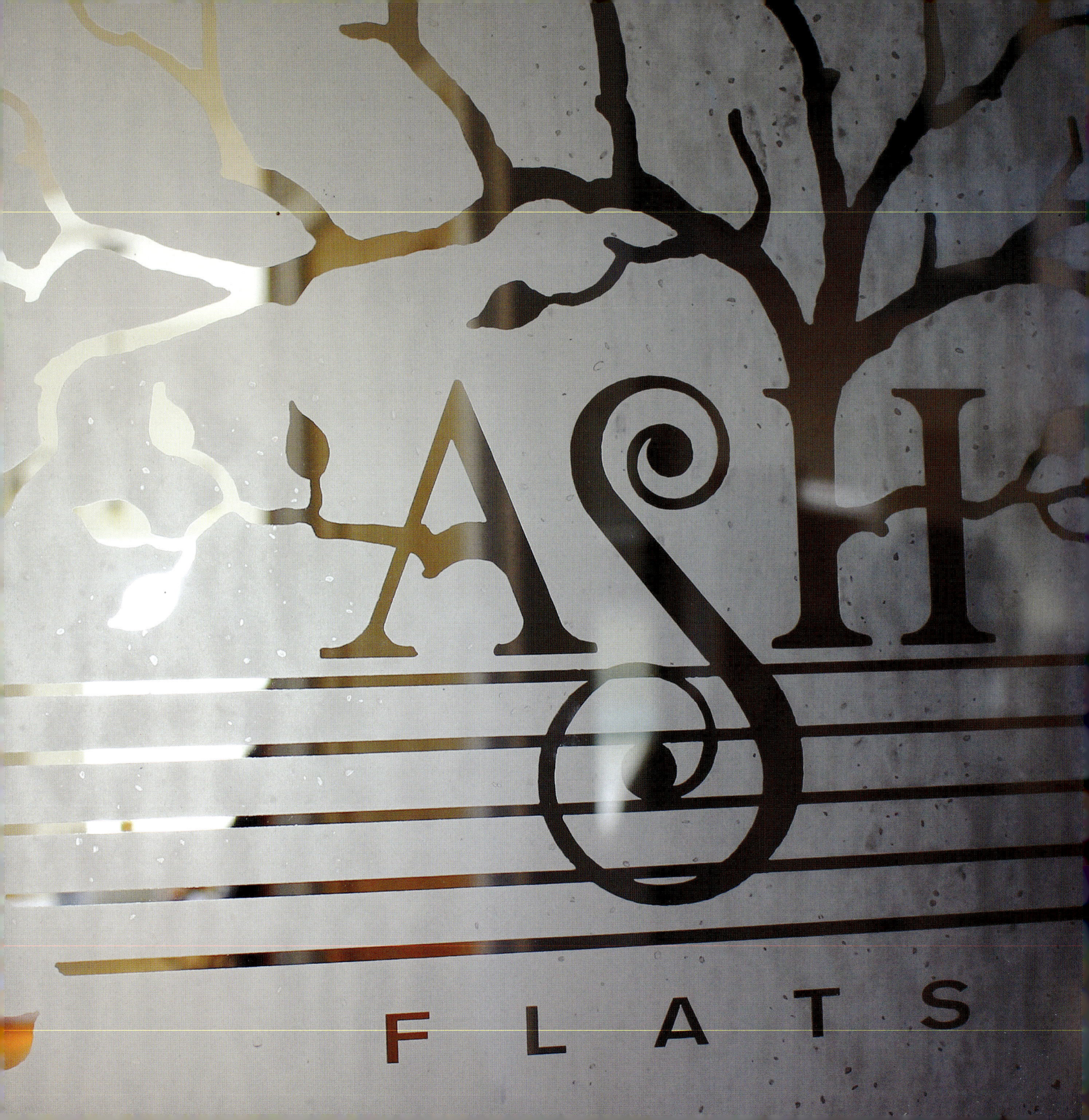
ASH
FLATS

GREAT CHANGES AT ASH FLATS

With my husband, Mark Smyth, my sister Ellen and her husband, Ken, I designed a home for two families. Creating this unusual domicile was the backdrop for 20 successful years of sharing life with the Hadley family. We named our home ASH FLATS, for this place where ash trees grew in abundance; it was also an anagram for surnames Abernethy, Smyth and Hadley.

In 2011 Mark was offered an enticing job in Vancouver. The position was too interesting to refuse and his extended family lived in the city. When he accepted the post, we began to invent a life in two places. That same summer our older son, Glen, packed his bags for Carleton University in Ottawa. Alex and I found the Flats very quiet and rather empty. Our housemates of 20 years, my sister Ellen and her husband Ken, were also re-inventing their lives elsewhere. Mark and I became sole owners of Ash Flats and I expanded my work into the well-lit, high-ceilinged Great Room that two families had shared.

With Mark away, I began to repaint the Flats. Refreshing my 'double home' was in part a welcome for my sister Jean, who came to live with me after 25 years in the United States. In making the east wing of the house my own I also tackled many unfinished edges that lingered from our construction years. In step, commissions that had been brewing for months all began to launch. In no time, my original studio and the Great Room studio were filled with projects. My routine was to work as many hours a day as possible, gravitating between the coffee pot and the woodstove. Sculpting near the fire kept the wax soft and it was much easier on the hands. Every night around midnight I'd call Mark to discuss events of the day.

> **"*Manning sump pumps and downspouts, befriending a pellet furnace and tackling laneway potholes were just a few tasks that prompted me to coin the phrase 'full-spectrum femininity'.*"**

Mario Bernardi

One of the most important pianists and conductors of his generation (the generation of Glenn Gould), Bernardi was a builder, a man who constructed several musical legacies in this country with his spirit, drive and discipline.

– Robert Harris, The Globe and Mail, *June 3, 2013*

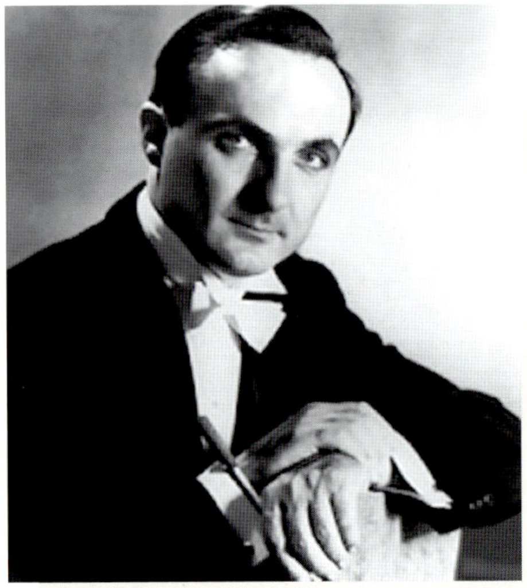

Mario Bernardi (1930–2013)

Conductor

Mario Bernardi was born in Kirkland Lake, Ontario. His prodigious musical talent was obvious early. As a young boy during World War II, he travelled with his mother to Austria for musical training. He graduated in piano and composition from the Venice Conservatory in Italy, and also from The Royal Conservatory of Music in Toronto. His skills flourished and later, as an established conductor in Europe, he was invited to Ottawa to form and lead the National Arts Centre Orchestra, set to launch in 1969.

Until age 80, Mr. Bernardi directed orchestras across Canada. He was a brilliant and demanding maestro who conducted Canada to musical maturity. He received honorary degrees from various universities and was recipient of the National Arts Centre Award and the Governor General's Performing Arts Awards. Mario's portrait was planned for the National Arts Centre foyer near the entrance to Southam Hall, where he'd made many musical memories.

Creation of Mario's portrait included memorable hours with his wife, Mona Kelly, an opera singer and an accomplished collaborator. Her observations were astute and to each session she brought new photographs, fresh eyes and a tremendous sensory memory of Mario's features. Once she'd approved the clay head study it was reproduced hollow, in wax. I built the wax head onto a carved jacket front with tie, creating a 'head and shoulders' portrait.

I sculpted Mario's beautiful hands from styrene and wax too, and the composite portrait was cast in bronze. Mona (on right) provided a photo poster that showed Mario's hands and it also confirmed their exact position, welded onto the bronze head and shoulders.

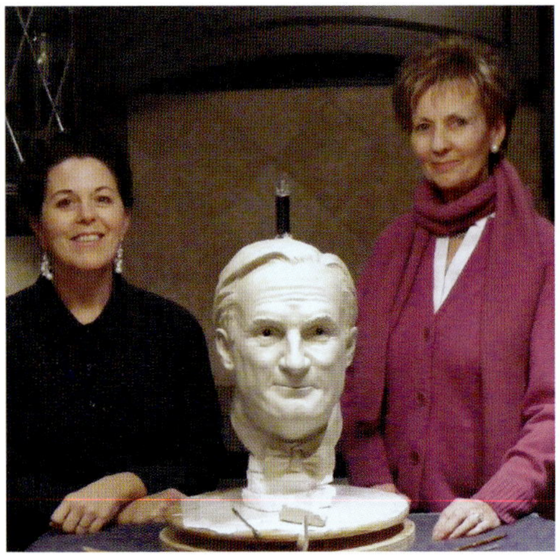

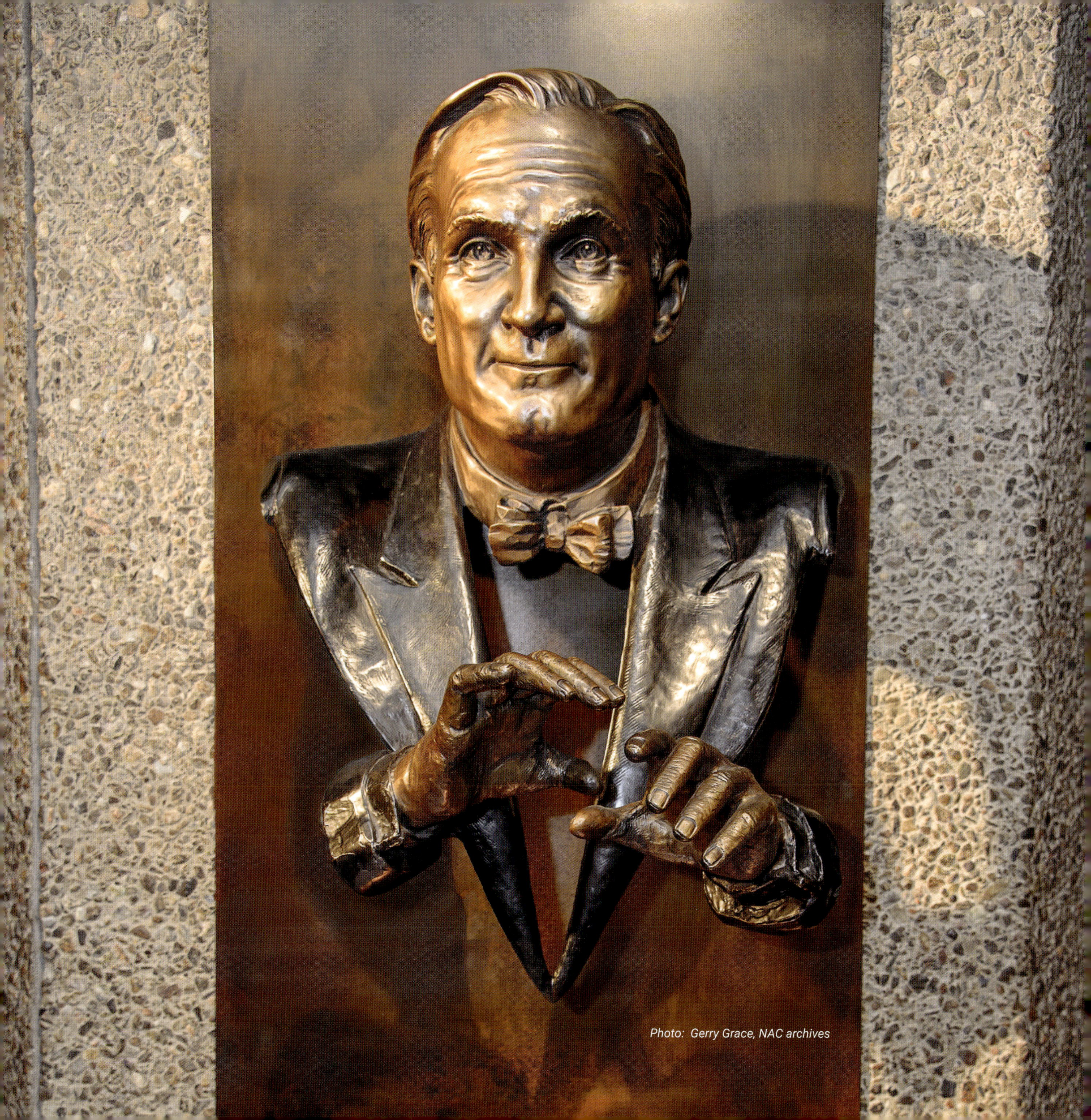
Photo: Gerry Grace, NAC archives

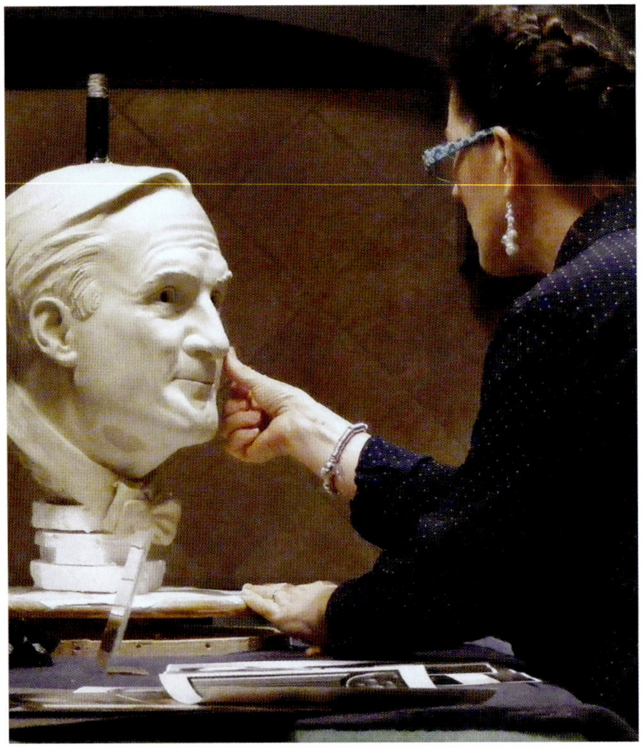

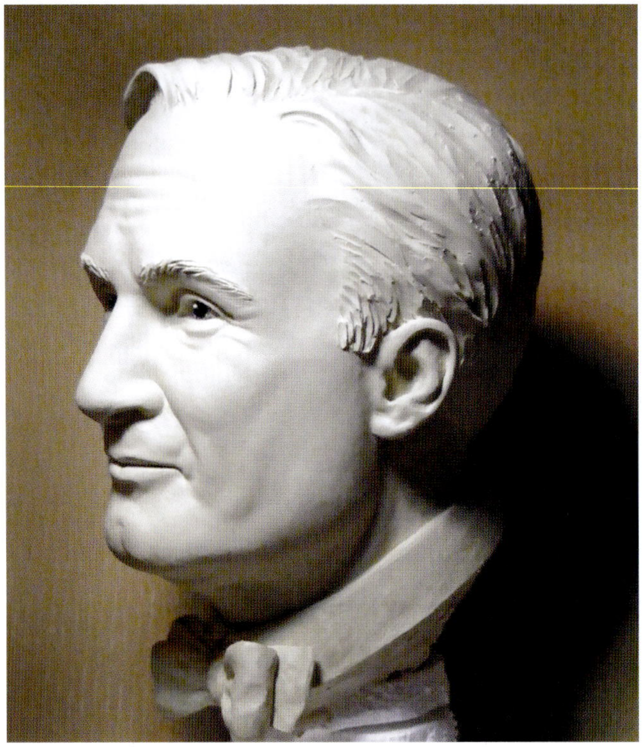

The bronze portrait had been completed for a few weeks when I got a request from Ottawa asking if a handful of veteran musicians could see it. I paled at the thought of a committee offering input on a finished casting! Changes were impossible without remaking the whole piece, but being obstinate never helps. I decided to share the bronze and the head study made of modelling clay. In the back of my mind, I reviewed diplomatic phrases to employ if the musicians had concerns about the likeness.

I arrived home from Vancouver the night before and I'd choreographed a plan for the six-hour drive to get the bronze to Ottawa for a 2:00 pm meeting. My new assistant, Cassandra, stayed overnight at the Flats and we made a very early departure. Cass steadied the heavy head on her lap while I drove, and our exit went exactly as planned. We avoided heavy freeway traffic into Toronto and across the city and headed out the far side of town with a sense of glee.

My glee dissipated in a heartbeat when I realized I'd forgotten to stop at the foundry near my home to pick up the bronze bust! After a few deep breaths to recover my wits, I stalled the Ottawa gathering with a phone call. My astonishing gaffe was overcome by the foundry's quick delivery of the bronze to the exact spot where we waited by the freeway. Only a portrait sculptor could confess to literally 'leaving her head behind'.

The handful of patient musicians met me in Ottawa with open hearts. Mario's players admired him immensely, despite the anxious and legendary moments of playing for him. Their response to the portrait was intense and moving. Quite simply, they loved the portrait as they had the man. I couldn't have been more pleased.

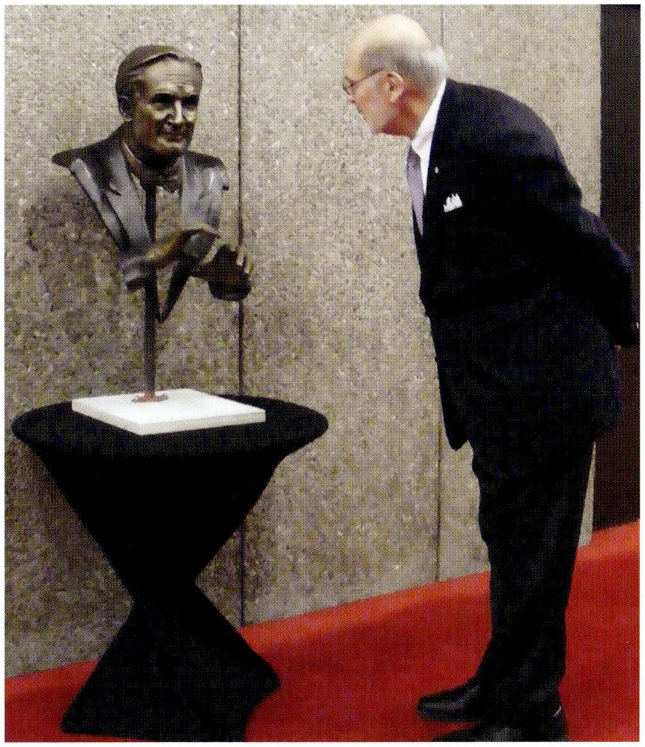

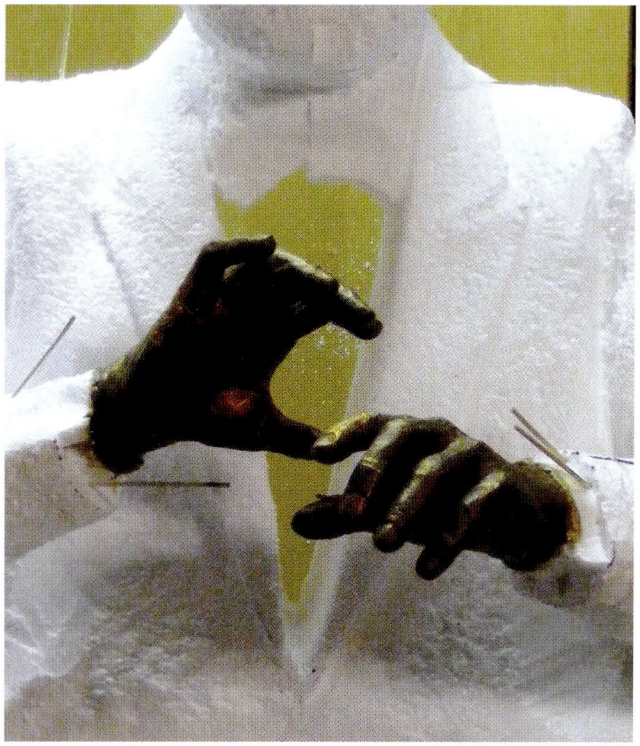

When we began this commission, Peter Herrndorf and I discussed Mario's presentation. Peter (shown above) had struggled for the best phrase to convey Mario's character and, gesturing with long, lean hands, he'd declared, "Mario could be . . . ferocious!" I'd caught the maestro's intensity just as we'd hoped. Peter's timing for the project was uncanny. Mario's death was just days before the portrait's dedication at the National Arts Centre. It was a gathering for celebration and memorial, in perfect harmony.

Actors' careers are rooted in recognition, but conductors spend many hours onstage with their backs to the audience. A traditionally sculpted head portrait of Mario offered little means to present his character. I suggested we include his hands to identify him as a conductor. Someone quipped to me that the design might have him mistaken for a magician, but if so, it's close enough to the truth.

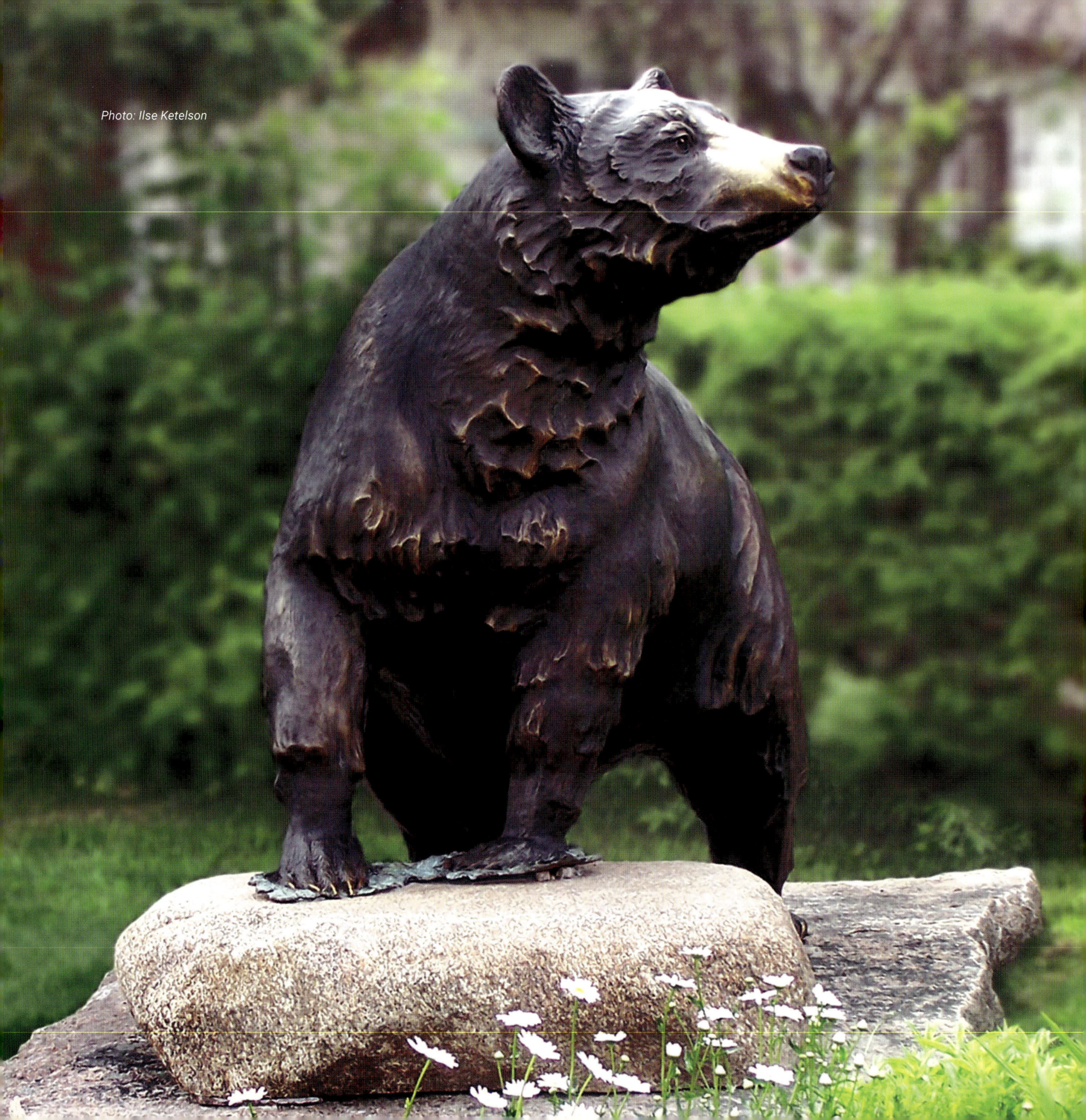

Photo: Ilse Ketelson

Duke the Bear

Duke the Bear roamed Riding Mountain National Park in central Manitoba where plentiful food supplies nurtured bears to exceptional growth. At his death, Duke was the largest black bear ever, weighing 812 pounds and estimated to stand nearly 8 feet tall. Then another huge bear was recorded—from the same area! Hibernation creates large fluctuations in a bear's body weight, and the two giants remained in contention for the title. They also prompted a biological study of their unique habitat.

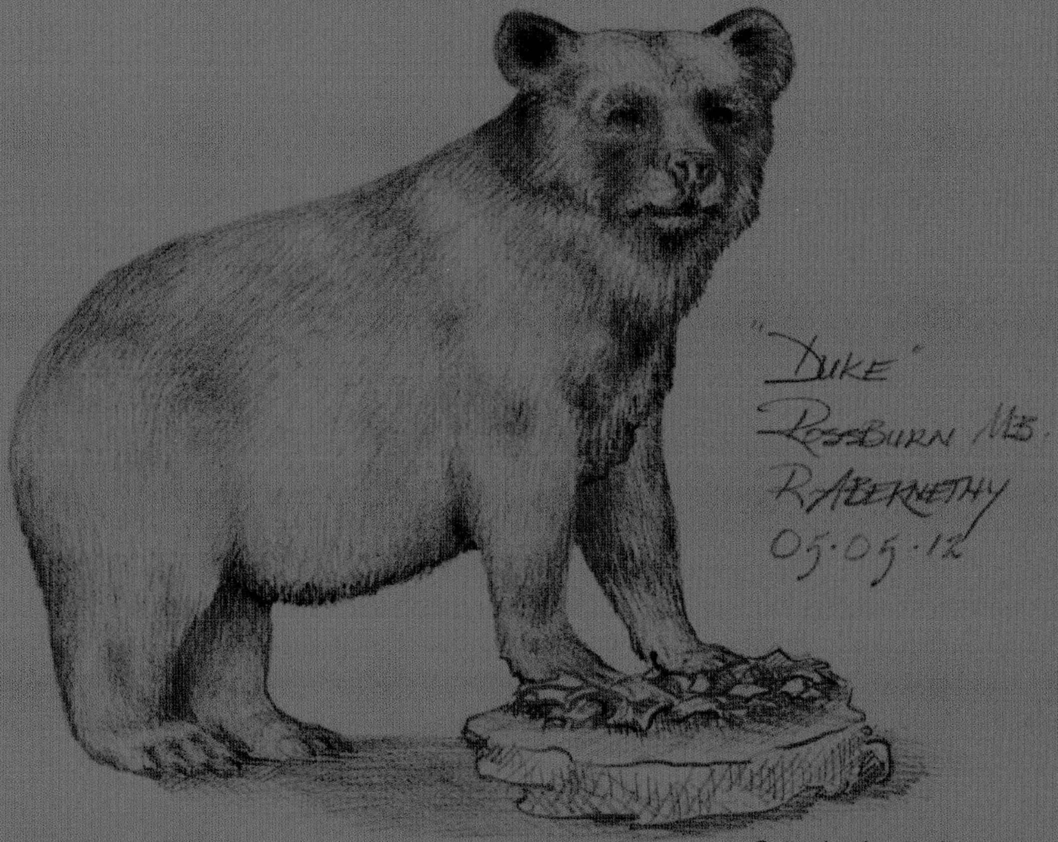

© Ruth Abernethy

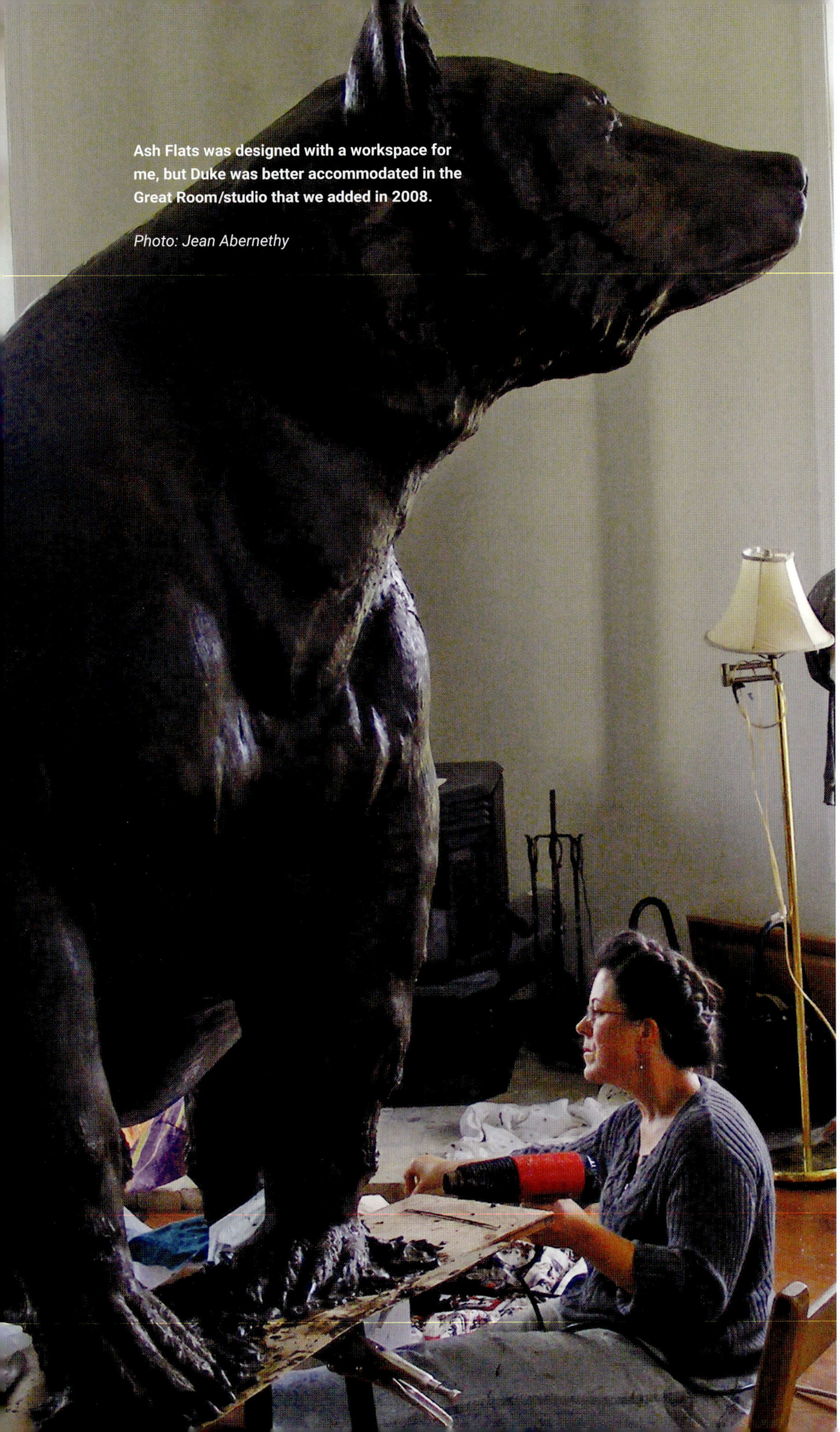

Ash Flats was designed with a workspace for me, but Duke was better accommodated in the Great Room/studio that we added in 2008.

Photo: Jean Abernethy

In February of 2008, an online Call to Artists from Rossburn, Manitoba outlined a story about Duke the Bear. It caught my attention because Rossburn is minutes from Russell, where my cousins had developed a line of prized cattle, the Primrose Herefords. And who wouldn't love the story of an enormous bear that grew to be nearly double the size of other black bears?

I responded to the Rossburn call, sending off a proposal in the spring of 2008. Several emails resulted, but I was left wondering about the end of the story until one day in 2012 when the phone suddenly rang.

"Hello," said a voice, "This is Walter, and I'd like to know if you might still be interested in sculpting a very large bear?"

Enough time had passed between my first sculpting estimate and the end of 2012 that the original proposal was unworkable. The shop that initially estimated sand casting patterns for bear-making no longer commanded a workspace that would hold this huge creature. Like everyone else, I'd fallen in love with Duke and couldn't face disappointing the generous couple who simply wanted a lasting gift for their community. There was nothing to do but invent a Plan B.

After discussion with Walter and Adelle Mychasaw, I resolved that lost wax casting was the preferred method. In styrene and wax, fabrication costs were within my control. I could create an original, easy-to-handle sculpture that had just enough texture in wax to make Duke adorable. Jim Wilson, with whom I'd worked for over a decade, was establishing Castaway Foundry and we were both willing to tackle this big furry fellow.

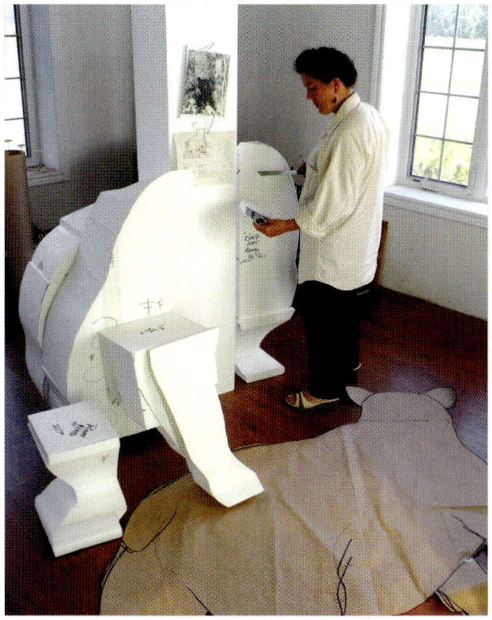

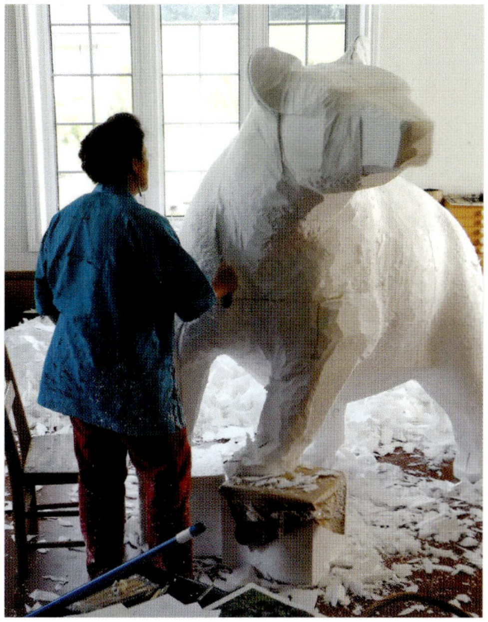

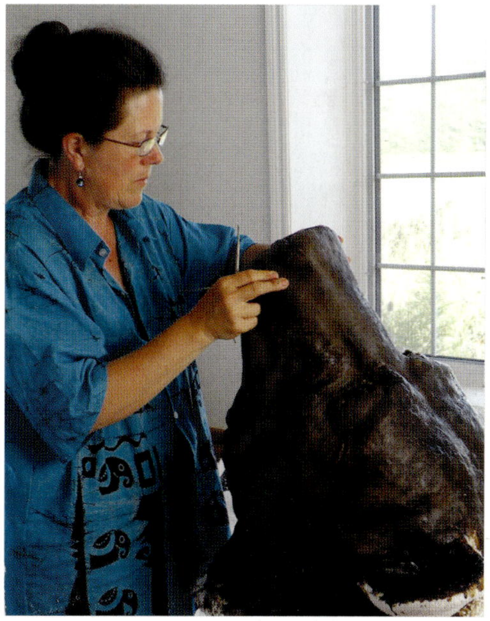

After carving Duke's body, I had to invent a surfacing technique for the fur coat that could be rendered on a large scale. A coarse brush, a heat gun and a steady hand put just the right amount of texture where I wanted it. Duke won our hearts with his huge features and his mighty bear-waddle. I enjoyed him throughout the process, as did everyone else. Jim confessed with a chuckle that so many guests began stopping by to see Mr. Bear that he could scarcely get foundry work done.

On July 2nd, 2013, Duke the Bear was dedicated in Rossburn, a village of 550 people. The community transformed a vacant lot into an elegant Memory Garden with cascading water, contemplative benches and beautiful plantings. An engraved stone tells of the giant bears of Riding Mountain National Park and the research that resulted from their legacy.

Beside a granite entrance, this grand fellow holds a place in the heart of his community—thanks to Walter and Adelle Mychasaw

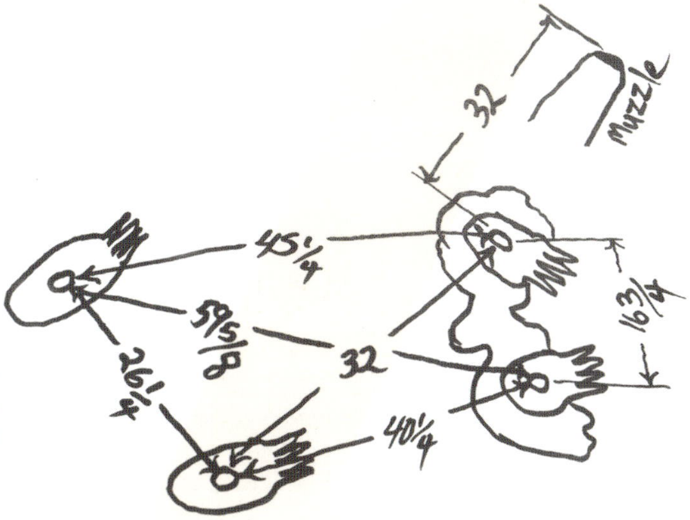

Positioning Duke on the boulder on a concrete base required many emails between the foundry, the studio, the stonemason and the town office in Rossburn.

Balancing Act

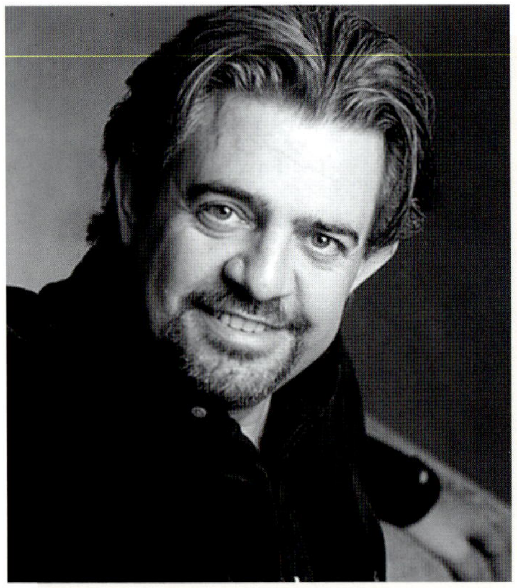

Alex Mustakas

Artistic Director

Alex Mustakas emigrated with his family from Cyprus to Canada when he was a child. He followed up his education at Wilfred Laurier University in Waterloo, Ontario with an Arts Administration degree at City University in London, England. Alex's talent onstage plus his innovative leadership put his Drayton Entertainment Company on the map. Drayton Entertainment presents comedies, dramas and Broadway musicals for all ages, at seven venues across Ontario. They are one of Canada's most successful professional theatre companies.

In the spring of 2011, I was contacted by Neil Aitchison and Bernie Melloul. We launched a discussion about portraying Drayton Entertainment's founder and Artistic Director, Alex Mustakas. Melloul Blamey Construction was currently building the company's newest theatre complex; it included workshops, rehearsal spaces and actor accommodations—an ambitious endeavour.

While sharing early ideas with Bernie and Neil, I said that I felt a 'career summary' portrait for Alex was lacklustre and far too staid for a leader in the arts. Alex was actively directing his company to creative heights on a grand scale. Alex, too, had personal concerns that a bronze portrait was somehow premature.

Understanding the conundrum and the multifaceted role of an artistic director, I suggested we present Alex 'in character' as a ringmaster, guiding his troupe of players. We all loved the concept and I especially loved the challenges in the design.

> *I wanted a theatrical portrait that hinted at life on a grand scale.*
>
> *– Ruth Abernethy*

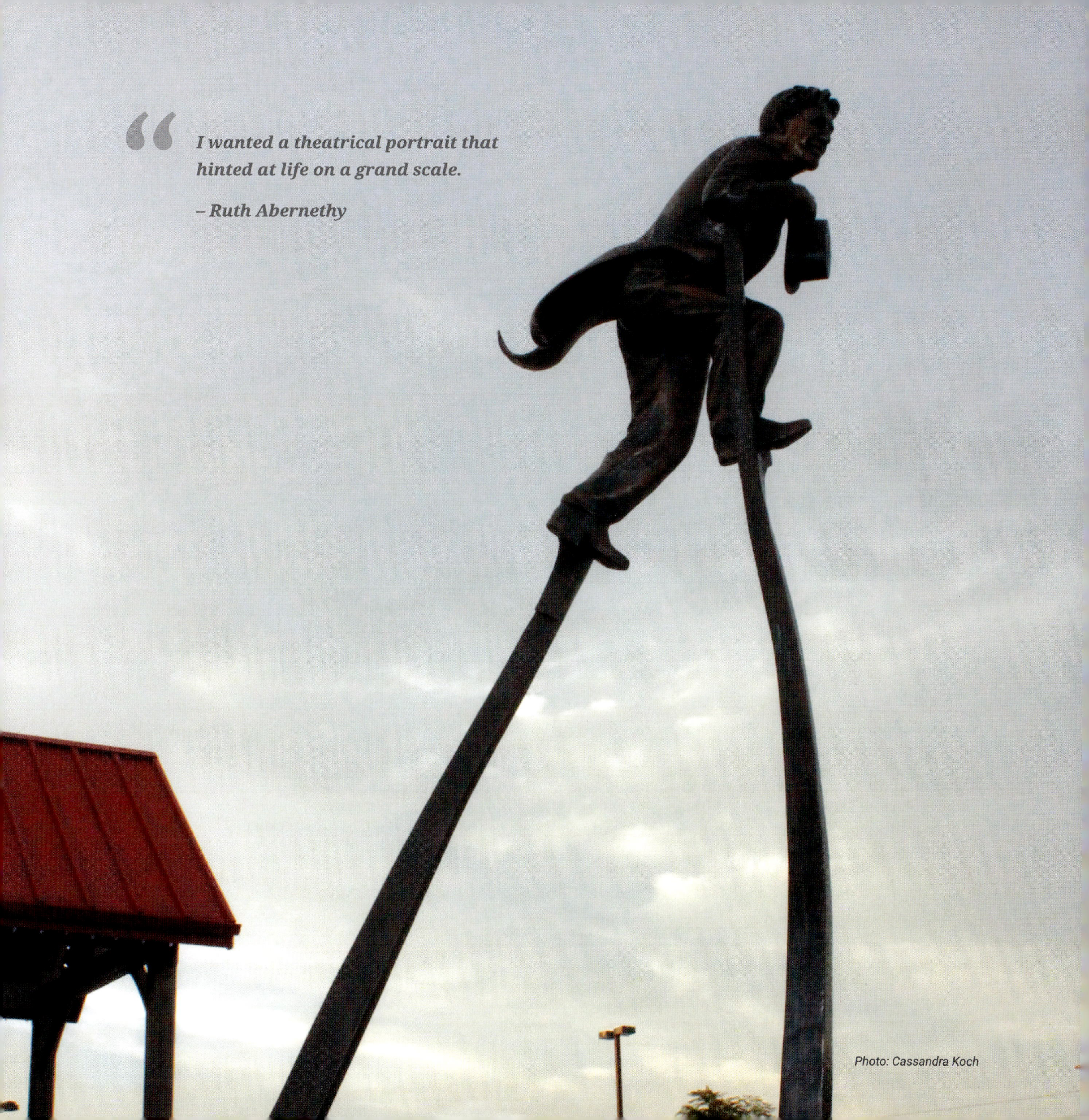

Photo: Cassandra Koch

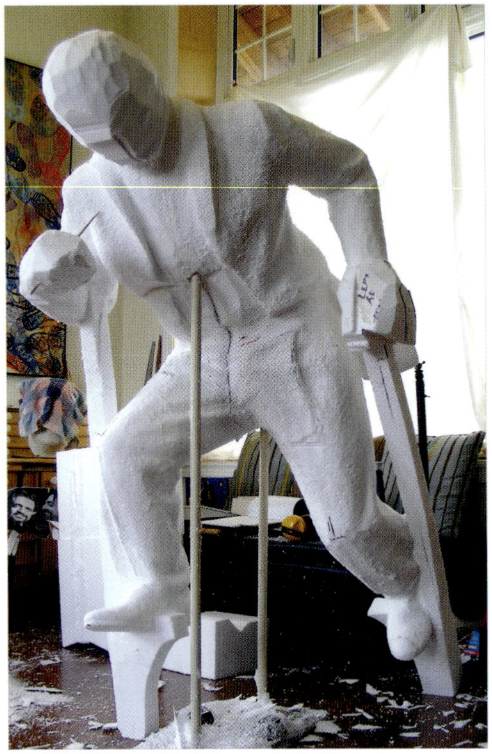

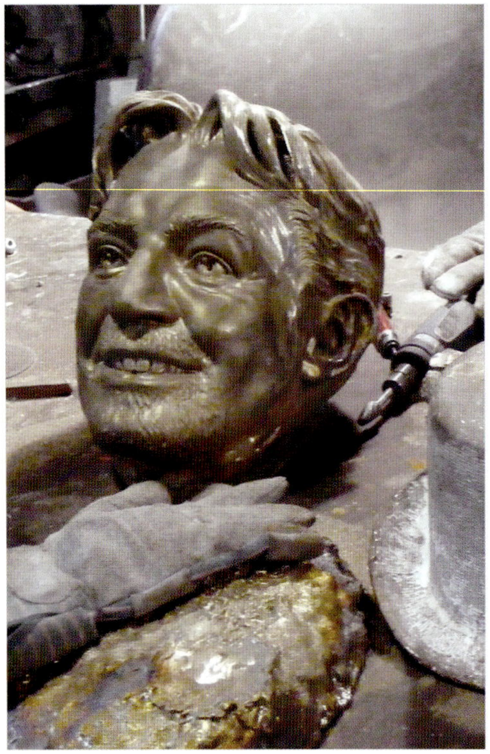

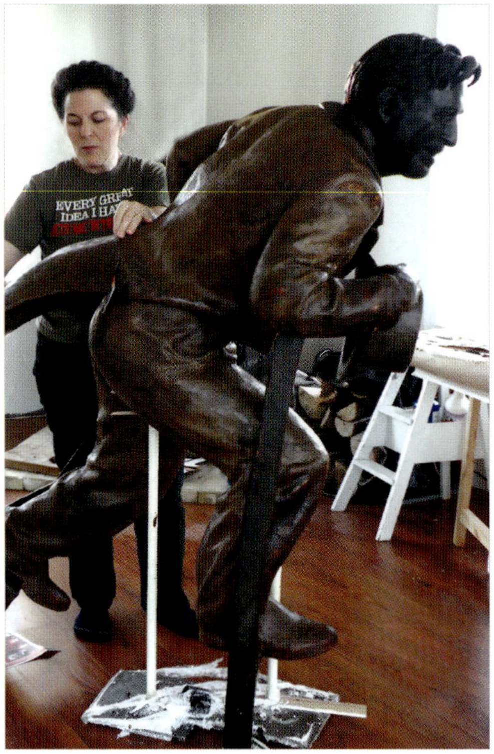

Photos: Jean Abernethy

There were many 'Eureka moments' as I wrapped my head around the creation of this work. I realized that the two stilts had to be different lengths. Neither the front nor side views of the stilts would appear as straight lines. Subtle curves implied shifting weight from one stilt to the other and added a sense of momentum to Alex's long, animated steps. I tapered the stilts to enhance the design's forced perspective, and the larger 'footprints' at grade allowed for secure attachment. In the studio I contrived a jig to position the figure exactly as it must be when elevated. The portrait had to appear to walk the earth and it was critical to establish the pull of gravity with my carving.

Alex and his wife provided their wedding photos for reference. I was honoured to share their beautiful day—even if my sharing was belated! I first tackled Alex's head study and then I laid out the figure in a wind-whipped tailcoat. I carefully positioned the bronze top hat so that it wouldn't fill with rainwater. Then, since this 'action figure' would be viewed from beneath and my studio jig was adjustable, I hoisted the carving right to the high ceiling of my workspace to examine the composition.

Shaping stilts required advances in pattern-making. I laid the paper outline of the figure on the floor and stretched long lengths of masking tape across the floor to 'draw' the long posts. Then I laid window screening over top. I traced the patterns and cut them out with scissors. The screen didn't twist or curl and the weave indicated a true/constant vertical. What a perfect example of deceptive simplicity!

I cut the ten-foot-long styrene stilts with the band saw. With a hand iron and very hot wax, I finished the surfaces and refined their long, tapered shapes. Assembled in the foundry, they looked incredibly tall and I loved the big stride.

The sculpture site was resolved outside the St. Jacobs Country Playhouse, where the piece would entertain throngs of people strolling to Waterloo Market. I'd imagined an installation that hinted at life on a grand scale, and it seemed eminently practical that this portrait stride across the space *on high stilts*. Distinctively, Alex would also be part of the audience that mingled beneath on the public terrace.

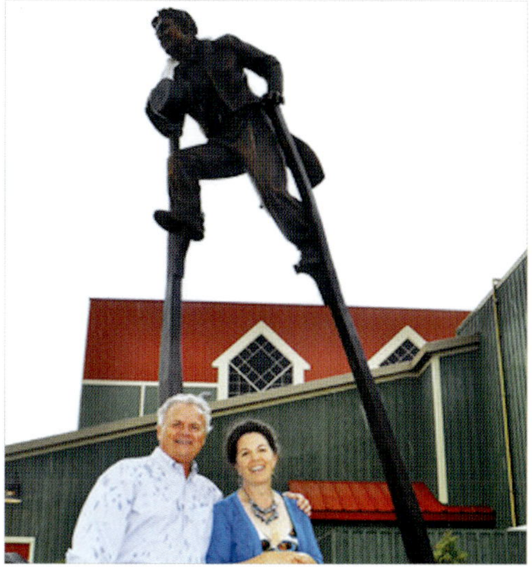

Here I am with project sponsor Bernie Melloul. Unveiling day in July 2013 began bright and glorious but winds brewed and clouds churned overhead. Moments after unveiling, the heavens opened and driving wind whipped around torrents of rain. A tornado whirled between Waterloo and Guelph to heighten the dramatic effect. Trees were uprooted across the region, but *Balancing Act* did not misstep!

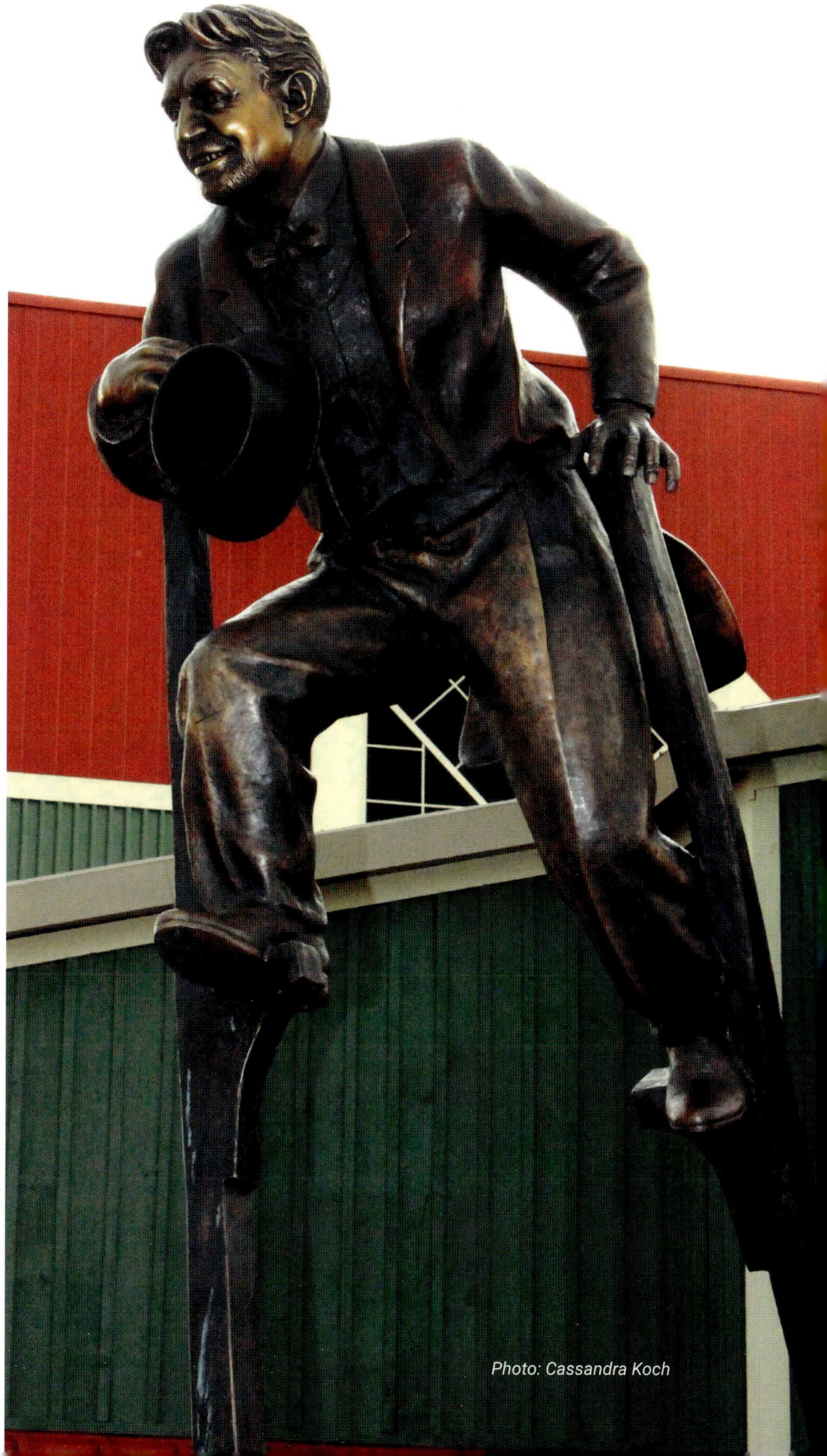

Photo: Cassandra Koch

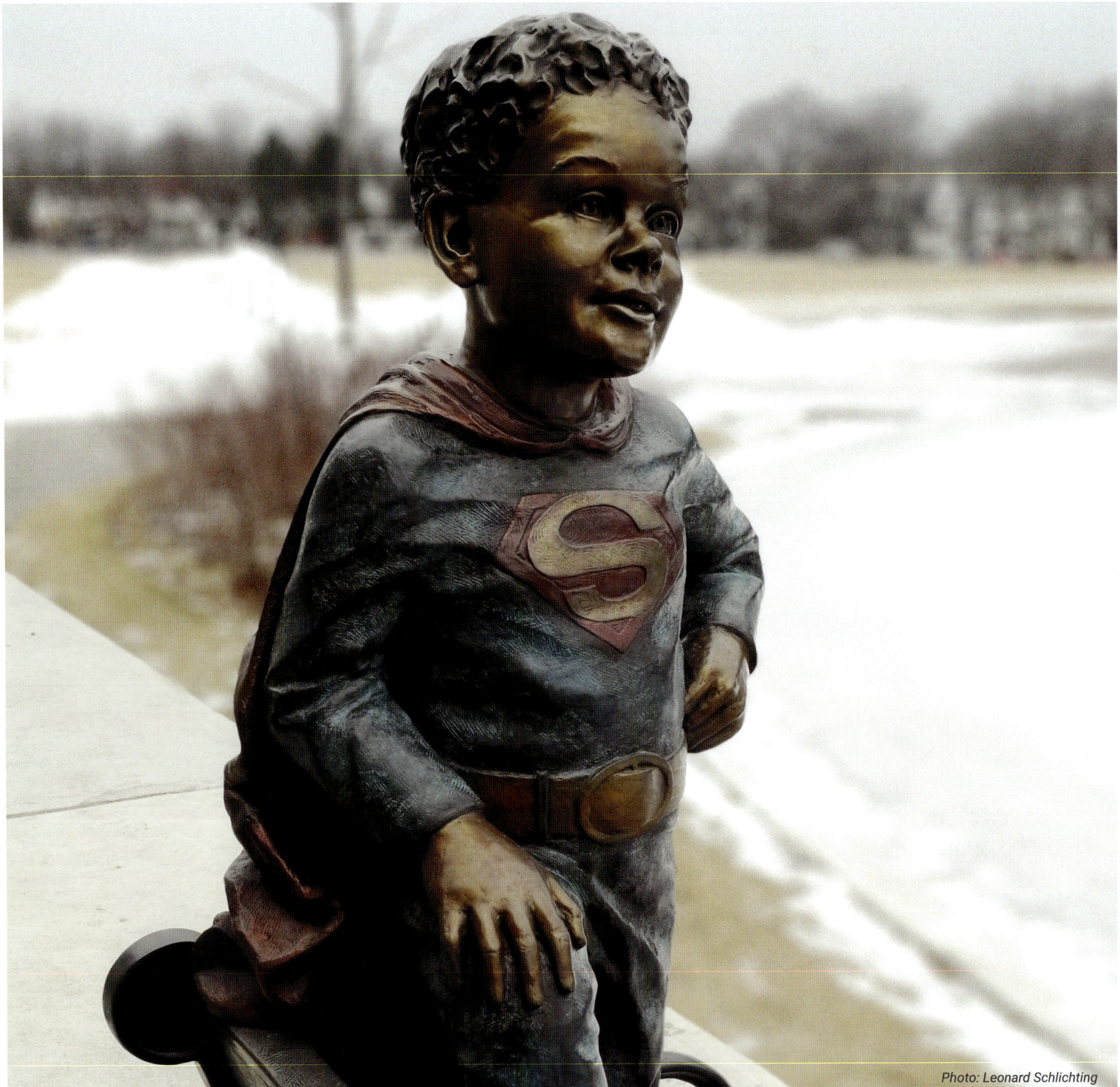
Photo: Leonard Schlichting

Jeffrey Baldwin

> *I have never created a portrait of someone about whom I chose to know so little.*

Jeffrey Baldwin's story is tragic. At the age of five, he died a lingering death in foster care. His situation was harder to accept, since he suffered this neglect in the hands of his own grandparents. Following Jeffrey's death a criminal trial resulted in convictions. Months later, news from the subsequent inquest brought public sentiment to the surface once again.

For me, Jeffrey Baldwin's tribute started in February of 2014. Todd Boyce of Carleton Place, Ontario, near Ottawa, had been profoundly moved by Jeffrey's story. This father of four had a son who shared Jeffrey's birthday. With his wife's encouragement, Todd researched online fundraising with the goal to create a permanent commemoration for Jeffrey. Crowdfunding posts online garnered donations from across the world. Seeking a bronze casting, Todd contacted the Artcast foundry. He and foundry staff invited me to be the artist. This firm had made numerous castings for me and our collaboration was straightforward. It certainly needed to be. Time was short and we had to keep costs within reach of Todd's funding.

The Sterling Room, in Toronto's Distillery District, stepped up to host a fundraising evening. Todd's online updates on portrait progress brought donations from an amazing list of places. Jeffrey's story, and Todd's careful presentation of it, garnered passionate interest from the press and from individuals everywhere. People needed to express and share emotions in a way I'd never experienced before. One surreal phone call reached me at the gym, where I hastily assembled thoughts for a meaningful exchange with two grieving brothers in St. Louis, Missouri. They'd heard about the portrait and simply wanted to express heartfelt gratitude for the work I'd undertaken.

It seemed obvious to dress Jeffrey in his beloved Superman costume. He'd delighted in wearing it and had bounced about his home in costume during his few years before foster care. Sadly, children who are not well loved are not well documented. The Superman photos were the best and almost the only reference I had—but they were charming and utterly *true*, with heartbreaking irony.

I decided that placing Jeffrey on a public bench would ensure he'd seldom be alone. Being only 42 inches tall, his little figure would've been lost standing at ground level in public space. Besides, I couldn't bear the thought of him being knocked and bumped by lawnmowers. On the bench, he would make eye contact with adults and with children who could stand beside him. I imagined young guests returning to visit the portrait once they'd become adults or parents. They'd certainly see Jeffrey with a changed perspective.

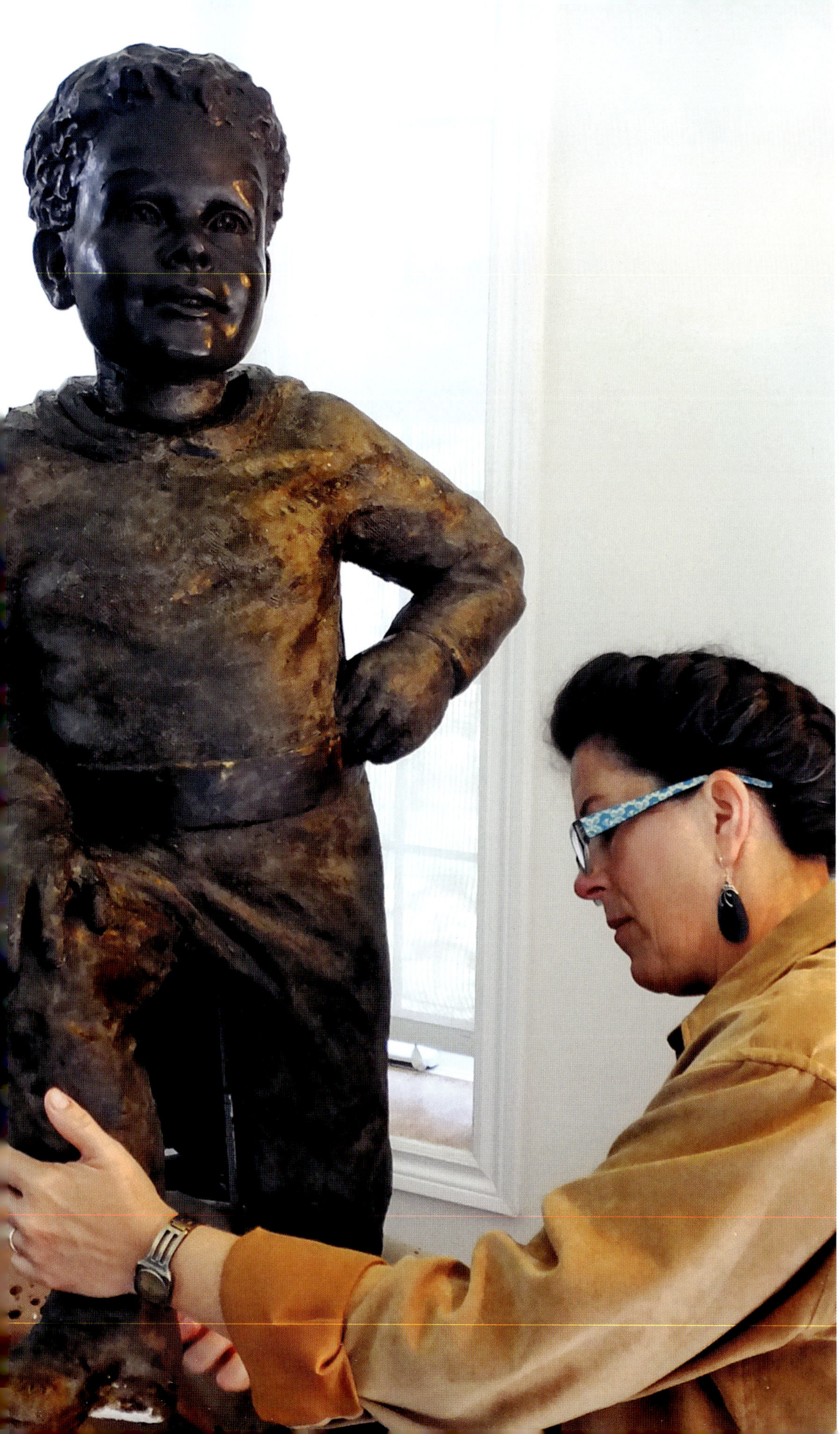

My husband's work in Vancouver, ongoing since 2011, put my practice partially there. I crafted many head studies in the workspace near English Bay, and Jeffrey would be one of them. The facts of Jeffrey's story made me cringe; the thought of focusing on his death for hours was unbearable. I purposefully avoided newscasts of the inquest. I fixed my thoughts firmly on joyful times with my own sons and loved this boy as best I could. In the end, I felt I caught some of the soft beauty that's bewitching about children.

The task was intimidating, in part because of the large audience Todd managed to attract, but also because of my own expectations for the work.

I was grateful for my experience in structuring humans so I could focus on the essence of this child.

Using bench measurements resolved at the foundry, I made a precise studio jig on which to carve Jeffrey's small form. The foundry cast individual planks and a bench support beneath each end. Jeffrey was beautifully assembled in bronze with feet and cape connecting exactly as planned.

My first quick portrait sketch had showed Jeffrey as a stalwart superhero. In my final studio assembly, I'd set Jeffrey's little wax head onto his sculpted shoulders where it settled, slightly off-balance. His quizzical expression was a beautiful fit with his gesture and the portrait was completed that instant. Never before had I shifted from my original composition of a subject, but his pert little face was potent. I hope the questioning pose helps speak Jeffrey's truth.

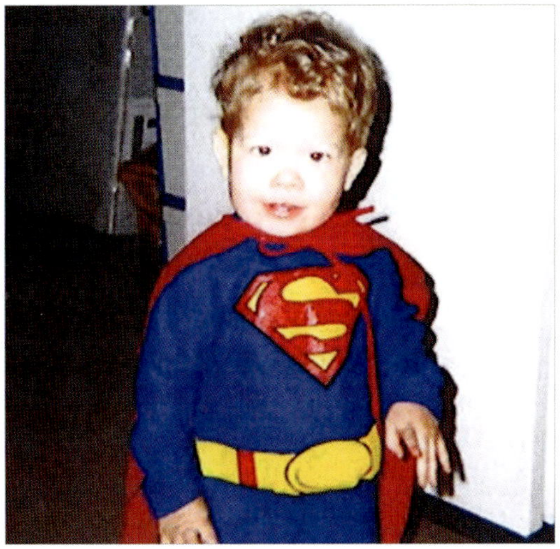

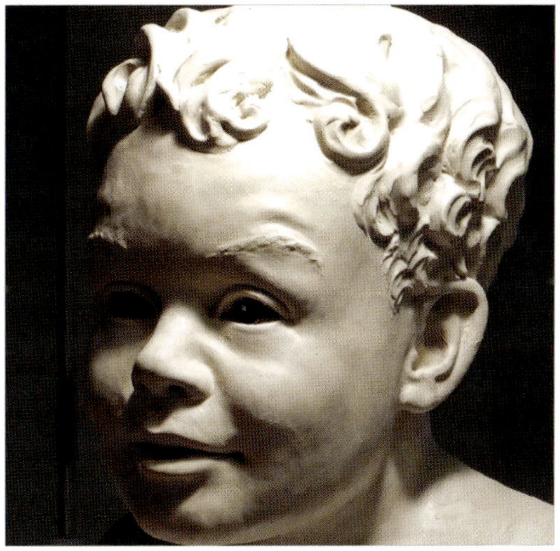

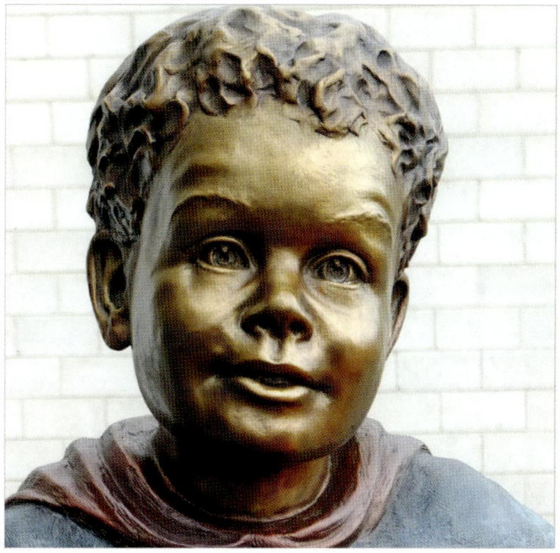

Photo: Leonard Schlichting

The Superman outfit in the photographs looked like a dime-store kiddy costume, unlikely to provide superpowers to anyone. Stamped across the front of the suit was the large 'S' shape, which someone told me was a Kryptonian symbol for hope. Permission to install the sculpture in public space relied on Todd getting written permission from DC Comics to use the Superman logo. The connection to child abuse made DC's first response a sharp refusal. At the foundry we scrambled to transpose the wax initial into a capital 'J'. But public outcry was deafening and DC Comics quickly reversed its decision! Sweet Jeffrey stands in Greenwood Park, in Toronto—an iconic Superman.

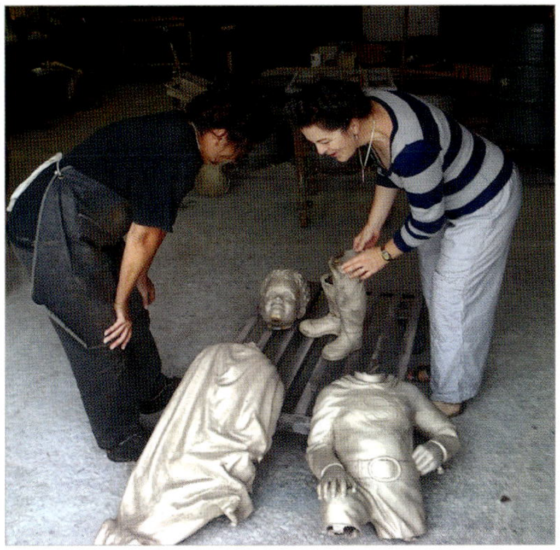

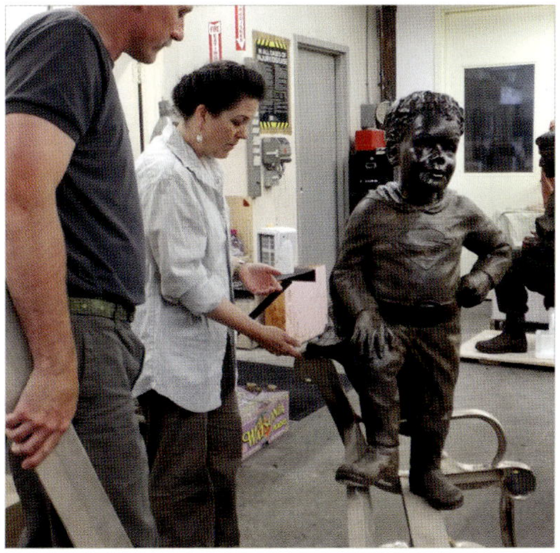

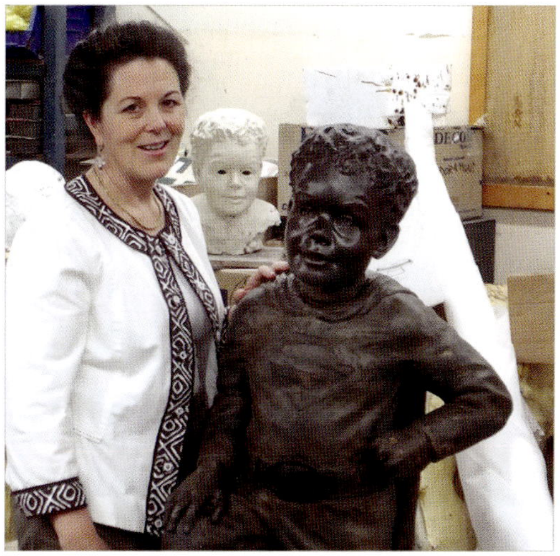

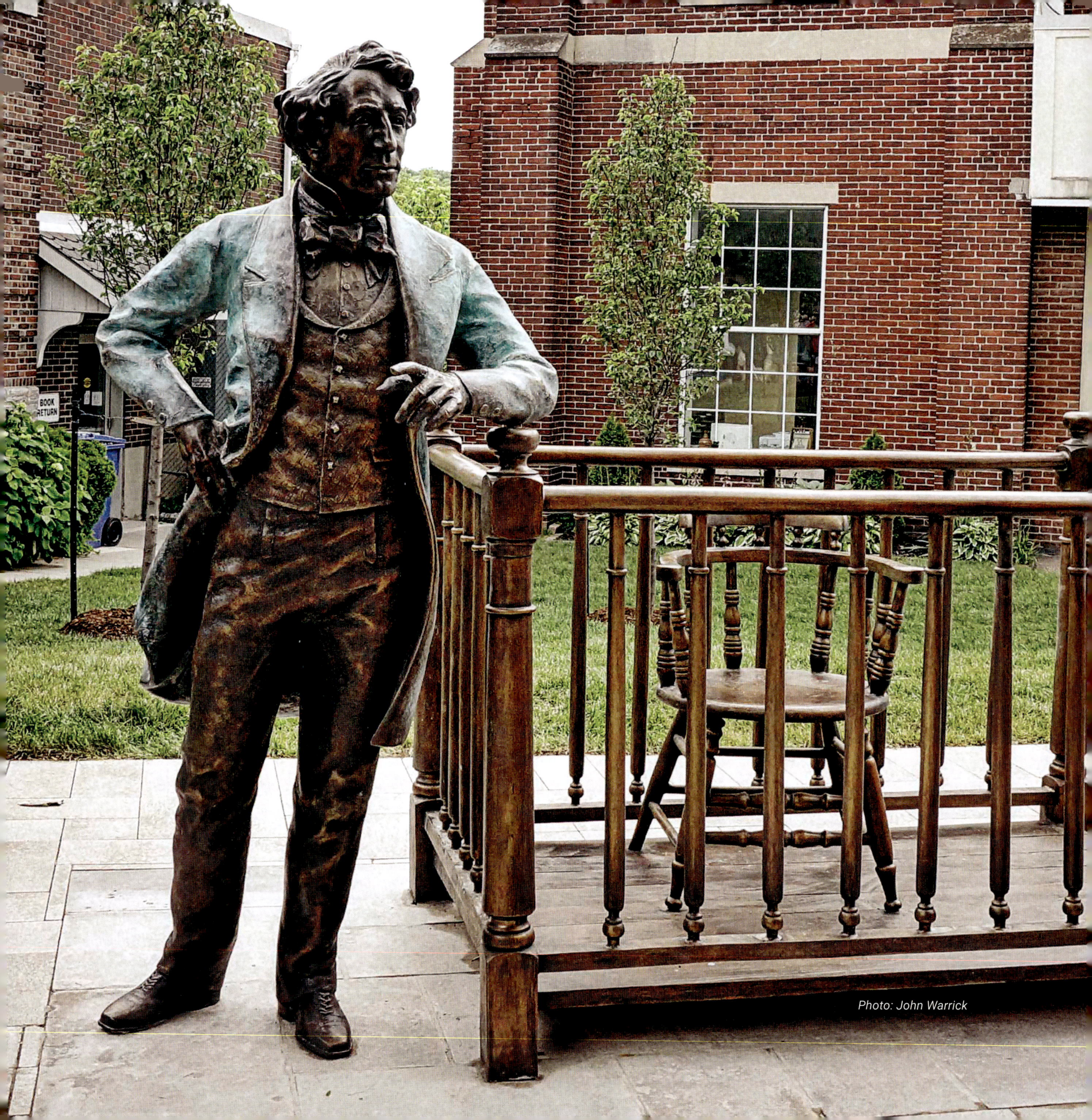

Photo: John Warrick

Holding Court

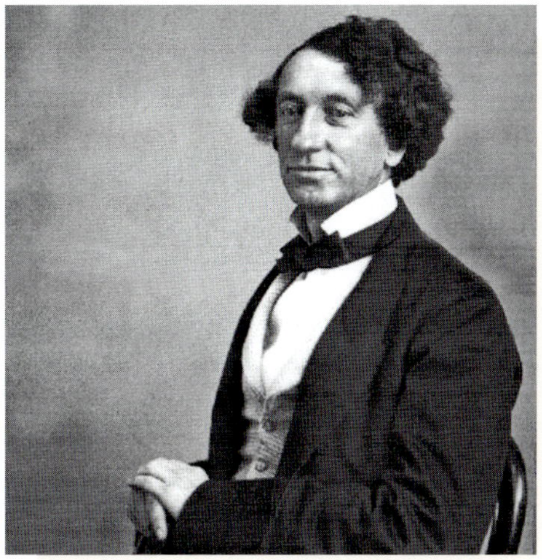

John A. Macdonald (1815–1891)

First Prime Minister of Canada

Sir John A. Macdonald was the first Prime Minister of Canada, serving 19 years in that role, the second-longest tenure of any Canadian prime minister. His political career lasted almost 50 years in total, during which time he was the main architect of *The British North America Act,* which united the provinces into Canadian Confederation. Macdonald also oversaw the expansion of the country from the Atlantic to the Pacific, and to the Arctic Ocean.

A few weeks after the Oscar Peterson unveiling in 2010, I received a phone inquiry. Would I consider undertaking a portrait of Canada's architect of Confederation, John A. Macdonald? The phone call was from David Warrick, chairman of a committee in Picton, Ontario. The committee had dubbed 2015 'The Year of Macdonald' and celebrations were planned for John A.'s 200th birthday year. They also wanted a figure portrait in the heart of Picton.

I met with the group for introductions and talk over a delicious dinner. Between first course and dessert, members of the committee relayed the story of Macdonald's first court appearance, which had happened in the courthouse just down the street. It was an engaging tale told over a jovial repast. Retired civil servants Alan Gratias and Gerry Raynor hilariously attempted jokes in Latin and ran delightfully roughshod over parliamentary procedure. On finishing the meal, they asked for my thoughts on how I'd present Macdonald.

I rose by my dining chair and demonstrated *the moment* when 19-year-old John A. brought fine logic to the courtroom and won over a jury of respected peers. Heads nodded and there were smiles around the table. We had our goal in sight.

My design, titled *Holding Court*, was resolved with details from the historic court case. Young John A. would be standing beside a prisoner's dock styled on the actual fixture in Picton's courthouse. In the dock was a chair that sat empty, since John A. was both the defendant and the accused.

Previous research and personal interest had acquainted me with life in Upper Canada in the 1830s. I read several biographies about Canada's first Prime Minister to absorb the characteristics of John A. Macdonald.

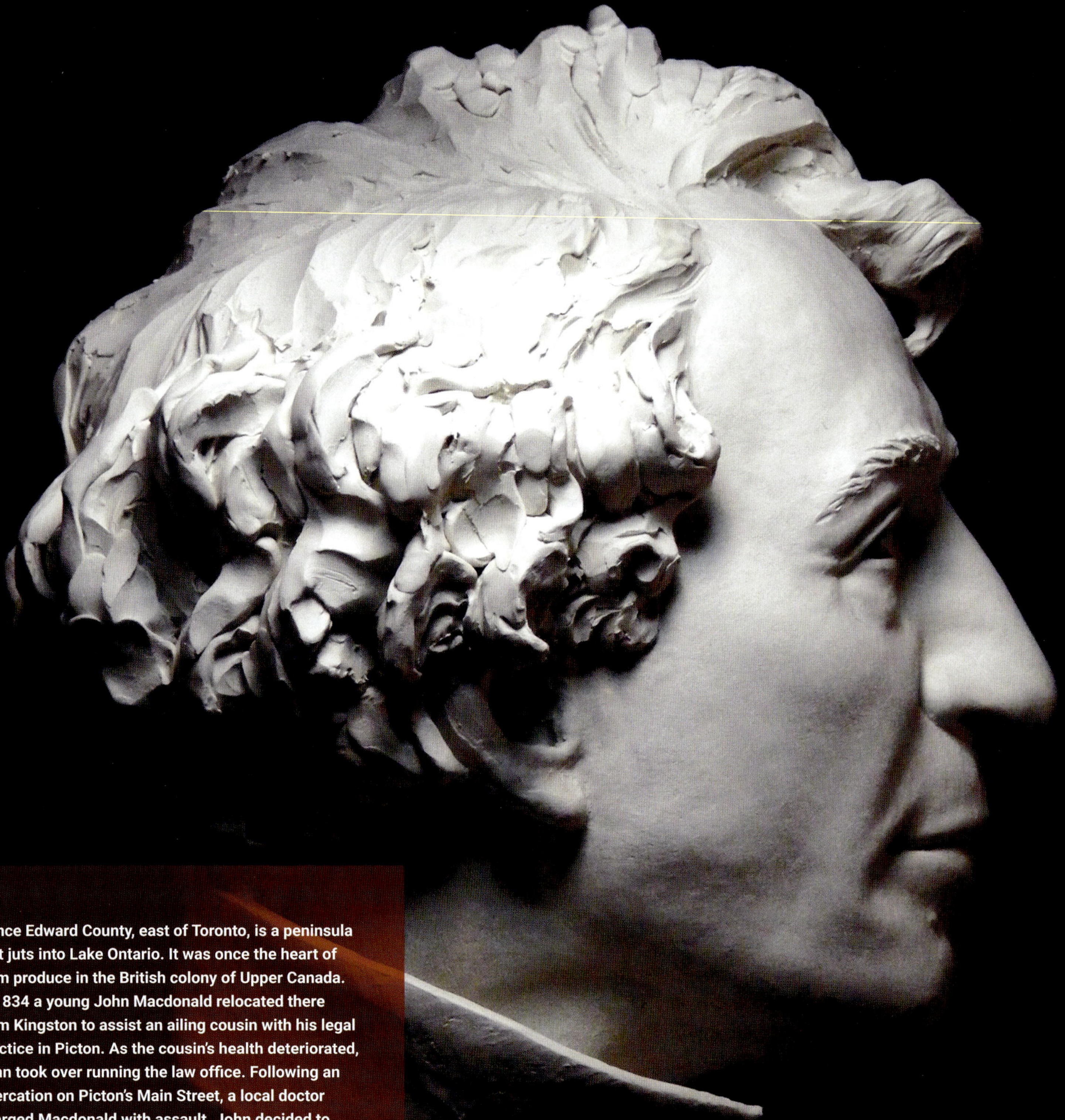

Prince Edward County, east of Toronto, is a peninsula that juts into Lake Ontario. It was once the heart of farm produce in the British colony of Upper Canada. In 1834 a young John Macdonald relocated there from Kingston to assist an ailing cousin with his legal practice in Picton. As the cousin's health deteriorated, John took over running the law office. Following an altercation on Picton's Main Street, a local doctor charged Macdonald with assault. John decided to defend himself. No transcripts of the trial exist, but Macdonald won the day with his logic that all colonists, not just landowners and British appointees, had the right to freedom of expression in a public place.

Author Richard Gwyn produced an illuminating two-volume biography on John A. Macdonald just prior to my sculpting of John A.'s distinctive face. I declared to Richard that, true to Canadian politics, his books "were so boring I couldn't put them down!" They were ideal background reading as I divided my time between the Wellesley studio and my workspace near English Bay in Vancouver, where John A.'s head study was sculpted. I'd built a large carton to carry the delicate portrait through airports and across the country. With Macdonald deep in the belly of the plane and me buckled in at 30,000 feet, I read the final chapters of his story. I could consider John A.'s accomplishments and the scope of Confederation while looking down at fluffy clouds, the Rockies and the immense Canadian landscape.

Back in the Wellesley studio, I began carving young Macdonald despite inflamed public discourse about the upcoming 'birthday boy'.

The process behind my sculpting of each portrait somehow reflected the real-life struggles of the characters I portrayed. Perhaps predictably, the making of John A. was set against a backdrop of vivid debate around his successes and failures.

The stalwart Picton committee members could occasionally insert a few facts into the conversation—like Macdonald's attempt to give women the vote as early as the 1880s.

Contrasting a fast and furious public discourse, my studio tasks were a series of pragmatic decisions about the cut and shape of John A.'s 1830s clothing. My friend Marvin Schlichting, an eminently knowledgeable theatre tailor, advised me. His sister, Lynette Schlichting, was my assistant at the time. She sculpted the components for the prisoner's dock and the period chair it held, using styrene and wax.

John A.'s finished portrait had charm and youthful energy—right from the start! The committee was delighted with the first photos. I polished John A.'s Civil War–style riding boots and sharpened the pleats on his jacket and drop-front pants. Along with the prisoner's dock and chair, he was trundled to the foundry to be made into bronze.

As guest speaker at the annual Macdonald Dinner of the Historical Society in Kingston, I presented photos of my research, which included my preliminary head study of John A. Later I added lapels to the head study and refined the work into a limited edition of portrait busts. These cast portraits were displayed across Canada to re-introduce Canadians to the Macdonald legacy.

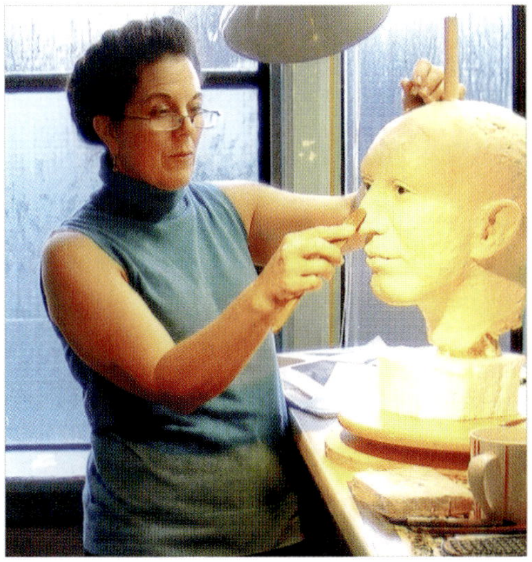

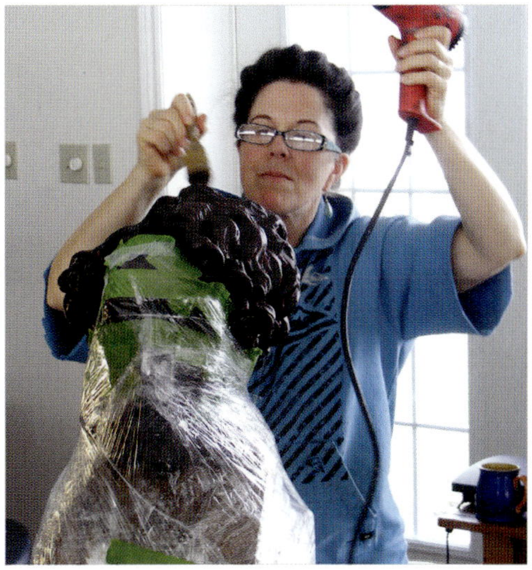

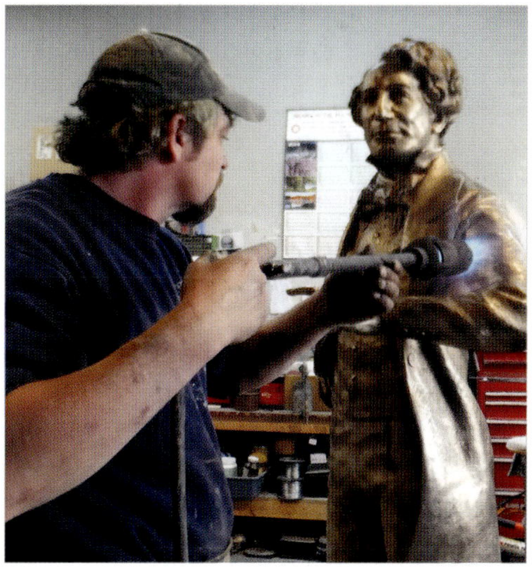

The Royal York Hotel Hosts Macdonald's 200th Birthday Bash

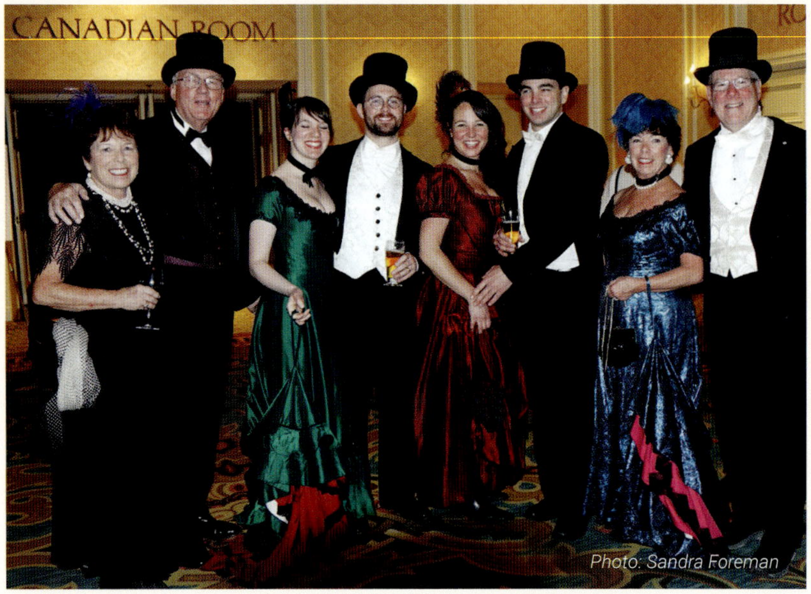

Left to right: Judy Groves, John Groves, Heidi Craig, Nathan Howard, Alynn Casgrain, Stuart Casgrain, Sheila Casgrain, Tim Casgrain.

In classic Canadian fashion, celebrating an elected leader was unduly difficult. Macdonald's nineteenth-century choices were not deemed politically correct today and the contemporary press seemed to focus on the historic 'errors'. There was little mention of his nineteenth-century accomplishments, yet Macdonald's continual re-election suggested that his ideas were shared and supported by the electorate.

To add momentum to the project's fundraising the committee staged a play in Picton. Judge Robert Sharpe had written a book based on a notorious 1884 double hanging in the historic Picton Courthouse. To the delight of a capacity audience, who booed and hissed at the characters just as they'd been instructed, the re-enactment created from Sharpe's *The Lazier Murder: Prince Edward County, 1884* unfolded. This rollicking summer event sparked new interest for the John A. project throughout Prince Edward county. At last heads, and the tide, began to turn.

The committee and I were welcomed at Queen's Park in Toronto, where members in the chamber offered resounding applause at the prospect of a new heritage installation in Picton. Also in Toronto, a group called the Friends of Macdonald collaborated with the committee on an unveiling of the new portrait at their annual John A. Dinner. The Royal York Hotel, one of the Canadian Pacific Railway Hotels, was a perfect venue.

The Canadian Pacific Railway had been central to Macdonald's dream of connecting the nation by rail from coast to coast. On January 11, 2015 the hotel's elegant Canadian Room held a resplendent gala gathering. Lanny Huff, of Huff Estates Winery, had supported the portrait project from its inception and he'd produced an excellent sparkling vintage that befitted a night of toasting, *"John A., you'll never die!"* Steve Paikin, a well-known television interviewer, hosted the evening in grand style. With nearly 500 guests, including Ontario Premier Kathleen Wynn, former Prime Minister Kim Campbell and many VIPs, Macdonald and *Holding Court* was celebrated at a spectacular 200th birthday party.

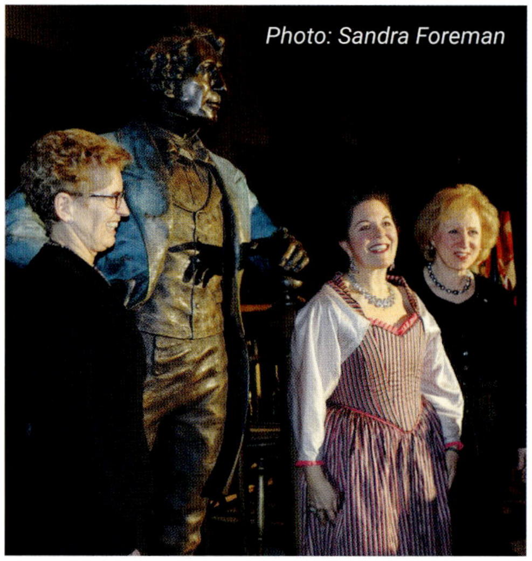

L to R: Premier of Ontario Kathleen Wynne, Ruth Abernethy and former Prime Minister of Canada Kim Campbell.

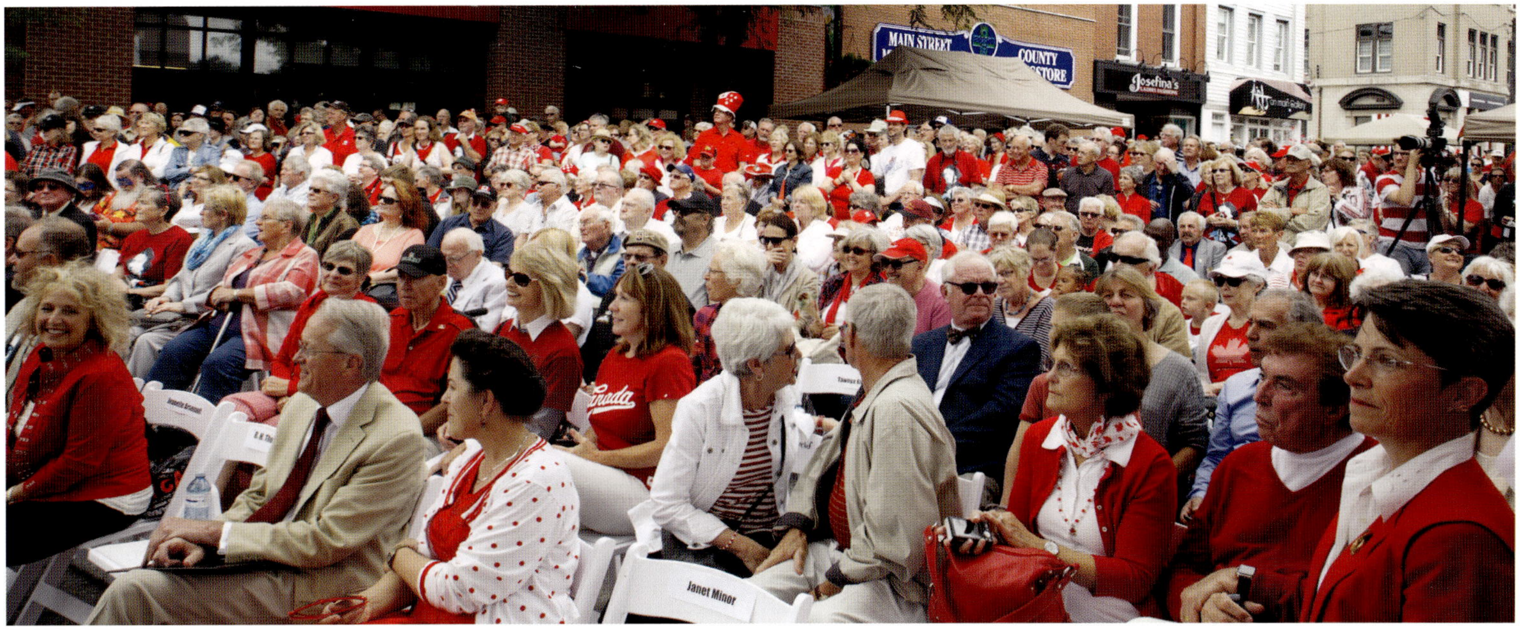

At Macdonald's dedication in Picton on July 1st, 2015, five thousand people gathered for a red-and-white party on Main Street.

Several months later the crew in Picton began final preparations for Macdonald's permanent site in front of the local Armoury. Canada's July 1st birthday dawned to a blustery grey sky but event planners for the red-and-white party proceeded bravely. The town outdid itself! Main Street filled with red-and-white revellers from end to end. The dedication ceremony was succinct and each speaker shared unique ideas about Macdonald's legacy. I was astonished by the multitude and that the crowd listened intently to what was said. We felt raindrops as R.H. Thomson, an accomplished actor and Canadian heritage activist, mesmerized the crowd with his presentation of Wilfred Laurier's eulogy to Macdonald. It was originally spoken after the leader's death on a rainy June 6th, 1891. As Thomson finished, the sky cleared and young John A. was revealed for photographs at last.

Dedication Day was a perfect demonstration of the new Macdonald Square as a gathering place in the heart of Picton. I'd learned a great deal about Macdonald through *Holding Court*, and even more about the complexities of celebrating Canada's elected leaders.

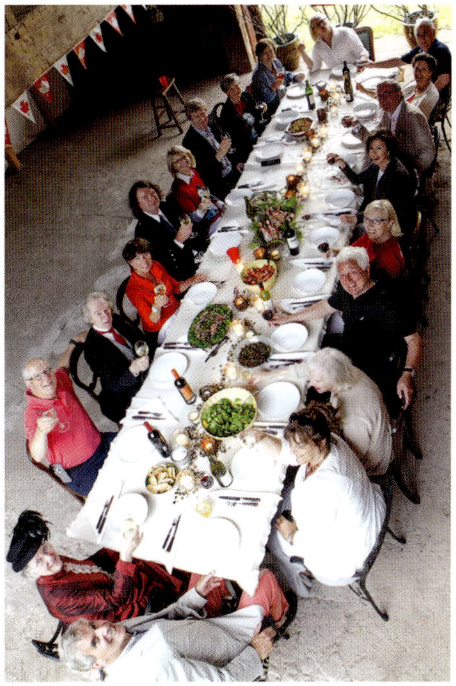

Photos: John Warrick

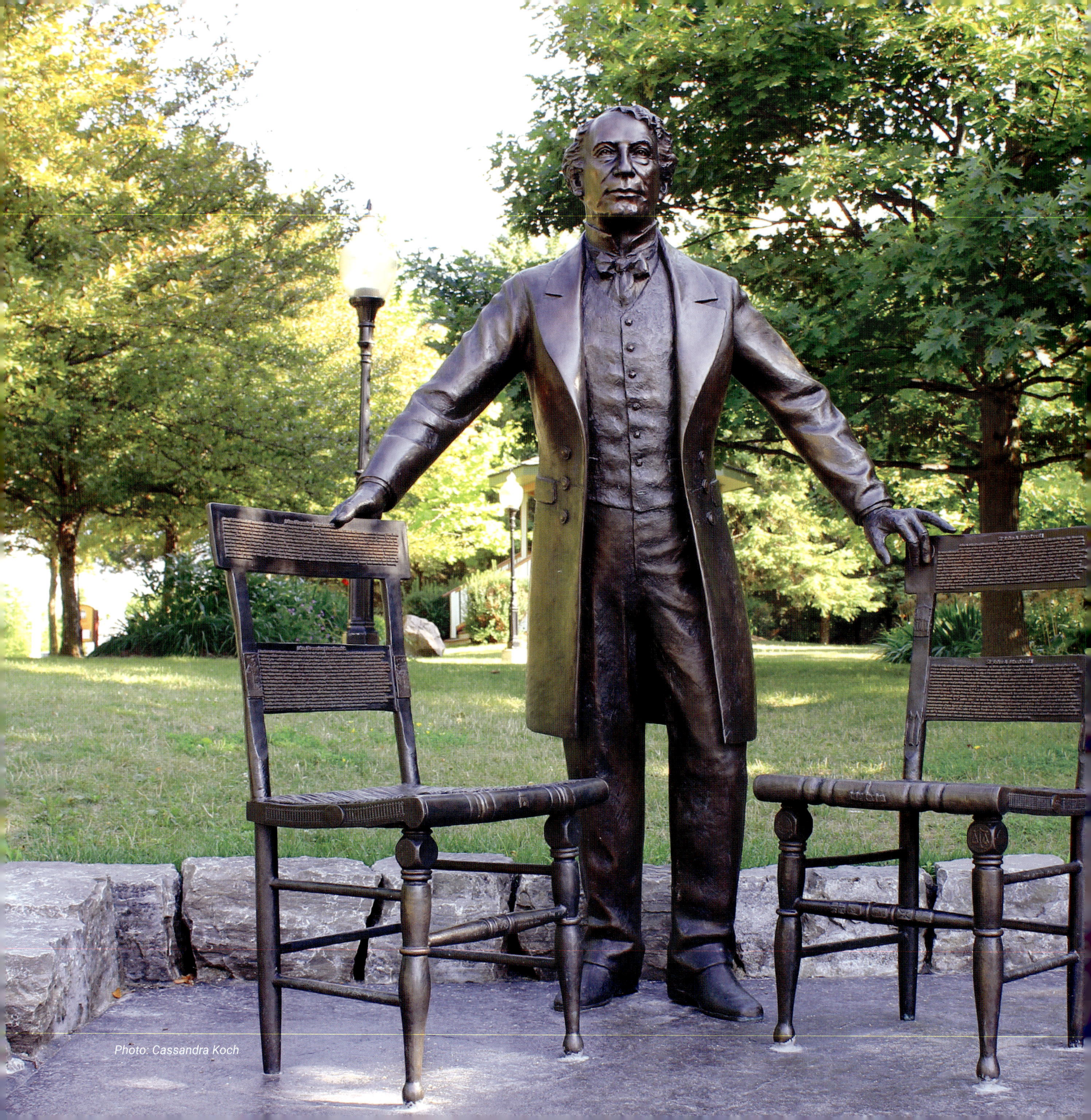

Photo: Cassandra Koch

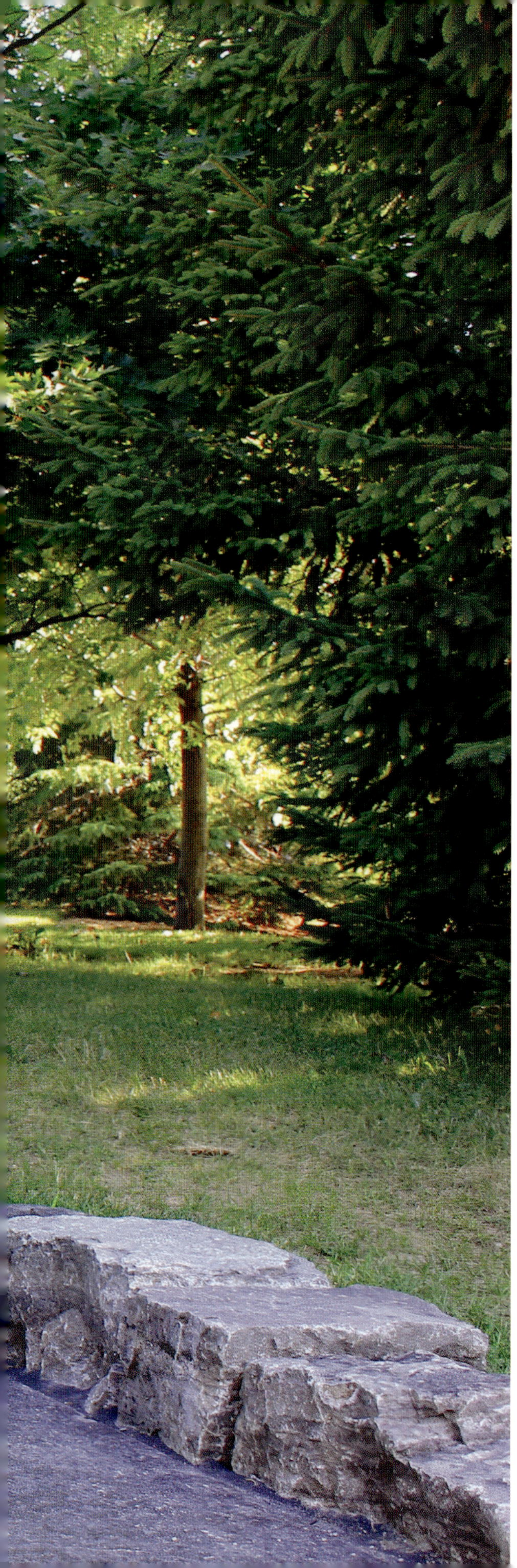

A Canadian Conversation

In 2004 Jim Rodger and I had collaborated on a portrait of William Lyon Mackenzie King, Canada's longest-serving prime minister, who grew up in Kitchener. Jim had heard I was sculpting a young John A. Macdonald for Picton. He and high-tech entrepreneur Dave Caputo invited my input on the Prime Ministers Portrait Collection planned for Waterloo Region.

Canada's forthcoming 150th anniversary in 2017 prompted conversations across the country about ways and means of celebrating. Jim and Dave proposed bronze portraits of all 22 prime ministers in contextual designs to illustrate each leader's role in the national narrative. The mandate of the Prime Ministers Portrait Collection was to stimulate discussions about leadership. As the architect of Canadian Confederation, Macdonald was an obvious first candidate for the endeavour. My task was to consider the public's encounter with John A. Macdonald and create a design that conveyed his formative leadership in Canada's early history.

Since Macdonald had grown up in the shadow of the Napoleonic Wars in Europe, the sensibilities he held within this small British colony were difficult for a contemporary audience. In 1867, the year of Confederation, Macdonald was 52 years old; he'd endured career challenges and personal tragedies. It was a big pleasure to retrieve my sculpted head study of young John A. and overlay his features with the more familiar etchings of age and worry.

I imagined 'my moment' with him as if he were awaiting a meal after official meetings had adjourned. I positioned John as a statesman, standing between two dining chairs, welcoming guests to join the discussion. I reasoned that nation-building inevitably happened across the dinner table, where fresh ideas were shared and considered over food; in consensus, there can be feasting.

> *In the design, titled* A Canadian Conversation, *John A. Macdonald invites you to sit. When you take a seat, you must have something to say—but you also must be prepared to listen.*

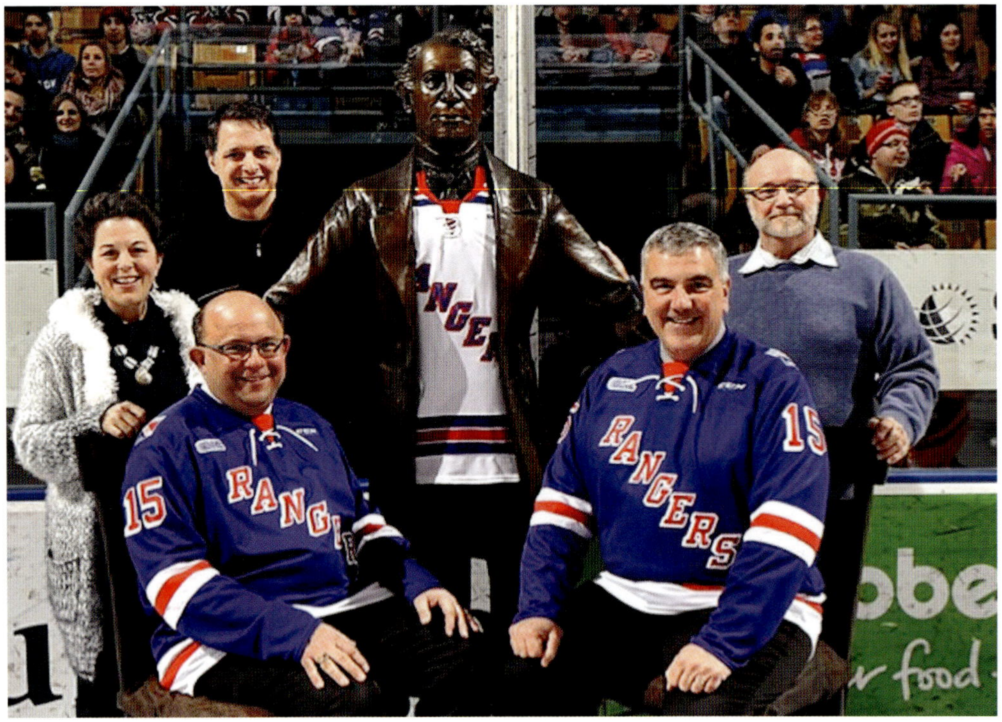

Macdonald's 200th birthday being celebrated in Kitchener Memorial Auditorium, with Dave Caputo standing left, Jim Rodger standing right. Seated, Kitchener Mayor Berry Vrbanovic and Dave Jaworsky, Mayor of Waterloo.

My portrait concept was met with immediate delight and satisfaction. The project leaders had hoped for an iconic presentation of the man, but also for a contextual design that conveyed the inclusive and often chaotic dilemma that is Canadian democracy. My assistants and I considered the portrait's tight timeline, then committed to completing it for Macdonald's 200th birthday.

Depicting statesman John A. Macdonald, I needed to present the changes in fashion from his earlier portrait set in 1834. My assistants, Lynette Schlichting and Cassandra Koch, settled into the lower studio and prepared pieces for two identical chairs. These held several dozen detailed symbols etched into their waxed surfaces for site guests to seek out. I heightened existing studio chairs for shaping Macdonald's hands precisely over the chair backs. In early September we jubilantly delivered JAM and his dining chairs to the foundry.

Project head Dave Caputo is a true innovator and the Ontario Hockey Association quickly supported his unique unveiling proposal. *A Canadian Conversation* was first shared in the most Canadian of venues, a hockey game in Kitchener Memorial Auditorium. The Kitchener Rangers faced off against the Belleville Bulls and all players sported a Macdonald badge on their jerseys. An enthusiastic crowd sang "Happy Birthday" to John A. Macdonald and the Rangers took the night with a score of 5–2.

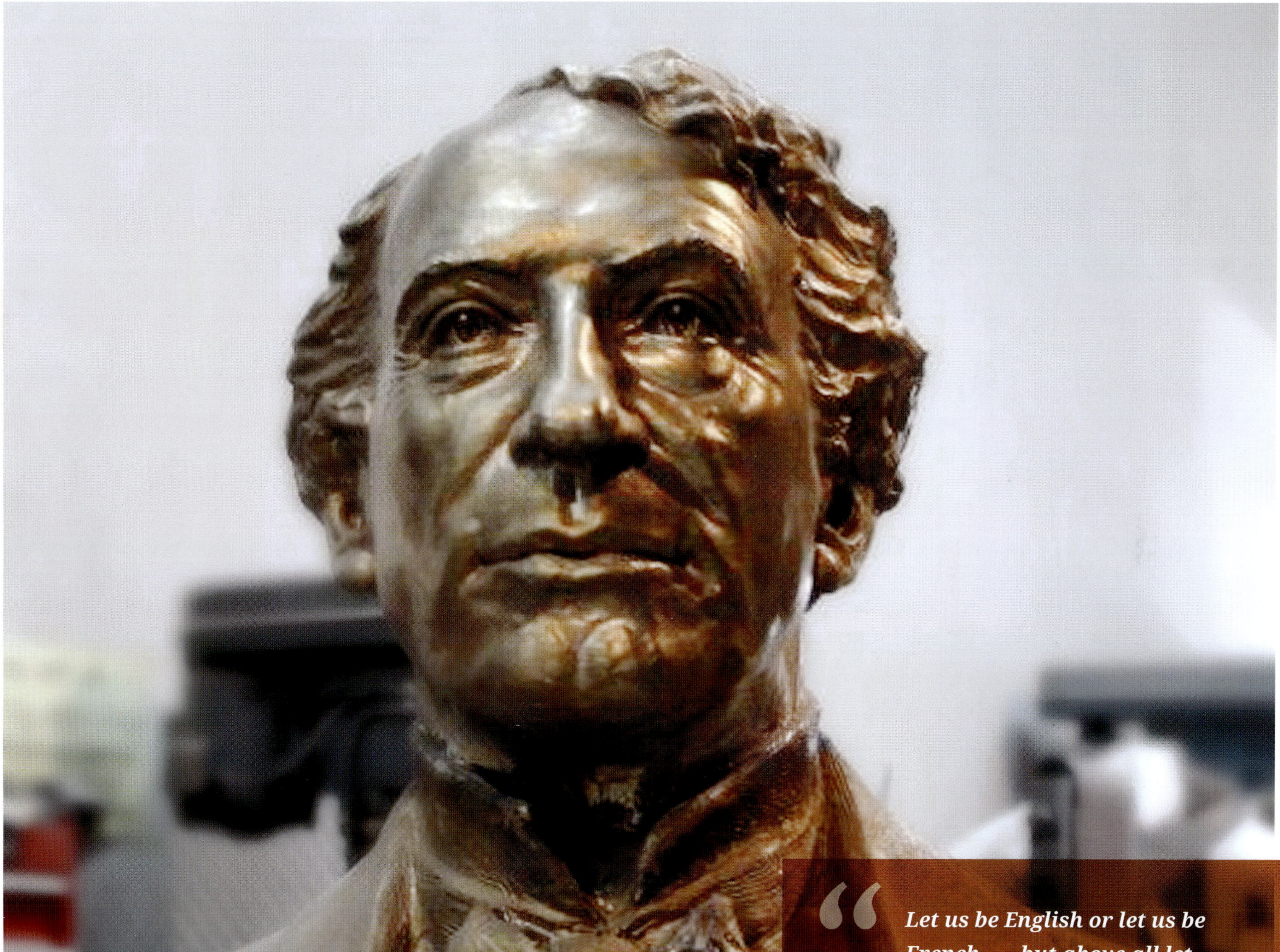

> *Let us be English or let us be French . . . but above all let us be Canadians.*
>
> *– John A. Macdonald*

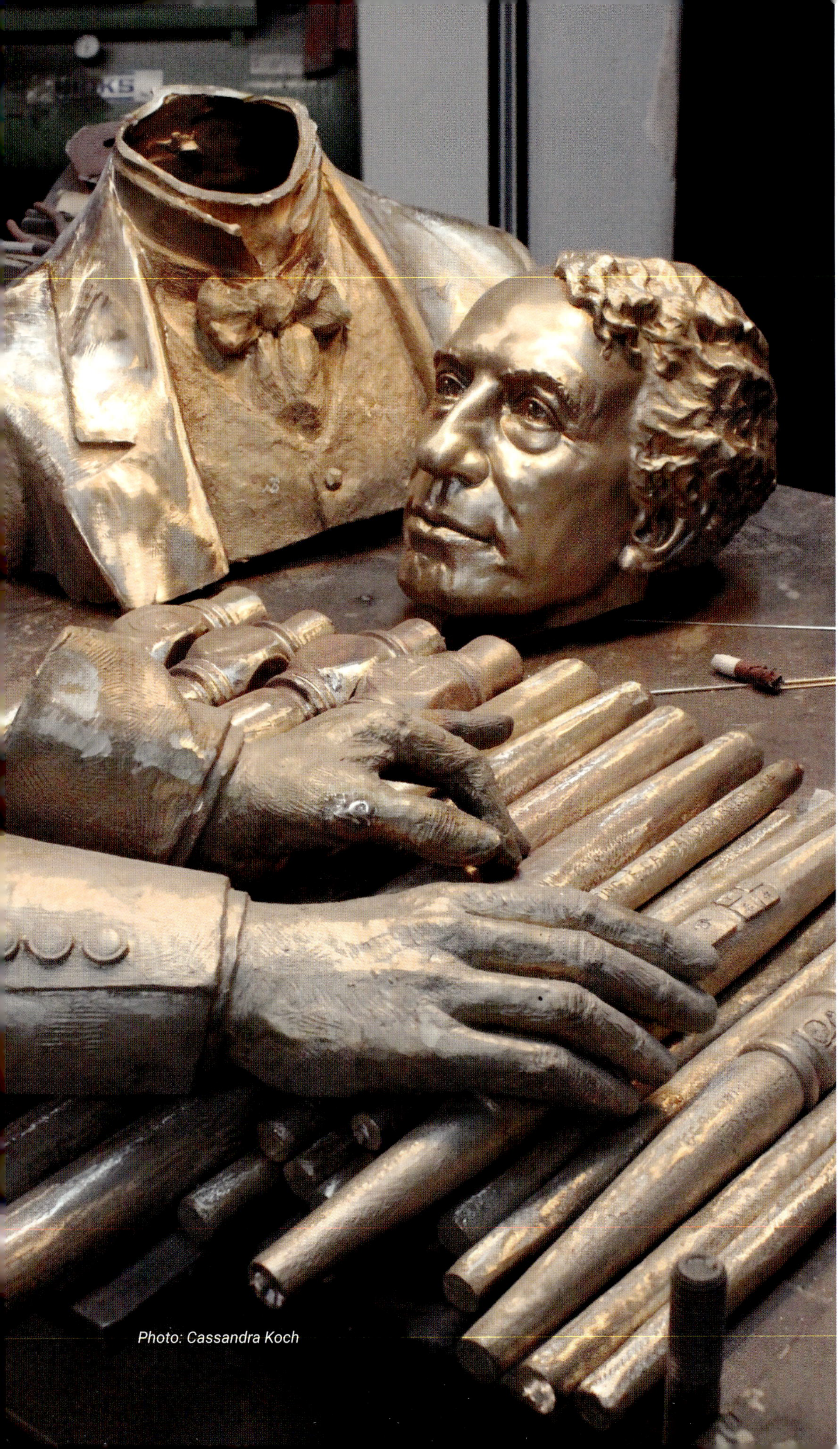
Photo: Cassandra Koch

The chairs that flank Macdonald in *A Canadian Conversation* had a vital role. I wanted them to allude to Canada's French and English heritage. They had to be dining chairs to suggest gathering for a meal. The design of the furniture specified its place in history. I reproduced heritage chairs that had been documented from Addington County near Kingston, Ontario circa 1850. The distinctive North American Hitchcock chairs had exquisite hand-painted stencil work rather than expensive inlay, as was fashionable in Europe at the time. They also had rush seats. In bronze the traditional chair stencils were replaced with symbols for events and people in Macdonald's personal and public life.

For a month after the hockey game, Macdonald drew fans into discussion at 'the Aud'. Students at Sir John A. Macdonald Secondary School enjoyed 'conversations' when John A. appeared at their school in Waterloo. Over winter break and through the spring of 2015*, A Canadian Conversation* prompted exchanges with passersby at the museum on King Street in Kitchener.

Despite often vitriolic public discourse over John A.'s habits and his nineteenth-century decisions, long-term planning for the PM Collection continued. These months of very Canadian conversations were highlighted by 50th-anniversary flashbacks to the selection of the Canadian flag in 1965. It was difficult to comprehend the aggravation across the nation over that red maple leaf that we now wholeheartedly embraced.

The Prime Minister Collection has been given a welcome at Castle Kilbride, in Baden, Ontario, where a nine-acre site surrounds a distinctive home built by James Livingston in 1877. Livingston was a member of parliament from 1882 to 1900 and would have known Macdonald and many of Canada's early statesmen. I expect he'd be fascinated by the bronze characters and equally intrigued by visitors' discussions of the Collection mandate: leadership in Canada.

Let the conversations begin!

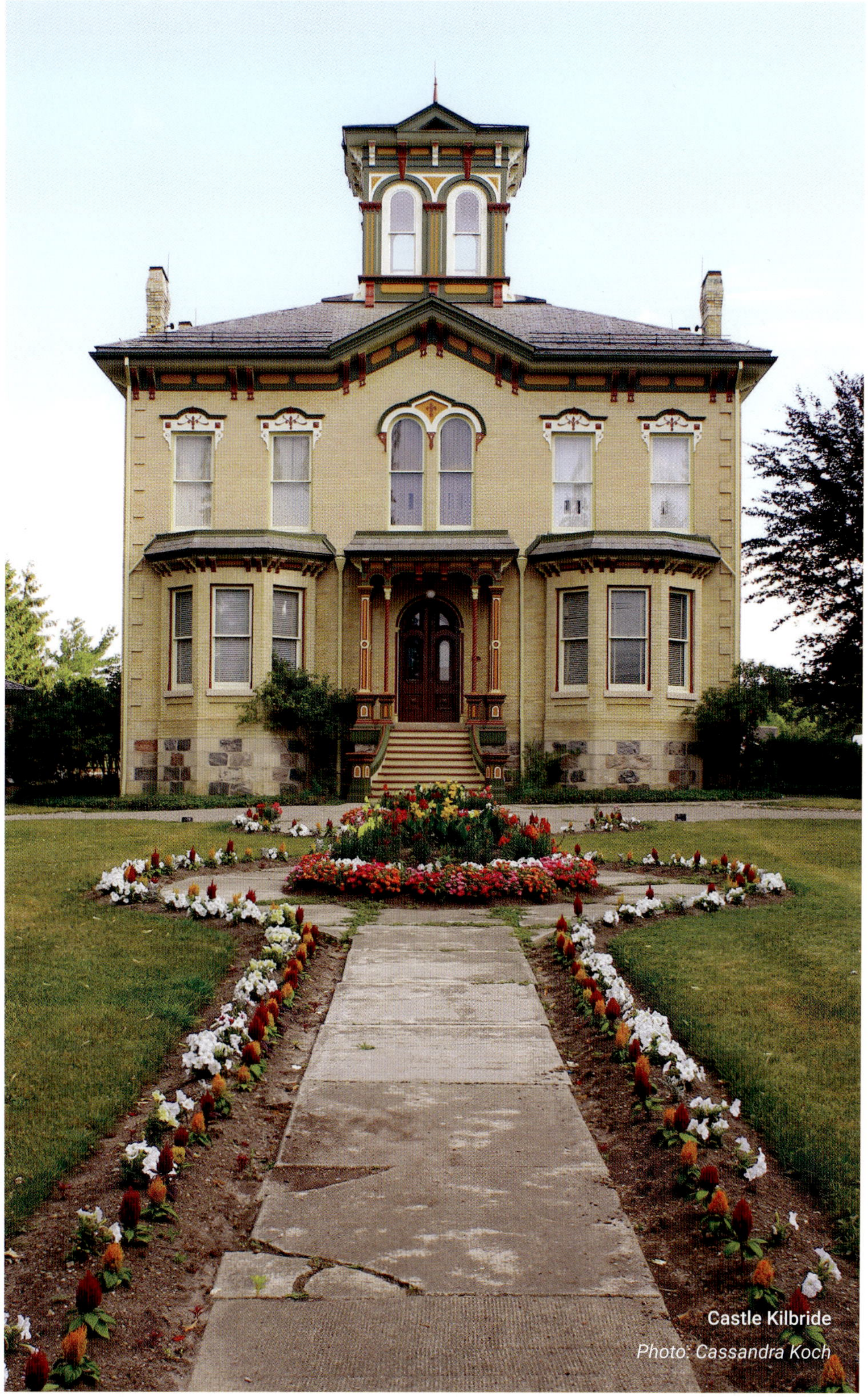

Castle Kilbride
Photo: Cassandra Koch

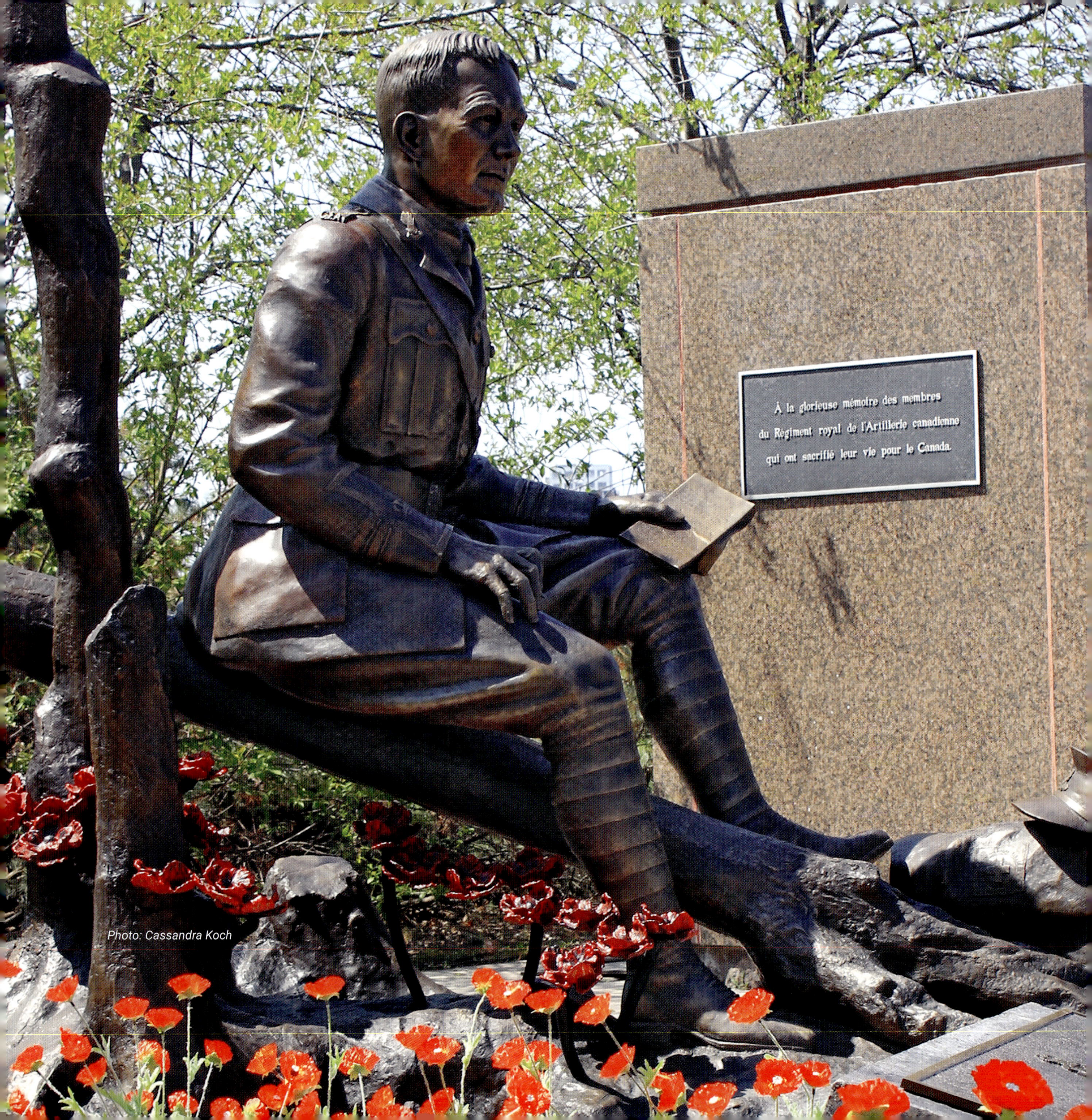

Photo: Cassandra Koch

Remember Flanders

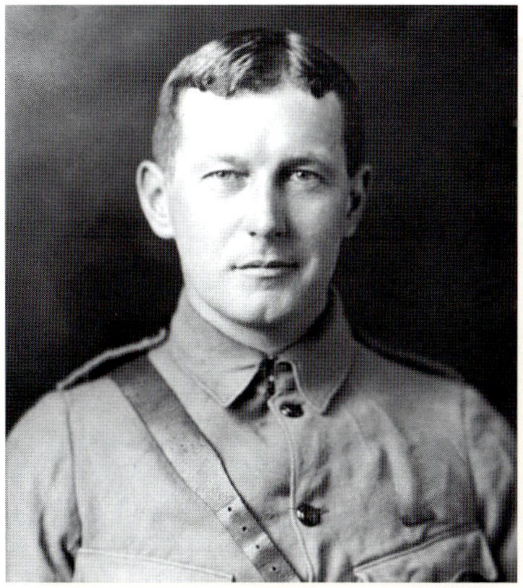

John McCrae (1872–1918)

Physician, Poet, Canadian Serviceman

Lieutenant Colonel John McCrae, MD was born in Guelph, Ontario. He trained as an artilleryman at the Royal Military College in Kingston and studied medicine at the University of Toronto. After serving in the Boer War, McCrae returned to Montreal, where he taught medicine at McGill University and wrote a textbook on pathology. Re-enlisting for service in World War I, he was quickly stationed as a field surgeon during the 2nd Battle of Ypres. A friend's death spurred him to write "In Flanders Fields." John McCrae died of pneumonia in January of 1918.

> *It's not often the Canadian military is honoured by something as transcendent as a poem.*

In the spring of 2012, a Call to Artists appeared in my inbox. May 3rd, 2015, would be the 100th anniversary of the poem "In Flanders Fields" written by Lieutenant Colonel John McCrae. Two identical portraits were planned, for Ottawa and for Guelph, Ontario, McCrae's hometown. I began to consider what moment I'd capture for this remarkable military poet.

The call specified that McCrae should be portrayed while writing his famous poem. He'd be in uniform and I imagined an uncontrived, trench-weary fellow, but I weighed the pros and cons of his demeanour quite carefully. The 'emotional architecture' had to ring true and I couldn't present a proud military man in a disheveled state.

In his journal, McCrae wrote about a dike road in Flanders over which all supplies were hauled into the base. He described the drovers spurring the horses along this road to stay ahead of relentless gunfire. McCrae's description gave me the idea of stark, battle-scarred saplings to hold the visual narrative of life and death at the front lines.

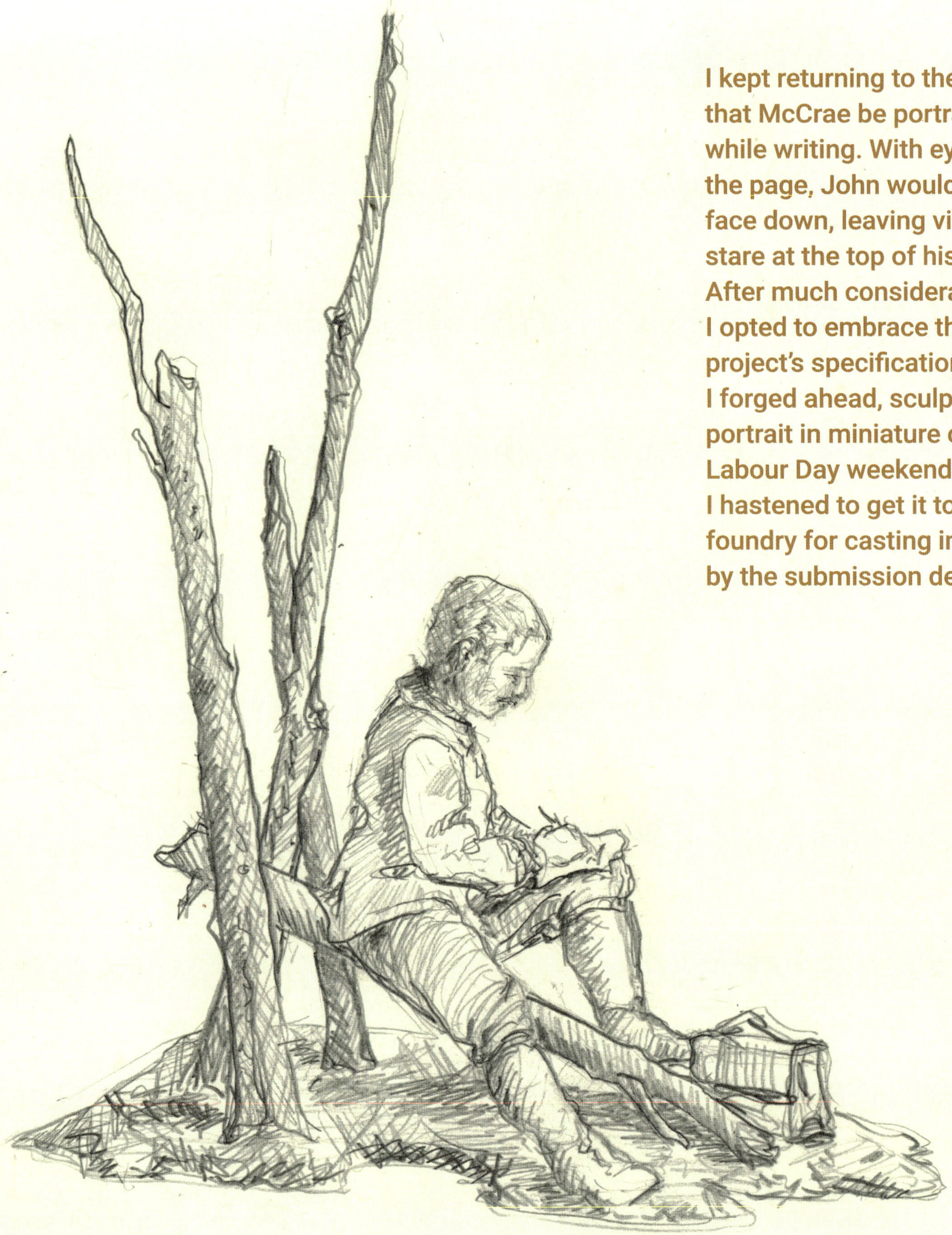

I kept returning to the request that McCrae be portrayed while writing. With eyes on the page, John would have his face down, leaving visitors to stare at the top of his head. After much consideration, I opted to embrace the project's specifications. I forged ahead, sculpting the portrait in miniature over the Labour Day weekend. I hastened to get it to the foundry for casting in bronze by the submission deadline.

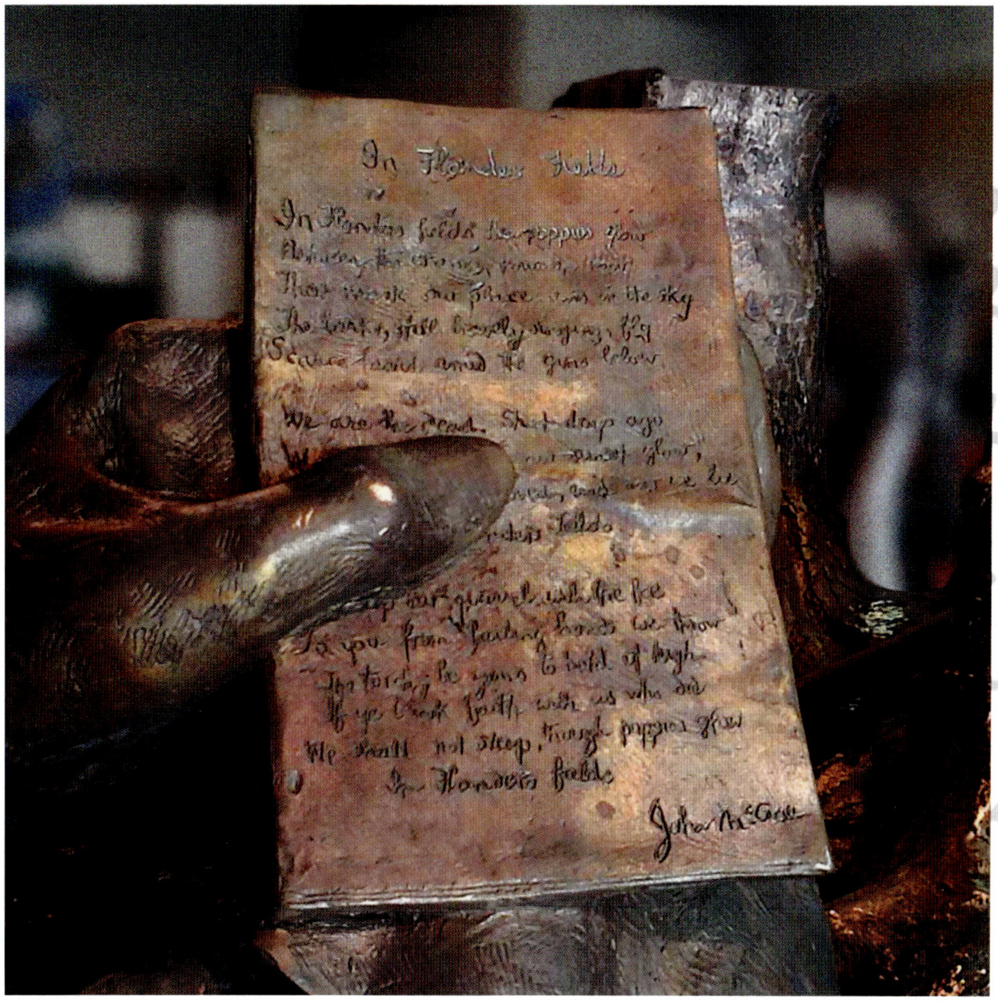

Once I was awarded the commission, I discussed McCrae's position with the commissioning chairman, Lieutenant Colonel Mike McKay. Mike understood my concerns and I revised the design to capture a moment with John McCrae *as he completed* writing the verse. After the last line was in place, he'd have signed his name and settled his writing hand, with pencil stub, onto his right knee. Drawing a deep breath, the artilleryman would look up in readiness to return to his duties. This portrait would have the logic and integrity that befitted our subject.

My revised design could include every line of the remarkable poem. I structured a notepad in McCrae's left hand that would be safer and stronger than a single page. "In Flanders Fields," in McCrae's own handwriting, would be copied, etched in wax and cast into bronze.

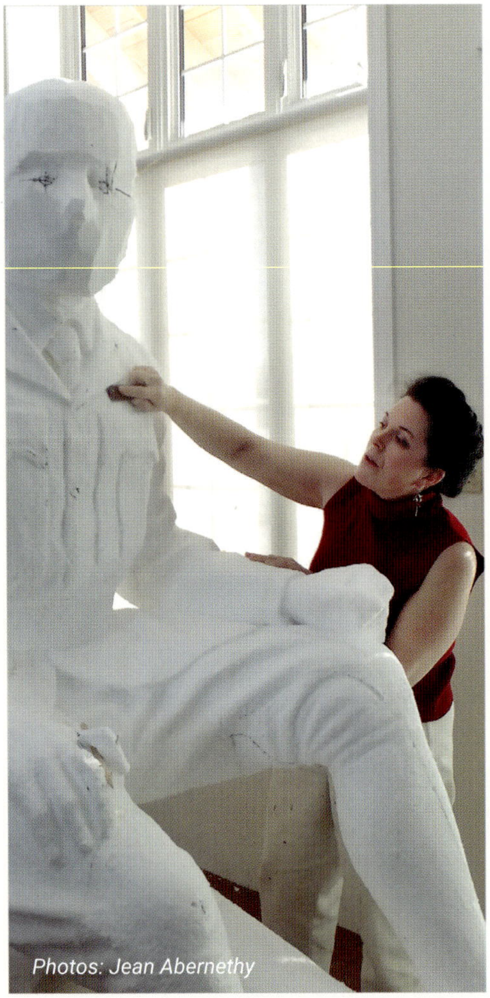

Photos: Jean Abernethy

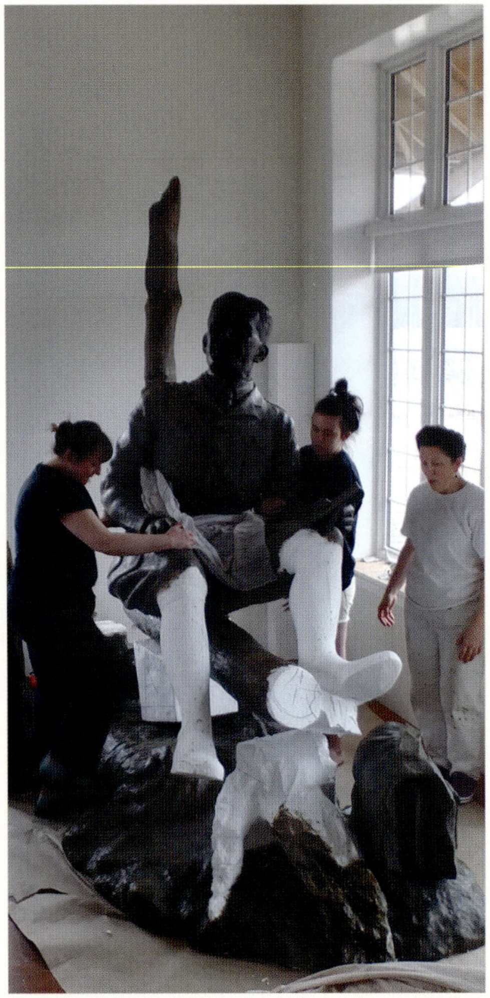

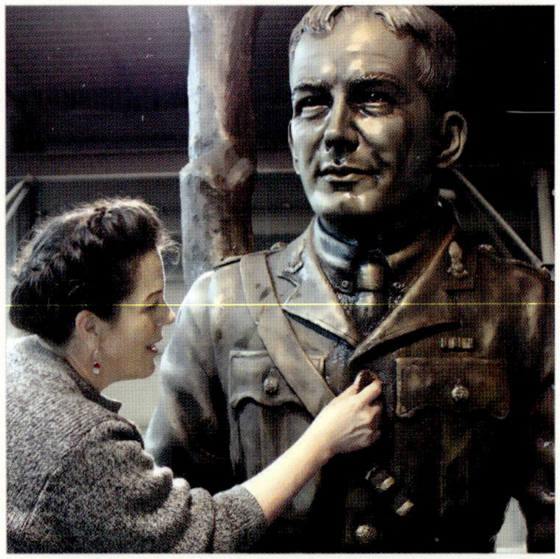

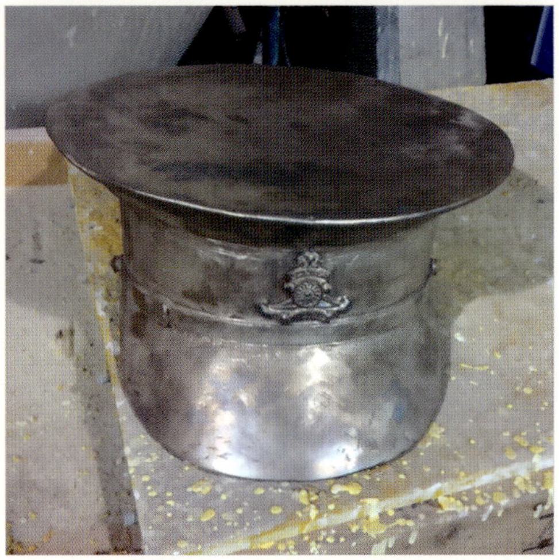

Since the portrait was to be 150 percent of life size, each item had to be hand-sculpted. I needed to create embossed uniform buttons in two sizes. There were brass collar pins, a delicate artillery badge and specific military regalia. The World War I jacket would be wide at the hem, designed for officers on horseback. I was keen to sculpt the weight of the worn woolen uniform and the fullness of the jodhpur riding pants, standard issue in 1915.

Research showed McCrae wore puttees. 'Puttee' was an English iteration of a word taken from British India, meaning a long strip of fabric. In military terms, puttees were the protective bands that wrapped the pant legs from knee to ankle. I learned they were wound onto each leg in opposite directions then tied with laces at the top and bottom. In bronze, all materials were made distinctive with texture: sleek leather, woolen cloth, military braid and of course McCrae's buttons that were buffed to a shine.

With help from military archives in Shilo, Manitoba, I researched McCrae's medical kit. Various utilitarian bags served on the front lines but there was no way of knowing what type of satchel McCrae had used. I chose one with a medic's crest and reproduced it precisely. On top of the kit, his officer's cap was placed precisely as though Dr. John had lifted it from his own head by the brim.

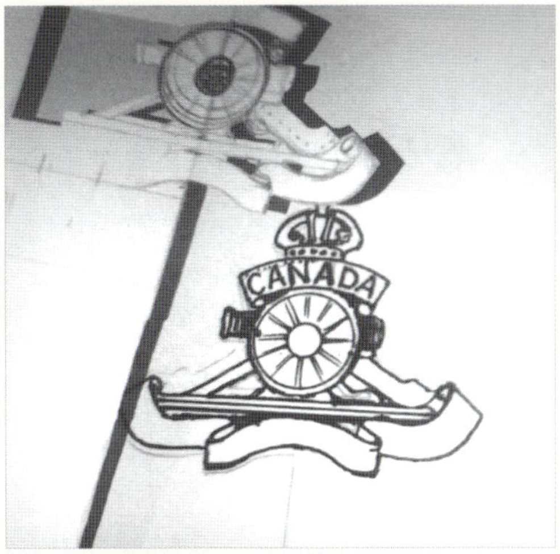

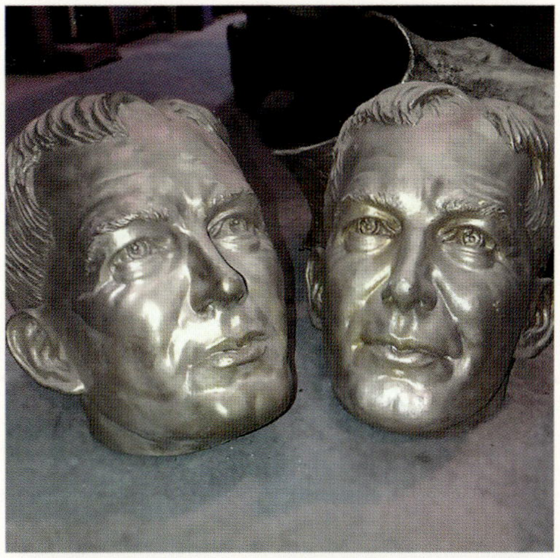

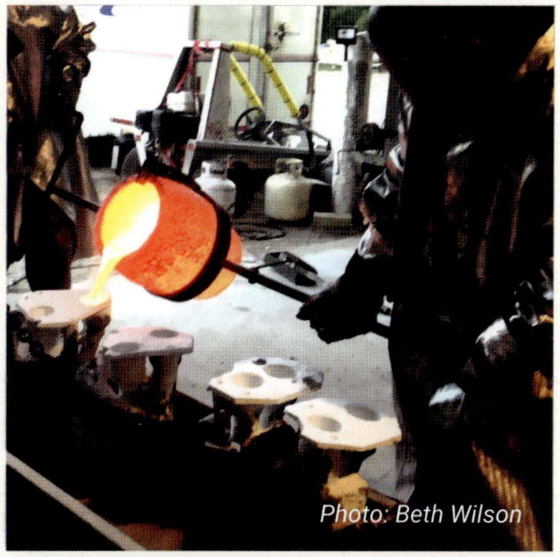
Photo: Beth Wilson

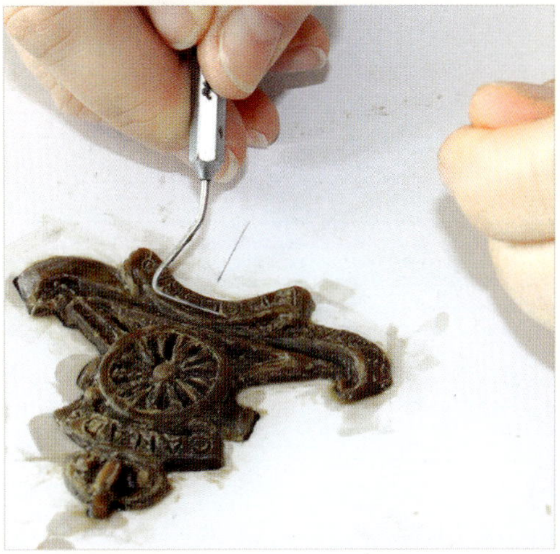

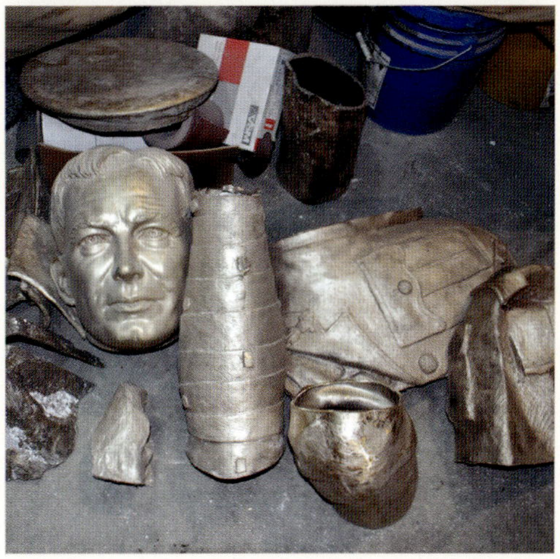

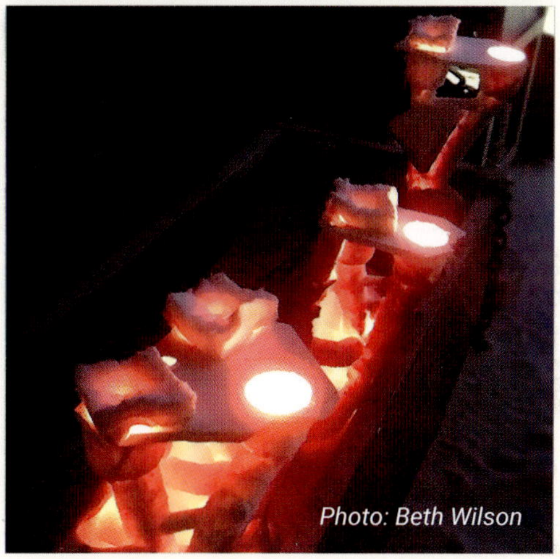
Photo: Beth Wilson

The fabrication steps were curiously identical in creating McCrae 8 inches tall and again 8 feet tall. I worked out the anatomy; I plotted it as a paper pattern in front and side views and traced the outlines onto columns of white styrene. John McCrae needed many blocks! As I shaped the figure portrait in the Great Room studio, my assistant Lynette formed the 'terra firma' sculpture base in the second studio. Cassandra Koch joined us when her term finished at the University of Guelph. She carved McCrae's tall, battered tree trunks, then refined and waxed their surfaces by hand. My arms and hands were weary but McCrae took shape as a truly endearing fellow.

The measurements I'd resolved at Christmas 2013 were put to the test in August when at last we fit the base and the figure together in the large studio. I couldn't have been more pleased. The pieces aligned so nicely that we took the components to the foundry and completed our final assembly.

McCrae was an enormous undertaking for Castaway Foundry, owned by Beth and Jim Wilson. Because we needed two castings, it was decided that the pieces for Ottawa would each be duplicated to create a second set of pieces for Guelph. For months, Beth counted and coded odd-shaped bronze segments from the first casting, transported them for reproduction and held her breath as each copied and original piece was counted and recounted on return. The pile of 'body parts' continued to grow. Jim's bronze work was exquisite! As the days and weeks flew by, two installation sites were prepared. There were a few tense moments in our schedule. To a number of people who sustained optimism and a sense of humour I am truly grateful.

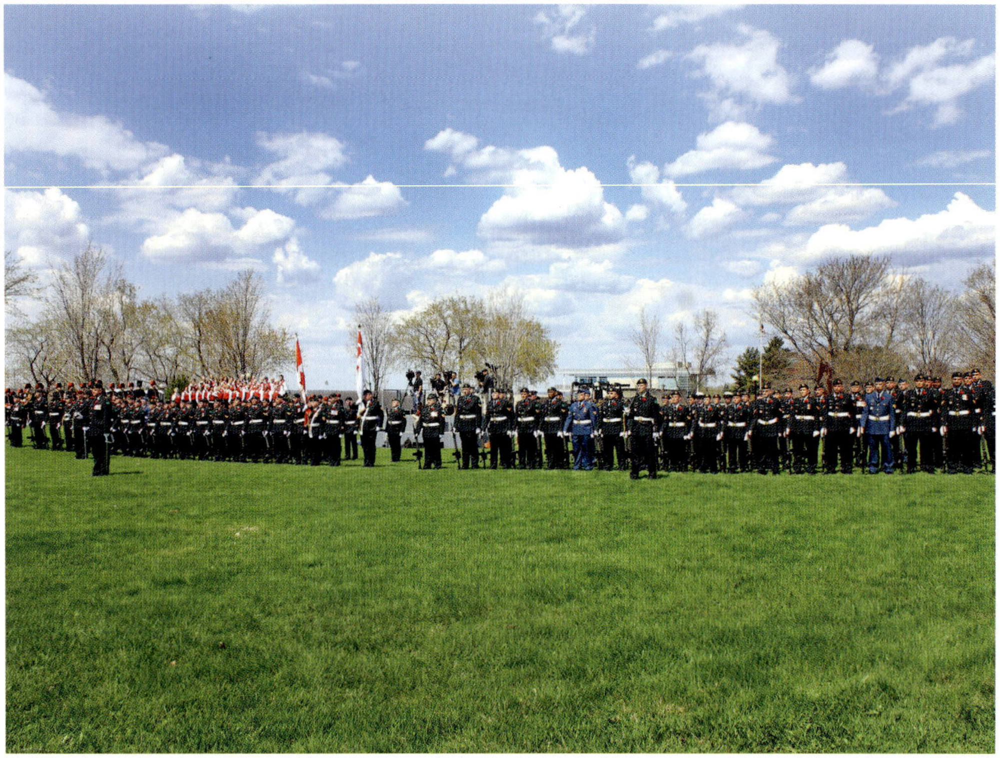

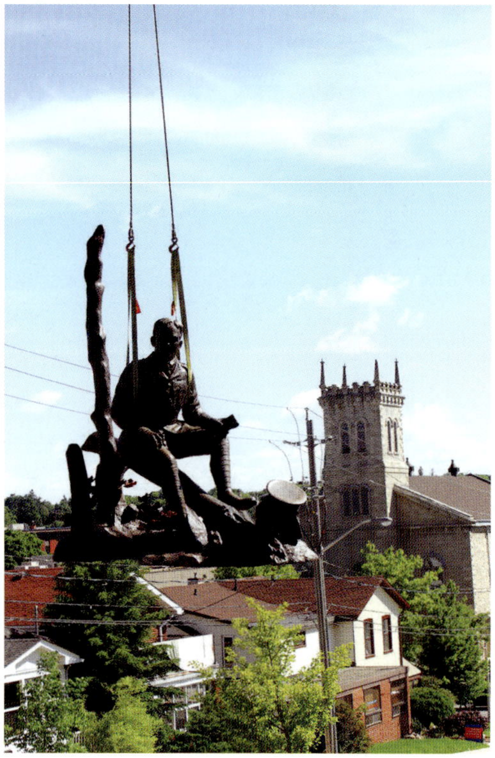

Photos: Cassandra Koch

The bronze had been requested large. At 150-percent life-size, a seated figure would be substantial enough to suit both the Ottawa and the Guelph installation sites. In Ottawa, the McCrae portrait was to install in Artillery Park, a narrow strip of land on Green Island. Sussex Drive runs past the park, past the international embassies, official residences and then to Rideau Hall, home of Canada's Governor General. The tall bronze saplings against the Ottawa skyline would make it easy to spot McCrae's portrait while driving past on this busy street.

Many guests and military personnel had a part in the national unveiling ceremony. Koen Verlaeckt, Belgian Secretary General for Foreign Affairs from Flanders, expressed heartfelt thanks from the people of his nation for Canada's war effort and their ". . . gratitude for the ultimate sacrifice that more than 14,000 young men from this great country made a century ago in Flanders Fields."

In Guelph the following month, the duplicate portrait sat at the top of a long slope from street level to the Guelph Civic Museum. The landscape was designed with a pattern of earthen trenches, and the plantings around them would become more exquisite with time. Lieutenant Colonel John McCrae commanded a panoramic view of his home town near the foot of its imposing stone basilica. Governor General David Johnston spoke to a large assembly on the Civic Museum terrace. His words unfolded around the ancient Greek meaning of the word 'poem'—'to create'. Surely McCrae's words to "In Flanders Fields" created coherence and resolution of the inherent dilemma of military service.

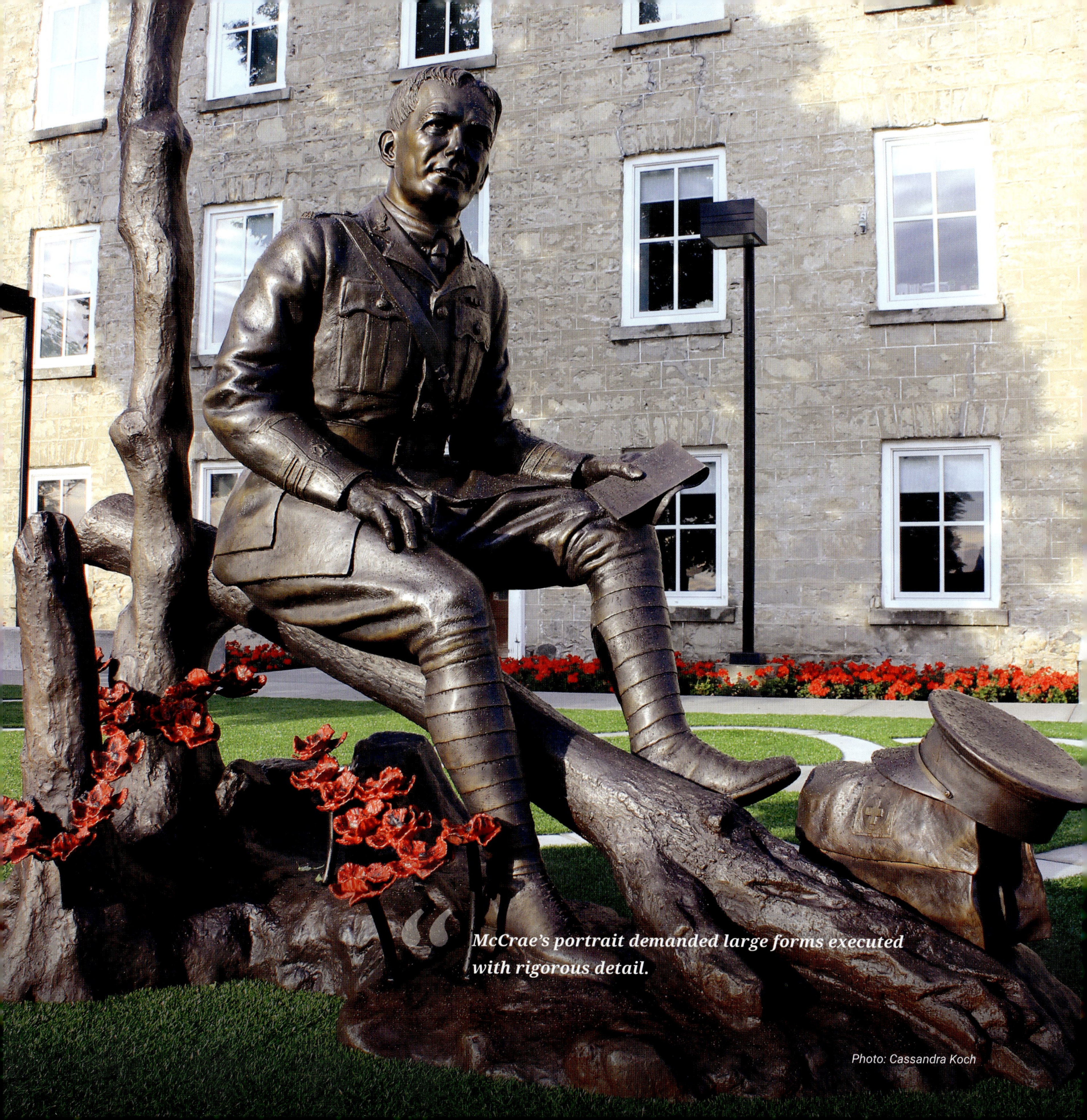

McCrae's portrait demanded large forms executed with rigorous detail.

Photo: Cassandra Koch

Work at the Trestle

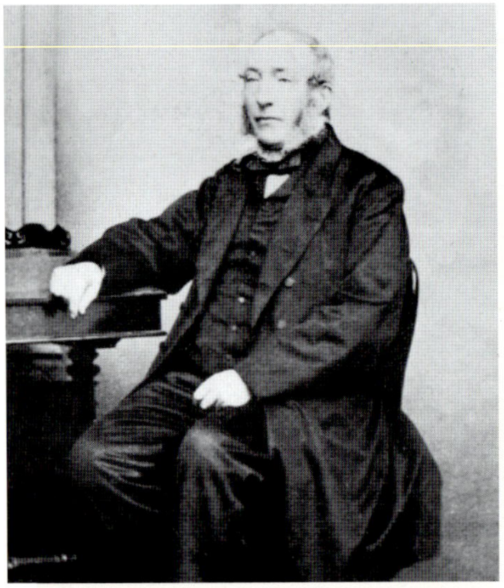

Thomas Timmis Vernon Smith (1824–1890)

Civil Engineer

Thomas Timmis Vernon Smith was born to one of the oldest families in England involved with the iron and steel trades. He apprenticed with Robert Stephenson, who built the world's first steam locomotives. Smith engineered railways in Russia and in Spain before reaching New Brunswick in 1857. Success with Maritime railways placed him at the centre of engineering for the railway infrastructure that connected Canadian provinces in the 19th century. Vernon Smith was elected a Member of the Canadian Society of Civil Engineers in the CSCE's inaugural year, 1887.

I met Vernon Smith's great-grandson in 2011. His name is Allen Eaves and he was interviewing my husband, Mark. After a decade of inventive engineering in Waterloo, Ontario, Mark had been offered a job in Vancouver. His biology study, machinist skills and training in robotics made him an excellent candidate to engineer and design automated lab equipment. The job was with Stemcell Technologies, founded by Allen Eaves, himself a pioneer in medical research and founder of the Terry Fox Laboratory of the BC Cancer Agency.

The annual industry conference brought Allen and his team to Toronto, where I was thoughtfully invited to join the group's meeting with Mark. After brief introductions, we exchanged business cards and Allen declared he'd been seeking a sculptor for an idea set in Wolfville, Nova Scotia. "How interesting," I responded. I had first cousins in Wolfville, where my aunt lived after she married a railway man. Allen's project revolved around the railway. My uncle had been stationmaster in Wolfville and my cousins had lived above the railway station until its closure in 1973. I'm not sure whether Allen or I was more astonished.

Mark and I were both impressed by the Stemcell team. He accepted the position and we began to rearrange our lives between Ash Flats and English Bay in Vancouver.

Allen Eaves and I soon launched our first commemorative project featuring his great-grandfather, Vernon Smith.

The sculpture was to be set in the Annapolis Valley in Nova Scotia. For the first time, the initiative was not guided by a local committee. I was tasked with creation, the background research and the site arrangements.

> *Smith was committed to completing the line, making it profitable and bringing new technology to Nova Scotia.*
>
> *– Marguerite Woodworth, History of the Dominion Atlantic Railway*
> *The Kentville Publishing Co., October 1936*

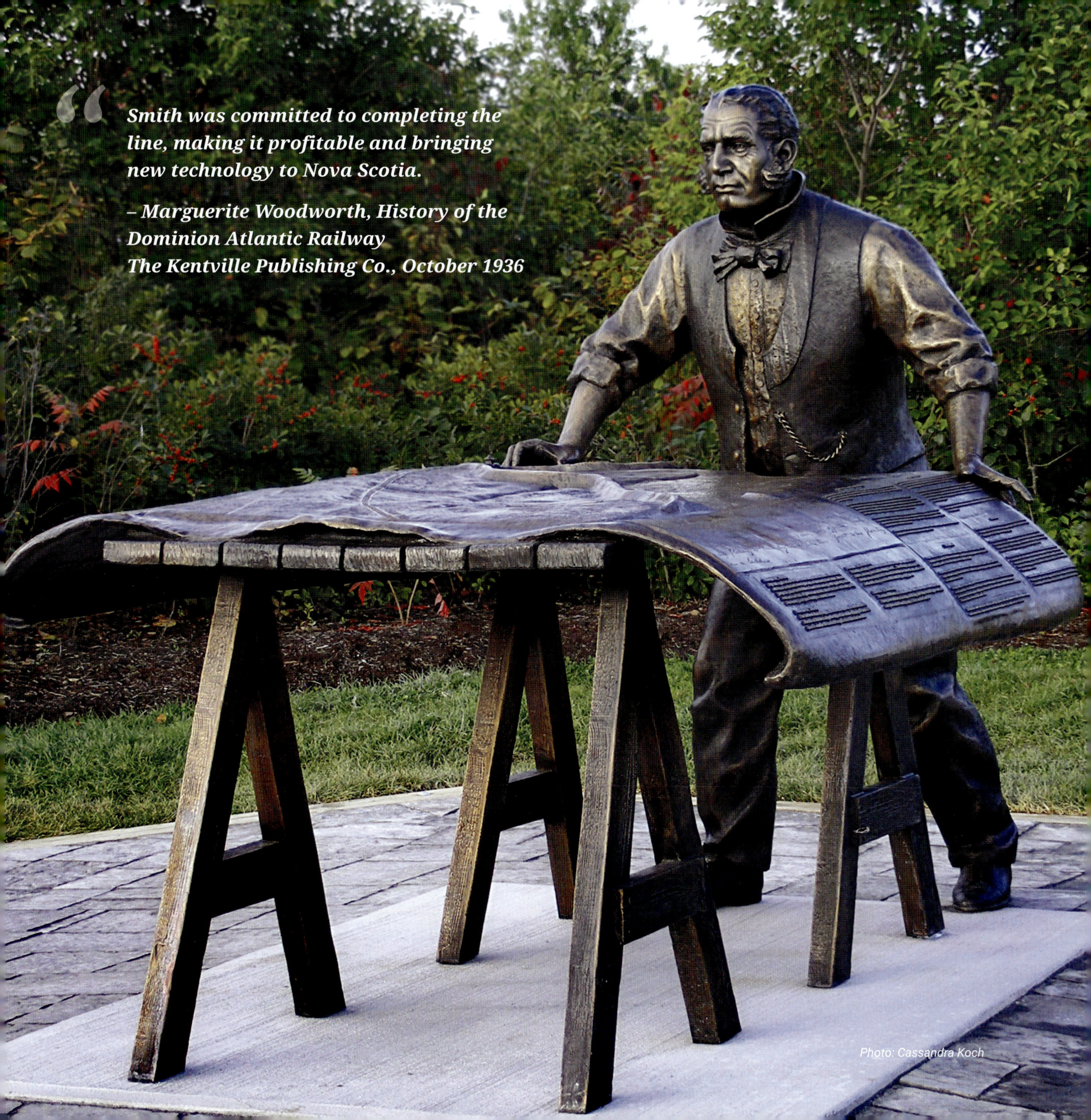

Photo: Cassandra Koch

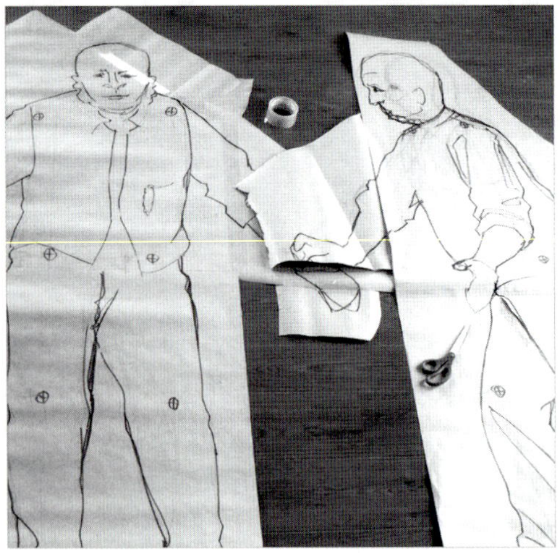

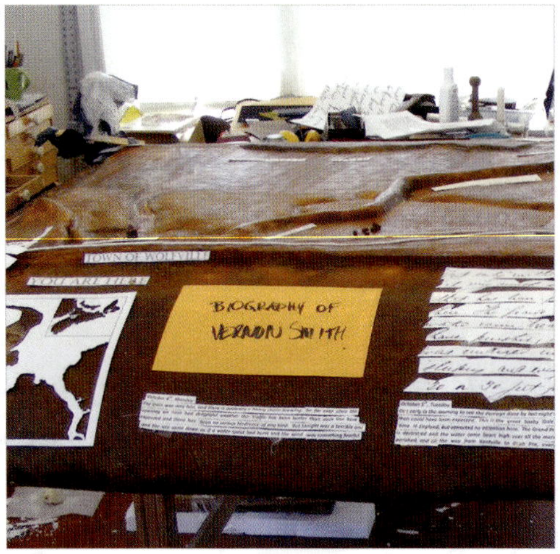

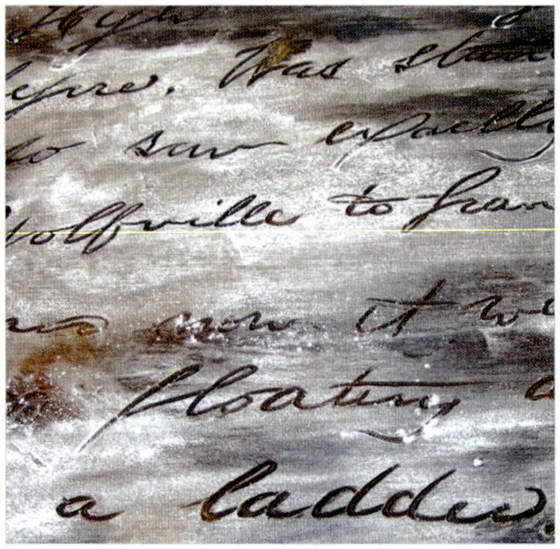

As a child, Allen had found intriguing journals, with illustrations of engines, trestles and equipment, stowed in the family attic. The family had donated these volumes and my search for them linked me to several museums and then to provincial archives in Halifax.

Engineering journals in the 1860s were all handwritten, and deciphering Vernon's tidy, rhythmic script was an absolute joy! He documented the inaugural run of the Dominion & Atlantic Railroad with pride, noting schedules and successes.

He wrote of an increasing storm in early October. His firsthand account of the hurricane's destruction on the morning of October 5th was startling.

Further research showed that Vernon's storm story started in England with Stephen Saxby's prediction of a terrible gale that would sweep the Atlantic Seaboard. Warnings had been printed in North American newspapers in 1868 and, despite his flawed logic, the gale arrived precisely as promised on October 5th, 1869. It struck the Bay of Fundy with full force, breaching dikes that protected acres of low farmland from the tide. Fearsome floods raged several miles inland and long sections of the newly-constructed Windsor & Annapolis Railway were washed out to sea.

A sculpture site was needed. It was summer in the Annapolis Valley and I was keen for a visit with my Aunt Ellen and the Van Blarcom cousins who lived there. I also wanted to revisit Nova Scotia's geography. I'd first seen this landscape when I was 15 years old, but didn't then appreciate the dike system and how it sheltered coastal communities. The Wolfville team, led by Mayor Bob Stead and town planner Gregg Morrison, were supportive at every step of the site selection process.

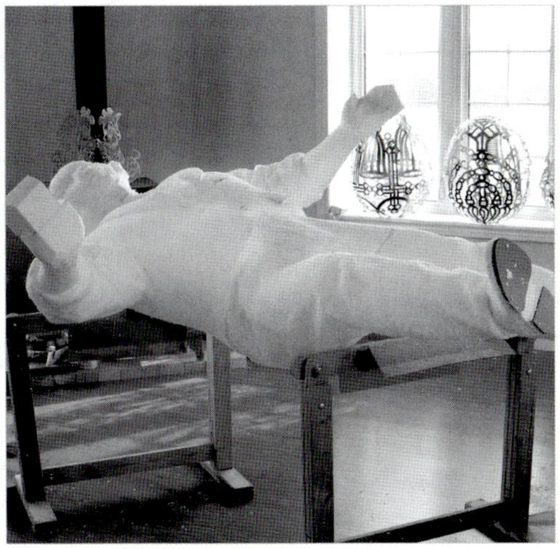

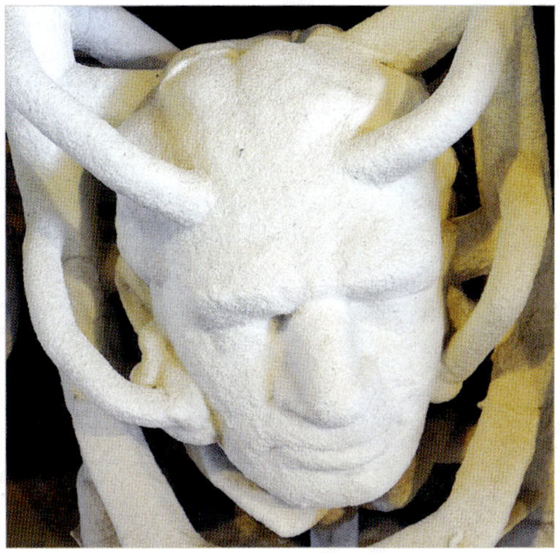

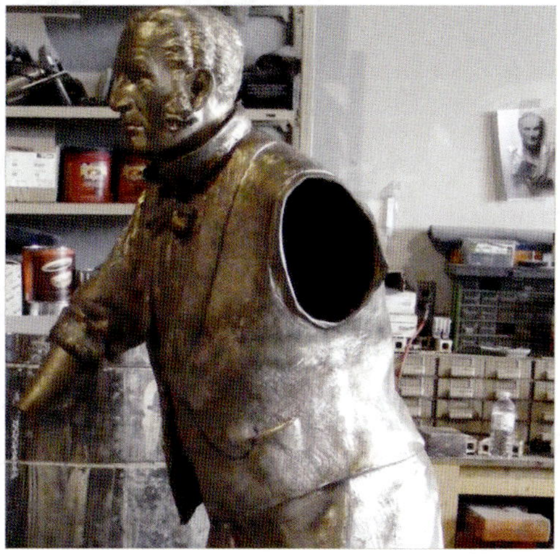

With Allen's input, I resolved the design for *Work at the Trestle*. Vernon would stare across a map spread over an emergency worktable. He'd cast an unyielding bronze gaze across the besieged dike lands to the east. Miraculously, a local railway historian, Jay Underwood, found a photo of Vernon Smith in the McGill University Archives and I began to sculpt.

Having read about Vernon's endless hours on the muddy tidal flats of the Minas Basin, I dressed him in heavy workpants. The cut of his shirt had to be accurate to the time period and I included the chain of an engineer's pocket watch. I decided that he'd removed muddy boots for his late-night engineering session. In decent leather shoes, Vernon would be perceived as a professional rather than a ruffian.

Orienting the foundation work for an installation hundreds of miles from the studio was a new challenge for which the internet was a perfect tool. My parents and sister Jean, happened to be in Nova Scotia while I was planning for Vernon in the studio. With a compass in Waterfront Park, they established an exact direction along the edge of a concrete walkway. That same walkway could be seen in an aerial map that I viewed online from Ontario. I could align the sculpture's foundation so that Vernon looked directly east toward Grand Pré.

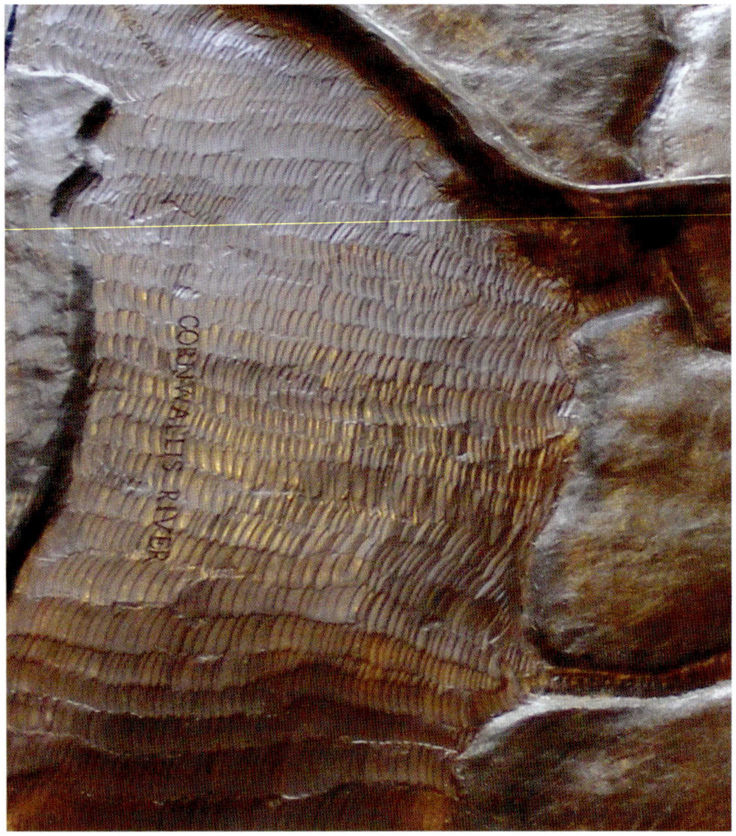

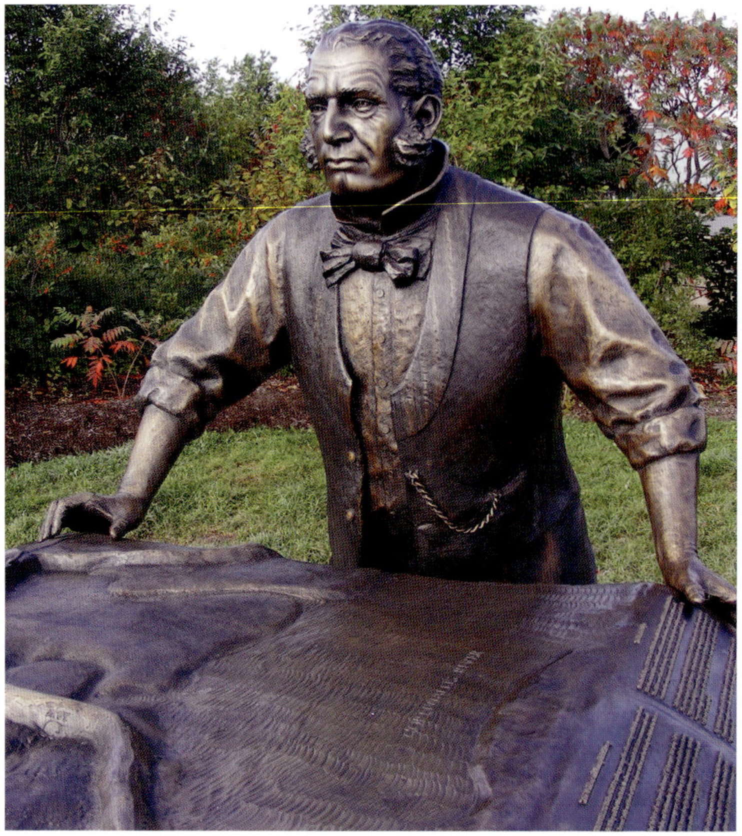

Vernon's large map was sculpted to scale and I chose to present the shoreline as it appeared in contemporary maps, rather than recreating waterfront shapes from the 1800s. The map's dimensional top surface showed Wolfville and the connecting railway embankment that continues to Grand Pré. The edges of the map held texts that told of Vernon Smith, the famous gale, the history of the W & A Railway and of the tidal dikes.

"Vernon's bronze map drains rainwater, just like the tide's patterns on the shore!" wrote one Californian guest to Wolfville's mayor. She was thrilled to see the landscape of the area demonstrated in an interactive bronze in a way she could not have imagined it by standing at the water's edge.

Mark and I headed east into the autumn sunshine with bronzed Vernon trussed carefully into a rental truck with his huge map and supporting trestles. We delivered the bronzes to Wolfville and the town's crew did a meticulous installation in Waterfront Park.

Dedication Day dawned still and golden, though Mark and I were startled awake by a phone call. The heavens had opened over Wellesley. Back home, the Flats was being rescued from floodwaters. Mark and I engaged in a series of tense phone calls over the following hour. At one point Mark dared to ask our exhausted house sitter just how big the rainfall was. Cathy Koch's answer was succinct: "Biblical!" Vernon was not the only one to battle rising waters.

Originally I'd suggested October 5th, the anniversary of the Saxby Gale, as our dedication date. This day was difficult for Allen and his wife, Connie, to arrange; instead they selected September 25th, 2013. How curiously perfect that they'd picked the 85th birthday of my Aunt Ellen Van Blarcom, whose Nova Scotia home had started our conversation.

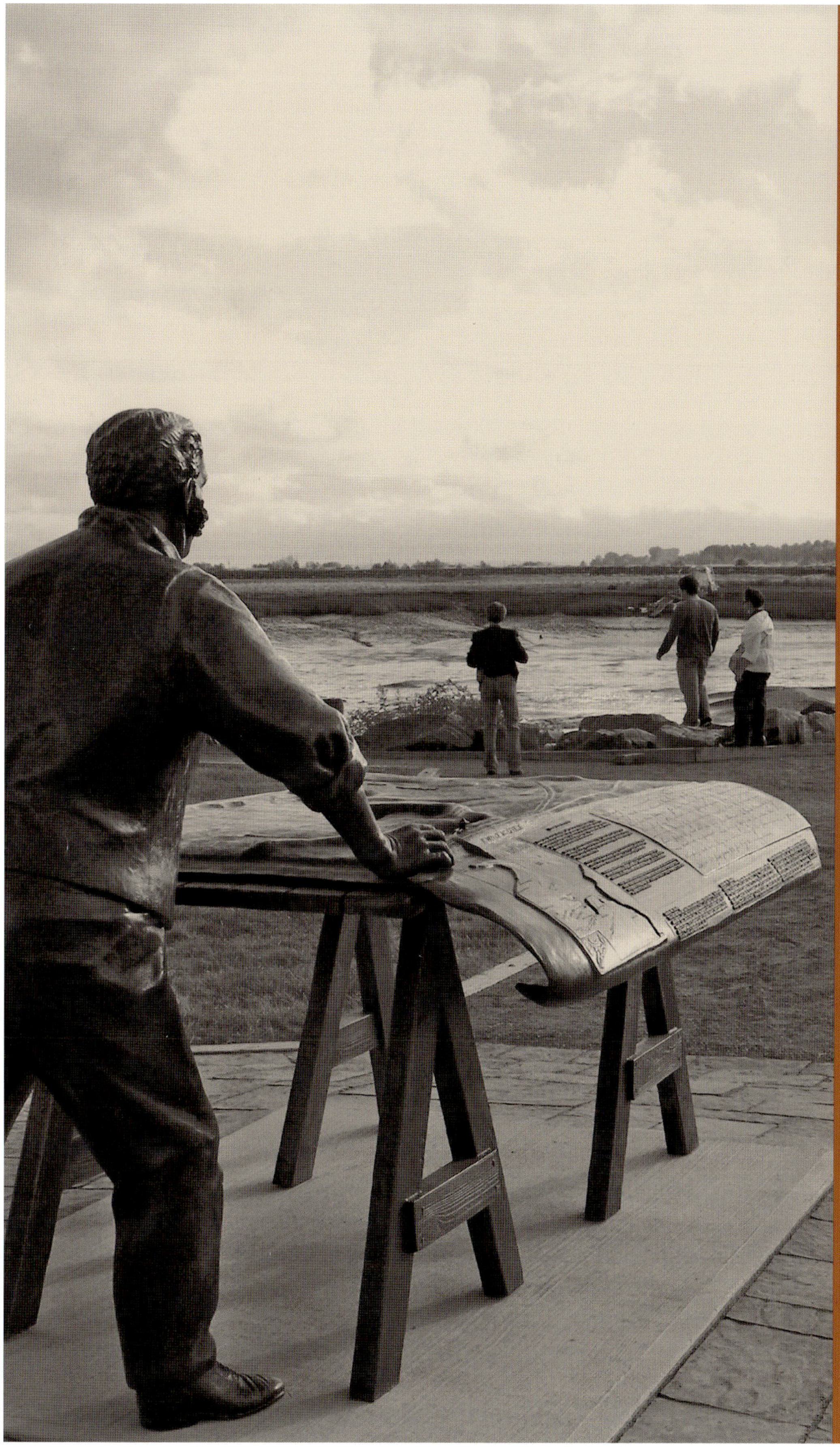

“Out early in the morning to see the damage done by last night’s storm and found it very much worse than could have been expected. This is the great Saxby Gale that has been predicted for some time in England, but attracted no attention here. The Grand Pré, or rather the Wolfville portion of it, is destroyed and the water came breast high over all the marshes. Cattle by hundreds must have perished, and all the way from Kentville to Grand Pré, every bridge was rendered impassable and east of Wolfville the railway track line, sleepers and everything was washed clear of the foundation and in places 20 or 30 feet from the foot of the embankment.

– T.T. Vernon Smith, October 5th, 1869

Dr. Apple

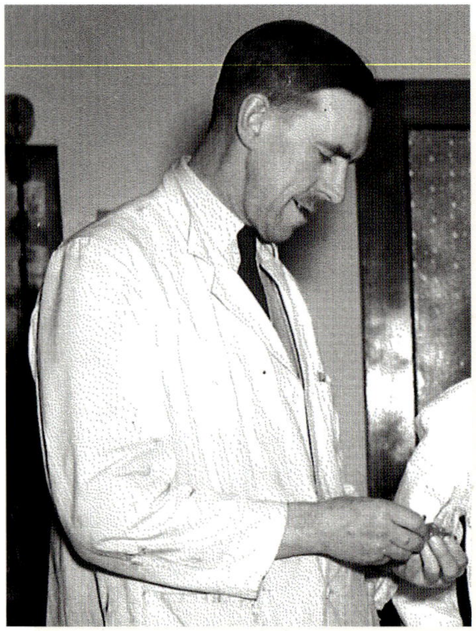

Charles Eaves (1908–2006)

Agricultural Scientist

Charles Eaves arrived in Canada from Liverpool, England in 1926. Educated at McGill University's Macdonald College in Montreal, he also studied plant pathology in Cambridge, UK. In 1934 Nova Scotia exported more than three million barrels of apples to the United Kingdom, so preserving the shelf life of fruit was an important matter. To it Charles Eaves turned his prodigious talents. His experiments exposed apples to high levels of carbon dioxide to lower their metabolic rate. He built the first controlled atmosphere storage in the western hemisphere in 1939 in Port Williams, Nova Scotia. After service in World War II, his research at the Kentville Experimental Farm established fruit storage methods that were adopted worldwide. Eaves did post-harvest work for the United Nations in Turkey and Brazil. In 2000 he was awarded an honorary doctorate by the Nova Scotia Agricultural College and Dalhousie University.

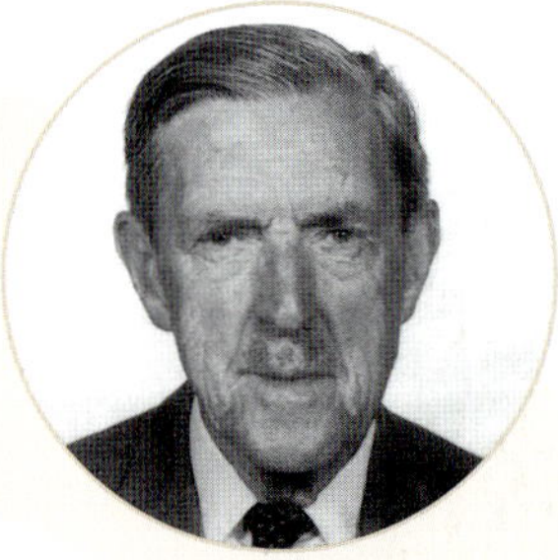

Discussions on a Charles Eaves portrait began as I completed *Work at the Trestle*, the portrait of railway man Vernon Smith. Allen Eaves, Vernon Smith's great-grandson and Charles Eaves' son, commissioned both projects. Charles' autobiography, *A Lively Tale* (Acadia University Library, 1994), was an understated volume about a remarkable life that brimmed with humour and adventure. I enjoyed the book, but as a sculptor I was smitten by the wonderfully angular face in the reference photos!

Allen and I resolved a simple design that showed Charles in his standard-issue lab coat. He'd be holding a test apple and glancing up, as though someone posed a question and he was keen to hear the answer. At his sides sat a stack of apple boxes and a traditional wooden apple barrel. These two items added context but they also provided surfaces on which to present text on Charles, his research and the history of the Kentville Research Centre. We included information on the history of fruit production in the Annapolis Valley. This unearthed such interesting details about the barrel-making industry that we added that too!

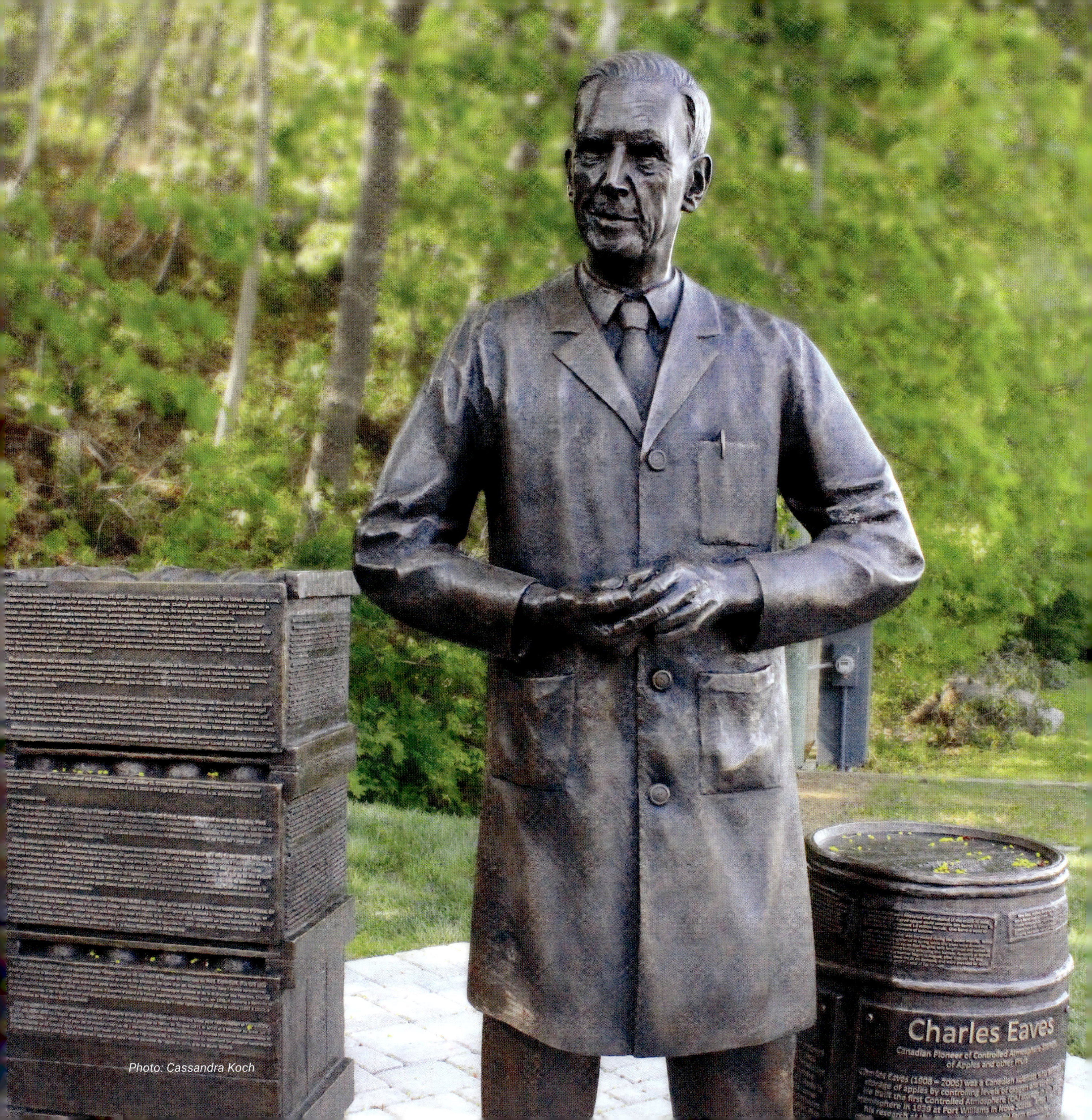

Photo: Cassandra Koch

> ***The likeness of his face is astonishing!***
>
> ***– Connie Eaves***

Interpretive texts are a complex undertaking. The sleuthing and drafting, editing, approving and French translation of Dr. Eaves' work involved easily a dozen individuals. Retired researcher Bob Prange and Avril Vollenhoven of Agriculture Canada Media Relations in Halifax played key roles, as did Susan Novosad and Dr. Mark Hodges at the Research Centre in Kentville. The many steps of compiling information were easily matched by the processes of transferring text into reverse-lettering polymer molds—formatted to size on the computer. I applied these flexible sheets, like small rubber mats, to the sculpted wax surfaces of the boxes and barrel, and then it was cast into bronze. Lengthy text is challenging to cast but the foundry captured bronze lettering that was crisp and legible.

Together with my assistant Cassandra Koch I sculpted the boxes, barrel and figure in my large Wellesley studio; the head study was done in Vancouver where it could be shared with the Eaves family. Allen seemed to enjoy the hand-sculpting process as much as the finished product.

The characteristic twinkle in Charles' eye was caught with the particular structure of my sculpted eyes combined with a very precise tension shaped around his mouth.

It was fun to work that out with Allen, who added insights and fresh details at every step.

It was a curious exercise to sculpt a thin man in a lab coat. Worn over top of other clothing, the simple garment is always oversized. This one needed to hang from Charles' shoulders to look right. Added details would distract from the portrait's presentation. I wanted the large shapes of the coat to contrast with the finesse of his hands and face.

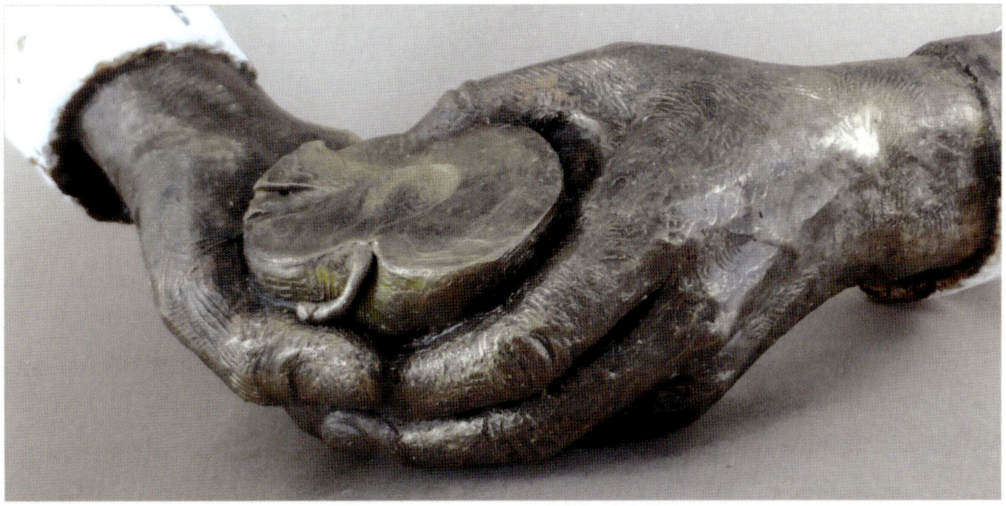

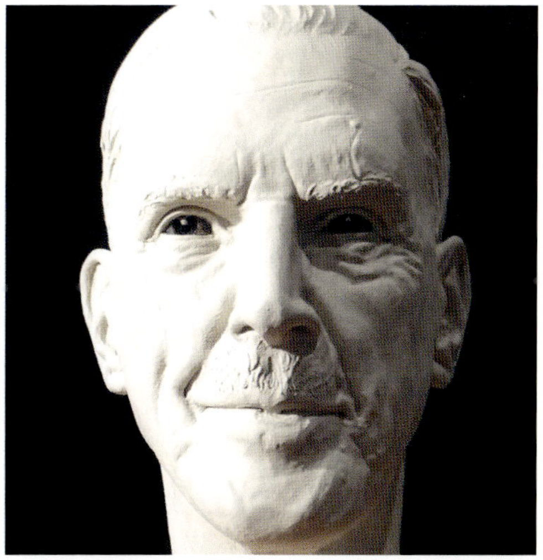

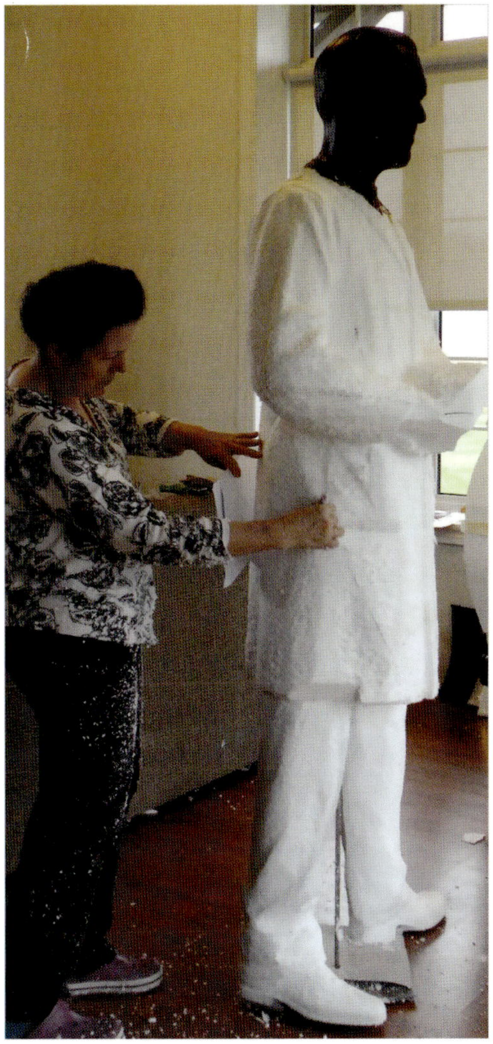

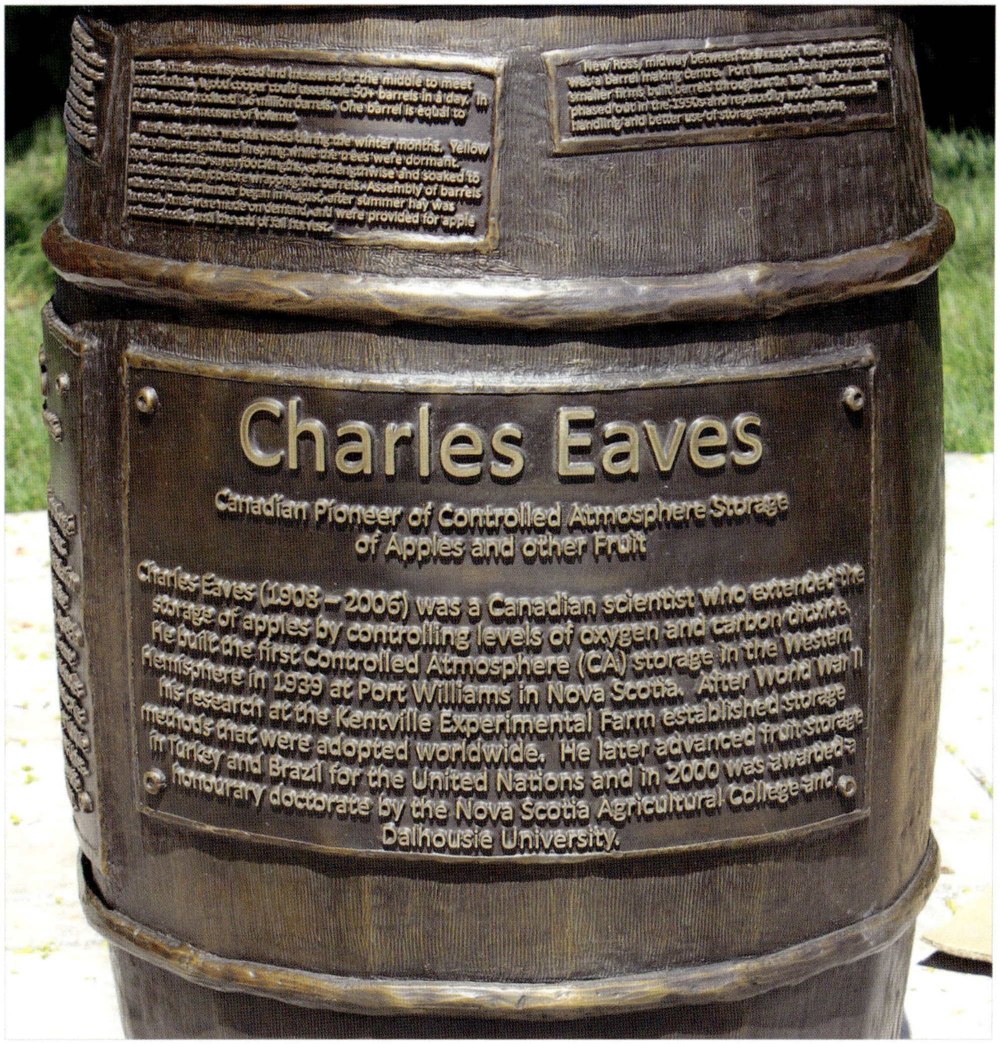

Charles Eaves
Canadian Pioneer of Controlled Atmosphere Storage of Apples and other Fruit
Charles Eaves (1908 – 2006) was a Canadian scientist who extended the storage of apples by controlling levels of oxygen and carbon dioxide. He built the first Controlled Atmosphere (CA) storage in the Western Hemisphere in 1939 at Port Williams in Nova Scotia. After World War II his research at the Kentville Experimental Farm established storage methods that were adopted worldwide. He later advanced fruit storage in Turkey and Brazil for the United Nations and in 2000 was awarded a honourary doctorate by the Nova Scotia Agricultural College and Dalhousie University.

It seemed that every time Charles' name was mentioned, somebody smiled! Throughout this project, people who'd known 'Charlie' recalled his dry wit and engaging approach to life. They were nearly at a loss to explain how much his friendship was valued, but each person gave a stalwart effort. It was rewarding to feel I'd captured some essence of Charles' energy and presence.

Spring finally arrived in May 2015 after a wet and frigid onslaught of winter storms across the Maritimes. By now my younger son, Alex, was a certified truck operator, having logged many hours. His big-rig experience wasn't needed for a U-Haul, but he was the perfect hire to get my castings to the Annapolis Valley. With the bronzes secured in the back and my assistant Cassandra secured in the front, Alex headed east on the Trans-Canada Highway. Mark was home from Vancouver for this road trip and with our older son, Glen, we fell in behind the eastbound rental truck. Our family times were now few and far between and this journey together was a big pleasure. My favourite 'Three Bears' brought considerable hands-on experience to the installation team in Kentville. Their strength and patience were invaluable in lowering the 400-lb. figure into exactly the right position.

Dedication Day was one of the first warm, glorious days of the season. Our unveiling was on the roster of Apple Blossom Festivities happening all across the Annapolis Valley. Fragrance hung in the air and I think there was a whiff of optimism in the Valley as we celebrated a new growing season.

Mayor David Corkum welcomed guests to a sheltered green space across the street from the Research Centre where, beneath the Welcome to Kentville sign, Charles stood with a smile and an apple. Now named Eaves' Hollow, this is an access area to the network of hiking trails that flank the protective dikes along the Cornwallis River.

After the ceremony Allen hosted a dinner, at which a number of people added remembrances of Charles' impact on their lives. One fellow recalled Charles as his scout leader. The man struggled, then chuckled, then dug deeper for just the right words to express his regard. Another woman had known Charles when he was resident in a seniors' home where she'd been a trainee. His kind wisdom redirected her career. She was eventually tasked with reforms in staff training specifically for geriatric care. Charles' lingering influence hung in the blossom-scented air.

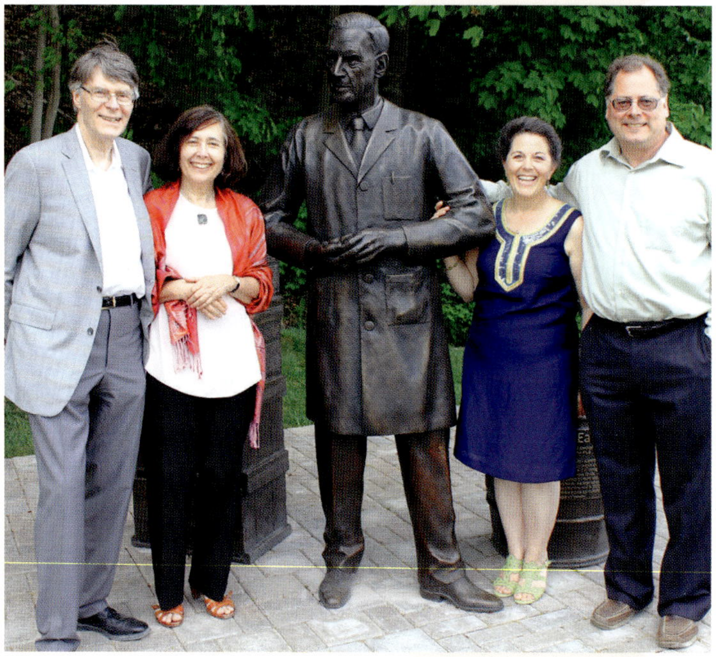

A successful installation is as good as Christmas, when the perfect gift is shared at last! Left to right: Allen Eaves, Connie Eaves, Ruth Abernethy and Mark Smyth.

Commemorating Ingenuity

Dedication Day wrapped up over dinner at the Old Orchard Inn, which lies surrounded by acres of fruit trees in blossom. Allen Eaves spoke to the assembled guests, recalling a visit to Nova Scotia some years earlier when he'd noticed a small plaque erected to describe the work of Abraham Gesner. Born in Cornwallis, NS, Gesner's noteworthy scientific investigations included the invention of kerosene. This new product stopped the killing of whales for their oil. Gesner was considered the father of the global petroleum industry. Allen was inspired to commemorate his father's and great-grandfather's contributions to science and technology, realizing that Gesner's significant invention was saluted by such a modest marker.

Vernon Smith's engineering was integral to the railway infrastructure that became the backbone of this new country. Charles Eaves' advancements in produce handling and storage had a global impact impossible to quantify. Allen was taken aback that such legacies were so easily forgotten when the results of applied science shaped life in contemporary Canada and created the wealth of the nation.

PART FIVE

The Company You Keep

Till and McCulloch

Lincoln Trio

Her Majesty

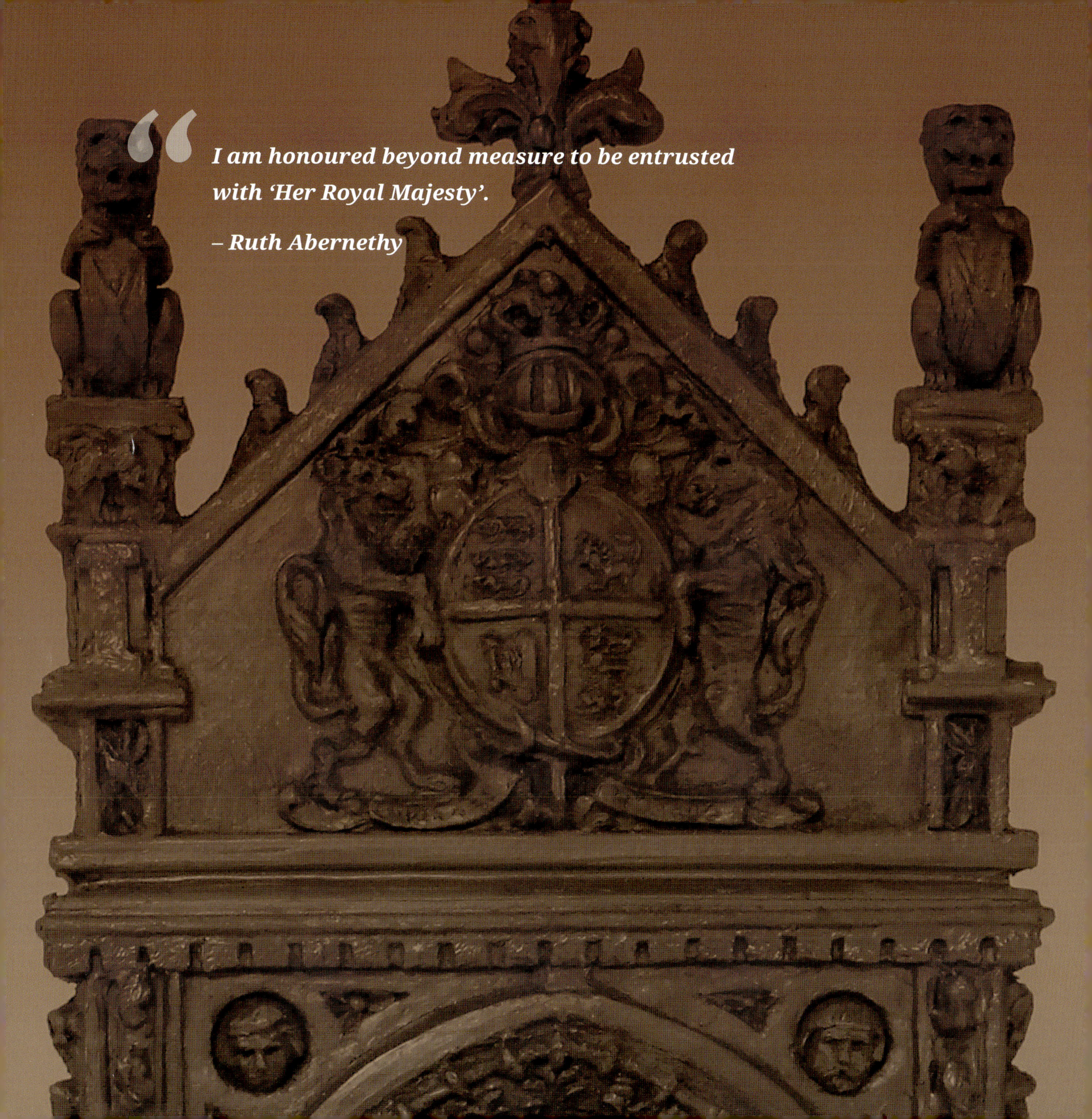

I am honoured beyond measure to be entrusted with 'Her Royal Majesty'.

– Ruth Abernethy

Till and McCulloch

Pioneers in Stem Cell Research

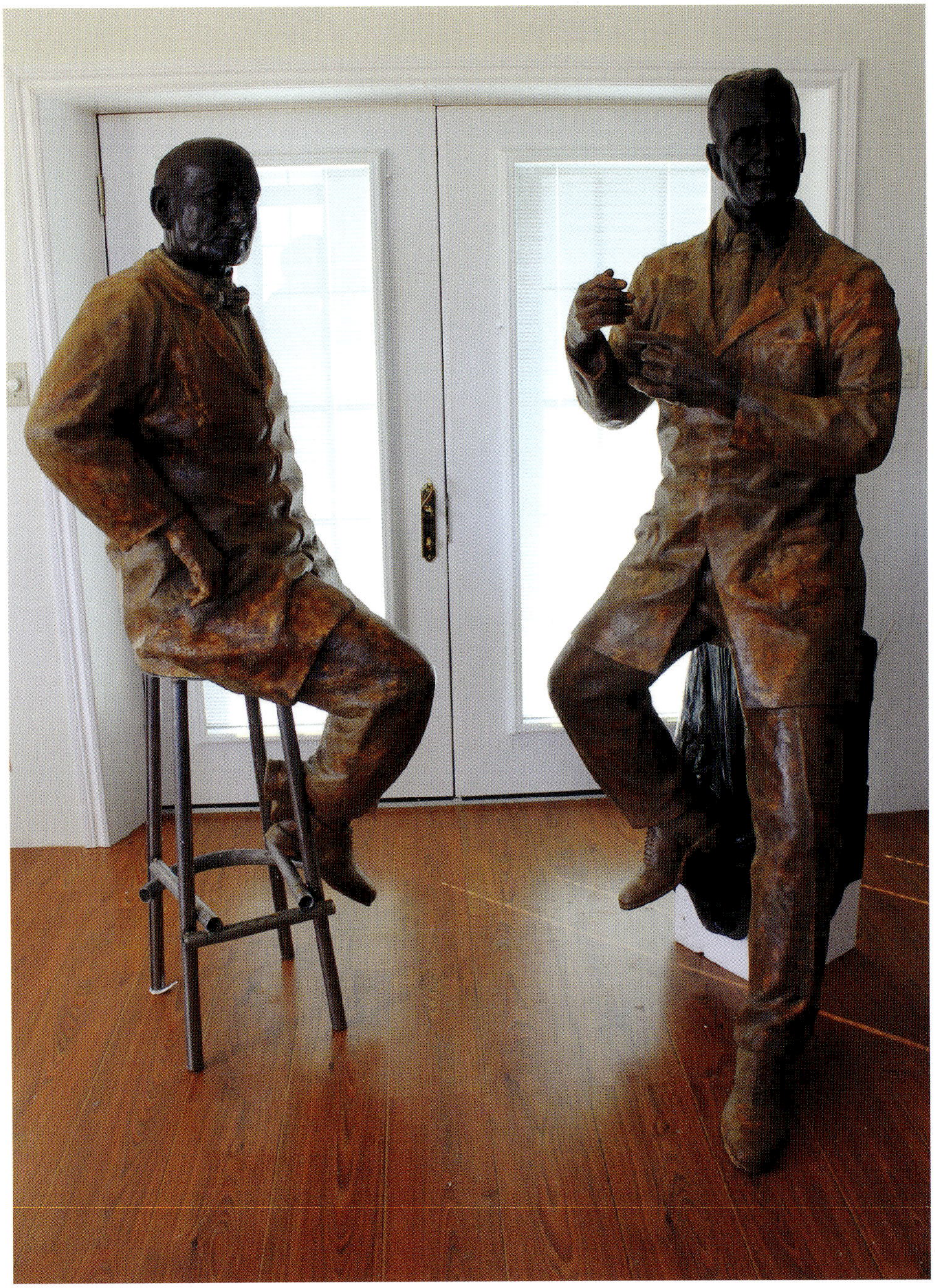

January of 1960 was a month of sequential snowstorms across Ontario. Rural mail in our area was reduced to three delivery days over the course of three weeks. My parents managed to reach the hospital for my birth but they felt lucky to do so.

The same year, a few hours away in Toronto, a new field of science was born.

In the Jarvis Street Laboratories of the Ontario Cancer Institute, James Till and Ernest McCulloch painstakingly studied the effect of radiation on the bone marrow of mice. Their observations lead to a method of measuring and characterizing multi-potent blood-forming stem cells. They proclaimed their find in a 'game-changing' academic paper in early 1961.

(Till, J.E.; McCulloch, E.A. (1961). "A direct measurement of the radiation sensitivity of normal mouse bone marrow cells". Radiation Research 14 (2): 213–22. doi:10.2307/3570892. JSTOR 3570892.)

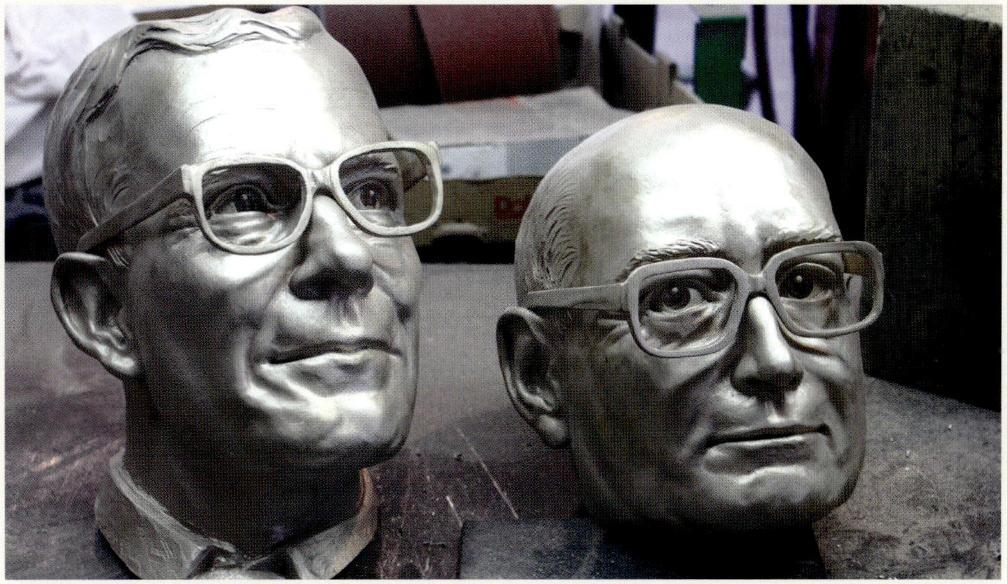

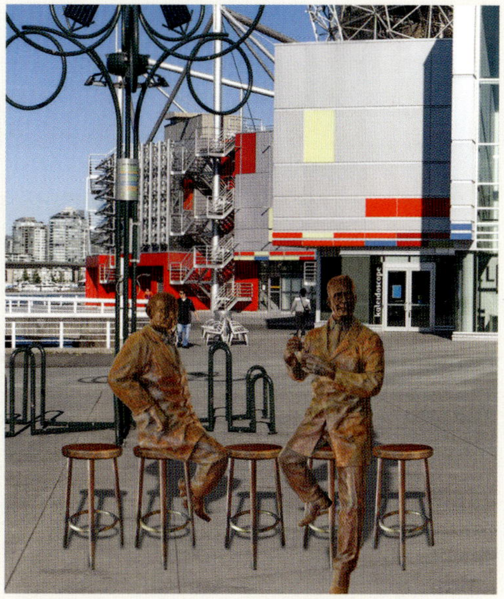

Installation mock-up at Science World in Vancouver, BC.

> ***James Till is not a household name in Canada. Not yet. But as one of the co-discoverers of stem cells, he should be. A Saskatchewan native, Till had been working on radiation therapy for cancer treatment in the early '60s at the Ontario Cancer Institute in Toronto, along with another Canadian, Ernest McCulloch (who died last year), when they discovered stem cells.***
>
> **– *Gustavo Vieira,* Maclean's, *March 26, 2012***

Through the following two decades the research and supporting methodology of James Till and Ernest McCulloch became the bedrock for a generation of scientists at the University of Toronto and beyond. The significance of their work garnered innumerable awards. Yet, as the Maclean's article quoted above stated, these two scientists were not publicly known.

Connie and Allen Eaves were two of the young scientists guided by James Till and Ernest McCulloch. Their postgraduate work at the University of Toronto, with the Ontario Cancer Institute in the Jarvis Street labs, launched two career paths that expanded stem cell study exponentially.

In 1979 Allen Eaves joined the British Columbia Cancer Agency, Vancouver General Hospital, and the staff at the University of British Columbia, where for 18 years he was Head of Hematology. In 1981 he established the Terry Fox Laboratories and in 1993 he launched Stemcell Technologies. Growing from a staff of eight employees, Stemcell Technologies became the largest biotech firm in British Columbia. The staff numbered about 300 when Allen hired my husband, Mark Smyth, to establish an engineering department within the firm. Less than five years later, Stemcell Technologies has grown to over 600 employees.

Connie Eaves followed her chemistry degrees at Queen's University with doctoral studies at Manchester University in the UK. After three years at the Ontario Cancer Agency, she was appointed Assistant Professor of Medical Genetics at the University of British Columbia (UBC) and Senior Scientist at the BC Cancer Institute (now Agency) in Vancouver. Since 1973 her work effectively expanded the legacies of Till and McCulloch in British Columbia and in laboratories around the globe. The Canadian website *women.gc.ca* describes her as a Canadian pioneer in science.

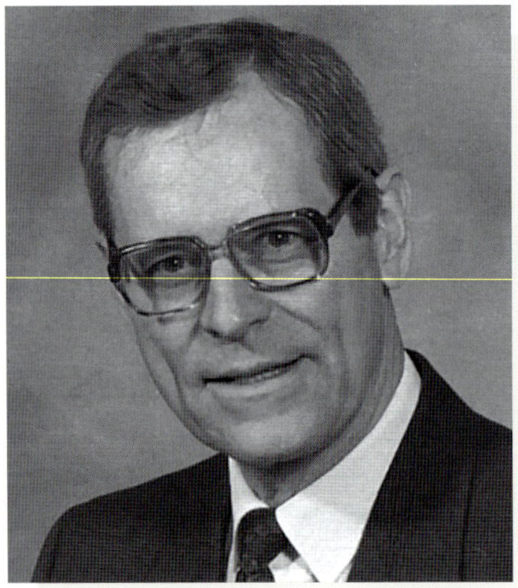

James Till (1931–)

Biophysicist, Medical Researcher

James (Jim) Till, OC, O. Ont, FRSC, was born in Lloydminster, Saskatchewan. After graduating from the University of Saskatchewan, the man described as 'analytical' and 'a straight arrow' continued studies at Yale University, earning a PhD in biophysics. Later, at the Ontario Cancer Institute, Jim's biophysics experience suited a working partnership with Ernest McCulloch's hematology skills. Intersecting points of view stimulated their pioneering stem cell discoveries and anchored years of insightful and rewarding inquiry. In 2005 they won the Albert Lasker Award for Basic Medical Research, widely considered a precursor to the Nobel Prize. In 2010 Jim was inducted into the Canadian Science and Engineering Hall of Fame.

"When I started to do research, I was surprised that one could be paid for doing something that I would have been willing to do for nothing . . ."

– James Till on science.ca

A list of the notable scientists mentored by Till and McCulloch is a who's who of Canadian medical scientists, including (but not limited to): former president of the Canadian Institute for Health Research, Alan Bernstein; the discoverer of the T-cell receptor, Tak Mak; and a world leader in the field of hematopoietic stem cell biology, Connie Eaves.

– science.ca

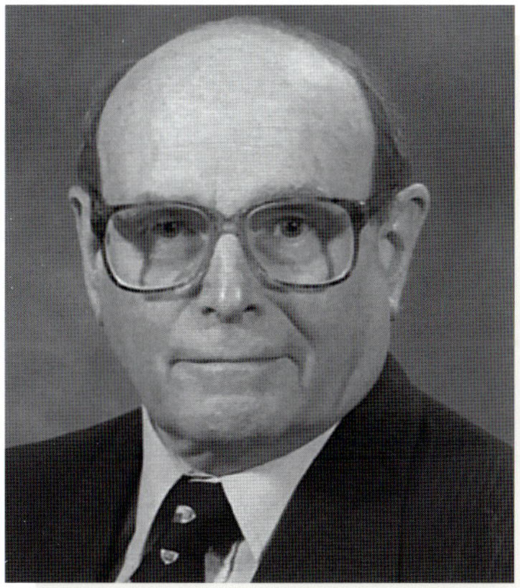

Ernest McCulloch (1926–2011)

Hematologist, Medical Researcher

Bold and extroverted, Ernest ('Bun') McCulloch, OC, O. Ont, FRS, FRSC, graduated from Upper Canada College and then medicine at the University of Toronto. After U of T he continued research at the Lister Institute in London, UK, with a special interest in plasma proteins. In 1957 Bun joined the Ontario Cancer Institute, where he teamed up with James Till. For their pioneering stem cell discoveries in 1961 they received the Albert Lasker Award in 2005. Bun was inducted into the Canadian Science and Engineering Hall of Fame in 2010. His droll humour and propensity for quoting poetry and Shakespeare made him a memorable mentor and valued friend.

"I learned enough about myself to settle on a career in medicine: I did not like discipline—therefore I wanted to work for myself—to be my own boss."

– Ernest McCulloch on science.ca

Allen Eaves and I discussed how to portray Jim Till and 'Bun' McCulloch. Their research certainly warranted attention, but I resolved my design around the connection between the two men and the way they engaged others. In the simplest possible configuration, I seated Jim and Bun in a row of lab stools as though they were engrossed in conversation. At the approach of friends the men looked up in greeting.

These two were a study in opposites. Jim's long, leggy stance contrasted Ernest's stocky silhouette. The moment of interruption I'd decided on required each man to glance to the side. I couldn't have them appear shifty or evasive but a 'frontal' portrait would not work. I reviewed the minutiae of eyeball rotation to catch exactly the expressions I had in mind.

Allen wanted two sculptures, to link the initial research done in Toronto with the ongoing biomedical advancements in Vancouver. To do so, we required a BC site. Andrea Durham, at Science World's iconic dome overlooking Vancouver's False Creek, offered a warm welcome. Near the main entrance, Till and McCulloch would be excellent diplomats for the Science World mandate of teaching British Columbians about science.

Elizabeth Hand guided her video crew to document the casting steps at In Bronze, a foundry near Vancouver where I'd shipped my original sculptures. Once molded and cast, the original wax figures returned east for creation of the second castings.

Near to Canada's centre in Toronto, the Till and McCulloch legacy was honoured by installation at MaRS, a centre that links medical research with applied therapy and commercial development. In the grand atrium at MaRS this dynamic duo has immense presence. They welcome past students and new devotees—just across the street from a building named for their scientific equals, Banting and Best.

Lincoln Trio

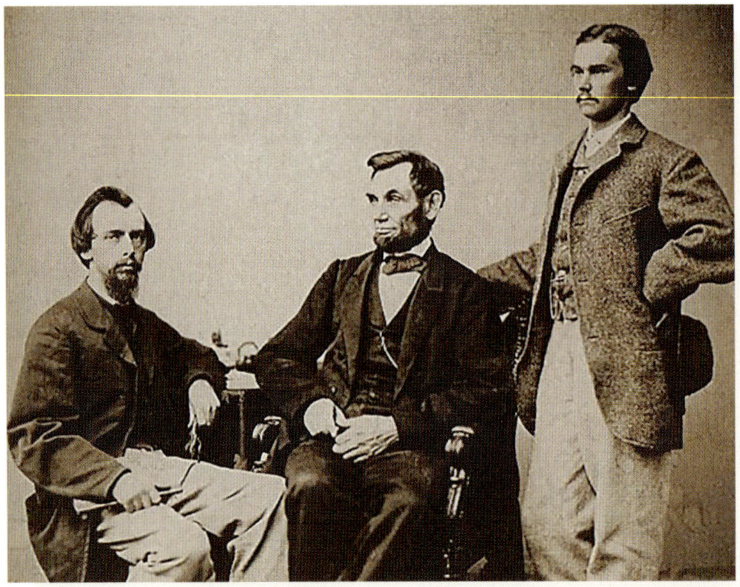

Abraham Lincoln (1809–1865)

Lincoln was born in Hodgenville, Kentucky, where he grew up in humble circumstances. He trained as a lawyer, was elected a member of the Illinois House of Representatives and became the 16th president of the United States.

He led the country through the Civil War—a moral, constitutional and political crisis from 1861 to 1865. He preserved the Union, abolished slavery, strengthened the Federal government and modernized the economy.

John Nicolay (1832–1901)

Abe Lincoln selected Nicolay to be his personal secretary. Shortly before his assassination Lincoln appointed Nicolay to a diplomatic post in France.

Nicolay and Hay collaborated on Lincoln's official ten-volume biography after the President's death.

John Hay (1838–1905)

Cheerful John Hay's political career, begun with Abe Lincoln, extended for 50 years. Under presidents William McKinley and Theodore Roosevelt he served as US Secretary of State.

Another unexpected phone call introduced portrait commissions to depict American president Abraham Lincoln and his two pivotal secretaries, John Hay and John Nicolay.

I thank Ken Burns for his remarkable documentary on the American Civil War. In this series the images of Abe Lincoln were illuminating; I could absorb every detail of his unusual and haunting face. On July 4th, 2016, the 'Lincoln Trio' was celebrated at a heritage site in Pittsfield, Illinois. My master copy of the bronze oversees the Lincoln Bedroom at Ash Flats!

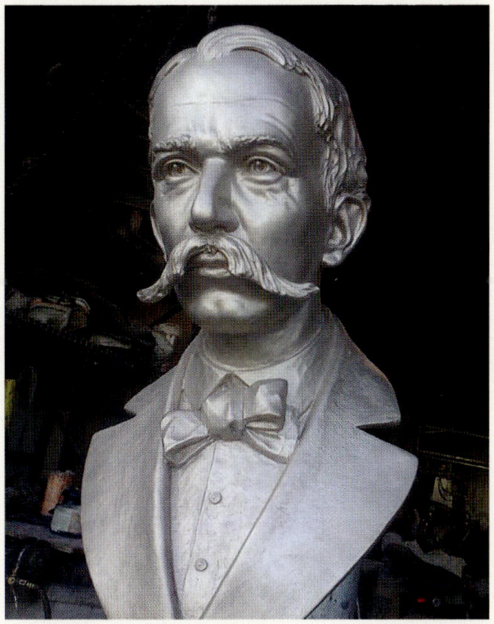

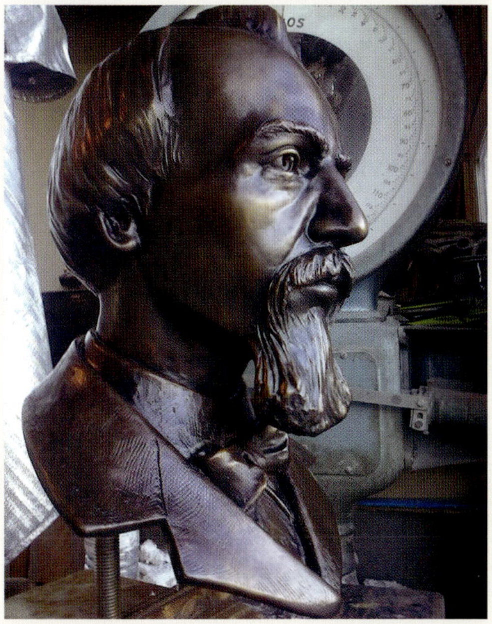

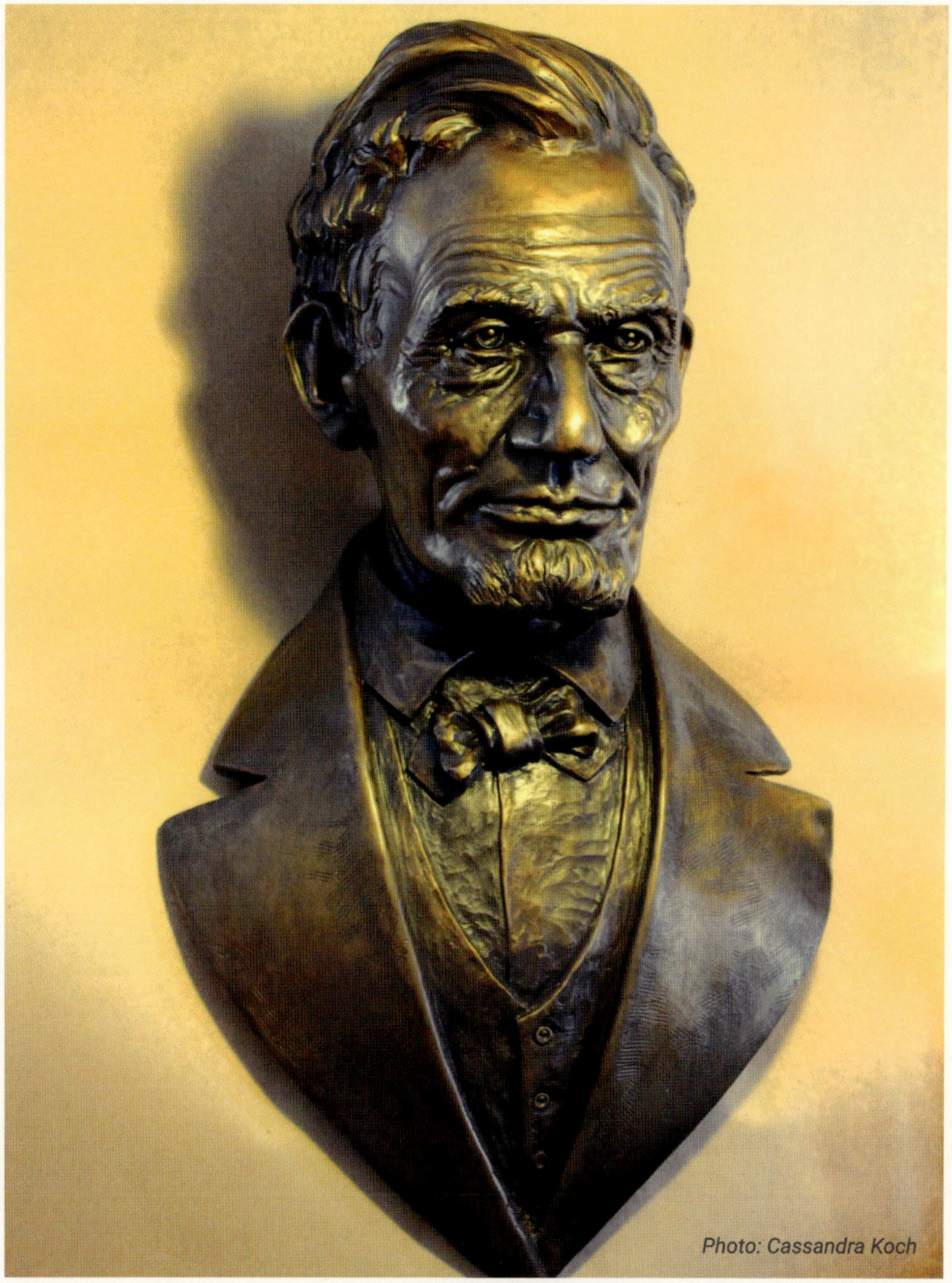

Photo: Cassandra Koch

> ***Most folks are as happy as they make up their minds to be.***
>
> ***– Abraham Lincoln***

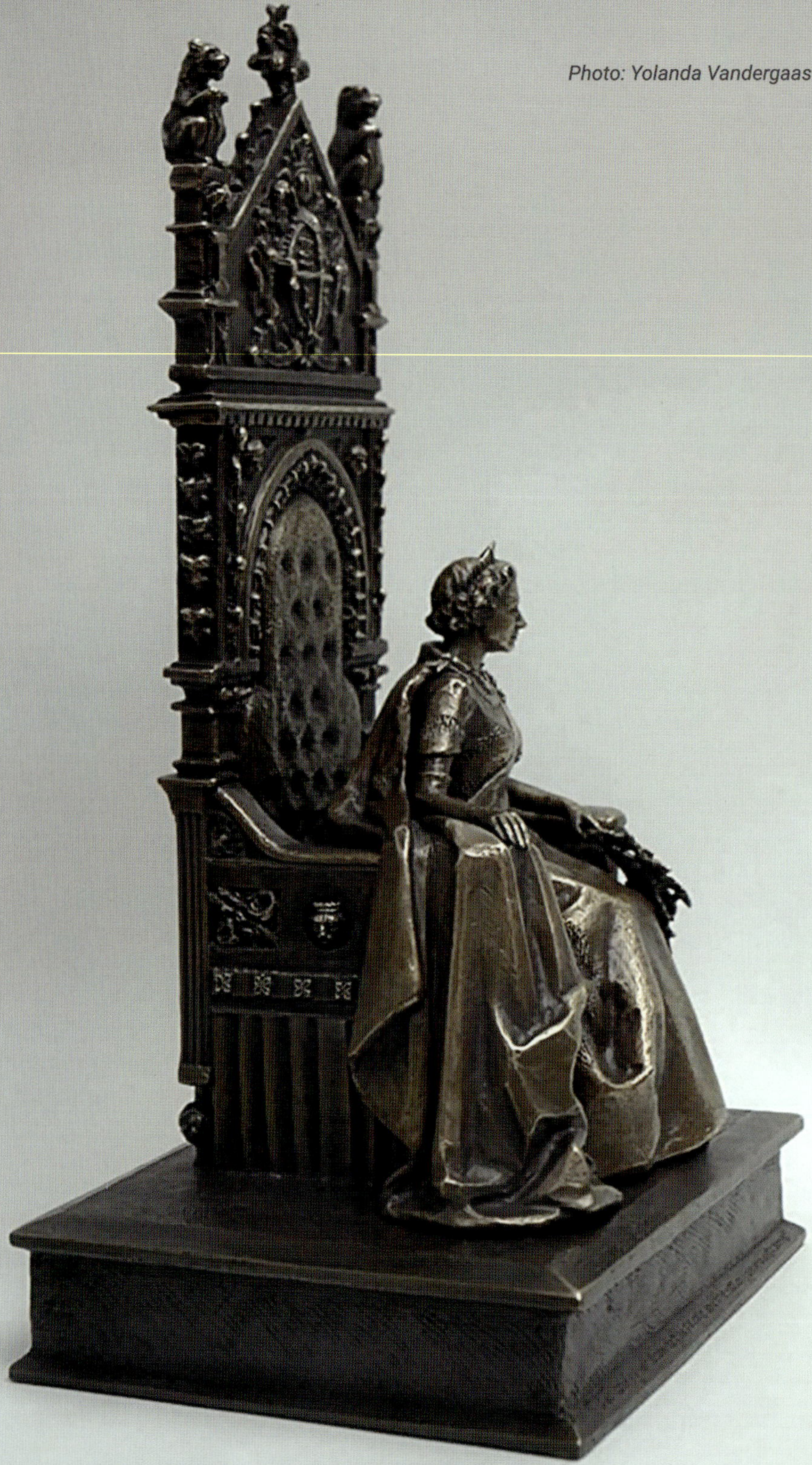

Photo: Yolanda Vandergaast

The Blue Sapphire design for Her Majesty's 65th anniversary on the throne is shown here in a bronze maquette, 18 inches high. Her Majesty received the first casting of the maquette for her 90th birthday.

Her Majesty

I was invited to submit a portrait proposal for Queen Elizabeth II in the spring of 2015. Her Majesty's Blue Sapphire Portrait was to commemorate 65 years on the throne. That anniversary coincided nicely with 150th anniversaries for the nation of Canada and the Province of Ontario. Model-building followed months of preparation, after which I was honoured to be entrusted with Her Majesty's portrait.

My design portrays the Queen seated on an enlarged replica of the Throne of Canada, which sits in the Senate Chamber in Ottawa. She's presented in a gown and jewelry that she wore for her address to Parliament in 1977. In her speech from this throne she quoted herself in an earlier address to Canada's Parliament in 1957.

With Cassandra Koch, my assistant and throne-maker extraordinaire, I look forward to Dedication Day at Queen's Park in Toronto on July 1, 2017.

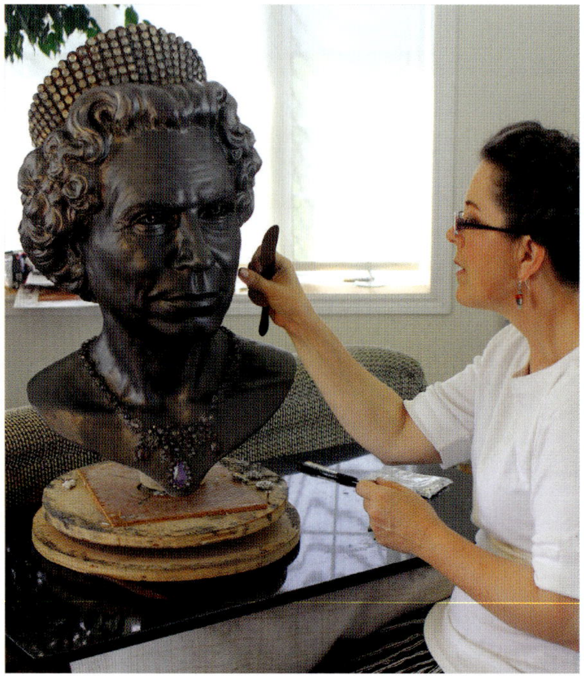

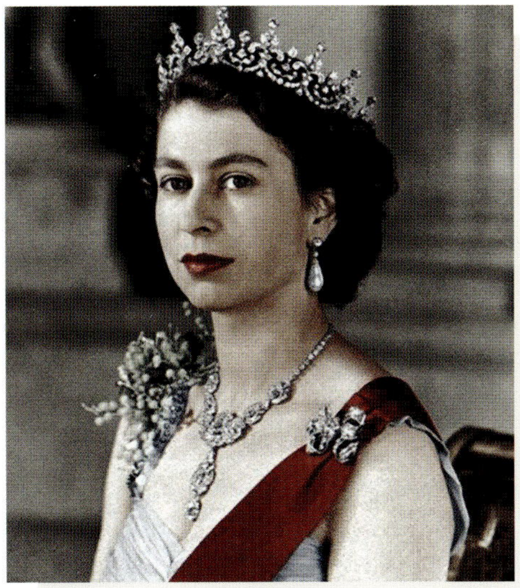

Queen Elizabeth II (1926–)

Queen of the United Kingdom, Canada, Australia and New Zealand and Head of the Commonwealth

Her Majesty's relationship to Canada began with her first Royal Tour in 1951 when she was Princess Elizabeth. Twenty-two additional tours have taken her into every province and territory of this nation. In 1957 and 1977 the Queen opened the Canadian Parliament by delivering the Speech from the Throne. In 1959 she inaugurated the new St. Lawrence Seaway with President Dwight D. Eisenhower. She celebrated Canada's Centennial in 1967 on Parliament Hill before a crowd of 70,000 people.

During Her Majesty's Golden Jubilee Tour of Canada in 2002 she expressed her relationship to this country that she holds dear with these words: "It is a privilege to serve you as Queen of Canada to the best of my ability, to play my part in the Canadian identity, to uphold Canadian traditions and heritage, to recognize Canadian excellence and achievement, and to seek to give a sense of continuity in these exciting, ever-changing times in which we are fortunate to live."

During Canada Day celebrations in Ottawa in 2010, the Queen stated in her speech: "During my lifetime, I have been a witness to this country for more than half its history since Confederation. I have watched with enormous admiration how Canada has grown and matured while remaining true to its history, its distinctive character and its values."

> ***"The upward course of a nation's history is due in the long run to the soundness of heart of its average men and women.***
>
> ***– Her Majesty Queen Elizabeth II***

PART SIX

The Backstory

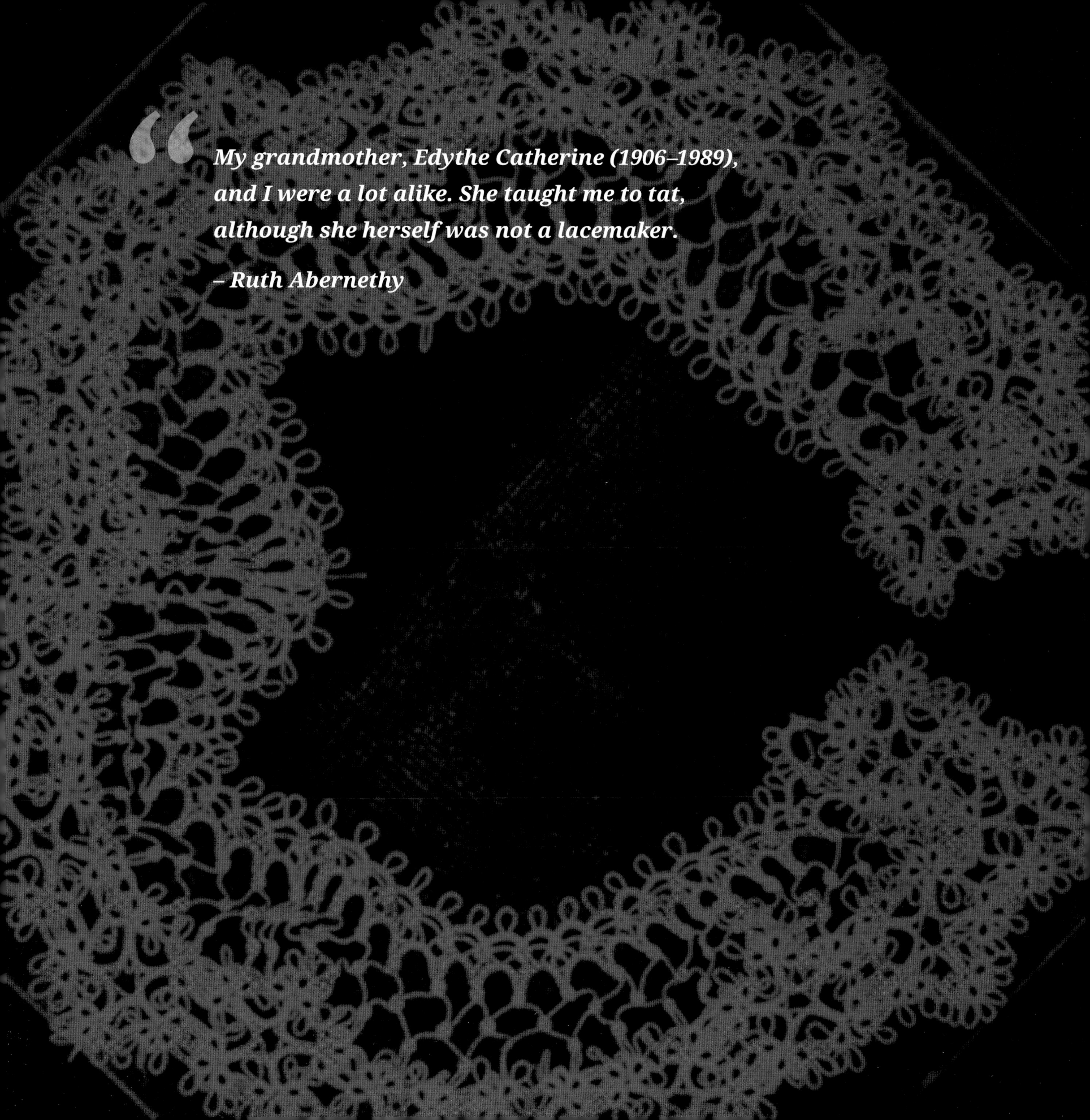

My grandmother, Edythe Catherine (1906–1989), and I were a lot alike. She taught me to tat, although she herself was not a lacemaker.

– Ruth Abernethy

Homelife

With glorious hindsight, I realized I sketched my first portrait on a small wooden board when I was eight years old. By then I'd spent hours with my grandfather in his workshop watching him record his thoughts on pieces of wood. Of course I did too. Grandpa and I shared a passion for structures, music and invention. We both had a refined spatial sense. I first noticed mine in the grocery checkout. I could scarcely keep my hands from packing purchases into cardboard boxes. I knew exactly where everything would fit!

I was enthralled by the ingenious mechanisms grandpa devised: the swivel-triggered live-rabbit trap he was building or the forms he made to laminate planks for a new arched-rafter barn. His jigs to hold wooden assemblies were logical and clever. Grandpa showed me how to make wooden turnings on the lathe; I hammered endless nails into a rough post at the top of his workshop stairs.

Years later I watched Grandpa build houses, with my father's help. They built places to work, to gather and to celebrate. Grandpa's magic conjured spaces that were simply not there before. His barn-building focused my growing interest in built spaces and as a result I sought drafting classes in high school in Lindsay, Ontario.

Lindsay was several hours northeast of Toronto and home to the Kawartha Summer Theatre. It turned out that my hand at carpentry with Grandpa was enough preparation for theatre founder Dennis Sweeting to hire me as Assistant Carpenter in the summer of 1977. Mr. Sweeting's Kawartha Company employed a stream of talented people who spent summers making live theatre in Lindsay. Dennis, a born storyteller, gleefully recounted the tale of young Donald Sutherland's audition for him. It ended with his succinct advice to Mr. Sutherland, "Don't give up your day job!"

My own 'audition' with Mr. Sweeting happened long before that 1977 summer job. Mom, Dad, my three siblings and I had performed as a family band in Dennis' winter variety shows at the Academy Theatre in Lindsay. My parents, Sandy and Shirley Abernethy, learned to play as young adults. Night after night, we four children drifted off to sleep while they practised accordion and fiddle in the downstairs rooms. Those melodies were in my cell structure.

When we were old enough to make music too, the house filled with instruments. I was perhaps 13 years old when we tackled our first full-evening dance. Despite the uncountable hours of practice, it was the best part-time job around. Our parents encouraged us; we were never pushed. My older sister Ellen, my brother Glen and my younger sister Jean could summon music from a toaster. I'm in awe of their talents on multiple instruments. I cannot imagine life without inventive people who speak music as a second language!

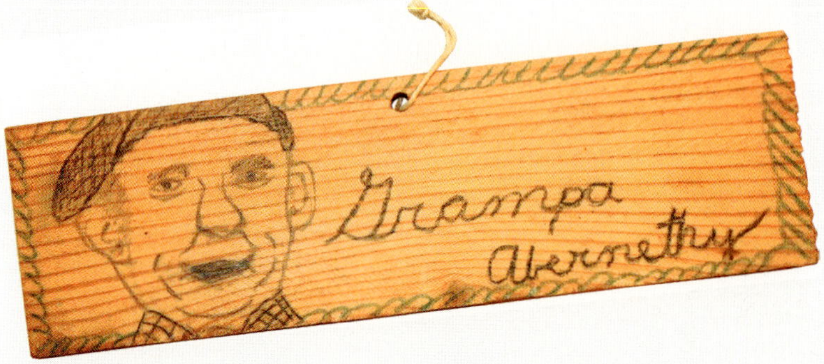

A Place to Grow

My grandparents lived across the hedge. They loved growing things; the more challenging the plant, the more rewarding. Grandma cross-pollinated incredible delphiniums, nurtured a yucca plant and grew a ginkgo tree. Grandpa planted windbreaks. By the time I was big enough to explore, the cedars had enclosed little 'kingdoms'. Grandpa also started hazelnut and butternut trees, grafted apple varieties and masterminded our huge kitchen gardens. The summer picking sequence included strawberries, raspberries, beans, peas, corn and tomatoes, followed by root vegetables and the storage and preserving of everything!

We were all playful and delighted in making each other laugh. Teamwork on the farm was mostly a pleasure. Work stopped only for mealtimes and music. We had farm pets, of course: ponies, dogs and cats. Those we could, we hitched up or dressed or slept with outside under the stars.

A bantam rooster named Jerebome was resident in the basement while he recovered from a broken leg. Timothy the flying squirrel scampered about in the evenings while we read stories. Mom protested only if he scrambled up the drapes. Pet crows snitched clothespins and my brother's tools and motor parts. They stalked the cats and flew alongside us as we four cruised back roads on two tandem bicycles that dad had welded together from four single bikes.

My grandmother, Edythe Catherine (1906–1989), and I were a lot alike. She taught me to tat, although she herself was not a lacemaker. (1987)

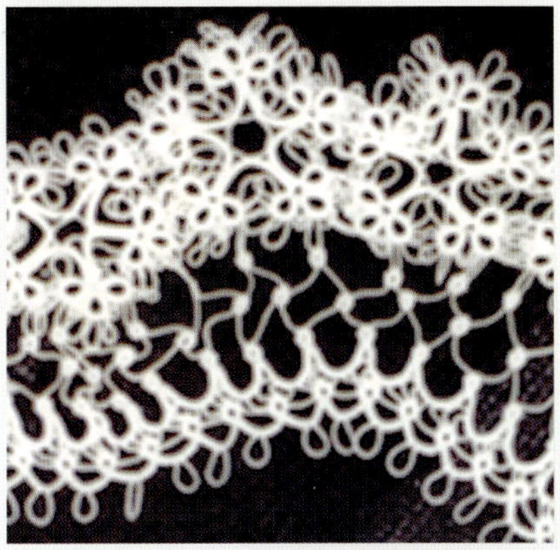

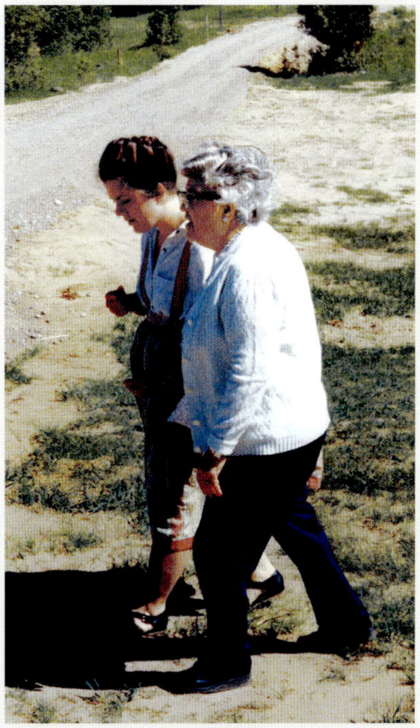

This was one of the few times I ever saw my grandfather ride a horse, although he had grown up with them. Here he's astride Prince and my sister Jean is riding Dusty. (1973)

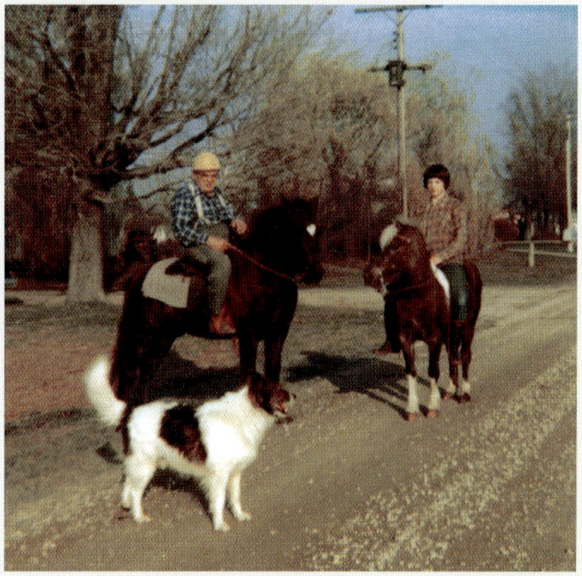

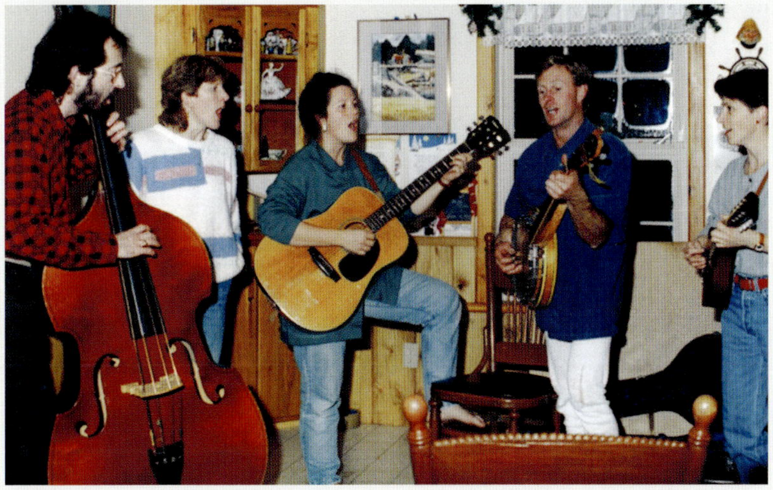

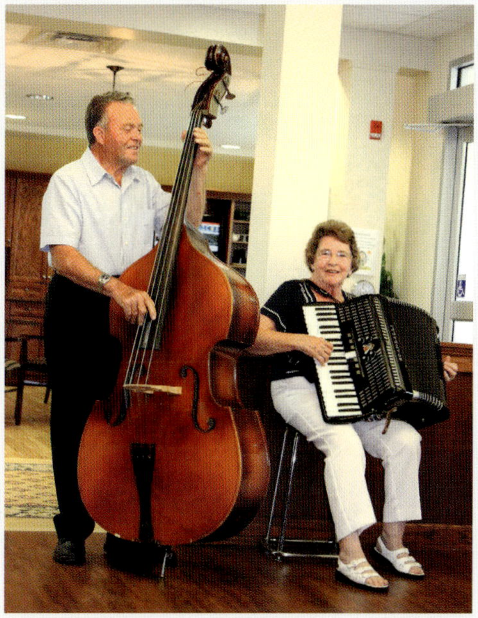

Building Suspense

Kawartha Summer Theatre staged an ambitious three-act play each week through July and August. In 1977 I was part of a crew that built costumes, props and scenery during the day and ran live performances each evening. My exhilarating rewards for this demanding schedule were the intense connections I forged with playful, quick-witted workmates.

Creating props, guided by a designer and script, connected the building of things to an intellectual narrative. I found that utterly satisfying. At summer's close my theatre friends dispersed to various provinces. Most of them continued as designers, playwrights, administrators and teachers, eventually holding key positions across Canada and beyond.

I headed back to my last year in high school confident the incredibly creative summer would play out in my life—somehow. I'd bought a stack of art books from Jennifer Barr and her stage-manager husband, Colin. I pored over them. I wanted to absorb the craft and beauty on the pages and re-invent it! I also found a tiny booklet entitled Design Education in Canada. From its pages of programs, I sent applications to half a dozen provinces. My first choice, from among multiple invitations, was a building and design course east of Edmonton.

Enter serendipity. My college was only a few miles from Mannville, Alberta, where my older sister Ellen had secured a nursing job. We loaded the car and headed west just days after she'd had her wisdom teeth extracted. She was nauseous the whole way and as green as the Qu'Appelle Valley!

After a few weeks in class, I realized I'd chosen engineering over creativity. I transferred to Malaspina College in Nanaimo, BC where I was back in theatre.

"It's just not a risk for a singer . . . to SING!"
– Ruth A.

Manitoba Theatre Centre

Heading east after my school term on Vancouver Island, I stopped in Winnipeg to visit Kari Hagness, a friend from my Kawartha Theatre summer. She gave me a personal introduction to the Manitoba Theatre Centre. In 'far off-Broadway Winnipeg', MTC got rights to new cutting-edge scripts that Toronto theatres were unable to obtain. These MTC productions drew seasoned directors, gifted designers and dynamic performers—and eventually me.

I'd done a little work at Tarragon, a small theatre in Toronto, but I craved the complex building that was done in larger workshops. With that goal in mind, it was logical to fly to Winnipeg in the February darkness of 1979 to volunteer with the top-notch MTC company.

In spite of my experience with props, I was reticent to claim myself as a props builder. Instead, I offered to sew. In the wardrobe department, Margaret Lamb, Carol Case and Marvin Schlichting topped a long list of experienced people who guided my skills. I felt I couldn't learn fast enough from scene painter Bill Chesney and prop builder Larry Demedash. Peter Wingate, Debra Hanson, Phillip Clarkson and a host of other designers put visions onstage. Within weeks I was part of the MTC team and finished the season in the wardrobe department.

Rainbow Stage in north Winnipeg employed me for the summer. In autumn 1980 I became Head of Props at the Manitoba Theatre Centre. Production Manager Dwight Griffin offered this amazing opportunity, confident I'd rise to the occasion. I turned 21 in Winnipeg, with a dozen long-stemmed roses from friends and a very good bottle of scotch! There was a great deal to celebrate.

The MTC Christmas production that year was *Alice Through the Looking Glass*. Props included huge flowers, masks for the March Hare and White Rabbit—and oversized everything! I worked uncountable hours, produced a great deal of work and resolved some uniquely challenging structures. My props looked just like the designer's sketches, which is the goal for any theatre shop.

The compliments for my building took me by surprise and I expressed this to carpenter Mark Playfair at the end of a long day. With a sage look and a stabbing forefinger, he insisted, "Enjoy every moment right now. Once people know what you can do, they'll expect to be 'wowed' every time and nothing short of brilliance will be enough!"

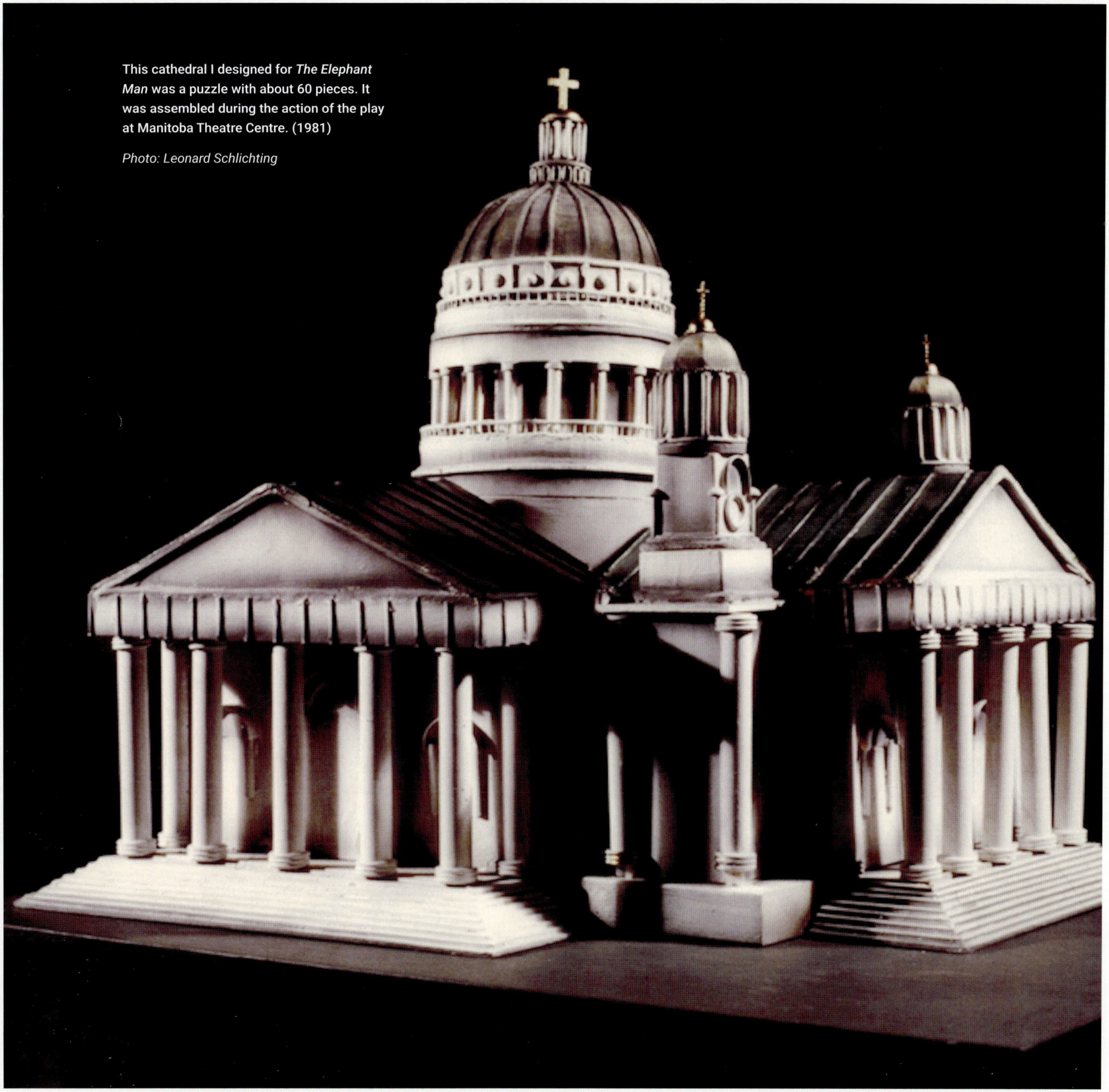

This cathedral I designed for *The Elephant Man* was a puzzle with about 60 pieces. It was assembled during the action of the play at Manitoba Theatre Centre. (1981)

Photo: Leonard Schlichting

Putting Down Roots

Stratford Festival Theatre

From Winnipeg I drove to Stratford, where I lodged in a tiny suite beside the river down a walkway awash in cosmos blossoms. The Festival's prop builders welcomed me while they madly prepared for the season that almost wasn't. A shift in the company's leadership had created delays in designs and stalled scenic building. Technicians pulled summer plays together in an unbelievably short time. At the insistence of Lloyd Axworthy, then Minister of Culture, a fellow named John Hirsch was finally appointed to lead the 1981 season. He was the Festival's first Canadian Artistic Director.

My inventive approach, and a broad range of established hand skills, set me up nicely as a member of the prop-building staff in Stratford. I was adept at exploring new materials. I'd employ the strength engendered by a simple fold of fabric or the flexible energy of springs. A wire structure covered with fake fur and a tiny face became an animated dancing dog in the eyes and minds of the audience. I loved the engineering and architecture of structures—the measuring and planning. Materials and methods had to weave together into believable and durable objects. The onstage illusions had to work for the actors while their 'reality' sustained the audience throughout the play.

What I learned in the Stratford Festival prop shop is impossible to quantify. Around the time of my arrival, someone tallied the collective experience among the shop's builders and it was into the hundreds of years. Such richness of talent in a well-equipped shop, making items that lasted for months of performances, put Stratford's prop department well ahead of other Canadian workshops at the time.

Being a 'full-time' member of the Stratford Company was, in one sense, misleading. Employment contracts spanned from January to July, leaving the rest of the year for other opportunities. I found my opportunities in Fredericton, London, Vancouver, Calgary, Edmonton and Banff. There was occasional film work, a season running the Shaw Festival prop shop, plus specialty building for the Louisville Ballet in Kentucky and the National Ballet in Toronto. The designers who worked in Stratford designed in regional theatres too. New shops in new cities offered lots to explore. Like many Canadian artists, I became familiar with the Trans-Canada Highway.

Returning to Stratford each time felt like coming home. Frank Holte ran the Stratford Festival's prop shop with a deft hand and he was brilliant. He often told stories of growing up in England and weekend jaunts to pubs in Liverpool to catch a start-up band named The Beatles. I hope his whistling of Beatles' tunes still echoes through the theatre after hours.

Each year in June, the openings for the early set of plays provided a week of heady excitement. In the middle of opening week in 1984, I arrived home from work to note a curious vintage station wagon outside my apartment. It commanded the entire street because it was hitched to a trailer holding two unusual motorcycles. Once inside my door, I was welcomed by two young men I'd never seen before. They were on a road trip; one was a university friend of my roommate. The 'friend' sweetly confessed to forcing entry through an upstairs window.

The station wagon owner, Mark Smyth, is now my husband and partner of thirty-plus years. He'd restored the 1968 Citroën I'd seen in the street (the African Safari model) and it eventually served as our wedding getaway car. In a clear moment that week in June 1984, I knew Mark was the perfect partner for me. Fourteen addresses later, Mark and I moved into the house we designed and built near Wellesley, Ontario.

In 1977 Daphne Dare's designs for *The Guardsman* were being constructed in the Festival prop shop. Frank Holte spied these offcut shapes as Georges Kamm cut out metalwork for the show. Georges welded together this assembly of figures and they've been striding across the prop shop window ever since.

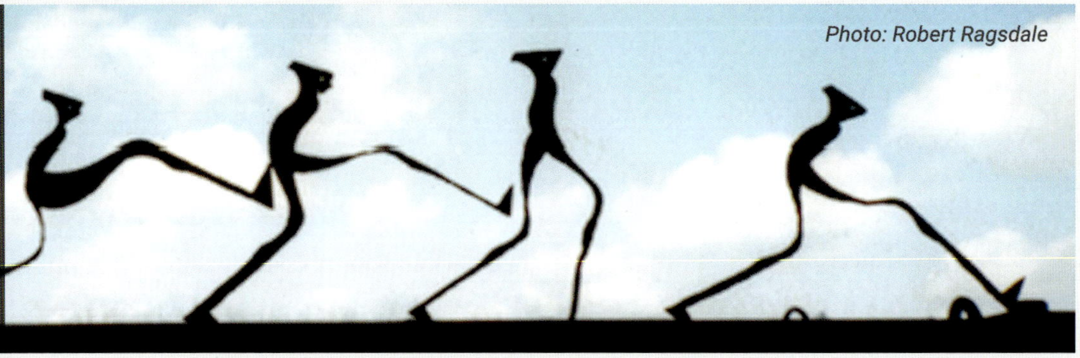

Photo: Robert Ragsdale

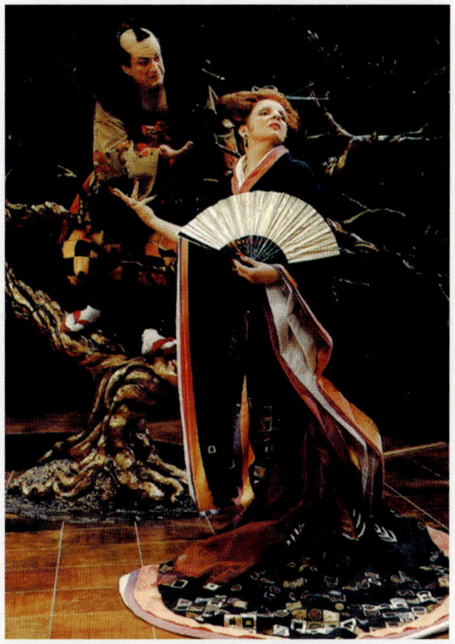

Georges Kamm and I created a bonsai tree for the Stratford production of *The Mikado*, 1982. It was one element in a remarkable design by Susan Benson. Shown here in character, Eric Donkin as Ko-Ko (left) and Christina James as Katisha (right).

Photo: Robert Ragsdale

A moment of fun with Frank Holte, head of the Festival Theatre prop shop.

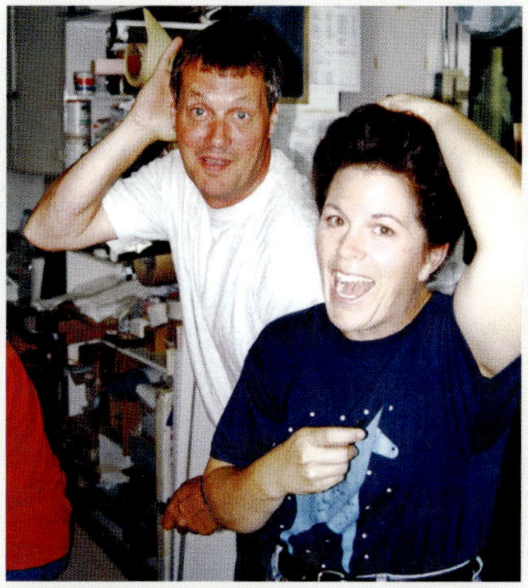

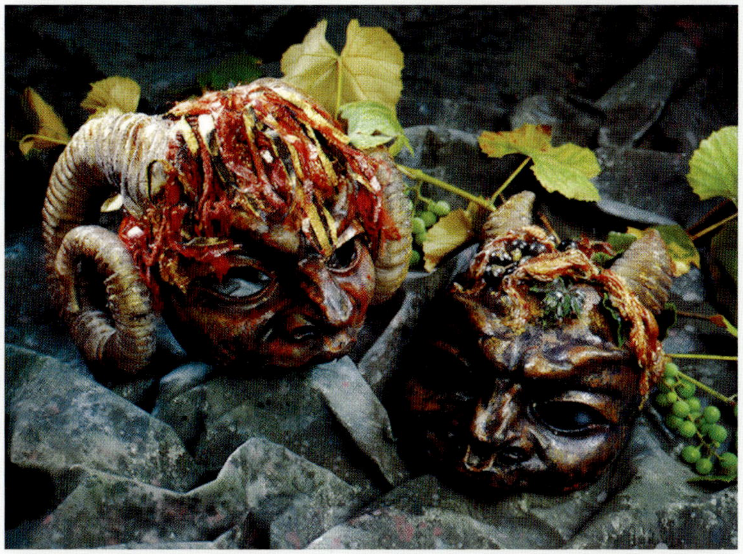

Masks for *Romeo and Juliet* were molded with buckram and tissue paper over sculpted character faces. Sliced fabrics and woven tubing over a wire form make the forelock and lightweight horns.

Photo: Stratford Festival Archives

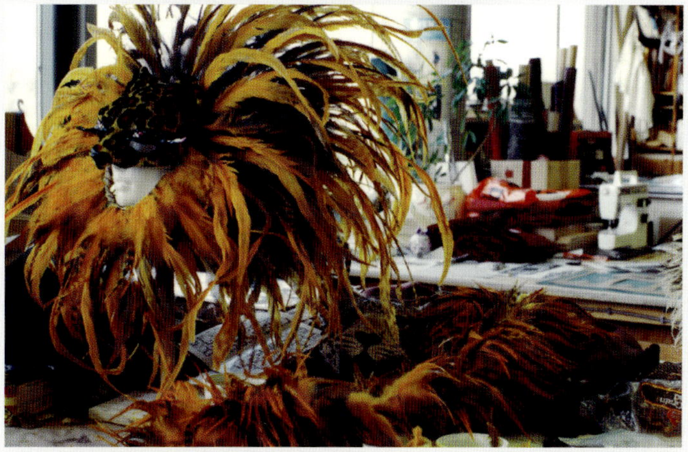

Leopard headdress/ mask, made with same methodology as an Elizabethan ruff.

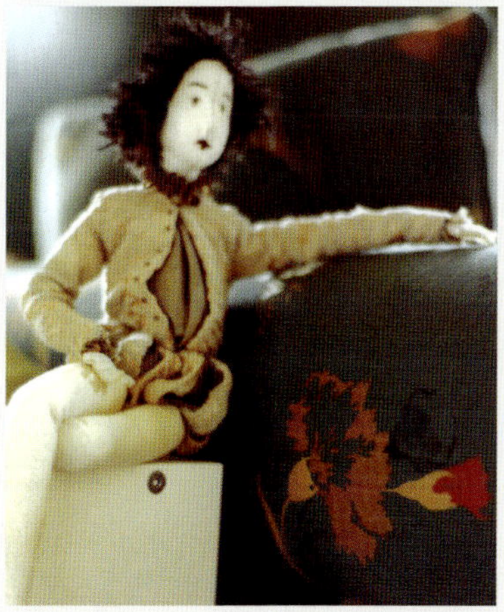

From costume sketches for the plays in Stratford, I created a series of 'dolls'. They were weighted and jointed for life-like movement and dressed in remnants of fabrics that were worn onstage.

Ash Flats

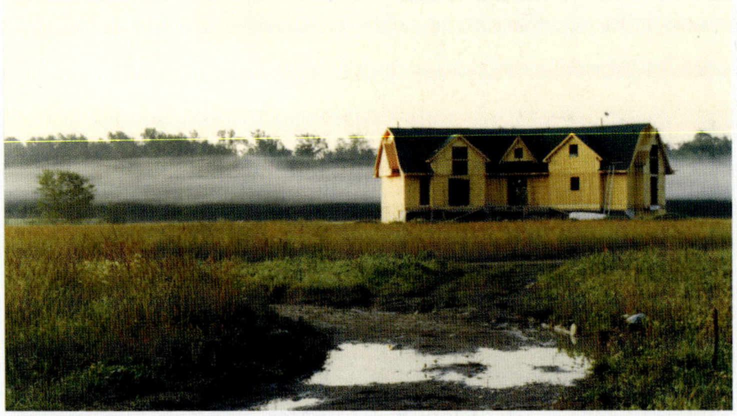

In 1984 when I met Mark, he had a home in Edmonton and worked at Cycle Works. It was a high-performance shop started by Canadian racing champions Don Galloway and Eddie MacDonald. Mark was a brilliant mechanic whose talents made snowmobiles and motorcycles go faster. Edmonton became my home until Mark undertook a career change. Robotics training took him to Peterborough, Ontario in 1987. I went 'home' to the Stratford Festival to build props. During this year in the east Mark came to love my family and developed a passion for planting trees. When he graduated he was immediately hired by a robotics firm in Burlington. Returning west made little sense.

I began to gather books on house design. David Suzuki's series, *A Planet for the Taking*, then airing on television, sparked the idea of a shared dwelling for the wiser use of resources. My sister Ellen was married to Ken Hadley, and with their children, Owen and Avory, they were outgrowing their small house; the time seemed right for us to dream large together.

Mark and I felt lucky to purchase 15 landlocked acres near Wellesley, Ontario. The first thing we did was to plant 1,200 walnut trees. We felt luckier still to purchase adjoining land with road frontage, which qualified our lot for building. I spent evenings in our rented place in nearby Cambridge designing a house at the drafting board, a feat which got harder as I became gradually more pregnant! As often as possible we spent evenings with Ken and Ellen resolving the design for an off-the-grid, two-family house. Our venture needed a name and A-S-H was perfect. It was an anagram for Abernethy, Smyth and Hadley. Ash trees grew in abundance and the acreage was flat as a pancake.

Working Out The Method

When I returned to Stratford for the 1987 season, show designs were well underway in the prop shop. I was given a large carving—also underway. I remember thinking it ludicrous to wade into an enormous block of styrene hoping to find a particular elbow! Surely there was a better method? For years I'd worked from blueprints showing front and side views of an object. I'd also employed the two-view idea from my high school drafting classes. I used it to make patterns for everything from fake food to dead animals. I now wanted to integrate the drafting idea with the woodworker's technique of cutting shapes from a cube of material.

On one face of a block, I'd trace the front view of an object from a paper pattern. I'd rotate the block and trace a side view of the same object onto the block from a side view pattern. Once I cut both outlines, the excess material on all sides fell away. The form that resulted looked curiously cubist but features were recognizable enough to guide further hand carving with a wickedly sharp knife.

I used the paper patterns to record physical features, like kneecaps or elbows, as exact points in a grid. I measured forward or backward, left or right from centre lines in each view, and an exact distance up from the floor. Cutting the outlines on the saw was the second part of the puzzle. The first step was to work out the anatomy of the figure that made each view and, with a framing square, project the lengths of limbs and align the two views. I extrapolated the lengths and proportions of limbs from photographs or measured for comparison from anyone who happened to be nearby in the prop shop.

Creating Ash Flats was unbelievably difficult. The home I'd designed with Mark and the Hadleys was ambitious enough in itself, but we added the more difficult goal of living off the electricity grid. With limited resources, work proceeded in fits and starts. There were tearful moments when it took every ounce of collective strength to keep momentum going. Still, continue we did—with music and laughter and charmed holidays with cousins and Christmas sleepovers that filled every bed for days at a time.

I loved building props, but it was a craft which felt limiting to me. My wise friend Carol Case said, "You're not unhappy working in theatre. You just shouldn't do it all the time!" She was right. My life now included Mark and baby Glen and then later another babe, Alex. I could no longer relocate for prop work. I had to believe that another livelihood would somehow materialize for me through the months when I was not at the Stratford Festival.

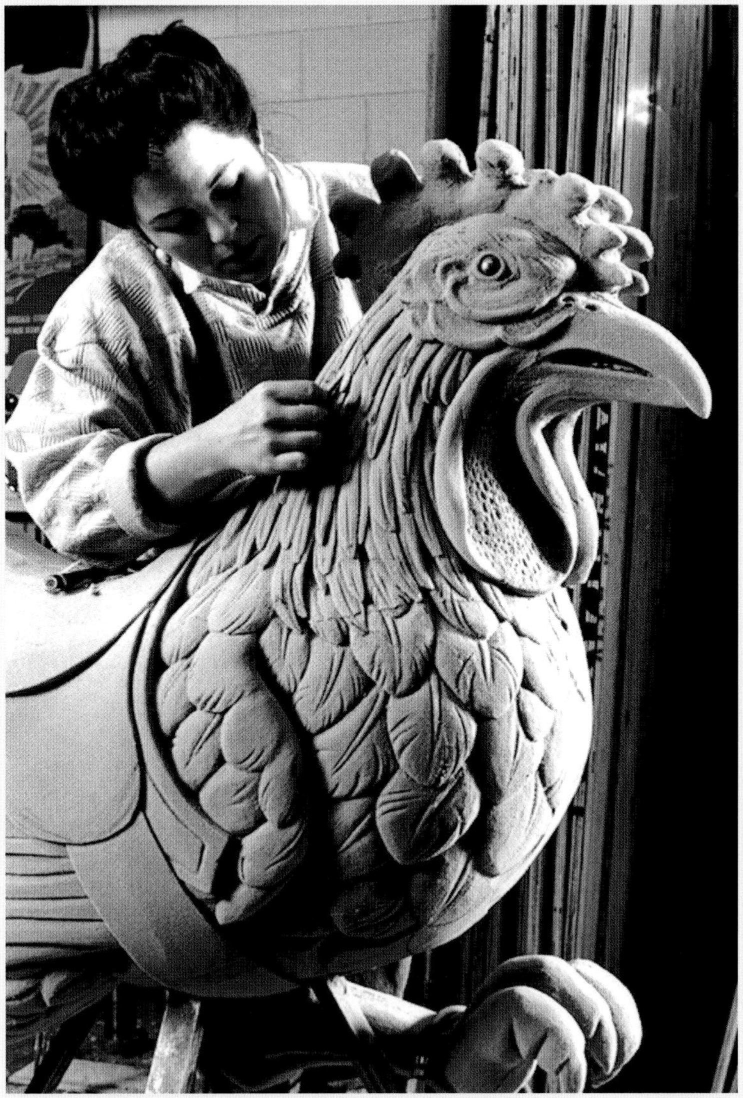

Animals for a Stratford production of *Carousel* were carved out of urethane foam, a material compatible with a fibreglass-and-resin finish.

Photo: Elisabeth Feryn

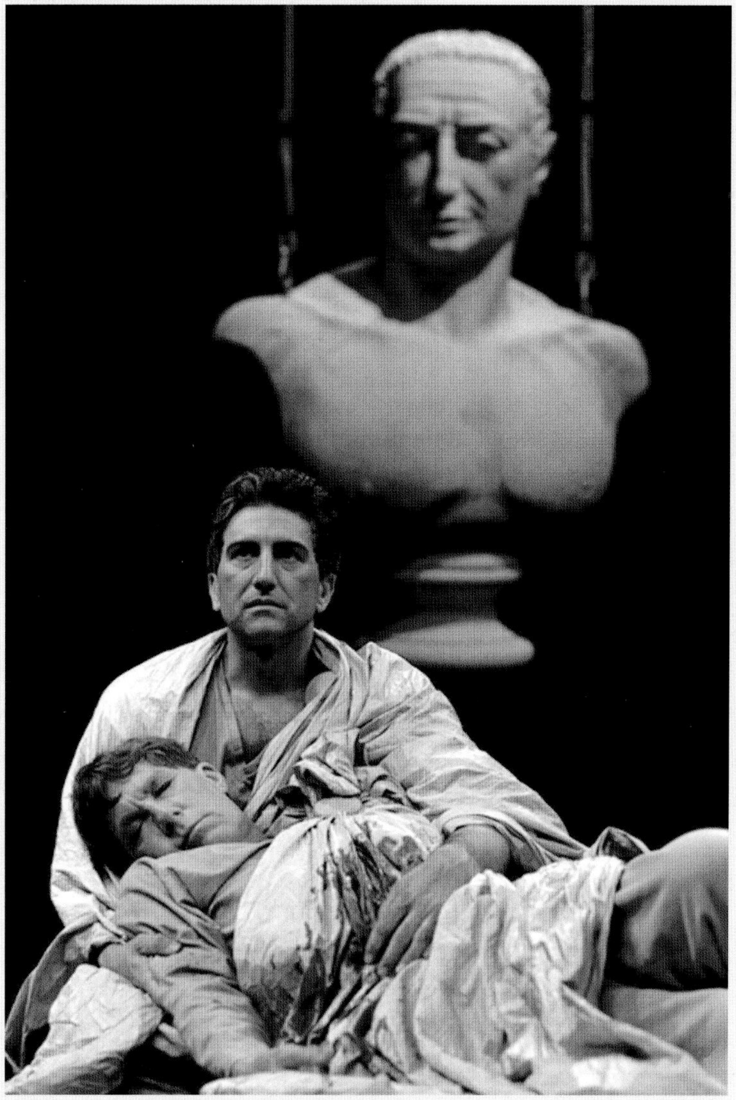

A bust of Julius Caesar overlooks his death scene in the Stratford Festival (Nicholas Pennell as Caesar in the arms of Scott Wentworth as Mark Antony). I carved the eight-foot-tall bust in styrene, then surfaced it with glued fabric and drywall paste—a classic prop finish. (1990)

Photo: David Cooper

Raising the Tent

"Better not look down
if you want to keep on flying."
– B.B. King lyric

By 1996 the Festival Theatre auditorium needed updating and a fundraising team sought funds to pay for renovations. Stage Designer Doug Paraschuk took on the task to create something akin to a 'United Way thermometer' to show contributions advancing toward the financial goal. Doug imagined 'small villagers' watching the Festival's performance tent being heaved into place. He asked if I would carve them. The design included a metal framework, curved like the Festival's seating, to hold plaques naming campaign contributors. The 'villagers' evolved into two large workmen and a young girl watching the action with her dog. Although the carving would be a delicious challenge, I worked full-time in the prop shop and had toddlers in my partly-finished home. I had no hours for an extracurricular job.

As Department Head, Frank Holte arranged for me to carve on this project in the prop shop. I worked as quickly as I could, not wanting to neglect my regular duties. Doug prepared numerous photographs to guide me. As I pored over the photos, a 'Eureka moment' showed the inherent flaw in each image—a figure posed for a photograph could not be in motion! In reality if the cables on which these men were hauling had suddenly been cut, the workmen would surely fall. I set the photos aside. I needed to create particular men, suspended in the action of a moment. Nothing else would have the right dynamics.

I rendered each of the three figures in about four days. For expedience I based them on characters in 'my Stratford story'. The standing man was Al Jones, who'd helped construct the Festival Theatre, then remained on staff as a scenic carpenter. Al had passed away just months before and it was a pleasure to remember him as I worked. The lower figure was Skip Manley, hired as foreman for tent-raising day because of his experience with Barnum & Bailey Circus. Katie Besworth, the daughter of two Festival staffers, was near at hand to model for the little girl.

I tried the front-view/side-view mapping I'd imagined, as it seemed the best method of controlled sculpting for 'action figures' in white styrene. When I finished the three figures, I struggled with an acrylic surface sealer. Prop maker Brian McLeod saved the day by applying a coating of durable fibreglass.

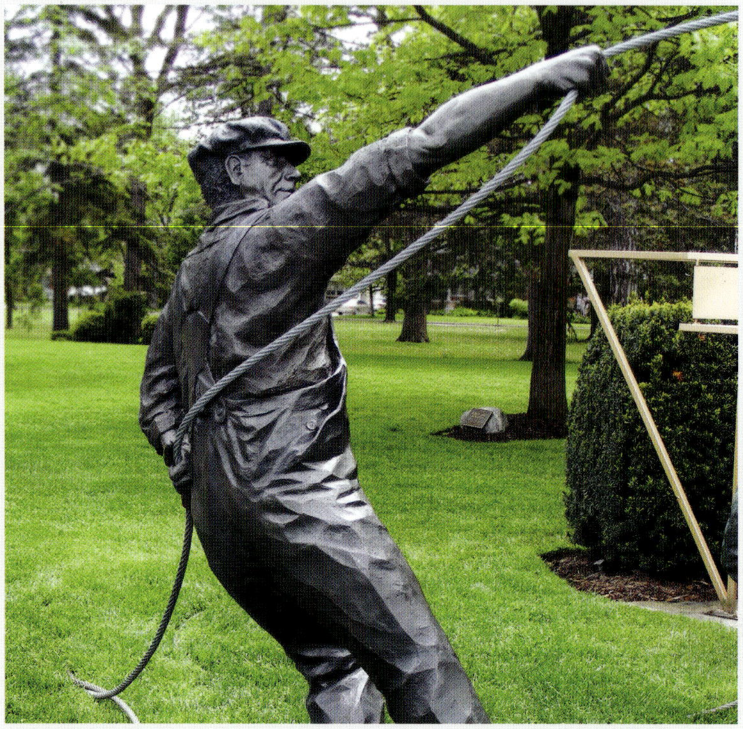

In the nick of time, in early June I watched as Stratford staff bolted the girl and her dog to the curved metal framework. The workmen's hands were rigged to grasp cables linked to the tilted tent pole. Over the months, a metal crown, like the one atop the theatre, pushed further and further up the tipped pole toward large numbers indicating the fundraising goal. It was a huge success!

By autumn several people had mentioned a bronze version of the temporary sculpture dubbed *Raising the Tent*, but by then my props contract had finished and I was at home with Glen and Alex. The buzz continued. Months later I learned that the $12-million campaign goal had been surpassed—to a total of $13.1 million. There was keen interest in commemoration.

In early December 1996, a small group gathered at the Festival Theatre for discussion about 'the bronze'. I'd invited Eric Knoespel of Artcast Foundry. The timelines we discussed dictated I'd have a month to create each figure. Artcast would have to produce three life-sized castings in just over four months. We took a long pause. Doug asked if I thought I could pull this together in the available time. This timeline seemed generous compared to the first set of carvings. I said YES. There were smiles and nods around the table and we set our sights on June 1997. *Raising the Tent* represented the theatrical momentum of this remarkable company of which I was proud to be a part.

Raising The Tent: Take Two

"It's a very public thing I do at home in private." – Ruth A.

I'd carved the first set of fundraising figures quickly by inventing a simple slicing style to shape the gesture, garments and anatomy all at once. Recreating them seemed straightforward. I refused to be distracted by the permanence of bronze. I'd ordered heavier styrene by mistake and as a result, carving was difficult; as well, my studio knife was nothing special. Nevertheless, I made progress and it was novel to work without the usual designer input. I did use the only sketch page Doug Paraschuk faxed over.
It showed one large circle and three small dots!

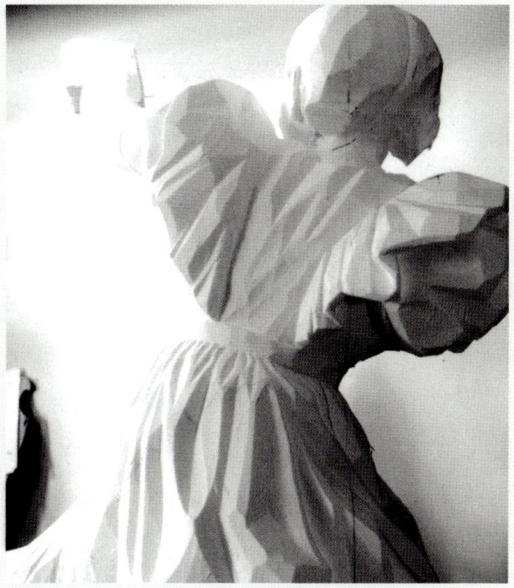

Although I had a designed home workspace, house-building had engulfed it. I managed to clear and guard a ten-foot-square area for carving. I used an electric fry pan to heat the wax for the surface of the styrene. That was a thrill in itself. After four years off the grid, and with unbelievably good timing, we'd connected Ash Flats to the public power grid only six weeks prior.

I began the first figure in early January, knowing that my workspace wouldn't hold all three figures. Once I completed each one, it was whisked to the foundry for casting. It was the only way to meet the June deadline. As I wearily trundled the final figure out of the studio, B.B. King came on the radio, crooning "Better not look down / If you want to keep on flying!"

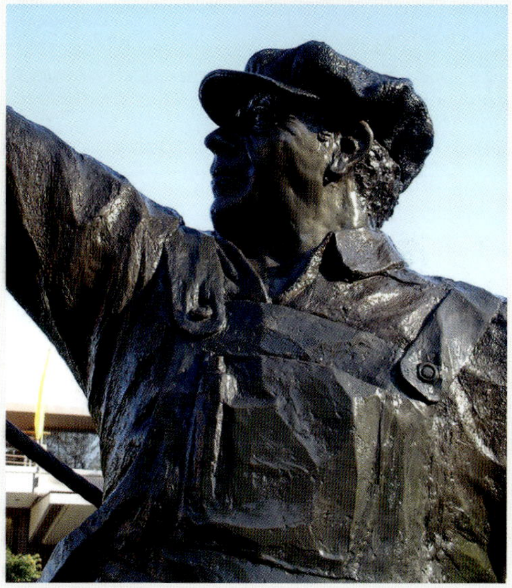

Discussion at the foundry soon revealed that the wax coating on my carved styrene was not thick enough to support the lost wax casting process. Mine was going to be a very public learning curve! Foundry staff rose to the occasion; patient hands guided me through waxwork. At first I hated the sticky, bulky wax but eventually I learned its magic and grew to love the warm, fluid surface.

There was no possibility of assembling the bronze sculptures before installation day, but I needed accurate alignments for multiple components. I'd traced a mounting template from the bleacher framework as it sat in the darkness of a storage van. The bronze girl had to bolt securely to its skeletal frame with only three points of contact. Two wire cables had to be capped at both ends. Since they'd been ordered weeks in advance, I'd calculated the length and crossed my fingers. Subgrade concrete was guesstimated into position. Amazingly enough, everything fit!

The most critical successes in this deceptively simple work were invisible, as were the efforts of the construction crew and key Festival staff, who aided wherever possible. Opening week at the renewed Festival in 1997 held a unique sense of celebration. My introduction to the foundry also offered a glimpse of life beyond the prop shop. With a sense of departure to an unknown destination, I tucked the project paperwork into a file simply titled 'Large bronzes'.

Lost Wax Casting

Bronze is a malleable alloy made primarily of copper—which gives it a relatively low melting point. Since it's easily worked with tools, bronze is ideal for casting. To reproduce a traditional clay sculpture in bronze, liquid rubber that is flexible when it dries is applied over the surface, making a mold. Then a harder ceramic material is carefully layered over top of the rubber. Both layers are removed. The flexible rubber layer peels easily off the complex shape of the original sculpture. The rigid ceramic 'mother mold' supports the flexible rubber and keeps it in the correct shape. This two-part mold is called 'the negative'.

Wax is like chocolate—solid at room temperature but easily melted to a paste or a liquid. Hot liquid wax is poured into the mold and swished around to coat the inside surface to at least 0.375 inches thick. This coating is allowed to harden. Thus a hollow wax copy of the artwork is formed (just like a hollow chocolate Easter bunny). Referred to as a 'wax', this structure is essential to the casting process. The hollow shape is delicate, must be kept cool and will shatter if dropped.

The 'wax' shape is dipped in alternate layers of ceramic slurry and sand until a solid coating forms. When this ceramic coating is fired in a kiln or oven, the wax inside melts away; hence it is 'lost'. This process, called 'lost wax casting', has been used in various forms all over the world for thousands of years. To make a hollow metal casting, the steps of coating the outer surface of a wax with ceramic and sand are repeated *inside* to essentially mold the space within the hollow wax. Between the outer mold and the inner mold is the space that will fill with bronze to make the 'wall' of a hollow metal shape. Molten bronze is poured into the mold's empty space and, when it cools, the ceramic shell surrounding the metal is broken away.

In my process, I apply the wax surface onto the styrene that I've carved. This 'core' is lightweight. If dropped, a styrene and wax carving won't shatter. If damaged, it is probably repairable. The styrene carvings burn away along with the wax that's melted and 'lost' in the bronzing process.

If only one copy of an artwork is needed, this styrene method bypasses making an expensive mold of the original sculpture. Large artworks are cast in many pieces, then reassembled and welded back together. Imperfections in the cast surface are resolved with sandblasting or tooling. The raw bronze is pale brown, but heat and acid washes add permanent subtle colours in a process called 'patination'.

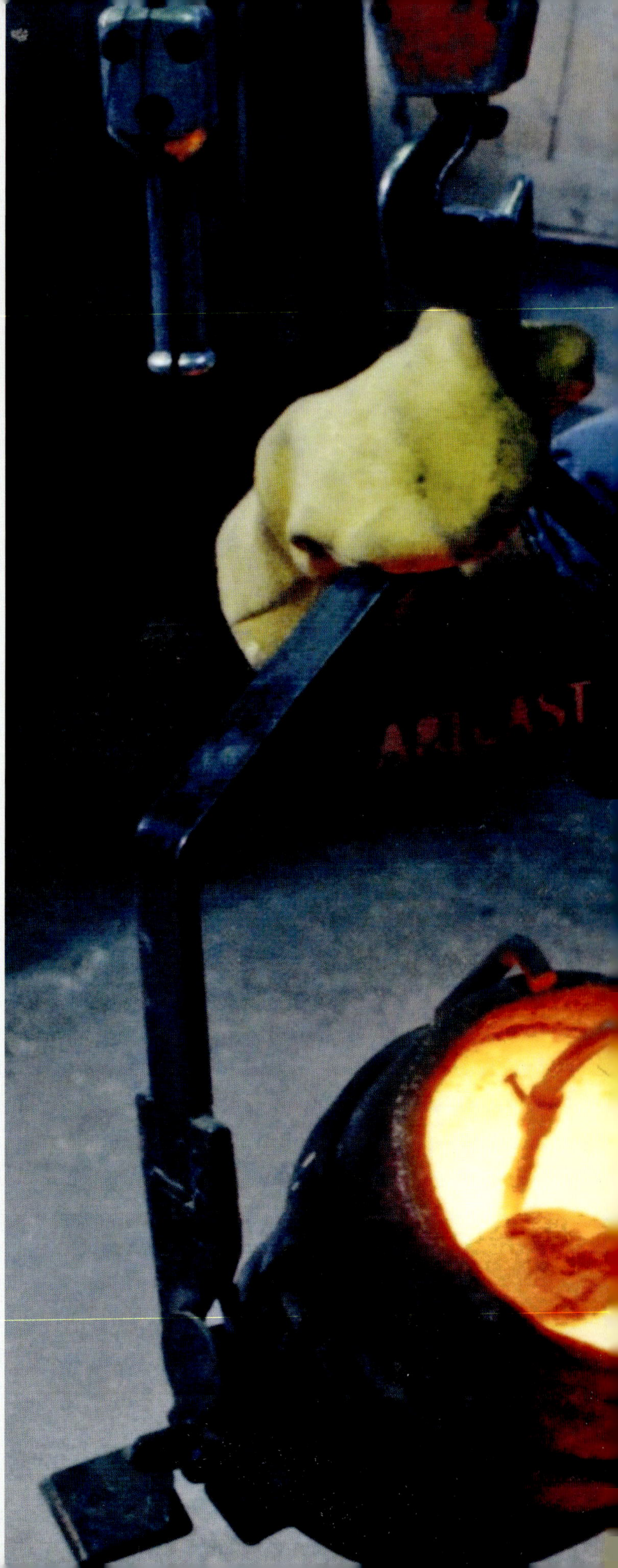

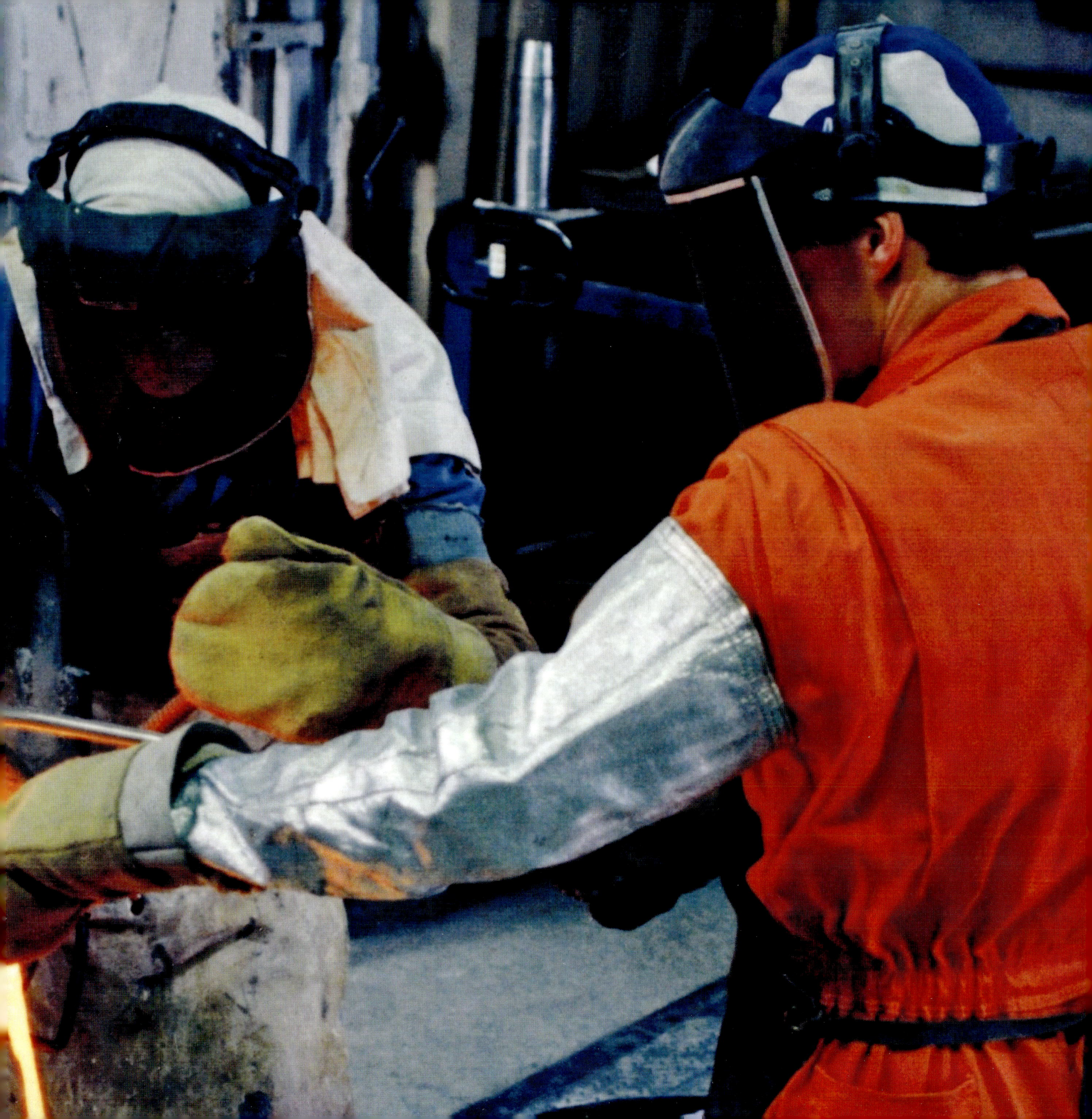

INDEX

ACKNOWLEDGEMENTS

This book would not have been realized without the enthusiasm of **Allen Eaves**. I cannot overstate my thanks for his encompassing support, direction and good spirits. I'd first met his invitation to create a sculpture album with reticence. At the time it seemed every hour in my days was spoken for. Eventually I embraced the idea, knowing that this challenging task would become even more difficult if I waited another ten years!

Early guidance from **George Vanderburgh** helped reveal the scale of this endeavour. As I wrote the manuscript and assembled photos it became clear that my view outward from the studio differed profoundly from what was seen by others looking in.

For book-making expertise I turned to **Jo Blackmore** and her team at **Granville Island Publishing**. Together we shaped the book's content. With assistance from **Kyle Hawke**, **Neall Calvert** and **Daniel Colmont** we relayed 40 years of creative output into what I hope is an engaging photo album with glimpses of my particular balance of life and art.

I also extend heartfelt thanks to the members of several dozen complex committees whose diligent contributions of time and resources supported my creation of public sculptures that might well last 10,000 years. You know who you are and how much you're appreciated.

Allen's encouragement and support included the talents of graphic designer **Maggie Woo**, whose thoughtful interpretation guided the text and photo selections into superb layouts. It was a delight to witness such objective clarity of vision. To you, Maggie, I am immensely grateful.

More than a decade ago, **Angie Littlefield** and I joked that she'd be my editor when I wrote my life story! With an eagle eye, quick wit and tender, tenacious coaching, she got me to the finish line. Another dear friend, **Anne Maley**, brought proofreading skills and a personal overview from our friendship of 30 years.

Karen Stothart and I worked closely on Paul Stothart's memorial. Karen articulated my creative approach. She understood the weaving of passions and that families are ongoing creations. They are threads in life's rewarding tapestry.

Through every step of this journal, profound thanks must go to my assistant **Cassandra Koch**, who has given many hours and a great deal of creative input. Her photos, plus those of **JR Ribee**, **Leif Norman**, **Trevor Lush**, **Eric Knoespel** and **Leonard Schlichting**, are glimpses of my work that are a beautiful substitute for personal encounters. I am grateful for archive photos provided by **Ellen Abernethy**, **Manitoba Theatre Centre** and **The Stratford Festival**. They illustrate my theatre creations, the making of ***Glenn*** (Gould) and my transition from theatre prop building into the sculpture studio via my introduction to the bronze foundry.

I would be remiss without a nod to serendipity; each step along my varied career path seemed to come into focus when needed. For patience, love and courage I thank my husband, **Mark**, and our sons, **Glen** and **Alex**. My life with you, my most favourite Three Bears, is richer than you could ever know.

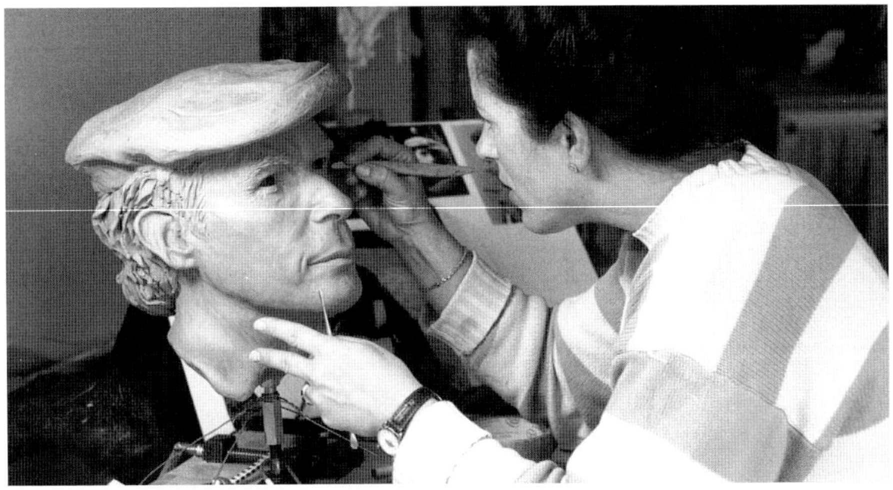

RUTH ABERNETHY was born in Lindsay, Ontario into an inventive and musical family. Hired at age 17 as a professional theatre technician, she subsequently worked in, and often headed, props departments across Canada. These 20 years of experience, including many at the Stratford Festival, inform her approach to sculpture and portraiture.

Ruth's first bronze commission in 1996 launched her solo art practice. Meanwhile she also designed her own off-the-grid home that included a studio where she refined her unique method of 'mapping' 3D figures before carving them in styrene. Her 1999 portrait of Glenn Gould touched off a series of distinctive commissions that included Mackenzie King, John A. Macdonald, Arnold Palmer and John McCrae. The National Portrait Collection acquired her bronze portrait of Al Waxman in 2003; Her Majesty Queen Elizabeth unveiled Ruth's bronze installation honouring Oscar Peterson at the National Arts Centre in 2010.

In addition to portraiture and private commissions, Ruth has created studio works combining textiles, handmade lace and stainless steel. Pieces from The Canadiana Collection were selected for exhibition in Ottawa's official residences; the Royal Ontario Museum acquired five works in 2009.

In Canada, Ruth's sculptures and installations grace public spaces municipally, regionally and nationally. Her sculptures have also been juried into exhibitions in Ireland, the United States, Australia and China. She recently received royal approval for a statue of Queen Elizabeth II seated on the Throne of Canada—to be unveiled in Toronto in 2017.

Ruth divides her time between her home/studio near Wellesley, Ontario and Vancouver, British Columbia.

www.ruthabernethy.com